HOSPITALITY FINANCIAL MANAGEMENT

HOSPITALITY FINANCIAL MANAGEMENT

Agnes L. DeFranco & Thomas W. Lattin

JOHN WILEY & SONS, INC.

Library of Congress Cataloging-in-Publication Data:

DeFranco, Agnes L., 1961–
    Hospitality financial management / by Agnes DeFranco & Thomas Lattin.
        p. cm.
    Includes index.
    ISBN-13: 978-0-471-69216-4 (cloth)
    ISBN-10: 0-471-69216-6 (cloth)
  1. Hospitality industry—Finance. I. Lattin, Thomas W. II. Title.
    TX911.3.F5D44 2006
    647.94068′1—dc22

                                                        2006007280

Printed in the United States of America

10 9 8 7 6 5 4 3 2 1

CONTENTS

PREFACE

Our goal in writing this book is to present a practical approach to hospitality financial management that provides students with a clear description of the financial management concepts, skills, and tools they need to become successful managers or entrepreneurs in the hospitality industry. The target audience for this applied finance book is undergraduate students taking a hospitality financial management course. However, it can also be used as a supplementary text in a graduate-level hospitality financial management course. *Hospitality Financial Management* is entrepreneurial in nature and emphasizes that to succeed in the world of business, whether you work for a large or small company, a public or private company, for others or yourself, you must always think like an owner while acting like a manager. The more you assume that the money you are spending, collecting, and investing is your own, the better business decisions you will make and the more financial rewards you will earn.

The unique and colorful image incorporated in the cover of this text is a photograph of the Portland Head Light, a famous and historic lighthouse in Cape Elizabeth, Maine, which was first lit in 1791. We chose this scenic landmark because it symbolizes the essence and entrepreneurial spirit of the hospitality industry and small business.

Pedagogical Features That Help Students

FEATURE STORY: Each chapter begins with a Feature Story, based on a real-world restaurant, hotel, or small business, that relates to the financial concepts presented within the chapter. An additional Feature Story is also included within the body of the chapter.

LEARNING OUTCOMES: A list of Learning Outcomes follows each chapter's Feature Story. This list highlights the key concepts covered in the chapter.

PREVIEW OF CHAPTER: A Chapter Preview outlines the main topics and subtopics within each chapter.

THE REAL DEAL: Boxed inserts in each chapter emphasize the relevance of the text content by relating financial concepts to fun facts relating to situations students either have or will encounter in their everyday lives.

FINANCE IN ACTION: Finance in Action problems provide real-world scenarios where a particular calculation or analysis relating to chapter-specific concepts is needed. A stepped-out solution is provided for each problem to walk the student through the necessary financial calculations.

APPLICATION EXERCISES: Application Exercises at the end of each chapter reinforce student comprehension of the key concepts presented in it.

CONCEPT CHECKS: Mini-cases with discussion questions based on real-world situations are included at the end of each chapter to enhance student understanding.

WHERE WE ARE GOING, WHERE WE HAVE BEEN: This section summarizes what has been covered in a particular chapter and what will be covered going forward in the text.

KEY POINTS: A bulleted list of the key concepts related to each of the learning outcomes presented at the beginning of each chapter appears within the end-of-chapter material.

KEY TERMS: These are bolded when they first appear within the chapter and then listed at the end of each chapter with their definitions.

Resources for Instructors

INSTRUCTOR'S MANUAL: Includes lecture outlines, quizzes, solutions to application exercises and concept checks, and a test bank.

COMPANION WEBSITE: Includes electronic files for the Instructor's Manual with Test Questions and PowerPoint slides containing lecture outlines for every chapter.

ACKNOWLEDGMENTS

Books are not written single handedly. We are grateful to Ms. Tanya Venegas and Ms. Jacqueline Lee, both graduates of the Conrad N. Hilton College, for their very able assistance in researching the feature stories that appear in each chapter and developing the exercises and concept checks that appear at the end of each chapter. We also wish to thank the following individuals for providing much of the material used for the numerous illustrations throughout the book: John Bowen, Cathleen Baird, Alan Gallo, Brian Hanna, David Manglos, R. P. Rama, Albert Ramirez, Arlene Ramirez, Michael Scott, and Rosa Tang.

Special thanks are also due to Randy Smith and Mark Lomanno of Smith Travel Research and Frank Wolfe of the Hospitality Financial and Technology Professionals for their generosity in sharing their knowledge and publications. We also wish to thank Joseph Jackson, Tom Latour, and Chuck Warczak for their valuable contributions, insights, and, most of all, their time and patience during our interviews. We also appreciate all the efforts Cindy Rhoads and Nigar Hale of John Wiley and Sons have made to make this project a pleasure.

Also, we would not be able to ensure this book will meet the needs of our target audience without the expertise and excellent suggestions provided by our reviewers. For this, our thanks go to: Rhomi Kher, International College of Hospitality Management; Woody Kim, School of Hotel and Restaurant Administration at Oklahoma State University; Don St. Hilaire, The Collins School of Management at California State Polytechnic University at Pomona; and Jenny Staskey, Northern Arizona University.

This book is dedicated to Dr. Gerald and Jean Lattin, who encouraged us to write it and have served as role models to both of us throughout our careers in the world of business and academics; to our spouses, Linda Lattin and John DeFranco, who have been so supportive and understanding of the many hours it has taken to write this book; and to the professors, teachers, and trainers who will, we trust, find this book a valuable and useful tool when preparing our young people for a career in the exciting and financially rewarding hospitality industry.

AGNES DEFRANCO
THOMAS LATTIN
University of Houston
Houston, Texas

FINANCE AND THE HOSPITALITY INDUSTRY

THE HILTON FAMILY

Perhaps the best-known hotel brand in the world is Hilton. When you think *hotel*, you think Hilton. The Hilton hotel chain was founded by Conrad Nicholson Hilton. His work is now carried on by his sons, Barron and Eric.

The child of a Norwegian immigrant father and a German-American mother, Conrad Hilton had a strong belief in the American dream. His philosophy and strength were derived from his faith in God, his belief in the brotherhood of man, his patriotic confidence in his country, and his conviction that natural law obligates all humankind to help relieve the suffering and distress of the destitute.

Conrad Hilton almost became a banker rather than a hotelier. He traveled to Cisco, Texas, in 1919, intending to purchase a local bank, but the deal fell through when the seller raised the purchase price higher than what Mr. Hilton would agree to pay. Instead, he purchased the Cisco Mobley Hotel when he discovered it was achieving high occupancies due to the influx of exhausted oil-seekers and railroad travelers. Mr. Hilton learned that the innkeeper of the Mobley was selling its rooms three times a day. Conrad went on to purchase three other existing hotels, which generated enough cash flow to help him construct his first new hotel, the Dallas Hilton, which opened on August 2, 1925.

Conrad Hilton was a fortunate man who had a knack for impeccable timing. During the Great Depression of the 1930s, when over 80% of the nation's hotels went into bankruptcy, he was able to maintain ownership of five of his eight hotels by convincing the Moody family of Galveston, Texas, to lend him $300,000, using the hotels as collateral. Incredibly, when he defaulted on the loan, the Moodys foreclosed on the hotels but offered him a one-third partnership with a salary of $18,000 per year in the newly created Moody hotel chain. While the partnership did not last long, Mr. Hilton was able to reacquire three of his five hotels from the Moodys with another loan of $95,000.

Conrad Hilton went on to expand his chain by purchasing other U.S. hotels including the Sir Francis Drake in San Francisco, the Plaza and Waldorf-Astoria hotels in New York City, and the Stevens, now known as the Chicago Hilton and Towers, and the Palmer House in Chicago.

The key to Mr. Hilton's success was his ability to purchase underperforming hotels and convert them into cash-flowing assets. He accomplished this by introducing innovative forecasting and cost control systems to the hotel industry. His hotel management team became experts at predicting the number of occupied rooms they would experience and scheduling their employees accordingly. This matching of business volume with employee hours resulted in high levels of guest satisfaction and significant cash flows for his company.

Internationally, Conrad Hilton developed his business by building hotels in such exotic places as San Juan, Madrid, Istanbul, Havana, Berlin, and Cairo and getting them financed by local partners. His corporate and personal motto became "World peace through international trade and travel." In a 1954 speech to students at Cornell University, he said:

> Each one of us . . . carries with us, wherever we go, a little of America. Whether we like it or not, we represent America, its culture, its faith and its history. . . . We are ambassadors in a true sense of the word and have got to act like ambassadors. . . . A hotel is a focal point for the exchange of knowledge between millions of people who want to know each other better, trade with each other and live with each other in peace.

Mr. Hilton also believed that tourism would stimulate international economies and provide jobs for many, thus generating kudos for the United States and reducing the amount of foreign aid it had to provide.

His sons, Barron and Eric, followed their father into the hotel business. In 1954, Barron assumed the position of president and chief executive officer of Hilton Hotels Corporation, and in February 1979 he became chairman of the board. He is credited with founding Hilton's credit card Carte Blanche and in developing the Hilton Inn franchise program. He led Hilton into the gaming business through the construction of the Vegas Hilton and the Flamingo Hilton hotels in 1970. These two casino hotels became so successful that they accounted for approximately half of Hilton Hotels Corporation's total operating income and vaulted the company onto the *Fortune 500* list. Hilton Hotels Corporation became the first gaming company traded on the New York Stock Exchange.

Conrad's other son, Eric, entered the family business at the bottom and worked his way up to the top. While still a high school student, he began his hospitality industry career as a hotel engineer working in the boiler room of the El Paso, Texas, Hilton. He also apprenticed as a bellman, a doorman, a steward, a cook, an elevator operator, a desk clerk, and a telephone operator. After serving his country in the army during the Korean War, and later enjoying a brief career as a professional baseball player, he renewed his Hilton career, becoming president of Conrad Hotels and vice chairman and director of Hilton Hotels Corporation.

Eric Hilton was also instrumental in the creation of the Conrad N. Hilton College of Hotel and Restaurant Management at the University of Houston. When its founding dean, Dr. James Taylor, first approached Eric with his vision for a new hotel school, Eric was receptive and convinced his father to contribute $1.5 million to the development of the college. The Hilton foundation has since provided over $45 million for the construction of classrooms, food laboratories, and an operating hotel to train students. This money has also funded scholarships and faculty chairs.

Hilton Hotels Corporation did not become one of the most successful hotel companies in the world without careful planning. Hilton's management is constantly working to increase its revenues and control its costs. Careful consideration is given to identifying companies to acquire, such as Promus, which brought Embassy Suites, Hampton Inns, and Doubletree Hotels into the Hilton family; new products to provide, like Hilton's new Garden Inn; where to open new Hilton-branded hotels; and how to finance the corporation's growth and expansion. Much of the information required to make these decisions is provided by the company's accounting, management information, and investment analysis systems, which utilize many of the concepts, techniques, and skills presented in this text.

SOURCES

Hilton, Conrad N. *Be My Guest.* Englewood Cliffs, N.J.: Prentice Hall, 1957.

———. Speech, Hotels International, April 21, 1954.

Hilton, Eric M. Hilton. Interview by Cathleen Baird, May 13, 1994.

Baird, Cathleen. Conrad N. Hilton: Innkeeper Extraordinary Statesman and Philanthropist, 1887 1979, 2005. Conrad N. Hilton Collection, Hospitality Industry Archives & Library, University of Houston, Texas.

Baird, Cathleen. Conrad N. Hilton: Nomination to the TIA Hall of Fame. July 1997. Conrad N. Hilton Collection, Hospitality Industry Archives & Library, University of Houston, Texas.

"Conrad N. Hilton, 1996 Hall of Honor Inductee of the Hospitality Industry Hall of Honor." http://www.hrm.uh.edu/home.asp?PageID=183.

"Barron Hilton," 1998 Hall of Honor Inductee of the Hospitality Industry Hall of Honor," http://www.hrm.uh.edu/home.asp?PageID=193.

Conrad N. Hilton Foundation Annual Report for 2004/2005. http://www.hiltonfoundation.org/reports/14.pdf.

"Vice Chairman Eric M. Hilton Retires After Nearly 50 Years of Service." http://www.hospitalitynet.org/news/4000513.print. March 31, 1997.

Learning Outcomes

1. Describe the nature of the book.
2. Note the book's target audience.
3. Explain the owner/manager alignment of interests theme of the book.

4. State the specific objectives of the book.

5. Discuss the financial challenges presented by the hospitality industry.

6. Present the structure and organization of the book.

7. Preview the contents of each chapter.

Preview of Chapter 1

1. INTRODUCTION

a. Nature of the book

b. Target audiences

c. "Think like an owner and act like a manager"

2. OBJECTIVES

a. Read, interpret, and analyze financial management reports

b. Manage working capital and profits

c. Understand the importance of growth and how to finance it

d. Become familiar with the sources, types, and costs of capital

e. Comprehend the concept of risk, reward, and value creation

f. Learn the skills and tools needed to perform investment analysis and make sound business decisions

g. Understand how an investment package is professionally prepared and presented to decision makers and financing sources

h. Learn how to structure and negotiate a new hospitality business venture

3. FINANCIAL CHALLENGES

a. Hospitality: A multifaceted industry

b. Low profit margins

c. Fluctuating sales volumes

d. Labor intensiveness

e. Capital intensiveness

f. Reliance on discretionary incomes

4. CHAPTER STRUCTURE

5. CHAPTER TOPICS

a. Managing revenues, expenses, cash, and profits

b. The need for growth and how to finance it

c. The time value of money, the mathematics of finance, and investment analysis

d. The investment package and the art of the deal

e. Increasing shareholder value

INTRODUCTION

Most financial management books focus on the world of big business and the corporate finance function. They are typically long, technical, and more theoretical than practical in their approach to finance. Their tables of contents feature chapters on the "Theory of Value Creation," the "Optimum Capital Structure," "Capital Expenditure Analysis," and "Public Trading in Stocks and Bonds." While some of these topics are relevant to the front-line hospitality industry manager, this book approaches them in a very different way. Several other important financial topics, unique to the hospitality industry, are also included in this book. As authors, we strived to make the content of the book concise, to the point, practical, and interesting. We hope you enjoy reading it and applying it to your personal career path.

The primary target audience for this financial management book is students who will soon graduate from a hotel/restaurant college and pursue a career in the hospitality industry. The book is also targeted at individuals currently working in the hospitality industry who want to advance their careers. It is intended as the primary text for undergraduate hospitality management courses and as a supplementary text for graduate-level courses.

A recurring theme throughout the book is to "think like an owner and act like a manager." Once this entrepreneurial mentality is learned, maintaining it will closely align the financial interests of both ownership and management, regardless of the size of the company, and greater financial rewards will result for both parties.

The more specific objectives of the book are to provide students with a clear understanding of:

1. The financial management reports they will encounter and rely on during their hospitality careers to more effectively manage their respective profit or cost centers.

2. The methodology used to accurately read, analyze, and apply the information contained in these reports to enable sound forecasting, pricing, and cost control decision making.

3. The skills and operating systems critical to the management of cash and the profitability of the business.

4. The importance of growing the business, and the growth strategies available to management to accomplish this goal.

5. The types, sources, and costs of capital available to a company to finance its growth, and the advantages, disadvantages, and risks involved.

6. The concepts of risk, reward, and value creation as they apply to investing in hospitality assets.

7. The financial analysis tools modern-day managers use to make sound investment decisions.

8. The importance and contents of a professionally prepared investment package for presentation to top management, owners, lenders, and outside investors to secure the capital needed for growth.

9. How to structure and negotiate a new hospitality business venture from the perspective of the project's sponsor.

10. How the practical application of the financial concepts, skills, and tools described in this book can increase shareholder value and achieve personal financial success for the hospitality manager.

THE REAL DEAL

According to the November 2004 Special Issue of *The Bottomline*, the official journal of Hospitality Financial and Technology Professionals, the average salary of a controller in the hospitality industry in 2004 was $74,143 as compared to $69,311 in 2003 and $66,550 in 2002. These numbers do not include bonuses or deferred compensation.

Assistant controllers reported average salaries of $52,916, $49,970, and $46,921 for the same three-year period. While the traditional career path for a property-level controller is to become a regional controller and then perhaps take a corporate-level position, some controllers become hotel general managers and, later, members of the corporate management team. So, the next time you contemplate your career path, consider using a position in accounting and finance as a springboard to an operations career. The more you know and can apply accounting and finance skills to your business, the more likely you are to become successful and perhaps even independently wealthy.

Source: Countryman, C., A. L. DeFranco, and T. Venegas. "The 2004 HFTP Compensation and Benefits Survey." *The Bottomline* 19(7):6–33.

Hospitality Industry Financial Challenges

Hospitality is an exciting and multifaceted industry that offers a variety of career opportunities to those who have earned a hotel/restaurant management degree. Careers with hotel, restaurant, airline, cruise line, gaming, and wine and spirit companies are readily available to such graduates. In addition, careers with service firms that support hospitality companies in the areas of accounting, consulting, real estate development, architecture, interior design, real estate brokerage, hotel valuation, investment banking, mortgage brokerage, insurance, advertising, and technology are also available to those with hospitality degrees.

FEATURE STORY

COLONEL HARLAND SANDERS—NEVER TOO OLD TO BECOME FAMOUS

One of the most unusual hospitality industry success stories is that of Colonel Harland Sanders. The Colonel's hospitality career began when most people start thinking about retiring, traveling the world, and playing with their grandchildren. At age sixty-five, Colonel Sanders embarked on a new small business venture that would grow and become one of the largest fast food empires in the world.

Colonel Sanders began his new enterprise by franchising his fried chicken recipe with equity provided by his $105 monthly Social Security check. That led to ownership of the international restaurant chain Kentucky Fried Chicken, today known as KFC.

Born in 1890, Mr. Sanders lost his father at age six and was forced to look after his three-year-old brother and baby sister while his mother worked. Having to cook most of the meals while his mother was away from home, he learned and mastered several regional cuisines at a young age. He was a farm worker at age twelve, a streetcar conductor at fifteen, and a soldier at sixteen. Later, he worked on the railroad, served as a justice of the peace, became an insurance salesman, operated a steamboat ferry, sold tires, and ran a service station.

At age forty, he began cooking for hungry travelers in the dining room of his living quarters connected to his service station in Corbin, Kansas. As the number of diners increased and his food volume grew through word-of-mouth advertising, he moved across the street to a motel and restaurant that seated 142 people. Over the next nine years, he perfected his secret blend of eleven herbs and spices and his pressure-cooking technique, which is still used today at all KFC restaurants.

Colonel Sanders was forced to auction off his restaurant business in 1950 when the new interstate highway bypassed Corbin. He was sixty-five years old at the time, and reduced to living off his Social Security check. The Colonel decided to hit the road to franchise his fried chicken recipe. He traveled by car across the country, going from restaurant to restaurant and cooking up batches of his chicken for restaurant owners and their employees. If their reaction was favorable, he entered into a handshake agreement with them which called for the owner to pay him a nickel for each serving of Kentucky fried chicken the restaurant sold. Using this unique franchising concept, the Colonel accumulated a large number of franchisees throughout the United States, which paid him a sizable amount of franchise fees each month. This proved to be a wise business decision on the Colonel's part; in less than ten years, the Kentucky Fried Chicken franchise network grew to a chain of more than 600 franchises. At this point, the Colonel cashed out on the value he had created in his business by selling his interest in KFC for $2 million while remaining as the company's most recognizable spokesperson and icon.

SOURCES

KFC. "About KFC: Colonel Harland Sanders." http://www.kfc.com/about/colonel.htm (accessed October 10, 2004).

"Colonel Harland Sanders, 2000 Hall of Honor Inductee of the Hospitality Industry Hall of Honor." http://www.hrm.uh.edu/home.asp?PageID=183.

Although dynamic and interesting, the business of hospitality presents many challenges. For example, hospitality businesses operate on low profit margins with fluctuating sales volumes. The ability to forecast revenues and control expenses is critical to achieving budgeted profits and a favorable return on investment for the owners of the company. Also, because hospitality businesses are labor intensive, scheduling employee hours so they are consistent with forecasted revenues and monitoring payroll cost daily are just two major management challenges.

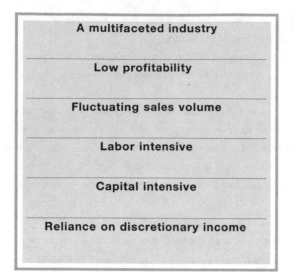

ILLUSTRATION 1-1
Hospitality Industry Financial Challenges

While a hospitality business typically requires a relatively low level of operating inventories, it requires a relatively high level of capital for its real estate component. This component often includes buildings, operating systems, guest room furniture, and restaurant equipment. Securing financing to acquire these assets is a continuing challenge for management.

Finally, hospitality businesses rely heavily on the discretionary income of their customers. During a weak economy, when household discretionary income is low, the hospitality industry usually suffers. High-end establishments, such as resorts and fine dining restaurants, normally feel the effects of a weak economy first, but eventually, the entire industry feels the financial pain. However, as soon as the economy takes a turn for the better, consumers return, discretionary spending increases, and the industry prospers. Accurately predicting these economic fluctuations, and knowing when to buy and sell hospitality assets, can be financially lucrative for the astute hospitality investor.

The financial tools utilized by modern-day management to address these challenges and opportunities are the focus of this book. Understanding of these financial tools and applying them to the challenges and opportunities they will soon face when they take jobs in the industry will serve hospitality graduates well throughout their business careers. Illustration 1-1 lists many of these challenges.

Chapter Structure

Each chapter in the book includes the following features:

- Two feature stories that describe the careers of hospitality professionals and how their knowledge of financial skills contributed to their personal business success
- Learning Objectives

- Chapter Preview
- Illustrations of important concepts and calculations
- "Finance in Action," an illustrative case study that relates to the concepts presented in the chapter
- "Where We've Been, Where We're Going," which provides a summary of what was covered within a chapter and what is covered in subsequent chapters
- Key Points, a bulleted list of the key concepts relating to the learning objectives provided at the beginning of each chapter
- Key Terms
- Application Exercises
- Concept Checks
- "The Real Deal," a financial vignette based on a real-life financial scenario
- Links to hospitality websites, where applicable, to supplement the text and keep it current

Chapter Topics

The text is organized into five modules. Chapters 2, 3, and 4 focus on managing revenues, expenses, cash, and the profitability of the hospitality business. Chapters 5 and 6 discuss the need for growth, growth strategies, and how to finance the growth of a company. Chapters 7, 8, and 9 deal with the concept of time value of money, the mathematics of finance, investment analysis, and how financial analysis tools are used by management to make wise investment decisions. Chapters 10 and 11 apply the knowledge gained in the prior nine chapters to the preparation of a professional investment package and the negotiation of a new business venture. Both internal capital and private financing requests are discussed. Finally, chapter 12 recaps the key concepts, skills, and tools presented throughout the book and provides a reference guide for the hospitality graduate. Illustration 1-2 highlights the building blocks of the book.

CHAPTER 2: FINANCIAL REPORTING

Chapter 2 focuses on the basic daily, weekly, and monthly management reports the hospitality manager receives and explains how to read and interpret each. The daily revenue report, daily payroll report, Smith Travel Research STAR report, food menu abstract report, rooms revenue forecast, income statement, and balance sheet are all explained. The chapter also reviews the principles of accounting on which a company's financial statements are based, the limitations of financial statements, and the Uniform System of Accounts for hotels, restaurants, and clubs. The impact of the Sarbanes-Oxley law on the hospitality industry is also discussed.

CHAPTER 3: ANALYZING FINANCIAL STATEMENTS

Chapter 3 begins with an explanation of how to analyze financial statements and management reports. Ratio analysis, both vertical and horizontal, is discussed in addition to how hospitality

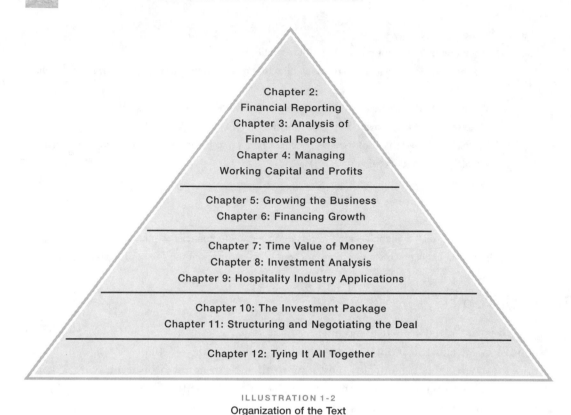

Chapter 2:
Financial Reporting
Chapter 3: Analysis of
Financial Reports
Chapter 4: Managing
Working Capital and Profits

Chapter 5: Growing the Business
Chapter 6: Financing Growth

Chapter 7: Time Value of Money
Chapter 8: Investment Analysis
Chapter 9: Hospitality Industry Applications

Chapter 10: The Investment Package
Chapter 11: Structuring and Negotiating the Deal

Chapter 12: Tying It All Together

ILLUSTRATION 1-2
Organization of the Text

managers compare the operating results of their department, or the business as a whole, to industry standards and norms. The chapter also explains how the financial statements and management reports discussed in chapter 2 are used for employee scheduling, budgeting, profit flexing, cost-volume-profit modeling, pricing, and revenue management.

CHAPTER 4: MANAGING WORKING CAPITAL AND CONTROLLING CASH

How effective management of working capital, product cost, and operating expenses leads to success in business is the focus of chapter 4. Internal controls, cash budgeting, accounts receivable management, accounts payable management, food and beverage cost control systems, and a unique profit management system called CP³ are also discussed. The CP³ System involves a monthly commitment budget prepared by department heads and approved by the general manager and the corporate office. It is a management reporting system that tracks and monitors revenues, expenses, and profits on a daily basis through an analysis of purchase orders, a daily recap of payroll hours and payroll expense by department, and a daily profit and loss statement.

CHAPTER 5: GROWING THE BUSINESS

Growing the business is the subject of chapter 5. The importance of growth and growth strategies are also discussed, including franchising, management contracts, mergers, and acquisitions.

CHAPTER 6: FINANCING GROWTH

Sources, characteristics, advantages, disadvantages, and the cost of debt and equity financing are discussed in chapter 6. Financing decisions related to both public and private financing vehicles and hospitality financing schemes such as condominium hotels are also discussed.

CHAPTER 7: THE TIME VALUE OF MONEY

Chapter 7 introduces the concept of time value of money and offers instruction on how to use formulas, interest factor tables, the business calculator, and the Excel spreadsheet to solve time value of money problems. The chapter provides detailed instruction on how to calculate the future value and present value of a single lump sum, an annuity, and an uneven stream of cash flow, in addition to the calculation of a loan amortization table.

CHAPTER 8: INVESTMENT ANALYSIS

Chapter 8 builds on the time value of money concepts discussed in chapter 7 and explains how hospitality managers use time value of money calculations to help make wise investment decisions. This chapter begins with a discussion of risk, reward, and value creation and then proceeds to the concepts of payback period, net present value (NPV), internal rate of return (IRR), and modified internal rate of return (MIRR). The advantages, disadvantages, and factors impacting each financial tool are also discussed. Detailed instruction on how to calculate payback, NPV, IRR, and MIRR using formulas, interest factor tables, the business calculator, and the computer is also provided. The capitalization and appraisal methods of valuation are also discussed.

CHAPTER 9: HOSPITALITY INDUSTRY APPLICATIONS OF TIME VALUE OF MONEY CONCEPTS AND SKILLS

Building on chapters 7 and 8, chapter 9 applies the aforementioned financial investment analysis tools to real-life hospitality situations. This chapter demonstrates how to use these financial analysis tools to determine the optimum loan size, the maximum debt service affordable, the amortization rate required, the maximum amount of equity that can be raised based on the cash flow projected, and the amount of ownership that must be offered to a new equity investor to meet the investor's hurdle rate. This chapter also explains how to analyze and compare multiple investment opportunities and perform sensitivity analyses of potential investments.

CHAPTER 10: THE INVESTMENT PACKAGE

Preparing a professional investment package and customizing it for both internal capital requests and external financing needs are the subjects of chapter 10. This chapter also provides information about how potential lenders and investors evaluate an investment package.

CHAPTER 11: CRAFTING AND NEGOTIATING THE DEAL

Chapter 11 explains how to structure and negotiate a new business venture, taking into consideration tax and liability issues, business entity options, the optimum mix of capital, and special ownership incentives for the sponsor.

CHAPTER 12: TYING IT ALL TOGETHER

This is the final chapter. It recaps the key concepts, skills, and tools discussed throughout the book and provides an easy reference guide for use when business opportunities and challenges present themselves.

WHERE WE'VE BEEN, WHERE WE'RE GOING

This chapter prepares us for what is to come. Toward the end of this chapter, there is a list of key terms in alphabetical order, and you will see such lists in the remaining eleven chapters of the book. Hospitality finance is a fascinating and challenging subject, applicable not only to the business you manage but also to your personal life. Take time to learn and enjoy the material.

Key Points

➤ This book presents financial management in a concise, to the point, practical, and interesting manner.

➤ The target audience for this book is undergraduate hospitality students and current employees of hospitality companies who want to advance their careers.

➤ "Thinking like an owner and acting like a manager" means adopting an entrepreneurial attitude. The primary goals of both owner and managers should be to increase shareholder value. When the interests and objectives of ownership and management are aligned, favorable financial results can be more easily achieved.

➤ The primary goal of this book is to teach the student how to manage revenues, expenses, cash and profits; generate, manage, and finance growth; analyze potential investment opportunities and make sound business decisions; structure and negotiate new business ventures; and increase shareholder value.

➤ Hospitality businesses operate on low profit margins, experience fluctuating sales volumes, are labor and capital intensive, and rely on the discretionary income of their customers to be successful.

➤ Each chapter in this book includes feature stories of hospitality leaders, learning objectives, a preview of the chapter, illustrations, "Finance in Action" case studies, a summary of key points, key terms, application exercises, concept checks, challenging case studies, real-life financial vignettes, and links to hospitality websites where applicable.

Application Exercises

1. In your own words, describe what hospitality finance is.

2. Why is hospitality a multifaceted industry and therefore a challenge to hospitality graduates?

3. What is the range of profit margins for each segment of the restaurant industry? Search the National Restaurant Association website at www.restaurant.org.

4. How does labor intensiveness complicate financial management of a hotel, restaurant, theme park, club, or any hospitality operation?

5. Do you believe the manufacturing industry or the hospitality industry carries a higher inventory level as a percentage of total assets? Please explain.

6. How does a boom or a bust in the economy impact the travel segment of the hospitality industry in terms of airlines, hotels, and rental cars?

7. The concept of time value of money is introduced in this chapter. As a follow-up exercise, please visit a local bank and ask for the current list of interest rates the bank pays a customer on a regular checking account, a three-month certificate of deposit, and a one-year certificate of deposit. Explain why the bank has different rates for each of these three investment instruments.

8. Interview at least three friends or family members who have the financial capacity to lend you $1,000. Ask them if you presented them with a business proposal, would they prefer to lend you $1,000 plus interest or to invest their $1,000 for an ownership position in your venture? Also ask them the rationale behind their decision.

9. Interview a controller of a hospitality business in your area and write a brief article on "A Day in the Life of a Controller."

10. **ETHICS** ✷ As a restaurant manager, Ian knows his business well and enjoys servicing his guests. He leaves all the financial dealings to his partner, Patrick. Ian's philosophy is that as long as customers are coming in to dine, his restaurant will do just fine. He entrusts all of the financial matters of the business to Patrick. From a financial standpoint, do you share Ian's view? Is there any downside to Ian not actively participating in the financial management of his restaurant? If so, please explain.

FINANCIAL REPORTING

TILLMAN J. FERTITTA

Tillman J. Fertitta's entrepreneurial spirit and financial astuteness have helped him create a highly successful $600 million restaurant company, Landry's Restaurants, Inc. *Business Week* recently listed Landry's Restaurants, Inc., as twenty-sixth on their list of the "Top 100 Growth Companies." *Forbes* listed Landry's fifth on its roster of "The 200 Best Small Companies in America." Landry's also received the *Nations Restaurant News* award as one of the nine "Hottest Concepts of the 1990s."

Born into a family of entrepreneurs, Fertitta is no stranger to starting new businesses. During his high school years he played the stock market; during college he started his own sales and marketing firm; and after graduation he became a real estate developer building million-dollar "spec" homes and developing restaurants and hotels.

Life was good for Tillman until the oil and real estate booms went bust during the mid-1980s. It was a double whammy for him, as his real estate business was concentrated in Houston, the oil capital of the world. Just like that, his financial statement showed him to be $10 million in debt, forcing him to negotiate by day with his creditors while sleeping by night in the multimillion-dollar home he had built but could now not afford.

Searching for a new direction, Fertitta went back to his seafood restaurant roots, using $1 million in promissory notes and the last of his personal cash to buy a 60 percent interest in two faltering Houston restaurants, Willie G's Oyster Bar and Landry's Seafood House. After turning both concepts into moneymakers, Fertitta chose to grow his company through public ownership and management rather than through franchising, as most other restaurant chains do. Tillman financed his company's growth in part by taking his ten-unit restaurant company public and raising over $60 million from two stock offerings.

Reflecting on his formula for success in the highly competitive restaurant business, Fertitta recently commented, "I learned the fundamentals of the seafood business from my dad and combined this knowledge with my own personal experience in real estate development. This combination of skills and hard work has enabled me to grow Landry's as quickly as I have."

Today, while he is still in the real estate business, Fertitta is now more recognized as a restaurateur. He prefers, however, to be characterized as "a businessman first and a restaurateur second." At age forty-seven, he is the chairman, president, and CEO of Landry's Restaurants, Inc. His restaurant empire includes over 300 full-service and limited-service restaurants throughout the United States, several hotels, and even an aquarium. Some of his company's most prominent restaurant concepts are Landry's Seafood House, Joe's Crab Shack, and the Rainforest Café.

SOURCES

http://www.landrysrestaurants.com/pages/about/pg_whoweare.htm.
http://www.landrysrestaurants.com/pages/news_events/published_news/99cfp-021599.htm.
Smith, Michelle L. "Fertitta Looks to the Future." *Pasadena Citizen,* February 2, 1999.

Learning Outcomes

1. Review the importance of accounting as the language of business and realize the value of the financial statements and management reports hospitality managers utilize.

2. Review the principles of accounting and the various systems of accounts used in the hospitality industry.

3. Describe the three basic financial statements—balance sheet, income statement, and statement of cash flow—and their usefulness to management.

4. Understand how hospitality managers use managerial reports to monitor and control key expenses and gauge the success of a hospitality business.

Preview of Chapter 2

Financial reporting in the hospitality industry

1. ACCOUNTING AS THE LANGUAGE OF BUSINESS

a. Accounting standards and principles

b. Uniform systems of accounts for lodging, restaurants, clubs, and spas

2. FINANCIAL STATEMENTS

a. Income statement

b. Balance sheet

c. Statement of cash flow

3. MANAGEMENT REPORTS

a. Daily revenue report

b. Daily payroll cost report

c. Rooms revenue forecast

d. Food and beverage menu abstract

e. Accounts receivable aging schedule

4. ACCOUNTING SYSTEM—CP³ SYSTEM

FINANCIAL REPORTING

The goals of chapter 2 are to introduce you to the financial and management reports you will encounter during your hospitality career and to teach you how to read and interpret them. The more you advance within your company, the more you will rely on these reports to succeed. The more familiar you are with the financial statements, management reports, and control systems presented in this chapter, the better your chances will be for promotion and the more effective you will be as a manager.

We begin the chapter with a brief review of the accounting principles and system of accounts that provide the foundation for the preparation of financial statements. We discuss new accounting rules affecting the hospitality industry today, and then focus the balance of the chapter on the management reports and control systems that will help you make informed financial business decisions and become a successful hospitality manager.

Accounting as the Language of Business

Many people in the hospitality industry find accounting and finance, which are considerably different from the operational areas of the hospitality business, tough to master. They find accounting and finance to almost have a language of their own. To some extent, this is true. The business world typically refers to accounting as *the language of business*. Just as you needed to learn the alphabet before you could read and write, you must learn the key accounting principles and terminology before you can effectively read and analyze financial statements and management reports.

THE REAL DEAL

Would you like to be certified as a Certified Hospitality Accountant Executive (CHAE)? The CHAE designation identifies an individual as having technical competence in the field of hospitality accounting and is a certification for the entire hospitality industry, including hotels, restaurants, clubs, tourism boards, cruise lines, theme parks, and other recreation facilities as well. To assist and encourage those who may want to enter the hospitality accounting and finance discipline, the CHAE examination is available for students who have earned at least 90 semester college credit hours and are within thirty semester hours of graduation. Once students pass all five parts of this examination, they have four years to accumulate the experience points required to become formally certified. Plan accordingly!

Accounting is divided into two parts: **financial accounting** and **managerial accounting.** The goal of financial accounting is to produce financial statements that accurately present the financial condition of the company and its operating results over time. The goal of managerial accounting is to provide more timely operating results related to revenues and expenses to help management maximize the operating performance of the business.

ACCOUNTING STANDARDS AND PRINCIPLES

The **Financial Accounting Standards Board (FASB),** together with the **Securities and Exchange Commission (SEC),** establishes the rules and regulations that govern all accounting and financial reporting. These principles are known as **Generally Accepted Accounting Principles (GAAP).** As a result of the 2002 Sarbanes-Oxley Act, hospitality companies are now investing large sums of financial and human resources to ensure these principles are correctly followed. Failure to apply these principles to the company's financial system properly can result in the termination, and in some cases imprisonment, of management, including the CEO of the company. Here is a brief recap of these principles:

The **cost principle** states that all transactions, including the purchase or sale of an asset, must be recorded at its transaction price (cost) rather than its market value. In addition, fixed assets, like hotel buildings, must be depreciated over time on the company's records. The application of this principle prevents management from arbitrarily inflating the value of an asset on the company's balance sheet and from artificially increasing profits on its income statement as the market value of the asset increases over time. Unfortunately, the application of this principle can result in the value of a company's assets being understated. An example of this is a hotel like the Waldorf-Astoria located in the heart of Manhattan. While its balance sheet shows the value of the hotel at its original cost less many years' worth of depreciation expense, the true market value of the hotel is significantly higher than the value shown on the balance sheet. Unless you are aware of how this principle works, you could significantly underestimate the true value of the company.

The **full disclosure principle** requires that all potential events that could impact a company's financial position or operating results be clearly reflected on the company's financial statements or noted within footnotes attached to the financial statements. For example, a pending lawsuit against the company involving its pension plan must be noted for those analyzing the financial statements to properly gauge the future profitability and value of the company.

The **revenue recognition principle** states that revenues should be recorded in the month they are earned, not when the contract is signed. For example, a controller should not recognize (record) $10,000 of room sales for a convention group until the convention actually takes place and the attendees have stayed in the hotel. Some companies violate this principle in an effort to show higher revenues and profit for a particular month.

The **matching principle,** following the revenue recognition principle, requires that all expenses incurred in order to generate a particular revenue are recorded in the period the revenue is earned, even if the expense has not yet been paid. For example, if a business incurs $10,000 in labor costs to generate $30,000 of banquet revenue, the $10,000 should be recorded as an expense in the current month even though it will not be paid until the following month.

The **monetary unit principle** states that only transactions that can be expressed in terms of money should be shown on a company's financial statements. It is because of this principle that businesses have begun to debate the feasibility of measuring human capital. No agreement, however, has been reached, and therefore the value of a company's employees cannot be reflected on its financial statements.

The **economic entity principle** separates the dealings of a business from the private dealings of its owners. It prevents the commingling of a company's assets, liabilities, and net worth with those of the owners. This principle protects limited partners from becoming the target of lawsuits filed by disgruntled guests or suppliers. For example, if a guest is injured, sues the hotel for damages, and wins the lawsuit, the only assets affected are those of the company. The guest cannot go after the owner's personal assets if he wins the lawsuit.

The **going concern principle** requires businesses to assume they will continue to operate long into the foreseeable future. Thus, assets that have a useful life of several years are depreciated over the life of the asset rather than when they are acquired. This is consistent with the matching principle in that the cost of a hotel building is matched against the revenues it helps generate over time. The going concern principle requires that the cost of all operating equipment be depreciated over its useful life rather than expensed in the month it was purchased.

The **time period principle** states that the company must set specific time periods for measuring its financial results. For example, a company could elect to prepare its financial statements monthly, quarterly, annually, or a combination thereof. In each case, the financial statements should clearly state the time period being reported.

The last accounting principle, **materiality,** states that if a revenue or expense is significant, it should have its own account on the income statement. For example, if banquets are an important source of revenue, a banquet revenue account should be included in the chart of accounts and shown on the income statement. On the other hand, if banquets are not a significant source of revenue, they should be recorded as part of food and/or beverage revenue.

A clear understanding of how the application of these accounting principles can impact a company's financial statements will enable you, as a hospitality manager, to effectively read, analyze, and interpret financial statements so you can make intelligent financial business decisions.

UNIFORM SYSTEMS OF ACCOUNTS

The three best-known systems of accounts used in the hospitality industry are the systems for lodging, foodservice, and club management.

LODGING INDUSTRY. The Uniform System of Accounts for Lodging was first published by the Hotel Association of New York in 1926 and included an expense dictionary that defined and categorized accounts. The ninth edition added industry trends. The tenth edition was published in 2006.

FOODSERVICE INDUSTRY. The Uniform System of Accounts for Restaurants, first published in 1927, is currently in its seventh edition. It provides sample financial statements, classifications of accounts, and an expense dictionary.

CLUB INDUSTRY. The club industry is self-regulating. Because a club's members are also its owners, accountability is of the utmost importance. The Club Managers Association of America, formed in 1927, published the Proposed Uniform System of Accounts for City Clubs in 1942. It was not until 1954, however, that the first Uniform System of Accounts for Clubs was adopted by the club management industry. Its most recent edition, the fifth, is known as the Uniform System of Financial Reporting for Clubs.

Other uniform systems are available to the hospitality industry, including systems for time-share entities, condominium developments, health, racquet, and sports clubs, and spas. The Uniform System of Financial Reporting for Spas, the newest uniform system of accounts, was published in 2005 to better monitor spa services for upscale hotels and resorts.

Financial Statements

While you, as an entry-level hospitality manager, may not initially come in direct contact with the business's financial statements, as you advance in the company you will. Knowing how to read, understand, and analyze a business's financial statements is a valuable skill that will serve you well in the future. While it is not critical that you know how each statement is prepared, if you understand the basic components and what information is contained on each, you can better determine how the business is performing, how financially healthy it is, and how its value might be increased through better management. The better your working knowledge of financial statements, the more informed you will be and the better decisions you will make. The three primary financial statements you should be familiar with are the **income statement,** the **balance sheet,** and the **statement of cash flow.**

INCOME STATEMENT

The income statement, which is often referred to as a *profit and loss statement,* presents the operating results of a business over a specific period, usually a month, a quarter, or a year. The results are usually shown for the current month and year-to-date, with budget and prior year results provided for the purpose of comparison. The income statement presents revenues, operating expenses, capital expenses, and the resulting profit or loss for the period.

All income statements begin with a revenue section. Revenues are the sales generated by the business. The primary sales categories for a hotel are rooms, food, beverage, telephone, and other. The income statement for a restaurant includes food revenues, beverage revenues, and retail sales.

The second section of an income statement is operating expenses. Operating expenses are expenditures directly related to the day-to-day operation of the business and include the cost of goods sold, payroll, marketing, repair and maintenance, and energy expense. These are also called *controllable expenses* because management has direct influence over how much is spent each period. For example, a manager can schedule more or less waitstaff, thereby controlling the amount of payroll cost. A manager can also work with his staff to conserve energy, thereby controlling the amount of energy expense.

For a hotel, operating expenses are subdivided into two sections: departmental expenses and unallocated expenses. **Department expenses** are those costs that can be charged directly to one department or profit center, while **unallocated expenses** are those costs that apply to two or more departments of the hotel. For example, the front office manager's salary is charged directly to the rooms department, while the general manager's salary is an unallocated expense.

The four standard departmental expense categories are rooms, food and beverage, telephone, and other. Food and beverage are combined, as many of the same employees sell and service both food and beverage items. The standard unallocated expense categories are administrative and general, marketing, property operations and maintenance, and utilities. It is important that you not only know these expense categories but also that you know what expenditures are charged to each. This knowledge enables you not only to flag problems when they occur but also to home in on specific expenses that may be out of line.

The last section of an income statement covers capital expenses. **Capital expenses** are primarily fixed costs related to the physical structure and include interest expense, property taxes, insurance, and depreciation expense. Capital expenses are sometimes referred to as *fixed costs* because they cannot be controlled on a daily or monthly basis by management. For example, once a bank loan is negotiated, the amount of the interest expense is fixed.

The last line on an income statement, often referred to as the **bottom line,** is net income, or profit and loss. If revenues exceed expenses, the business shows a profit. If revenues fall short of expenses, the business shows a loss. Illustration 2-1 shows a standard income statement for a hotel. Illustration 2-2 shows a standard income statement for a restaurant.

BALANCE SHEET

The **balance sheet** is also referred to as the *statement of financial condition.* It provides a snapshot of a company's financial position as of a certain date. It consists of three categories of accounts: assets, liabilities, and equity. On a balance sheet, total assets equal total liabilities plus total equity. In other words, for every dollar of assets, creditors have first claim, then whatever is left goes to the equity holders.

Assets are items of value the company owns, such as cash, inventories, land, buildings, and equipment. Assets are subdivided into current assets and fixed assets. **Current assets** have an estimated life of one year or less, while the estimated life of a **fixed asset** is more than one year. Assets are listed in the order of their **liquidity.** An asset's liquidity relates to how easily and quickly it can be converted into cash.

Liabilities are obligations the company owes government, lenders, vendors, suppliers, and employees. Liabilities are divided into current and long term. Current liabilities are obligations

Sample Hotel
Income Statement
For the Year Ended December 31, 2008

			%
Revenues:			
Rooms	$	1,512,732	64.38
Food		512,650	21.82
Beverage		265,200	11.29
Telecommunications		22,122	0.94
Other Operated Departments		25,088	1.07
Rental and Other Income		12,000	0.51
Total Revenues	$	2,349,792	100.00
Departmental Expenses:			
Rooms	$	361,745	23.91
Food		435,753	85.00
Beverage		159,120	60.00
Telecommunications		27,653	125.00
Other Operated Departments		11,540	46.00
Total Departmental Expenses	$	995,810	42.38
Gross Operating Income	$	1,353,982	57.62
Undistributed Operating Expenses:			
Administrative and General	$	187,921	8.00
Marketing		192,326	8.18
Franchise Fees		113,455	4.83
Property Operations and Maintenance		117,490	5.00
Utilities		93,992	4.00
Total Undistributed Operating Expenses	$	705,183	30.01
Gross Operating Profit (House Profit)	$	648,798	27.61
Management Fee	$	70,494	3.00
Fixed Expenses			
Property Taxes	$	101,379	4.31
Reserve for Capital Improvements	$	93,992	4.00
Insurance		50,000	2.13
Interest Expense		30,000	1.28
Total Fixed Charges	$	275,371	11.72
Net Operating Income (NOI)	$	373,427	15.80

ILLUSTRATION 2-1
Sample Hotel Income Statement for the Year Ended December 31, 2008

Sample Restaurant
Income Statement
For the Year Ended June 30, 2008

			%
Revenues:			
Food	$	890,000	78.20
Beverage		220,000	19.33
Others		28,100	2.47
Total Revenues	$	1,138,100	100.00
Cost of Sales:			
Food	$	320,400	36.00
Beverage		48,400	22.00
Others		15,455	55.00
Total Cost of Sales	$	384,255	33.76
Gross Profit:			
Food	$	569,600	50.05
Beverage		171,600	15.08
Others		12,645	1.11
Total Gross Profit	$	753,845	66.24
Operating (Controllable) Expenses:			
Salaries and Wages	$	352,811	31.00
Employee Benefits		105,843	9.30
Direct Operating Expenses		68,286	6.00
Marketing		39,834	3.50
Utilities		44,386	3.90
Administration and General		28,453	2.50
Repairs and Maintenance		25,038	2.20
Music and Entertainment		31,867	2.80
Total Operating Expenses	$	696,517	61.20
Operating Income	$	57,328	5.04
Other (Noncontrollable) Expenses:			
Rent	$	8,000	0.70
Depreciation		20,470	1.80
Interest		4,500	0.40
Total Noncontrollable Expenses	$	32,970	2.90
Income Before Income Taxes	$	24,358	2.14

ILLUSTRATION 2-2
Sample Restaurant Income Statement for the Year Ended June 30, 2008

due within the period being reported, while long-term liabilities have due dates longer than the subject period.

The numerical difference between assets and liabilities is called **equity.** Equity is the amount of capital invested in the business plus retained earnings. If the business is a corporation, the investment is called *common* or *preferred stock.* If the business is a partnership, the investment is called *partnership interests.* Retained earnings are prior-year profits that have not been paid out to owners as dividends.

It is important to note that the amount of equity shown on a balance sheet is shown at cost and may not be the true market value of the company. As we discuss later in this book, the true value of a business is a function of the cash flow it generates or is projected to generate. Don't be misled and assume that *equity* is synonymous with *value.* Illustration 2-3 provides an example of a balance sheet.

STATEMENT OF CASH FLOW

A third financial statement is the **statement of cash flow,** also known as the *sources and uses of funds statement.* If you refer to Illustration 2-4, you will see why this is its name. The statement presents cash flow from operations, cash flow from investing activities, and cash flow from financing activities. As shown in Illustration 2-4, the Danforth Hotel has generated a cash flow of $4,560. Also note that retained earnings have increased by $7,980. Question: How did the hotel increase cash flow by only $4,560 when it generated a profit of $7,980? When managing a business, it is important to note that generating a profit does not automatically create cash flow. This is why the statement of cash flow is important.

In the case of Danforth, the company received funds from its owners while paying down long-term debt. A net amount of $2,000 was generated from financing activities. The $4,560 increase in cash is a result of a series of activities involving cash, not net income alone.

THE REAL DEAL

The statement of cash flow is a useful and insightful tool. It not only ties the income statement and balance sheet together but also deals with the most important asset a business can have: cash. However, it has not always been a required statement. Not until the Tax Reform Act of 1986 was passed that the statement of cash flow finally became a required statement like the income statement and the balance sheet. Currently, any filing with the SEC must include this statement.

Management Reports

As a new hospitality manager, you will likely encounter several managerial reports immediately. Knowing how to read and analyze these reports will make you a better manager.

Danforth's Hotel
Balance Sheets
As of December 31, 2007 and 2008

Cash	$ 8,000.00	$ 12,560.00
Accounts Receivable	2,000.00	4,000.00
Marketable Securities	6,000.00	6,000.00
Inventory	13,150.00	15,000.00
Prepaid Rent	10,000.00	13,500.00
Total Current Assets	39,150.00	51,060.00
Furniture, Fixture, and Equipment (FF&E)	8,560.00	17,500.00
Accumulated Depreciation (FF&E)	(3,030.00)	(4,000.00)
Building	20,000.00	20,000.00
Long-term Investments	30,000.00	15,000.00
Total Long-term Assests	55,530.00	48,500.00
Total Assets	**$ 94,680.00**	**$ 99,560.00**
Accounts Payable	$ 15,000.00	$ 12,460.00
Accrued Payroll	7,500.00	8,000.00
Accrued Taxes	8,560.00	5,500.00
Total Current Liabilities	31,060.00	25,960.00
Long-term Debt	22,500.00	15,000.00
Owner's Equity	31,120.00	40,620.00
Retained Earnings	10,000.00	17,980.00
Total Owner's Equity	41,120.00	58,600.00
Total Liabilities and Owner's Equity	**$ 94,680.00**	**$ 99,560.00**

ILLUSTRATION 2-3
Danforth's Hotel Balance Sheets as of December 31, 2007 and 2008

DAILY REVENUE REPORT

The first management report you will probably work with is a form of the **daily revenue report.** As a hotel front office manager, you will want to know what your hotel's occupancy, average daily rate, and revenue per available room (RevPAR) are each day, how current performance compares with last year's performance, and how it compares to the budget. As the manager of a private country club, you will be interested in guest fees, golf cart rentals, food and beverage revenues, and the membership dues collected.

Illustration 2-5 shows the daily operations report for the All Sports Resort. All Sports is a large hotel corporation that manages over 100 properties worldwide. As you can see, the All

Danforth's Hotel
Balance Sheets
As of December 31, 2007 and 2008

	2008	2007	Increase or (Decrease)
Cash	$ 8,000.00	$ 12,560.00	$ 4,560.00
Accounts Receivable	2,000.00	4,000.00	$ 2,000.00
Marketable Securities	6,000.00	6,000.00	$
Inventory	13,150.00	15,000.00	$ 1,850.00
Prepaid Rent	10,000.00	13,500.00	$ 3,500.00
Total Current Asset	39,150.00	51,060.00	
Furniture, Fixtures, and Equipment (FF&E)	8,560.00	17,500.00	$ 8,940.00
Accumulated Depreciation (FF&E)	(3,030.00)	(4,000.00)	$ (970.00)
Building	20,000.00	20,000.00	
Long-term Investments	30,000.00	15,000.00	$ (15,000.00)
Long-term Assets	55,530.00	48,500.00	
Total Assets	$ 94,680.00	$ 99,560.00	
Accounts Payable	$ 15,000.00	$ 12,460.00	$ (2,540.00)
Accrued Payroll	7,500.00	8,000.00	$ 500.00
Accrued Taxes	8,560.00	5,500.00	$ (3,060.00)
Total Current Liabilities	31,060.00	25,960.00	
Long-term Debt	22,500.00	15,000.00	$ (7,500.00)
Owner's Equity	31,120.00	40,620.00	$ 9,500.00
Retained Earnings	10,000.00	17,980.00	$ 7,980.00
Total Owner's Equity	41,120.00	58,600.00	
Total Liabilities and Owner's Equity	$ 94,680.00	$ 99,560.00	

Danforth's Hotel
Income Statement
For the Year Ended December 31, 2008

Revenues:		
Rooms		$ 109,000.00
Food and Beverage		22,000.00
Others		2,810.00
Total Revenues		$ 133,810.00
Cost of Sales:		
Rooms		21,800.00
Food and Beverage		7,700.00
Others		1,545.50
Total Cost of Sales		31,045.50
Gross Profit:		
Rooms		87,200.00
Food and Beverage		14,300.00
Others		1,264.50
Total Gross Profit		102,764.50
Operating (Controllable) Expenses:		
Salaries and Wages		42,819.20
Employee Benefits		12,417.57
Direct Operating Expenses		7,894.79
Marketing		5,084.78
Utilities		5,084.78
Administration and General		3,345.25
Repairs and Maintenance		2,676.20
Music and Entertainment		3,612.87
Total Operating Expenses		82,935.44
Operating Income		19,829.06
Other (Noncontrollable) Expenses:		
Rent		7,800.00
Depreciation		970.00
Interest		1,084.00
Total Noncontrollable Expenses		9,854.00
Income Before Income Taxes		9,975.06
Less: Taxes		1,995.06
Net Income		$ 7,980.00

Danforth's Hotel
Statement of Cash Flow
For the Year Ended December 31, 2008

Cash flows from operations:		
Net Income	$ 7,980.00	
Increase in depreciation	970.00	
Increase in accounts receivables	(2,000.00)	
Increase in inventory	(1,850.00)	
Increase in prepaid rent	(3,500.00)	
Decrease in accounts payable	(2,540.00)	
Increase in accrued payroll	500.00	
Decrease in accrued taxes	(3,060.00)	$ (3,500.00)
Cash flows from investing activities:		
Purchase of FF&E	(8,940.00)	
Sale of long-term investments	15,000.00	$ 6,060.00
Cash flow from financing activities:		
Payment of long-term debt	(7,500.00)	
Increase in owner's equity	9,500.00	$ 2,000.00
Total cash flows		$ 4,560.00
Beginning cash balance		8,000.00
Add changes in cash		4,560.00
=Ending cash balance		$ 12,560.00

ILLUSTRATION 2-4

Danforth's Hotel Balance Sheets as of December 31, 2007 and 2008, Income Statement for the Year Ended December 31, 2008, and Statement of Cash Flow for the Year Ended December 31, 2008

	Today		ALL SPORTS RESORT			Run date: 11/10/2XX8	
						Run time: 8:35 am	
			As of Friday, 11/10/2xx8				
	Today		KEY METRICS		Period-to-Date		
Actual	Budget	Last Year		Actual	Budget	Last Year	
70.3%	90.4%	91.8%	TOTAL OCCUPANCY %	70.4%	80.0%	72.2%	
76.8%	91.2%	92.5%	AVAILABLE OCCUPANCY %	76.7%	80.6%	73.4%	
391	391	391	TOTAL ROOMS	10,948	10,948	10,948	
275	353	359	ROOMS SOLD	7,706	8,753	7,900	
279	357	362	OCCUPIED ROOMS	7,818	8,835	7,971	
4	3	4	COMPLIMENTARY ROOMS	112	82	74	
29	0	0	OUT-OF-ORDER ROOMS	784	0	119	
112	34	28	VACANT ROOMS	3,130	2,113	2,974	
358	388	388	AVAILABLE ROOMS	10,052	10,866	10,758	
65.97	86.09	71.25	NET AVERAGE RATE	93.97	91.67	94.09	
46.40	77.83	65.42	REVPAR	66.14	73.29	67.90	
248	N/A	267	ARRIVALS	4,382	N/A	4,382	
122	N/A	218	DEPARTURES	4,149	N/A	4,087	
522	N/A	636	GUESTS	9,482	N/A	9,734	
46	78	136	ROOMS SOLD-Transient	3,243	4,297	4,212	
172	220	183	ROOMS SOLD-Group	3,131	2,870	2,365	
57	59	39	ROOMS SOLD-Contract	1,332	1,586	1,335	
85.61	111.06	81.29	AVERAGE RATE- Transient	117.97	111.06	113.44	
66.14	85.41	72.09	AVERAGE RATE- Group	87.04	85.40	89.72	
49.23	49.34	47.18	AVERAGE RATE- Contract	48.57	49.34	49.00	
	Today		DEPARTMENT		Period-to-Date		
Actual	Budget	Last Year		Actual	Budget	Last Year	
3,938	8,647	11,056	Rooms-Transient	382,569	477,239	477,795	
11,375	18,785	13,193	Rooms-Group	272,525	245,110	212,179	
2,806	2,929	1,840	Rooms -Contract	64,696	78,253	65,411	
18,119	30,361	26,089	FULL DAY - ROOMS	719,790	800,602	755,385	
(15)	0	0	ALL SPORTS REWARDS (NET)	(450)	0	(2,896)	
0	0	0	PART DAY	1,808	0	1,287	
898	125	0	OTHER REVENUE	8,468	3,100	0	
(861)	(55)	(511)	ROOM-OTHER REBATES	(5,518)	(1,350)	(10,428)	
18,142	30,432	25,578	NET ROOM SALES	724,098	802,352	743,347	
112	1,018	(1,065)	TELEPHONE	18,046	25,200	20,318	
112	1,018	(1,065)	TELEPHONE	18,046	25,200	20,318	
286	744	415	GIFT SHOP	10,075	18,413	12,431	
286	744	415	GIFT SHOP	10,075	18,413	12,431	
52	583	(861)	RENTS & COMMISSIONS	8,290	14,439	7,578	
52	583	(861)	RENTS & COMMISSIONS	8,290	14,439	7,578	
70	(40)	57	TRADEOUT	(2,094)	(997)	(750)	
70	(40)	57	TRADEOUT	(2,094)	(997)	(750)	
0	0	0	AUDIO VISUAL	(156)	0	0	
0	1	0	Local Audio Visual	7,458	14,153	8,080	
0	1	786	Group Audio Visual	14,148	11,503	17,508	
0	2	786	AUDIO VISUAL	21,450	25,656	25,588	
1,613	2,631	2,150	CASUAL RESTAURANT	65,678	65,158	51,901	
1,613	2,631	2,150	CASUAL RESTAURANT	65,678	65,158	51,901	
2,593	1,868	1,778	ENTERTAINMENT LOUNGE	46,224	46,248	39,737	
2,593	1,868	1,778	LOUNGES	46,224	46,248	39,737	
0	0	0	BANQUETS	(1,829)	0	0	
599	13	(36)	Local Banquet	108,240	129,754	108,876	
111	10	1,698	Group Banquet	77,789	98,867	86,209	
710	22	1,662	BANQUETS	184,200	228,621	195,085	
517	1,062	1,011	ROOM SERVICE	17,829	26,289	23,286	
517	1,062	1,011	ROOM SERVICE	17,829	26,289	23,286	
5,433	5,585	7,387	TOTAL FOOD AND BEVERAGE	335,382	391,972	335,596	
24,095	38,321	31,511	TOTAL SALES	1,093,796	1,251,379	1,118,519	
	(14,226)	(7,416)	TOTAL SALES VARIANCE (+/-)		(157,583)	(24,722)	

ILLUSTRATION 2-5

Daily Operations Report for All Sports Resort

			ALL SPORTS RESORT				Run date: 11/10/2XX8
							Run time: 8:35 am
			As of Friday, 11/10/2xx8				
	Today		ROOM SEGMENTATION		Period-to-Date		
Rooms	Revenue	Avg Rate		Rooms	Revenue	Avg Rate	
			WEEKDAY				
0	0	0.00	Premium	382	62,252	162.96	
0	0	0.00	Corporate	657	97,251	148.02	
0	0	0.00	Special Corporate	953	111,113	116.59	
0	0	0.00	Transient	30	2,862	95.40	
0	0	0.00	Other Discounts	312	30,844	98.86	
0	0	0.00	Leisure	68	5,467	80.40	
0	0	0.00	Weekend	1	95	95.00	
0	0	0.00	Govt/Military	131	9,715	74.16	
0	0	0.00	AARP	60	8,259	137.65	
0	0	0.00	Travel Industry	77	9,212	119.64	
0	0	0.00	All Sports Employees	17	873	51.35	
0	0	0.00	All Sports Rewards	27	534	19.78	
0	0	0.00	TOTAL TRANSIENT	2,715	338,477	124.67	
0	0	0.00	Corporate group	881	95,431	108.32	
0	0	0.00	Association group	145	15,537	107.15	
0	0	0.00	Other group	1,113	92,994	83.55	
0	0	0.00	TOTAL GROUP	2,139	203,962	95.35	
0	0	0.00	CONTRACT	977	47,488	48.61	
0	0	0.00	TOTAL WEEKDAY	5,831	589,927	101.17	
			WEEKEND				
2	328	164.00	Premium	25	3,359	134.36	
0	0	0.00	Regular	0	(363)	0.00	
4	606	151.50	Corporate	16	2,637	164.81	
4	419	104.75	Special Corporate	56	6,069	108.38	
7	632	90.29	Transient	83	7,289	87.82	
5	340	68.00	Other Discounts	75	5,279	70.39	
0	0	0.00	Package	6	474	79.00	
17	1,294	76.12	Leisure	150	11,637	77.58	
0	0	0.00	Weekend	1	94	94.00	
0	0	0.00	Govt/Military	21	1,540	73.33	
3	225	75.00	AARP	20	1,606	80.30	
0	0	0.00	Travel Industry	21	2,625	125.00	
1	49	49.00	All Sports Employees	27	1,471	54.48	
3	45	15.00	All Sports Rewards	27	375	13.89	
46	3,938	85.61	TOTAL TRANSIENT	528	44,092	83.51	
0	0	0.00	Corporate group	76	5,886	77.45	
0	0	0.00	Association group	34	2,342	68.88	
172	11,375	66.14	Other group	882	60,335	68.41	
172	11,375	66.14	TOTAL GROUP	992	68,563	69.12	
57	2,806	49.23	CONTRACT	355	17,208	48.47	
275	18,119	65.89	TOTAL WEEKEND	1,875	129,863	69.26	
275	18,119	65.89	TOTAL ROOMS	7,706	719,790	93.41	

ILLUSTRATION 2-5
(Continued)

Sports daily revenue report provides information related to occupied rooms, average rate, RevPAR, departmental revenue, and market segmentation, with actual results compared with the prior year and to the budget.

DAILY PAYROLL COST REPORT

Because labor cost is a significant expense for most hospitality operations, it is usually monitored and controlled daily. Illustration 2-6 presents a **daily payroll cost report** for a conference hotel.

Date: 6/5/08

	Regular Hours	Overtime Hours	Total	Payroll	Daily %	Month-to-Date Regular	Overtime	Hours Total	M-T-D Payroll	M-T-D Payroll %	Budget Payroll %
Rooms											
Front Desk	38.10	0.00	38.10	$565.79	2.10	671.98	1.67	673.65	$9,930.64	3.99	3.49
Reservations	13.03	0.00	13.03	$206.70	0.77	269.27	14.66	283.93	$4,131.34	1.66	1.74
Guest Services	22.03	0.00	22.03	$252.39	0.94	338.09	15.84	353.93	$4,412.27	1.77	1.98
Housekeeping	85.70	0.00	85.70	$905.15	3.35	1,685.39	125.35	1,810.74	$19,480.01	7.82	9.50
Management	0.00	0.00	0.00	$0.00	0.00	0.00	0.00	0.00	$0.00	0.00	0.30
Total Rooms	*158.86*	*0.00*	*158.86*	*$1,930.03*	*7.15*	*2,964.73*	*157.52*	*3,122.25*	*$37,954.26*	*15.24*	*16.70*
Food and Beverage											
Culinary	66.11	0.00	66.11	$1,073.73	7.68	1,453.06	147.04	1,600.10	$25,255.33	8.86	8.32
Stewarding	56.16	0.00	56.16	$533.95	3.82	683.82	101.99	785.81	$7,496.51	2.63	2.87
Banquet Service	10.37	0.00	10.37	$154.37	1.10	1,279.19	155.28	1,434.47	$10,259.48	3.60	2.96
In-room Dining	17.00	0.00	17.00	$122.87	0.88	123.16	10.51	133.67	$1,107.43	0.39	0.82
Cuisine	86.94	0.00	86.94	$913.31	6.54	1,655.17	87.27	1,742.44	$17,676.80	6.20	6.05
Casual	7.67	0.00	7.67	$46.02	0.33	134.99	0.00	134.99	$849.70	0.30	0.57
General	21.36	0.00	21.36	$314.55	2.25	371.83	18.51	390.34	$6,768.40	2.37	2.59
Pantry	24.34	0.00	24.34	$111.54	0.80	316.83	22.51	339.34	$1,644.71	0.58	0.40
Total F&B	*289.95*	*0.00*	*289.95*	*$3,270.34*	*23.40*	*6,018.05*	*543.11*	*6,561.16*	*$71,058.36*	*24.93*	*24.58*
Conference Service											
Conf. Management	24.78	0.00	24.78	$563.84	2.06	349.35	7.67	357.02	$8,351.13	4.10	6.91
Audio Visual	61.03	0.00	61.03	$992.95	3.63	497.60	65.95	563.55	$10,569.75	5.20	6.59
Conf. Attendants	27.00	0.00	27.00	$140.44	0.51	209.50	46.67	256.17	$1,543.19	0.76	1.86
Conf. Floor	17.33	0.00	17.33	$266.69	0.97	189.99	40.49	230.48	$3,864.09	1.90	2.28
Concierge	22.17	0.00	22.17	$268.79	0.98	239.02	8.01	247.03	$3,058.06	1.50	2.76
Total Conf. Service	*152.31*	*0.00*	*152.31*	*$2,232.71*	*8.16*	*1,485.46*	*168.79*	*1,654.25*	*$27,386.22*	*13.46*	*20.39*
Telephone	*8.17*	*0.00*	*8.17*	*$102.62*	*7.54*	*88.17*	*1.51*	*89.68*	*$1,135.88*	*15.03*	*37.86*
Transportation	*7.50*	*0.00*	*7.50*	*$76.05*	*0.00*	*104.01*	*21.67*	*125.68*	*$1,384.28*	*1977.54*	*211.45*
Fitness Center	*0.00*	*0.00*	*0.00*	*$0.00*	*0*	*0.00*	*0.00*	*0.00*	*$0.00*	*0.00*	*0.07*

ILLUSTRATION 2-6

Daily Payroll Report for Florencia Hotel and Conference Center

A&G	Regular Hours	Overtime Hours	Total	Payroll	Daily %	Month-to-Date Regular	Overtime	Hours Total	M-T-D Payroll	M-T-D Payroll %	Budget Payroll %
Executive	19.09	0.00	19.09	$638.90	0.91	248.96	0.00	248.96	$8,864.51	1.08	1.53
Accounting	41.91	0.00	41.91	$833.46	1.19	598.12	10.17	608.29	$12,333.28	1.50	2.01
Security	9.50	0.00	9.50	$109.25	0.16	99.00	21.34	120.34	$1,506.62	0.18	0.59
Purchasing	5.70	0.00	5.70	$147.29	0.21	97.10	0.00	97.10	$2,509.08	0.31	0.36
MIS	5.70	0.00	5.70	$191.81	0.27	96.20	0.00	96.20	$3,267.45	0.40	0.40
Total A&G	81.90	0.00	81.90	$1,920.71	2.75	1,139.38	31.51	1,170.89	$28,480.94	3.47	4.89
Human Resources	19.08	0.00	19.08	$461.75	0.66	268.08	0.00	268.08	$6,817.00	0.83	1.04
Sales	43.85	0.00	43.85	$1,183.21	1.69	635.92	1.34	637.26	$17,572.66	2.14	2.68
Property Operations	51.88	0.00	51.88	$935.16	1.34	690.85	20.69	711.54	$12,850.46	1.56	2.17
Laundry	31.50	0.00	31.50	$305.61	0.44	302.83	0.00	302.83	$2,979.13	0.36	0.48
Cafeteria	12.17	0.00	12.17	$118.54	0.17	190.18	60.67	250.85	$2,708.06	0.33	0.36
Total Property	857.17	0.00	857.17	$12,536.74	17.94	13,887.66	1,006.81	14,894.47	$210,327.25	25.60	31.77

Today's Stats

Ttl Rooms	144
Bqt Cvrs	3
Cuis Cvrs	287
IRD Cvrs	17
Wats Cvrs	11
CB Cvrs	203
Ttl Cvrs	521
Conf. Gsts	203

M-T-D Stats

Ttl Rooms	1,593
Bqt Cvrs	3,109
Cuis Cvrs	4,629
IRD Cvrs	222
Wats Cvrs	115
CB Cvrs	2,189
Ttl Cvrs	10,264
Conf. Gsts	2,189

ILLUSTRATION 2-6
(Continued)

	Regular Hours	Overtime Hours	Total	Payroll	Labor Cost Cost/Room	Month-to-Date Regular	Month-to-Date Overtime	Hours Total	M-T-D Payroll	M-T-D Labor Cost Cost/Room	Budget Labor Cost Cost/Room
Rooms											
Front Desk	38.10	0.00	38.10	$565.79	$3.93	671.98	1.67	673.65	$9,930.64	$6.23	$5.29
Reservations	13.03	0.00	13.03	$206.70	$1.44	269.27	14.66	283.93	$4,131.34	$2.59	$2.64
Guest Services	22.03	0.00	22.03	$252.39	$1.75	338.09	15.84	353.93	$4,412.27	$2.77	$3.00
Housekeeping	85.70	0.00	85.70	$905.15	$6.29	1,685.39	125.35	1,810.74	$19,480.01	$12.23	$14.43
Management	0.00	0.00	0.00	$0.00	$0.00	0.00	0.00	0.00	$0.00	$0.00	$0.45
Total Rooms	*158.86*	*0.00*	*158.86*	*$1,930.03*	*$13.40*	*2,964.73*	*157.52*	*3,122.25*	*$37,954.26*	*$23.83*	*$25.36*
Food and Beverage					*Cost/Cover*					*Cost/Cover*	*Cost/Cover*
Culinary	66.11	0.00	66.11	$1,073.73	$2.06	1,453.06	147.04	1,600.10	$25,255.33	$2.46	$2.51
Stewarding	56.16	0.00	56.16	$533.95	$1.02	683.82	101.99	785.81	$7,496.51	$0.73	$0.87
Banquet Service	10.37	0.00	10.37	$154.37	$51.46	1,279.19	155.28	1,434.47	$10,259.48	$3.30	$2.91
In-room Dining	17.00	0.00	17.00	$122.87	$7.23	123.16	10.51	133.67	$1,107.43	$4.99	$9.83
Cuisine	86.94	0.00	86.94	$913.31	$3.18	1,655.17	87.27	1,742.44	$17,676.80	$3.82	$3.85
Coasters	7.67	0.00	7.67	$46.02	$4.18	134.99	0.00	134.99	$849.70	$7.39	$6.72
General	21.36	0.00	21.36	$314.55	$0.60	371.83	18.51	390.34	$6,768.40	$0.66	$0.78
Pantry	24.34	0.00	24.34	$111.54	$0.55	316.83	22.51	339.34	$1,644.71	$0.75	$0.71
Total F&B	*289.95*	*0.00*	*289.95*	*$3,270.34*	*$6.28*	*6,018.05*	*543.11*	*6,561.16*	*$71,058.36*	*$6.92*	*$7.41*
Conference Service					*Cost/Cnf Gst*					*Cost/Cnf Gst*	*Cost/Cnf Gst*
Conf. Management	24.78	0.00	24.78	$563.84	$2.78	349.35	7.67	357.02	$8,351.13	$3.82	$5.82
Audio Visual	61.03	0.00	61.03	$992.95	$4.89	497.60	65.95	563.55	$10,569.75	$4.83	$5.55
Conf. Attendants	27.00	0.00	27.00	$140.44	$0.69	209.50	46.67	256.17	$1,543.19	$0.71	$1.56
Conf. Floor	17.33	0.00	17.33	$266.69	$1.31	189.99	40.49	230.48	$3,864.09	$1.77	$1.92
Concierge	22.17	0.00	22.17	$268.79	$1.32	239.02	8.01	247.03	$3,058.06	$1.40	$2.32
Total Conf. Service	*152.31*	*0.00*	*152.31*	*$2,232.71*	*$11.00*	*1,485.46*	*168.79*	*1,654.25*	*$27,386.22*	*$12.51*	*$17.18*

ILLUSTRATION 2-6
(Continued)

The top part of the report details the daily and month-to-date regular hours, overtime hours, and total payroll by department. The totals are also compared to the budget. The bottom part of the report includes rooms sold and foodservice covers to measure labor productivity. Three common productivity measures are labor cost per room, cost per cover, and cost per conference guest. With recent hospitality technology advances, most hospitality operations utilize electronic time management systems to record payroll hours incurred and to control labor cost.

ROOMS REVENUE FORECAST

The **rooms revenue forecast** is generated to help ensure the proper number of employees are scheduled each day and to achieve labor productivity goals. Illustration 2-7 shows two forms of rooms forecast. The top form is a twelve-day rooms revenue forecast for the Huntington Hotel for the first twelve days of December. The bottom form summarizes the actual results for that period. As each day is completed, the actual number of rooms sold and rooms revenue generated are entered along with actual occupancy percentage, average daily rate, and revenue per available room.

Accurate forecasting is an extremely important skill for every hospitality manager to learn, whether he or she works in lodging, a restaurant, a club, or another related field in the hospitality industry. The better you plan and forecast your business, the better you will service your guests and control labor cost.

FOOD AND BEVERAGE MENU ABSTRACT

A useful report for food and beverage operations is the **food and beverage menu abstract.** The menu abstract tracks the popularity and the profitability of menu items to help management make menu changes as appropriate. The menu abstract can also be of value in calculating the theoretical food cost for a restaurant, which is then compared with the actual food cost for the period being analyzed.

Illustration 2-8 shows that Mexicana Cantina offers sixty-six lunch menu items. The most popular appetizer is chili con queso with jalapeños, with 778 portions sold, representing 5.56 percent of total sales. The most popular entrée is tacos al carbon, with 901 portions sold. Please note, however, that while only 286 portions (2.04 percent of sales) of chicken fajita quesadillas were sold, this menu item netted $1,981 in gross profit compared to the chili con queso gross profit of $2,723. The more interesting analysis is of the entrées. The 901 tacos al carbon (most popular entrée) sold netted Mexicana $7,713. The combination fajita platters, while not even ranked in the top ten items, sold 299 portions, which contributed $5,689.97 to Mexicana's bottom line and was its second most profitable item. This is a good indication of why the menu abstract is helpful in making smart food and beverage menu decisions.

FORECAST: as of 11/30/08

City: Los Angeles
Property: Huntington - Airport
Rooms: 86
Division: Rooms

Huntington Los Angeles Airport

12-Day Forecast Report	12/1/08	12/2/08	12/3/08	12/4/08	12/5/08	12/6/08	12/7/08	12/8/08	12/9/08	12/10/008	12/11/08	12/12/08
Avail Rooms	86	86	86	86	86	86	86	86	86	86	86	86
Forecast #	55	53	26	25	36	48	46	53	53	65	23	23
Forecast Occ. %	63.95%	61.63%	30.23%	29.07%	41.86%	55.81%	53.49%	61.63%	61.63%	75.58%	26.74%	26.74%
Net Rooms Revenues	6215	5313	2653	2724	4050	5272	4741	5313	5157	6153	2300	2473
Average Rate	$ 113.00	$ 100.25	$ 102.04	$ 108.96	$ 112.50	$ 109.83	$ 103.07	$ 100.25	$ 97.30	$ 94.66	$ 100.00	$ 107.52
REVPAR	$ 72.27	$ 61.78	$ 30.85	$ 31.64	$ 47.09	$ 61.30	$ 55.13	$ 61.78	$ 59.97	$ 71.55	$ 26.74	$ 28.76

ACTUAL: as of 12/13/08

City: Los Angeles
Property: Huntington - Airport
Rooms: 86
Division: Rooms

Huntington Los Angeles Airport

12-Day Forecast Report	12/1/08	12/2/08	12/3/08	12/4/08	12/5/08	12/6/08	12/7/08	12/8/08	12/9/08	12/10/008	12/11/08	12/12/08
Avail Rooms	86	86	86	86	86	86	86	86	86	86	86	86
Forecast #	55	53	26	25	36	48	46	53	53	65	23	23
Forecast Occ. %	63.95%	61.63%	30.23%	29.07%	41.86%	55.81%	53.49%	61.63%	61.63%	75.58%	26.74%	26.74%
Forecast Net Rms Rev	6215	5313	2653	2724	4050	5272	4741	5313	5157	6153	2300	2473
Forecast Average rate	$ 113.00	$ 100.25	$ 102.04	$ 108.96	$ 112.50	$ 109.83	$ 103.07	$ 100.25	$ 97.30	$ 94.66	$ 100.00	$ 107.52
Actual Occ Rooms	59	51	25	23	34	46	43	51	58	63	22	25
Actual Occ Rate	68.60%	59.30%	29.07%	26.74%	39.53%	53.49%	50.00%	59.30%	67.44%	73.26%	25.58%	29.07%
Actual Net Rms Rev	6799	5218	2533	2624	3738	5064	5088	5230	5757	5806	2253	2749
Actual Average Rate	$ 115.24	$ 102.31	$ 101.32	$ 114.09	$ 109.94	$ 110.09	$ 118.33	$ 102.55	$ 99.26	$ 92.16	$ 102.41	$ 109.96
REVPAR	$ 79.06	$ 60.67	$ 29.45	$ 30.51	$ 43.47	$ 58.88	$ 59.16	$ 60.81	$ 66.94	$ 67.51	$ 26.20	$ 31.97

ILLUSTRATION 2-7
Rooms Revenues Forecast for Huntington Los Angeles Airport

					Food Menu Abstract (Sales Mix)		
						Date: January-March, 2xx8	
Restaurant: Mexicana Cantina				Meal	Period: Lunch		

Menu Item Name	Number Sold (MM)	Menu Mix %	Item Food Cost	Item Selling Price	Item CM	Menu Costs	Menu Revenues	Menu CM
Bean, Cheese, and Jalapeño Nachos	170	1.21%	$2.44	$7.25	$4.81	$414.80	$1,232.50	$817.70
Beef, Bean, Cheese, and Jalapeño Nachos	180	1.29%	$2.78	$8.50	$5.72	$500.40	$1,530.00	$1,029.60
Chicken Fajita, Bean, Cheese, and Jalapeño Nachos	222	1.59%	$2.83	$9.95	$7.12	$628.26	$2,208.90	$1,580.64
Beef Fajita, Bean, Cheese, and Jalapeño Nachos	253	1.81%	$3.28	$9.95	$6.67	$829.84	$2,517.35	$1,687.51
Cheese Quesadillas	195	1.39%	$1.64	$7.75	$6.11	$319.80	$1,511.25	$1,191.45
Chicken Fajita Quesadillas	286	2.04%	$2.02	$8.95	$6.93	$577.72	$2,559.70	$1,981.98
Beef Fajita Quesadillas	259	1.85%	$2.48	$8.95	$6.47	$642.32	$2,318.05	$1,675.73
Shrimp and Scallop Quesadillas	158	1.13%	$3.82	$11.50	$7.68	$603.56	$1,817.00	$1,213.44
Shrimp Quesadillas	176	1.26%	$3.44	$11.50	$8.06	$605.44	$2,024.00	$1,418.56
Spinach Quesadillas	125	0.89%	$1.83	$8.50	$6.67	$228.75	$1,062.50	$833.75
Mixed Vegetable Quesadillas	91	0.65%	$1.75	$8.50	$6.75	$159.25	$773.50	$614.25
Mixed Vegetable Queso Flameado	37	0.26%	$1.24	$7.50	$6.26	$45.88	$277.50	$231.62
Chorizo Queso Flameado	117	0.84%	$1.47	$7.95	$6.48	$171.99	$930.15	$758.16
Chicken Fajita Queso Flameado	41	0.29%	$1.42	$8.25	$6.83	$58.22	$338.25	$280.03
Beef Fajita Queso Flameado	92	0.66%	$1.76	$8.25	$6.49	$161.92	$759.00	$597.08
Shrimp Queso Flameado	42	0.30%	$2.49	$10.25	$7.76	$104.58	$430.50	$325.92
Chili con Queso with Jalapeños	778	5.56%	$1.45	$4.95	$3.50	$1,128.10	$3,851.10	$2,723.00
Chili con Queso with Ground Beef and Jalapeños	293	2.09%	$1.59	$6.50	$4.91	$465.87	$1,904.50	$1,438.63
Chili con Queso with Chorizo and Jalapeños	210	1.50%	$1.79	$6.50	$4.71	$375.90	$1,365.00	$989.10
Christina's Queso	210	1.50%	$2.17	$6.95	$4.78	$455.70	$1,459.50	$1,003.80
Black Bean Soup	74	0.53%	$0.66	$4.25	$3.59	$48.84	$314.50	$265.66
Yucatan Tortilla Soup	366	2.62%	$2.65	$4.25	$1.60	$969.90	$1,555.50	$585.60
Caldo de Pollo	177	1.26%	$2.42	$4.25	$1.83	$428.34	$752.25	$323.91
Taco Salad with Ground Beef	115	0.82%	$1.89	$9.50	$7.61	$217.35	$1,092.50	$875.15
Taco Salad with Chicken Fajita	141	1.01%	$2.05	$9.50	$7.45	$289.05	$1,339.50	$1,050.45
Taco Salad with Beef Fajita	102	0.73%	$2.61	$9.50	$6.89	$266.22	$969.00	$702.78
Chicken Salad	208	1.49%	$1.76	$9.50	$7.74	$366.08	$1,976.00	$1,609.92
Chicken Fajita Platter 1/2 lb.	385	2.75%	$1.56	$11.95	$10.39	$600.60	$4,600.75	$4,000.15
Beef Fajita Platter 1/2 lb.	300	2.14%	$2.36	$13.95	$11.59	$708.00	$4,185.00	$3,477.00
Combination Fajita Platter 1/2 lb.	359	2.57%	$1.96	$12.95	$10.99	$703.64	$4,649.05	$3,945.41
Chicken Fajita Platter 1 lb.	161	1.15%	$3.07	$20.95	$17.88	$494.27	$3,372.95	$2,878.68
Beef Fajita Platter 1lb.	172	1.23%	$4.56	$24.90	$20.34	$784.32	$4,282.80	$3,498.48
Combination Fajita Platter 1 lb.	299	2.14%	$3.87	$22.90	$19.03	$1,157.13	$6,847.10	$5,689.97
Fajita Mixta Platter	395	2.82%	$2.71	$14.95	$12.24	$1,070.45	$5,905.25	$4,834.80
Chicken Alambres	372	2.66%	$1.46	$10.95	$9.49	$543.12	$4,073.40	$3,530.28
Pechugas de Pollo con Rajas de Chili con Queso	308	2.20%	$1.56	$10.95	$9.39	$480.48	$3,372.60	$2,892.12
Chicken Mole	329	2.35%	$0.94	$11.95	$11.01	$309.26	$3,931.55	$3,622.29
Progreso Mesquite Grilled Shrimp	296	2.12%	$3.09	$12.95	$9.86	$914.64	$3,833.20	$2,918.56
Camarones Diablos	510	3.64%	$5.97	$15.95	$9.98	$3,044.70	$8,134.50	$5,089.80
Camarones a la Mexicana	70	0.50%	$3.65	$14.95	$11.30	$255.50	$1,046.50	$791.00
Pasta Mariscos	54	0.39%	$4.09	$13.50	$9.41	$220.86	$729.00	$508.14
Pajaros a la Parilla (2)	98	0.70%	$4.40	$11.95	$7.55	$431.20	$1,171.10	$739.90
Pajaros a la Parilla (3)	32	0.23%	$6.15	$14.95	$8.80	$196.80	$478.40	$281.60
Cochinita Pibil	352	2.52%	$1.85	$14.95	$13.10	$651.20	$5,262.40	$4,611.20
Puerco Chops	222	1.59%	$2.23	$11.95	$9.72	$495.06	$2,652.90	$2,157.84
Sword Fish	31	0.22%	$3.57	$16.95	$13.38	$110.67	$525.45	$414.78
Mexicana's Combo Plate w/ crispy beef	95	0.68%	$1.58	$10.95	$9.37	$150.10	$1,040.25	$890.15
Mexicana's Combo Plate w/ crispy chicken	75	0.54%	$1.74	$10.95	$9.21	$130.50	$821.25	$690.75
Mexicana's Combo Plate w/ beef fajita	244	1.74%	$2.16	$10.95	$8.79	$0.00	$0.00	$0.00
Mexicana's Combo Plate w/ chicken fajita	85	0.61%	$1.70	$10.95	$9.25	$144.50	$930.75	$786.25
Cheese Enchiladas	317	2.27%	$1.52	$9.50	$7.98	$481.84	$3,011.50	$2,529.66
Chicken Enchiladas	96	0.69%	$2.82	$9.95	$7.13	$270.72	$955.20	$684.48
Beef Enchiladas	164	1.17%	$1.52	$9.95	$8.43	$249.28	$1,631.80	$1,382.52
Chicken Fajita Enchiladas	129	0.92%	$1.61	$10.50	$8.89	$207.69	$1,354.50	$1,146.81
Beef Fajita Enchiladas	164	1.17%	$2.17	$10.50	$8.33	$355.88	$1,722.00	$1,366.12
Chicken Enchilada Verdes	237	1.69%	$1.71	$10.50	$8.79	$405.27	$2,488.50	$2,083.23
Seafood Enchiladas	115	0.82%	$4.18	$11.95	$7.77	$480.70	$1,374.25	$893.55
Shrimp Enchiladas	106	0.76%	$3.35	$11.95	$8.60	$355.10	$1,266.70	$911.60
Spinach Enchiladas	68	0.49%	$1.31	$9.50	$8.19	$89.08	$646.00	$556.92
Mixed Vegetable Enchiladas	62	0.44%	$1.31	$9.50	$8.19	$81.22	$589.00	$507.78
Tacos al Carbon	901	6.44%	$1.39	$9.95	$8.56	$1,252.39	$8,964.95	$7,712.56
Tacos Pibil	507	0.02%	$1.01	$10.05	$0.01	$068.97	$5,551.65	$4,583.28
Flautas	236	1.69%	$1.36	$9.50	$8.14	$320.96	$0.00	$0.00
Chicken Fajita Burritos	212	1.51%	$1.81	$9.50	$7.69	$383.72	$2,014.00	$1,630.28
Beef Fajita Burritos	212	1.51%	$2.38	$9.50	$7.12	$504.56	$2,014.00	$1,509.44
Shrimp and Scallop Burritos	106	0.76%	$4.38	$11.95	$7.57	$464.28	$1,266.70	$802.42
	N							
Column Totals	13994	100.00%						

ILLUSTRATION 2-8

Food Menu Abstract for Mexicana Cantina Restaurant

PAPPAS FAMILY: PUBLIC, PRIVATE, OR BOTH?

Did you know that only 20% of businesses in the United States are public companies? In the foodservice industry, the percentage is even smaller. The Houston-based Pappas Restaurants, Inc., is a unique example of a successful private company that manages a public company. This close-knit, family-run business owns and operates more than 80 restaurants throughout the United States featuring several concepts, including Pappas Bros. Steakhouse, Pappadeaux Seafood Kitchen, and Pappasito's Cantina, in major cities like Houston, Dallas, San Antonio, Austin, Atlanta, Chicago, Denver, and Phoenix.

The family business, founded by Jim and Pete Pappas in 1967, started out as a refrigeration equipment company. Their first restaurants were the Dot Coffee Shop and the Brisket House, now known as Pappas Bar-B-Q. Today, Jim's sons, Harris and Chris Pappas, manage the chain of restaurants their father and uncle started. As their chain continues to grow, somewhat surprisingly, the brothers prefer to do nearly everything in-house rather than out source key functions. As Chris noted in 1997, "We have an attitude that we can do it better ourselves."

The Pappas family does all of the business's accounting in-house, operates its own restaurant supply company, and makes its own uniforms. The chain also creates its own specialized restaurant equipment and software programs.

While going public may seem like the logical next step to take the family enterprise to the next level, neither brother is in favor of it. They say they are having too much fun being in charge of their own private company. They believe there is a huge advantage to staying private rather than going public. The burden of providing short-term favorable financial results to public shareholders can be daunting. At best, they believe public company managers often are prone to make business decisions based solely on maximizing short-term operating results. Some top executives of public companies have indeed taken their responsibilities to the extreme by resorting to unethical window-dressing practices in an effort to improve short-term operating results at the expense of long-term performance. As a Pappas competitor, Tillman Fertitta, founder of the public company Landry's, Inc., observed: "I have to build a restaurant in four months and get it open quicker than I'd like to. They can take eighteen months to build a restaurant and throw as much labor as they want at it. They don't have to report quarter-to-quarter earnings."

While the Pappas prefer to keep their family business private, they have invested in, and now manage, Luby's Cafeterias, Inc., a large public company. Prior to the Pappas' investment, Luby's was struggling with cash flow problems and a tired product. In 2000, Harris and Chris purchased 1.3 million shares of Luby's stock, which represented approximately 6 percent ownership of the company. After dissident shareholders staged a proxy battle in March 2001, the brothers ousted corporate management, took control of the company, and lent Luby's $10 million in the form of convertible subordinated notes maturing in 2011.

Following the takeover, they sold the poorest-performing units to reduce debt and give the company more financial flexibility. In addition, they restructured Luby's default bank debt, which had been inherited from prior management, with a new $50 million revolving credit line and a $27.9 million secured loan. Operationally, they revamped the remaining units with new menus, new food presentations, more personal service, improved marketing, and better cost controls. As the result of their creativity and sound management skills, the Pappas have turned Luby's around and made the company profitable again. Luby's has shown seven consecutive quarters of same-store sales growth and recently announced it will open two new locations in 2007, another positive sign the company has fully recovered from its financial woes. The Pappas brothers' creativity and superior management turned the ailing company around. Today, the Pappas family owns approximately 20% of Luby's stock.

The Pappas family continues to resist the lure of Wall Street and chooses to keep the restaurant business they inherited from their father and uncle private to better maintain their identity and tradition. They continue to gain public company experience, however, by managing and growing Luby's Cafeterias, Inc. Will the lure of Wall Street eventually win them over, or will the advantages of operating a private company overrule? Only time will tell, as the brothers aren't talking. We'll all have to stay tuned to discover their next move.

SOURCES

Britton, N. "1919 Pete Harris Pappas 2005: A Leader in Houston's Restaurant Scene." *Houston Chronicle,* December 21, 2005.

Ruggless, R. "Chris Pappas: Minding the Family Business One Store at a Time." *Nation's Restaurant News,* (January 1997): 174–175.

Kaplan, D. "Pappas Brothers Find Ways to Reinvigorate Luby's While Keeping the Comfort Food." *Houston Chronicle,* November 5, 2005.

Ruggless, R. "Luby's Inc. Reverses Earnings Erosion, Cures Debt Default." *Nation's Restaurant News,* (June 2004).

Albright, M. "Luby's Serve Last Meal to Bay Area Wednesday—New Management Is Struggling to Repair the Troubled Texas Cafeteria Chain." *St. Petersburg Times,* October 16, 2001.

"Pappas Bros. Make Investment in Luby's." http://www.lubys.com/aboutusNews.asp?ID=41.

"Pappas Brothers Join Luby's Management." http://www.lubys.com/aboutusNews.asp?ID=43.

"Total Number of US Businesses." http://www.bizstats.com/businesses.htm.

ACCOUNTS RECEIVABLE AGING SCHEDULE

If you work at a full-service hotel, whether you work in the rooms, catering, or marketing department, sooner or later, you will likely come in contact with an **accounts receivable aging schedule.** Outstanding accounts are aged based on how far along they are in the collection process. It is the responsibility of the hospitality manager to collect the outstanding accounts receivable for his or her department as soon as possible.

Illustration 2-9 presents an accounts receivable aging schedule for a small hospitality business. In this example, while DeCarlo's account is not yet due, it is deemed to have a 1.5% chance of not being collected. Pratel's $335 account has more "age" and thus has a 20% chance of not being collected. Each category is assigned an uncollectible percentage based on past history. Total estimated bad debt expense is calculated by multiplying the total of each category by the estimated percentage. In this example, $1,527 is estimated to be uncollectible.

Members	Total $	Current	Number of Days			
			1–30	31–60	61–90	Over 90
C. DeCarlo	200	$200				
T. Vangard	450		$450			
J. Samuel	100					$100
F. Engel	320					$320
M. Pratel	335				$335	
M. Morgan	600			$600		
Others	26,875	$14,000	$10,000	$1,000	$200	$1,675
Total	28,880	$14,200	$10,450	$1,600	$535	$2,095
Estimated percentage uncollectible		1.5%	2.0%	10%	20%	40%
Total bad debts estimated	$1,527	$213	$209	$160	$107	$838

ILLUSTRATION 2-9

Aging Schedule for Hanover Country Club

Accounting System–CP³ System

A management tool that has become popular with hotel management companies over the years is the *CP³ system*. This system comprises the following components:

1. A monthly Commitment budget
2. A Purchase order system
3. A daily Payroll system
4. A daily Profit and loss statement

MONTHLY COMMITMENT BUDGET

The first component of the CP³ system is the **monthly commitment budget,** which is a day-by-day forecast of all revenues and expenses that appear on the hotel's monthly income statement. Each department head prepares his or her portion of the commitment budget, personally signs it, commits to achieving the budgeted cash flow for the upcoming month, and submits it to the hotel general manager for approval.

PURCHASE ORDER SYSTEM

The second element of the CP³ system is the **purchase order component.** While the purchase order component is similar to most purchase order systems you may be familiar with, it has one unique feature: The purchase order in the CP³ system is the source document for all of the company's expenses recorded in its accounting system. In other words, it is the document that the hotel controller uses to charge expenses on the hotel's books. Normally, an invoice is the source document that authorizes such an accounting entry.

The purchase process begins with a purchase order request, initiated by a department head who wants to purchase a product or service. The purchase order request is submitted to the hotel general manager, who checks to see if the purchase of the requested product or service is within the remaining monthly budget for that expense category. If it is, and he or she approves the purchase order, the general manager instructs the hotel controller to immediately enter it into the accounting system as an expense for the month rather than waiting for the invoice to arrive. This procedure eliminates the need for monthly adjusting entries.

DAILY PAYROLL SYSTEM REPORT

The next pertinent component of the CP³ system is **payroll cost.** Let us go back to Illustration 2-6. On May 8, Korvick, a full-time employee, was scheduled to work an eight-hour shift but called in sick. George, who was scheduled to work a four-hour shift, also did not show up for work. Landau and McGregor were therefore asked to work two extra hours to make sure all guest rooms were cleaned. O'Brian and Randon also worked extra hours to help out. You can see that by not showing up for work, Korvick and George caused labor cost for the week to be over budget.

DAILY PROFIT AND LOSS STATEMENT

The final component of the CP³ system is the **daily profit and loss statement.** Each day, the hotel controller prepares a daily profit and loss statement based on the actual revenues for the day, all approved purchase orders, and the daily payroll computations submitted by the department heads, and distributes it to each member of the management team. The headings for the daily profit and loss statement are shown in Illustration 2-10.

In addition to the summary profit and loss statement, a daily departmental profit and loss statement with identical column headings is prepared for each profit and cost center of the hotel and distributed to the department head in charge of each.

One final note: While most expenses are triggered by approved purchase order requests prepared by the department heads, a special monthly purchase order is prepared by the controller that allocates, by day, certain fixed expenses such as insurance, rent, and interest.

ADVANTAGES OF THE CP³ SYSTEM

The CP³ system offers several advantages in management's quest to achieve budgeted cash flow.

1. *No surprises:* By using the purchase order as the source document for expenses, the general manager and department heads are in complete control of the timing and amount of expenses that appear on

Summary Profit and Loss Report for January 15, 2007

	Today						Month-to-date					
	Actual	Actual	Budget	Budget	Variance	Variance	Actual	Actual	Budget	Budget	Variance	Variance
	$	%	$	%	$	%	$	%	$	%	$	%
Revenues												
Rooms												
Food												
Beverage												
Telecommunications												
Other Operated Departments												
Total Revenues												
Departmental Expenses												
Rooms												
Food												
Beverage												
Telecommunications												
Other Operated Departments												
Total Departmental Expenses												
Undistributed Operating Expenses												
Administrative and General												
Marketing												
Franchise Fees												
Property Operations and Maintenance												
Utilities												
Total Operating Expenses												
Gross Operating Profit (Loss)												

ILLUSTRATION 2-10

Profit and Loss Report for January 15, 2007

their profit and loss statements. There are no surprises created by invoices arriving late, monthly journal entries, and special adjusting entries involving expenses booked by the accounting department.

2. *Payroll control:* Payroll cost, including overtime expense, is controlled daily, allowing department heads to make changes in the weekly staffing schedule before it is too late.

3. *Flexing:* If actual revenues for the month are running behind forecast, the department head can hold back certain purchase order requests and make cutbacks in labor hours to meet budgeted cash flow. This is called *financial flexing.*

4. *Teamwork brings focus:* A certain amount of peer pressure and teamwork is created by this system, as department heads see how their peers are faring with respect to departmental budgets each day. If a particular department head is not meeting commitments for the month, other department heads have the opportunity to step in and assist in helping that head meet the hotel's cash flow goal for the month.

5. *Alignment of interests:* The active participation of each member of the management team, and the assurance that the numbers on the daily profit and loss statement are truly the operating results by which they will be evaluated, helps align managers' interests with those of ownership. Both groups are clearly focused on achieving budgeted cash flow each and every month.

6. *Timeliness of financial data:* Because ownership and management receive their copies of the monthly profit and loss statement immediately at month-end, they can react to problems without delay.

Finance in Action

Development of Restaurant Income Statement and Balance Sheet

The Caribou Restaurant, privately owned and operated by Mr. Ivan Medom, was opened over a decade ago and has prospered ever since. The current owner has decided it is time to retire and wants to sell the restaurant. Samuel Lightree, vice president of development for a major restaurant company, has contacted the current owner with interest in purchasing the property. Samuel has requested a copy of the most recent income statement and balance sheet to help determine if the property would fit into his company's portfolio of restaurants. The following financial information has been provided by Mr. Medom:

Information from the Income Statement for December 2008

■ Past year, revenues were $2.2 million with food accounting for 80% of sales.

■ Total cost of sales was 32.6% of total sales, with a food cost of 37.1% and beverage cost of 14.7%.

■ Expenses as a percentage of total sales were also provided by Mr. Medom.

Salaries and Wages	30.0%	Employee Benefits	3.9%
Depreciation	2.0%	Direct Operating Expenses	5.7%
Interest	0.5%	Music and Entertainment	0.1%

Marketing	2.1%		Utilities	2.5%
Rent	7.0%		General and Administrative	3.0%
Repairs and Maintenance	2.0%			

Information from the Balance Sheet as of Year End 2008

Furniture, Fixtures, and Equipment	$356,758	Current Portion of Long-term Debt	$17,941
Long-term Investments	$363,961	Prepaid Expenses	$31,611
Accounts Payable	$104,233	Building	$100,388
Accounts Receivable	$35,455	Accrued Expenses	$43,572
Accumulated Depreciation (FF&E)	($281,514)	Owner's Equity	$56,021
Other Current Liabilities	$25,203	Cash	$66,213
Inventory	$50,834	Retained Earnings	$187,533

QUESTIONS

1.   Develop a standardized income statement based on the information provided by Mr. Ivan Medom for the Caribou Restaurant.

   First, you must identify the major sections of a restaurant income statement, which are Sales, Cost of Sales, Gross Profit, Operating (Controllable) Expenses, and Operating (Noncontrollable) Expenses. Let's start with the first section: Sales. Over the past year, the Caribou Restaurant earned $2,200,000, with $1,760,000 ($2,200,000 × 80%) attributed to food sales and $440,000 ($2,200,000 × 20%) attributed to beverage sales. That takes care of the first section of the income statement.

   Next, there is the Cost of Sales section. Mr. Medom provided the total cost of sales percentage, food cost percentage, and beverage cost percentage. Utilizing this information and the sales figures, we can determine that the Total Cost of Sales is $717,200 ($2,200,000 × 32.6%). Food and beverage costs are calculated in the same manner. To calculate food costs, multiply $1,760,000 × 37.1%, and to calculate beverage costs simply multiply $440,000 by 14.7%.

   The next section to cover is Gross Profit. Because you have already calculated Sales and Cost of Sales, Gross Profit is a simple subtraction calculation. For food profit, subtract $652,652 from $1,760,000, and for beverage profit subtract $64,548 from $440,000. To calculate Total Gross Profit, there are two options. In option #1, you can subtract Total Sales from Total Cost of Sales to arrive at $1,482,800, or you can add the gross profits from food ($1,107,348) and beverage ($375,452) together to arrive at the same answer.

   The next section to tackle is Operating (Controllable) Expenses. Mr. Medom has provided the percentages for all of these expenses. To calculate these expenses, multiply Total Sales by the percentage provided. The answers can be found in the completed income statement. After you are finished calculating the costs, add them all together to get Total Operating Expenses. The next line in the income statement is Operating Income, which can be calculated by subtracting Total Operating Expenses ($1,085,326.21) from Gross Profit ($1,482,800).

   The final major section of the restaurant income statement is Other (Noncontrollable) Expenses, which consists of Rent, Depreciation, and Interest. Again, multiply these expense percentages by Total

Sales to arrive at the actual expense amounts. The last line of the income statement is Income Before Income Taxes, which is calculated by subtracting Other (Noncontrollable) Expenses ($208,808.77) from Operating Income ($397,473.79). This leaves us with Income Before Income Taxes of $188,666.02.

Caribou Restaurant
Income Statement
For the Year Ended December 31, 2008

	$	%
Sales		
Food	$ 1,760,000.00	80.0
Beverage	$ 440,000.00	20.0
Total Sales	**$ 2,200,000.00**	100.0
Cost of Sales		
Food	$ 652,652.00	37.1
Beverage	$ 64,548.00	14.7
Total Cost of Sales	**$ 717,200.00**	**32.6**
Gross Profit		
Food	$ 1,107,348.00	50.3
Beverage	$ 375,452.00	17.1
Total Gross Profit	**$ 1,482,800.00**	**67.4**
Operating (Controllable) Expenses		
Salaries and Wages	$ 660,000.00	30.0
Employee Benefits	$ 85,800.00	3.9
Direct Operating Expenses	$ 125,400.00	5.7
Music and Entertainment	$ 2,200.00	0.1
Marketing	$ 46,200.00	2.1
Utility Services	$ 55,000.00	2.5
General and Administrative	$ 66,640.78	3.0
Repairs and Maintenance	$ 44,085.44	2.0
Total Operating Expenses	**$ 1,085,326.21**	**49.3**
Operating Income	**$ 397,473.79**	**18.1**
Other (Noncontrollable) Expenses		
Rent	$ 154,128.16	7.0
Depreciation	$ 43,572.82	2.0
Interest	$ 11,106.80	0.5
Total Noncontrollable Expenses	**$ 208,807.77**	**9.5**
Income Before Income Taxes	**$ 188,666.02**	**8.6**

2. Develop a standardized balance sheet for the Caribou Restaurant.

As Mr. Medom has already given us the amounts for each account, we just need to make sure each account is put in the right place and add up the totals. The easiest way to do this is to look at the sample balance sheet for the Danforth Hotel (see Illustration 2-3). There were five major sections in this example, including Current Assets, Long-term Assets, Current Liabilities, Long-term Debt, and Owner's Equity. Now, set up an empty balance sheet and start placing each account under its appropriate heading. For example, Cash, Accounts Receivable, Inventory, and Prepaid Expenses all fall under Current Assets. You can look at the finished balance sheet for the Caribou Restaurant as a guide. When you have completed inputting all of the accounts, you are ready to add up the totals, which are shaded gray in the example. Remember, Total Assets must equal Total Liabilities plus Owner's Equity.

Caribou Reataurant
Balance Sheet
As of Year Ended 2008

Cash	$ 66,213	Accounts Payable	$ 104,233
Accounts Receivable	$ 35,455	Current Portion of Long-term Debt	$ 17,941
Inventory	$ 50,834	Accrued Expenses	$ 43,572
Prepaid Expenses	$ 31,611	Other Current Liabilities	$ 25,203
Total Current Assets	$ 184,113	Total Current Liabilities	$ 190,949
Furniture, Fixtures, and Equipment (FF&E)	$ 356,758	Long-term Debt Less Current Portion	$ 289,203
Accumulated Depreciation (FF&E)	$ (281,514)		
Building	$ 100,388	Owner's Equity	$ 56,021
Long-term Investments	$ 363,961	Retained Earnings	$ 187,533
Long-term Assets	$ 539,593	Total Owner's Equity	$ 245,554
Total Assets	$ 723,706	Total Liabilities and Owner's Equity	$ 723,706

WHERE WE'VE BEEN, WHERE WE'RE GOING

This chapter serves as a quick review of the more important accounting principles, statements, and reports you should be familiar with from your accounting classes. The CP^3 system, in particular, is useful for managers and owners alike, as it combines the financials for major areas of an operation to provide the essential managerial information for decision making. It is also a good reminder to all that the hospitality industry is highly organized in terms of accounting and financial practices. The various uniform systems are good indicators of how advanced this industry has become. In the next chapter, you will see how these financial statements can be further analyzed and what industry services and benchmark products are available for you to better manage your operation.

Key Points

➤ A business's financial statements summarize how the business has performed over time.

➤ A number of accounting principles form the foundation for all accounting practices. Some of the more important principles are cost, full disclosure, revenue recognition, matching, monetary unit, economic entity, going concern, time period, and materiality.

➤ The three primary financial statements you should be familiar with are the income statement, balance sheet, and statement of cash flow.

➤ The income statement, or profit and loss statement, presents a company's operating results over a specific period, usually a month, a quarter, or a year. The results are usually shown for the month and year-to-date and are often compared to the budget and/or the prior year.

➤ The balance sheet is also called the *statement of financial condition.* It is a snapshot of the company's financial strength as of a certain date.

➤ The statement of cash flow links the income statement and the balance sheet and provides management with a summary of the company's cash inflows and outflows from operations, investing activities, and financing activities.

➤ Managerial reports help hospitality managers understand the efficiency and effectiveness of their operations. The daily revenue report summarizes the sales from various outlets. Payroll is a major expense for a hospitality company and must be controlled daily. The rooms forecast projects the number of occupied rooms and average daily rate (ADR) for the upcoming period, while a food and beverage menu abstract provides management with a listing of the most popular items and their profitability.

➤ The CP^3 system comprises a monthly commitment budget, a purchase order system, a daily payroll system, and a daily profit and loss statement.

➤ The CP^3 system offers several advantages to hospitality financial managers in their quest to achieve budgeted cash flow. With proper daily management of revenues and expenses, surprises are held to a minimum. Utilization of the CP^3 system also creates positive peer pressure and teamwork; all department heads see how their peers are faring in their efforts to achieve budgeted profit for the period on a daily basis.

Key Terms

FINANCIAL ACCOUNTING: Produce financial statements that accurately present the financial condition of the company and its operating results over time.

MANAGERIAL ACCOUNTING: Provide more timely operating results related to revenues and expenses to help management maximize the operating performance of the business.

FINANCIAL ACCOUNTING STANDARDS BOARD (FASB): Has the responsibility for developing accounting principles in the United States.

SECURITIES AND EXCHANGE COMMISSION (SEC): An U.S. government agency, established in 1933 to administer laws and regulations relating to the exchange of securities and the publication of financial information by U.S. businesses.

GENERALLY ACCEPTED ACCOUNTING PRINCIPLES (GAAP): A set of standards and rules that are recognized as a guide for financial reporting in the United States.

COST PRINCIPLE: Assets purchased should be recorded at cost, or the price paid.

FULL DISCLOSURE PRINCIPLE: Requires that events that make a difference to the financial statement users be disclosed.

REVENUE RECOGNITION PRINCIPLE: Revenue should be recognized in the period in which it is earned.

MATCHING PRINCIPLE: Match expenses to the appropriate revenue stream.

MONETARY UNIT PRINCIPLE: Only transactions that can be expressed in terms of money can be included in the accounting records.

ECONOMIC ENTITY PRINCIPLE: Dictates that each operation is its own entity and should be kept separate.

GOING CONCERN PRINCIPLE: Assumes the operation will continue to operate into the foreseeable future.

TIME PERIOD PRINCIPLE: Suggests that businesses set their own time periods for measuring their activities.

MATERIALITY PRINCIPLE: States that if something is material enough, it must have its own account.

INCOME STATEMENT: A statement that summarizes the revenues and expenses of an operation during a specified period.

DEPARTMENT EXPENSES: Costs that can be charged directly to a department or profit center.

UNALLOCATED EXPENSES: Costs that apply to two or more departments of a business and therefore cannot be allocated to a single department.

CAPITAL EXPENSES: Fixed costs related to the physical structure of the business such as interest expense, property taxes, insurance, and depreciation expense.

BOTTOM LINE: Net income, the profit or loss.

BALANCE SHEET: A financial statement that reports a snapshot of the financial condition of an operation in terms of assets, liabilities, and equities.

ASSETS: Items of value the company owns.

CURRENT ASSETS: Assets that have an estimated life of one year or less.

FIXED ASSETS: Assets that have an estimated life of more than one year.

LIQUIDITY: The quickness of an asset being converted into cash.

LIABILITIES: Obligations the company owes.

EQUITY: Amount of capital invested in the business plus retained earnings.

STATEMENT OF CASH FLOW: A financial statement that breaks cash flow into three categories—operating, investing, and financing activities—and shows how cash flows in and out of these three categories in a given company for a specified period.

DAILY REVENUE REPORT: A report that summarizes revenues earned by each department within an operation.

DAILY PAYROLL COST REPORT: A report that details payroll costs by position and assists management in monitoring payroll and overtime effectively.

ROOMS REVENUE FORECAST: A report that projects the number of rooms to be sold during the upcoming period and the average room rates associated with the projections.

FOOD AND BEVERAGE MENU ABSTRACT: A report that tracks the popularity of menu items and their profitability.

ACCOUNTS RECEIVABLE AGING SCHEDULE: A schedule that details how long an account receivable has been outstanding or unpaid. The longer an account is unpaid, the older or more aged that account becomes.

CP³ SYSTEM: A tool that can help managers and owners budget cash properly. This system comprises four components: a monthly Commitment budget, a Purchase order system, a daily Payroll system, and a daily Profit and loss statement.

Application Exercises

1. Manuel is a good negotiator and is able to persuade the seller to give him a discount on the furniture for the lobby lounge of his hotel for $82,000 rather than the list price of $100,000. If he follows the principles of GAAP, which amount should he record on his balance sheet under "Furniture"? Which accounting principle is he following in this situation?

2. Juan is a meticulous accountant and wants to make sure everything is allocated correctly in its own line item or account. However, he also observes GAAP. According to which principle would he *not* use a separate account for a $10 expense for purchasing plastic forks, plates, and napkins for the annual office Christmas party?

3. Identify the three sections of the Statement of Cash Flow and give at least one example of cash inflow and one example of cash outflow for each of the three sections.

4. Explain why depreciation expense should be added back when compiling the statement of cash flow. If there is an amortization expense account, how would you treat it?

5. If beverage inventory increases from $150,000 on December 31, 2008, to $165,000 on December 31, 2009, will this constitute a cash inflow or cash outflow for W.S. Sports Bar in its cash flow from operations?

6. Gabi's Grill purchased a new ice machine in March. In Gabi's cash flow statement for that month, is this a cash inflow or outflow, and in which section of the statement of cash flow will the purchase appear?

7. Consider the following aging table. What will be Christian Catering's total estimated bad debts?

Christian Catering

Customer		Current	1–30	31–60	61–90	Over 90
				Number of Days		
M. Saryee	100	100				
B. Davis	350			350		
G. Francis	2,500	2,500				
C. Duncan	375				375	
J. Janik	300					300
B. Arredondo	470					470
Others	20,000	10,000	7,000	1,000	500	1,500
Total	$24,095	12,600	7,000	1,350	875	2,270
Estimated percentage uncollectible		1.0%	1.5%	10%	20%	50%

8. Discuss the advantages and disadvantages of adopting the CP^3 system for an independent restaurant and a country club.

9. **ETHICS** ✳ Esther knows from her accounting classes that revenues must be recognized only when they are earned. However, her boss wants to show that the theme park is doing well in June and asks Esther to recognize a $9,000 revenue entry related to a group he has booked for the next January. A contract has been signed with a provision that if the group cancels for any reason, it will pay the theme park a $1,000 fee. Esther's manager believes that because of this clause, this group will definitely show up, so recognizing the revenue earlier than January is of no consequence. What would you do if you were Esther?

10. **EXPLORING THE WEB** ✳ Visit the web page for the Securities and Exchange Commission at www.sec.gov. This is a valuable tool for students to access financial information for public companies. Select a hospitality company and download its latest quarterly filing.

Concept Check ✓

Rosabella

Rosabella Restaurants is a popular Italian restaurant chain located in the southwestern United States. Typical Italian food such as ravioli, lasagne, and fettuccine Alfredo can be purchased at a reasonable price at these family-friendly restaurants. All of the restaurants are owned and operated by Rosabella Restaurants, Inc.

Ms. Jennifer Churchman, a regional controller for Rosabella Restaurants, has seen decreasing profits from one of the properties in her region and is in the process of determining the cause of this problem. Ms. Churchman requested financial information from the property, including a food menu abstract, to get the entire picture of the restaurant's operations. The restaurant general manager provided all of the requested information. Below is the food menu abstract for dinner entrées over the last three months.

Rosabella Restaurant on Martin Street
Food Menu Abstract (Sales Mix)

Date: July–September, 2008
Meal Period: Dinner Entrées

Menu Item Name	Number Sold (MM)	Menu Mix %	Item Food Cost	Item Selling Price	Item CM	Menu Costs	Menu Revenues	Menu CM
Baked Ziti	125	3.85%	$ 1.75	$ 8.39	$ 6.64	$ 218.75	$ 1,048.75	$ 830.00
Cheese Ravioli	378	11.65%	$ 3.64	$ 7.99	$ 4.35	$ 1,375.92	$ 3,020.22	$ 1,644.30
Chicken Fettuccine Alfredo	280	8.63%	$ 2.10	$ 9.99	$ 7.89	$ 588.00	$ 2,797.20	$ 2,209.20
Chicken Marsala	65	2.00%	$ 2.25	$ 13.29	$ 11.04	$ 146.25	$ 863.85	$ 717.60
Chicken Parmigiana	115	3.54%	$ 1.98	$ 9.99	$ 8.01	$ 227.70	$ 1,148.85	$ 921.15
Eggplant Parmigiana	198	6.10%	$ 1.75	$ 7.99	$ 6.24	$ 346.50	$ 1,582.02	$ 1,235.52
Fettuccine Alfredo	286	8.81%	$ 1.85	$ 6.99	$ 5.14	$ 529.10	$ 1,999.14	$ 1,470.04
Grilled Chicken with Garlic Herb Pasta	156	4.81%	$ 2.10	$ 8.29	$ 6.19	$ 327.60	$ 1,293.24	$ 965.64
Grilled Salmon	225	6.93%	$ 1.10	$ 12.99	$ 11.89	$ 247.50	$ 2,922.75	$ 2,675.25
Lasagne	415	12.78%	$ 2.30	$ 7.99	$ 5.69	$ 954.50	$ 3,315.85	$ 2,361.35
Manicotti	186	5.73%	$ 1.95	$ 7.39	$ 5.44	$ 362.70	$ 1,374.54	$ 1,011.84
Seafood Fettuccine Alfredo	45	1.39%	$ 3.20	$ 11.99	$ 8.79	$ 144.00	$ 539.55	$ 395.55
Seafood Ravioli	83	2.56%	$ 3.35	$ 10.39	$ 7.04	$ 278.05	$ 862.37	$ 584.32
Shrimp Scampi	124	3.82%	$ 3.10	$ 10.99	$ 7.89	$ 384.40	$ 1,362.76	$ 978.36
Spaghetti with Meatballs	318	9.80%	$ 2.10	$ 8.29	$ 6.19	$ 667.80	$ 2,636.22	$ 1,968.42
Three-meat Cannelloni	81	2.50%	$ 2.45	$ 8.99	$ 6.54	$ 198.45	$ 728.19	$ 529.74
Vegetarian Lasagne	166	5.11%	$ 2.08	$ 8.99	$ 6.91	$ 345.28	$ 1,492.34	$ 1,147.06

Ms. Churchman has asked you to analyze the food menu abstract and given you the following questions to answer:

QUESTIONS

1. Do there appear to be any abnormalities with the report? Look for any items that seem unusual, such as item food cost.
2. Analyze the report. Which items have the highest contribution margin? Which items have the lowest contribution margin?
3. What advice can you provide to the restaurant manager for improving the restaurant's sales mix?

Concept Check

The Canyon Hotel and Meeting Center is a popular property among the many local corporations that hold meetings there. This hotel is conveniently located near a major metropolitan area, with easy access from several major highways. Because the majority of the business is done during the day, room totals do not tend to coincide with food sales and the number of meeting guests. For example, on November 20, the hotel sold 213 rooms and 703 food covers, and serviced 512 meeting guests.

Mr. Stan Domla is the general manager of the Canyon Hotel, and one of his responsibilities is to review the daily payroll report created by the department heads at the property. Mr. Domla has to check the reports for inconsistencies and make sure each department is meeting its budgeted goals. Not only does he need to look at today's numbers but also at the month-to-date calculations to determine if there are any trends. As of November 20, the Canyon Hotel and Meeting Center sold 1,593 rooms and 11,980 covers, and serviced 3,645 meeting guests.

Daily Payroll Report
Canyon Hotel and Meeting Center
November 20, 2009

Category	Daily Hours Regular	Overtime	Total	Daily Payroll $	Labor Cost Cost/Room	Cost/Cover	Cost/Meeting Gst	M-T-D Regular	Overtime	Hours Total	M-T-D Payroll $	M-T-D Labor Cost Cost/Room	Cost/Cover	Cost/Meeting Gst	Budget Labor Cost Cost/Room	Cost/Cover	Cost/Meeting Gst
Rooms																	
Front Desk	46.02	0.50	46.52	$694.53				698.58	9.00	707.58	$10,574.44				$5.68		
Reservations	18.01	0.00	18.01	$285.64				273.39	0.00	273.39	$4,335.99				$2.75		
Guest Services	26.70	1.08	27.78	$324.55				405.31	16.20	421.51	$4,923.28				$3.00		
Housekeeping	125.00	4.32	129.32	$1,388.43				1,897.50	86.40	1,983.90	$21,406.18				$12.87		
Total Rooms																	
Food and Beverage																	
Banquet Service	60.53	3.06	63.59	$969.64				918.85	105.32	1,024.17	$16,033.93					$2.91	
In-room Dining	24.00	0.00	24.00	$173.52				364.32	16.00	380.32	$2,807.55					$9.83	
Greenleaf Restaurant	105.35	0.00	105.35	$1,107.23				1,599.21	12.35	1,611.56	$17,002.43					$3.85	
Flower Café	18.95	0.00	18.95	$113.70				287.66	6.08	293.74	$1,780.69					$6.72	
General	233.84	3.16	237.00	$3,514.28				7,597.18	143.27	7,740.45	$115,072.08					$0.78	
Total F&B																	
Meetings																	
Meeting Management	42.40	2.35	44.75	$1,024.79				466.40	32.05	498.45	$11,704.31						$3.25
Audio-visual	56.00	0.00	56.00	$921.12				616.00	3.60	619.60	$10,110.18						$3.46
Meeting Attendants	96.00	3.65	99.65	$527.67				1,056.00	65.32	1,121.32	$6,000.70						$1.45
Meeting Floor	116.35	0.00	116.35	$1,790.63				1,279.85	0.00	1,279.85	$19,696.89						$5.60
Meeting Concierge	107.25	4.09	111.34	$1,374.23				1,179.75	12.05	1,191.80	$14,517.64						$2.32
Total Meetings																	

QUESTIONS

1. Calculate the labor cost per unit for November 20 and the month-to-date labor cost per unit, and then total each column. (Fill in the gray shaded areas in the daily payroll report provided.)

2. Analyze the daily payroll report, noting any major departures from the budgeted amounts.

3. If you were the general manager for this property, what actions would you take and why?

ANALYZING

FINANCIAL

STATEMENTS

FEATURE STORY

HOWARD SCHULTZ—SHARING COFFEE
WITH THE WORLD

While Howard Schultz was not the founder of Starbucks, his vision for the company and his creativity put Starbucks on the map. He saw the potential the company had well beyond the vision of its founders, Jerry Baldwin, Zev Siegel, and Gordon Bowker. Schultz took the six-store Seattle coffee company and grew it into a $23.7 billion S&P 500 and NASDAQ-100 conglomerate.

When Schultz first entered the picture, Starbucks Coffee, Tea, and Spice was a small coffee retailer with four stores in the Seattle area. Schultz, then vice president and general manager of the U.S. division of Hammarplast, a Swedish maker of plastic products, traveled to Seattle to investigate the small coffee company that was placing larger orders than Macy's for Hammarplast's drip coffeemaker. The New Yorker came away impressed with the passion the owners had for selling and educating people about top-quality, fresh-roasted whole-bean coffee. "It was just wonderful meeting people from a great young company. . . . I walked away from that meeting saying, 'God, what a great company, what a great city! I'd love to be part of that.'"

Schultz spent the next year trying to convince the owners to hire him as their marketing manager and buy into his vision of taking their coffee company international. He even offered to take a salary cut in exchange for a small equity stake in the business. But his grand vision and brazenness scared them so much they rejected his offer. Schultz, however, would not take no for an answer. And he said, "I think that sometimes the difference between success and failure, winning and losing, is a very fine line between those people who will continue to move forward and those who give up. I have a history of people closing doors and me saying, 'No, it's still open.'"

Changing tactics, Schultz made a last-ditch appeal with a scaled-down expansion plan and was hired the next day. Six months into his employment, Schultz had another revelation; this one formed the basis for Starbuck's future success. While he was in Milan, Italy, for an international housewares show, he noticed that there were espresso cafés on almost every street corner of the city. Each café had a barista (bartender) who was a great performer and served as the host. The café patrons were also part of the show, chatting away and having a good time while enjoying their coffee in an elegant setting with Italian opera playing in the background. Schultz made a quick calculation. If there were 1,500 coffee bars in Milan alone and a total of 200,000 in all of Italy, the global business potential for similar cafés was astronomical.

Ecstatic about his discovery, he returned to Seattle to share his revelation and ideas for modifying the format with the owners of Starbucks stores. To his surprise, they were not interested, pointing out to Schultz that Starbucks was a retailer, not a restaurant or bar. They feared that serving drinks would put them in the beverage business and dilute the integrity of Starbucks' mission as a coffee store. Upon Schultz's insistence, they reluctantly allowed him to test his concept at their recently opened sixth Starbucks store. Without any marketing or publicity blitz, 400 customers showed up at the café the first day. Within two months, the volume doubled. Even on their best days, the other five Starbucks stores averaged only 250 customers per day. Armed with the impressive results of his test, Schultz went back to the owners and implored them to expand his new concept chainwide, but they refused his request. In late 1985, the dejected marketer left the company to open his own coffee bar business.

Howard needed to raise $1.65 million in capital to start his new company, but after talking to over 200 potential investors, "ninety-nine percent of them said no." Eventually he raised the money, the majority of which was contributed by nine investors, including his former boss. His first Il Giornale store opened in April 1986 in downtown Seattle. Within six months, it was serving more than 1,000 customers per day. In October, he opened a second store in another downtown Seattle building. Another six months later, his third Il Giornale opened for business in Vancouver, Canada. The Vancouver store dispelled any doubt about the concept's transferability outside of Seattle and proved the international market potential for the concept. With three successful cafés under his belt, it was relatively easy for Schultz to convince his investors and bankers to provide him with the $3.8 million he needed to acquire the Starbucks Coffee, Tea, and Spice Company when the owners decided to cash out and pursue other business opportunities. Following the acquisition, Schultz renamed the company Starbucks Corporation.

The next five years saw the first phase of Starbucks' expansion. Between 1987 and 1992, Schultz opened 148 cafés with over $32 million of new venture capital from existing and new investors. While the company reported losses for the first three years, the investors stood by Schultz, as his business proposal had anticipated losses during the expansion phase. The second phase of expansion kicked in during June 1992, when Schultz took the company public. Going public at $17 a share, he raised a total of $273 million. The company raised another $80.5 million in debt by offering convertible debentures. A second common stock offering was completed in 1994. This influx of cash was used to aggressively expand Starbucks cafés throughout the country and internationally.

Today, Starbucks has more than 10,240 stores in over thirty countries through direct ownership, partnership arrangements, and licenses. It has also entered the grocery market through strategic alliances and acquisitions, and has expanded its product offerings to include tea, chocolate, liquors, and music CDs. In 2005, in spite of a high labor cost as the result of providing health insurance to employees working twenty or more hours weekly, the company still reported a gross margin of 59.10%, an operating margin of 11.05%, a net profit of 7.8%, and a return on investment of 21.68%. In contrast, Starbucks' competitors, Caribou Coffee Company and Diedrich Coffee, Inc., managed only 26.07% and 14.79% gross margins, 1.01% and −11.09% operating margins, −1.84% and −3.84% profit margins, and a negative return on investment.

In spite of his success, Schultz has an even greater vision for his coffee empire. "It's still so early on for us. We're in the embryonic stages of the growth of the company. Our dream is to continue to grow the company and become one of the most recognized and respected brands in the world."

Starbuck's total revenue grew by 20.3% in 2005. The previous year, the company showed growth in sales of approximately 30%. These growth figures are on par with the company's three- to five-year target of 20%. The coffee retailer opened 1,672 new stores in fiscal 2005 and plans to open another 1,800 stores in 2006. Given such a favorable track record, Schultz's dream definitely appears to be achievable. Let's drink to his continued success!

SOURCES

"Starbucks 2005 Annual Report, Part Two." http://www.starbucks.com/aboutus/Annual_Report_2005_part2.pdf.

"Company Timeline, August 2005." http://www.starbucks.com/aboutus/CompanyTimelineFeb05.pdf.

Thompson, A.A., Jr., and A.J. Strickland. "Online Cases: Starbucks Corporation." In *Strategic Management,* 11th ed., Student Resources. McGraw-Hill http://www.mhhe.com/business/management/thompson/11e/case/starbucks.html.

"Biography: Howard Schultz, Starbucks." http://www.myprimetime.com/work/ge/schultzbio/index.shtml.

"Howard Schultz for Hire." http://www.myprimetime.com/work/solo/content/pm_schultz/index.shtml.

"Howard Schultz: Not Your Average Joe." http://www.brandchannel.com/careers_profile.asp?cr_id=47.

"Interview: Howard Schultz." http://www.roadtripnation.com/interviews/72.

"Stories of Entrepreneurs: Howard Schultz." http://www.cecunc.org/entre/stories/howard-schultz.html.

Learning Outcomes

1. Interpret and analyze financial statements using vertical, horizontal, trend, and ratio analyses.
2. Use financial analysis methods to determine the financial health of a business and quantify its upside potential.

3. Apply financial analysis skills to scheduling, pricing, revenue management, profit flexing, and cost-volume-profit decisions.

4. Learn how unethical companies can manipulate financial statements to mislead readers.

Preview of Chapter 3

Reading and analyzing financial statements

1. READERS OF FINANCIAL ANALYSIS

2. TYPES OF ANALYSIS

  a. Vertical or common-size
  b. Horizontal or comparative
  c. Trends analysis
  d. Ratios analysis
  e. Industry averages and norms

3. USE OF FINANCIAL INFORMATION IN MANAGEMENT DECISION MAKING

  a. Scheduling
  b. Pricing
  c. Revenue management
  d. Profit flexing
  e. Cost-volume-profit modeling

4. BE AWARE OF

  a. Window dressing
  b. Off-balance-sheet financing
  c. Capitalization of current operating expenses
  d. Improper revenue recognition

ANALYSIS OF FINANCIAL STATEMENTS

The financial statements of a company are used to measure its current financial condition and operating results over a specified period. A more thorough and skilled interpretation and analysis of these statements, however, can provide the reader with a great deal more information on the company's operating performance, financial health, and likelihood of future success. The better you, as a hospitality manager, can read, interpret, and analyze the balance sheet and income statement for your business, the better business decisions you will make.

Readers of Financial Statements

A company's balance sheet and income statement are two important financial documents that are provided to, and read by, a number of groups, including the following:

- Owners: Track and evaluate management's performance.

- Lenders: Determine the risk of the business defaulting on its loan.

- Managers: Compare actual results with the budget for the period, the prior year, competitors, and industry norms, and flag problem areas for follow-up actions.

- Government: Ensure that the proper taxes have been calculated and paid.

- Suppliers: Track the growth of the business, its cash in flow and out flow, and evaluate its ability to pay its obligations on a current basis.

- Investment analysts: Evaluate the company's recent performance versus its market segment and competitors, determine important trends, and project future earnings for the company.

- Merger and acquisition candidates: Present the financial story of the company, highlighting its financial strengths, upside potential, and future value.

Types of Analyses

Analysis of financial statements can be horizontal or vertical. The operating results of the company may also be compared with industry averages, norms, and standards.

VERTICAL OR COMMON-SIZE ANALYSIS

Vertical analysis, also known as *common-size analysis,* is most often used to analyze and control variable expenses that appear on a hospitality company's income statement. Because variable expenses should increase or decrease with the level of sales, the percentage relationship between the expense item and its respective revenue category is the key to good variable cost control. For example, food cost and rooms payroll are both variable expenses. As more food is sold, food cost increases. As more rooms are sold, housekeeping payroll increases. While the actual dollar amount of each expense should increase with sales, the percentage relationship between the expense and revenue should remain approximately the same. If the percentage increases, a problem probably exists and should be researched immediately. Vertical analysis does not automatically solve cost control problems, but it does help flag potential problems. All expenses should be tracked and compared with either total revenue or the appropriate departmental revenue such as rooms, food, or beverage.

When using vertical analysis, all accounts are sized using total revenue or departmental revenue as the common base. The amount of each expense is divided by the revenue amount to derive its percentage. For example, marketing expense is analyzed as a percentage of total revenue because the marketing department sells products and services for all profit centers. Illustration 3-1 presents the same income statement for Shae's Restaurant Company that you read in chapter 2 with a percentage column added to facilitate the vertical analysis of its operation.

As you analyze the income statement, you should note that Shae's derives most of its revenue from food—78.2%—and only 19.33% from the sale of beverages. Shae's ran a 36% food cost (cost of food sold divided by food revenue), a 22% beverage cost (cost of beverages sold divided

Shae's
Income Statement
For the Month Ended June 30, 2008

Revenues:		Amount	Percent
Food	$	890,000	78.20
Beverage		220,000	19.33
Others		28,100	2.47
Total Revenues	$	1,138,100	100.00
Cost of Sales:			
Food	$	320,400	36.00
Beverage		48,400	22.00
Others		15,455	55.00
Total Cost of Sales	$	384,255	33.76
Gross Profit:			
Food	$	569,600	64.00
Beverage		171,600	78.00
Others		12,645	45.00
Total Gross Profit	$	753,845	66.24
Operating (Controllable) Expenses:			
Salaries and Wages	$	352,811	31.00
Employee Benefits		105,843	9.30
Total Labor Cost		458,654	40.30
Direct Operating Expenses		68,286	6.00
Marketing		39,834	3.50
Utlities		44,386	3.90
Administration and General		28,453	2.50
Repairs and Maintenance		25,038	2.20
Music and Entertainment		31,867	2.80
Total Operating Expenses	$	696,517	61.20
Operating Income	$	57,328	5.04
Other (Noncontrollable) Expenses:			
Rent	$	8,000	0.70
Depreciation		20,470	1.80
Interest		4,500	0.40
Total Noncontrollable Expenses	$	32,970	2.90
Income Before Income Taxes	$	24,358	2.14

ILLUSTRATION 3-1

Shae's Income Statement for the Month Ended June 30, 2008

by beverage revenue), and a 40.3% labor cost (salaries and wages plus employee benefits divided by total revenue) for the month. The company's operating income for June was just over 5%, and its income before income tax was 2.14% of total revenue. Based on industry standards, while its food and beverage costs appear to be in line with industry norms, its higher-than-normal 40.3% payroll cost raises a red flag and suggests that one or more of its restaurants may be causing the problem. The red flags also suggest that the restaurant chain's forecasting, employee scheduling, and payroll cost control system should be reviewed.

Illustration 3-2 provides an example of a vertical analysis of the December 31, 2007, balance sheet for Danforth Hotels. Danforth is a hotel corporation with hotels all around the world. The dollar amounts in Illustration 3-2 are expressed in millions. Please note that Danforth's current assets account for 10.68% of its total assets, with 89.32% falling in the long-term category. A

Danforth Hotels
Vertical Analysis of the Balance Sheet
As of December 31, 2007
(in millions)

	Amount	Percent
Cash	$ 82.00	1.20
Accounts Receivable	288.00	4.23
Marketable Securities	100.00	1.47
Inventory	193.00	2.83
Other current assets	64.00	0.94
Total Current Assets	727.00	10.68
Furniture, Fixture, and Equipment, net	3,641.00	53.47
Management and Franchise Contracts, net	383.00	5.62
Goodwill	1,240.00	18.21
Long-term Investments	558.00	8.20
Other Long-term assets	260.00	3.82
Total Long-term Assets	6,082.00	89.32
Total Assets	**$ 6,809.00**	**100.00**
Accounts Payable and Accrued Expenses	$ 540.00	7.93
Current maturities of long-term debt	329.00	4.83
Accrued Taxes	4.00	0.06
Total Current Liabilities	873.00	12.82
Long-term Debt	3,709.00	54.17
Total Liabilities	4,582.00	67.29
Owner's Equity	1,807.00	26.54
Retained Earnings	420.00	6.17
Total Owner's Equity	2,227.00	32.71
Total Liabilities and Owner's Equity	**$ 6,809.00**	**100.00**

ILLUSTRATION 3-2
Danforth Hotels: Vertical Analysis for the Balance Sheet as of December 31, 2007 (in millions)

vertical analysis also determines that the hotel is financed with approximately 67% debt, 54% of which is long term, and 33% of equity. This mix of debt and equity is quite conservative for most hotels.

HORIZONTAL OR COMPARATIVE ANALYSIS

While vertical analysis is used to analyze the relationship between expenses and revenues on an income statement or to analyze the capital structure of a company as presented on its balance sheet, **horizontal analysis** tracks and analyzes both income statement and balance sheet line items over a specified period. Horizontal analysis can also be useful in identifying trends in sales performance, profit margins, cash balances, accounts receivable balances, and inventory levels. Comparisons with industry averages and norms can also be of value. Horizontal analysis focuses on both dollar and percentage changes over time.

Illustration 3-3 expands the information presented in Illustration 3-1 by adding a column for Shae's July operating performance. By analyzing the dollar and percentage change columns, you can quickly determine the following:

1. While both beverage revenue and other revenue declined during the period, total revenue increased slightly as the result of food revenue increasing by 4.16%.

2. However, while food revenue increased by 4.16%, food cost increased by 11.95%.

3. The negative trend in gross profit is also a red flag. Food, beverage, and other gross profit declined during the period.

4. The decrease in operating expenses of $11,601 would normally be viewed as a favorable trend. Upon closer review, however, the reason for the decrease is a cutback in marketing expense and repair and maintenance. These are two critical areas where cutbacks should be closely evaluated.

Aside from analyzing the change in dollar amounts from period to period, a horizontal analysis of the changes in expenses as a percentage of departmental revenue can also be of value. The last three columns in Illustration 3-3 provide this information. Note the potential red flags for food cost, marketing expense, and repair and maintenance expense.

The horizontal analysis of the Danforth Hotel balance sheets as of December 31, 2007 and 2008 is provided in Illustration 3-4. The analysis indicates that total assets will increase by 2.09% from 2007 to 2008, the result of an increase in current assets of $200 million and a decrease in long-term assets of $58 million, netting a $142 million increase in total assets.

On the debt and equity side, the corresponding $142 million increase is a result of a decrease in current liabilities of $150 million, a decrease in long-term liabilities of $299 million, and an increase in owner's equity of $441 million. This change is a positive one for Danforth, as it now has less debt and more equity than in the previous year. Thus, Danforth's balance sheet is stronger than a year ago and will therefore assist the company in securing additional financing for growth. This positive change is also reflected in the last three columns of Illustration 3-4. Note that total liabilities have decreased, and total equity has increased by 5.68 percentage points.

Shae's
Income Statement
For the Months Ended June 30 and July 31, 2008

	June	July	$ change	% change	June %	July %	change in percentage
Revenues:							
Food	$ 890,000	$ 927,000	$ 37,000	4.16	78.20	80.31	2.11
Beverage	220,000	201,100	(18,900)	(8.59)	19.33	17.42	(1.91)
Others	28,100	26,150	(1,950)	(6.94)	2.47	2.27	(0.20)
Total Revenues	$ 1,138,100	$ 1,154,250	$ 16,150	1.42	100.00	100.00	–
Cost of Sales:							
Food	$ 320,400	$ 358,700	$ 38,300	11.95	28.15	31.08	2.92
Beverage	48,400	48,000	(400)	(0.83)	4.25	4.16	(0.09)
Others	15,455	15,010	(445)	(2.88)	1.36	1.30	(0.06)
Total Cost of Sales	$ 384,255	$ 421,710	$ 37,455	9.75	33.76	36.54	2.77
Gross Profit:							
Food	$ 569,600	$ 568,300	$ (1,300)	(0.23)	50.05	49.24	(0.81)
Beverage	171,600	153,100	(18,500)	(10.78)	15.08	13.26	(1.81)
Others	12,645	11,140	(1,505)	(11.90)	1.11	0.97	(0.15)
Total Gross Profit	$ 753,845	$ 732,540	$ (21,305)	(2.83)	66.24	63.46	(2.77)
Operating (Controllable) Expenses:							
Salaries and Wages	$ 352,811	$ 353,000	$ 189	0.05	31.00	30.58	(0.42)
Employee Benefits	105,843	105,900	57	0.05	9.30	9.17	(0.13)
Direct Operating Expenses	68,286	69,578	1,292	1.89	6.00	6.03	0.03
Marketing	39,834	35,000	(4,834)	(12.13)	3.50	3.03	(0.47)
Utilities	44,386	45,900	1,514	3.41	3.90	3.98	0.08
Administration and General	28,453	28,453	1	0.00	2.50	2.47	(0.03)
Repairs and Maintenance	25,038	15,040	(9,998)	(39.93)	2.20	1.30	(0.90)
Music and Entertainment	31,867	32,045	178	0.56	2.80	2.78	(0.02)
Total Operating Expenses	$ 696,517	$ 684,916	$ (11,601)	(1.67)	61.20	59.34	(1.86)
Operating Income	$ 57,328	$ 47,624	$ (9,704)	(16.93)	5.04	4.13	(0.91)
Other (Noncontrollable) Expenses:							
Rent	$ 8,000	$ 8,000	$ –	–	0.70	0.69	(0.01)
Depreciation	20,470	20,470	–	–	1.80	1.77	(0.03)
Interest	4,500	2,250	(2,250)	(50.00)	0.40	0.19	(0.20)
Total Noncontrollable Expenses	$ 32,970	$ 30,720	$ (2,250)	(6.82)	2.90	2.66	(0.24)
Income Before Income Taxes	$ 24,358	$ 16,904	$ (7,454)	(30.60)	2.14	1.46	(0.68)

ILLUSTRATION 3-3

Shae's Income Statement for the Months Ended June 30th and July 31, 2008

Danforth Hotels
Horizontal Analysis of the Balance Sheets
As of December 31, 2007 and 2008
(in millions)

	2007	2008	$ change	% change	2007%	2008%	change in percentage
Cash	$ 82.00	$ 298.00	$ 216.00	263.41%	1.20%	4.29%	3.08%
Accounts Receivable	288.00	269.00	(19.00)	—6.60%	4.23%	3.87%	—0.36%
Marketable Securities	100.00	112.00	12.00	12.00%	1.47%	1.61%	0.14%
Inventory	193.00	158.00	(35.00)	—18.13%	2.83%	2.27%	—0.56%
Other current assets	64.00	90.00	26.00	40.63%	0.94%	1.29%	0.35%
Total Current Assets	727.00	927.00	200.00	27.51%	10.68%	13.34%	2.66%
Furniture, Fixture, and Equipment, net	3,641.00	3,520.00	(121.00)	—3.00%	53.47%	50.64%	—2.83%
Management and Franchise Contracts	383.00	347.00	(36.00)	—9.40%	5.62%	4.99%	—0.63%
Goodwill	1,230.00	1,230.00	0.00	0.00%	18.06%	17.70%	—0.37%
Long-term Investments	568.00	599.00	31.00	5.46%	8.34%	8.62%	0.28%
Other long-term assets	260.00	328.00	68.00	26.15%	3.82%	4.72%	0.90%
Long-term Assets	6,082.00	6,024.00	(58.00)	—0.95%	89.32%	86.66%	—2.66%
Total Assets	**$ 6,809.00**	**$ 6,951.00**	**$ 142.00**	**2.09%**	**100.00%**	**100.00%**	**0.00%**
Accounts Payable and Accrued Expenses	$ 540.00	$ 601.00	$ 61	11.30%	7.93%	8.65%	0.72%
Current maturities of long-term debt	329.00	118.00	(211.00)	—64.13%	4.83%	1.70%	—3.13%
Accrued Taxes	4.00	4.00	0.00	0.00%	0.06%	0.06%	0.00%
Total Current Liabilities	873.00	723.00	(150.00)	—17.18%	12.82%	10.40%	—2.42%
Long-term Debt	3,709.00	3,560.00	(149.00)	—4.02%	54.47%	51.22%	—3.26%
Total Liabilities	4,582.00	4,283.00	(299.00)	—6.53%	67.29%	61.62%	—5.68%
Owner's Equity	1,807.00	1,998.00	191.00	10.57%	26.54%	28.74%	2.21%
Retained Earnings	420.00	670.00	250.00	59.52%	6.17%	9.64%	3.47%
Total Owner's Equity	2,227.00	2,668.00	441.00	19.80%	32.71%	38.38%	5.68%
Total Liabilities and Owner's Equity	**$ 6,809.00**	**$ 6,951.00**	**$ 142.00**	**2.09%**	**100.00%**	**100.00%**	**0.00%**

ILLUSTRATION 3-4

Danforth Hotels: Horizontal Analysis for the Balance Sheets as of December 31, 2007 and 2008 (in millions)

TREND ANALYSIS

For a hotel, occupied room-nights, revenue per available room, food sales, beverage sales, food cost, beverage cost, and payroll cost are some of the most important items to track and analyze. However, each department should monitor its own revenues and expenses, flag negative trends that appear, and capitalize on the positive ones. **Trend analysis** represents calculations and data points over a specified period. Financial information can be presented on line graphs and bar charts to visually highlight the trends the company is experiencing. Again, useful decisions can then be made with meaningful analysis.

RATIO ANALYSIS

Ratio analysis is a quick way to assess the financial health of a company. A ratio is simply an expression of one number divided by another. For example, dividing current assets by total assets provides a ratio of how much of the company's assets will be converted into cash within a year. There are five types of ratios:

- **Liquidity:** Measures an operation's ability to meet its short-term obligations (one year or less).
- **Solvency:** Measures an operation's ability to meet its long-term obligations (over one year).
- **Activity:** Used to gauge the effectiveness of how assets have been managed.
- **Operating:** Assists management in determining how efficient the operation is.
- **Profitability:** Measures management's effectiveness in achieving profit margins and return-on-investment goals.

The financial ratios presented in Illustration 3-6 are based on the information taken from the income statement, balance sheets, and parts of a statement of cash flow in Illustration 3-5.

LIQUIDITY RATIOS. Liquidity ratios include the current ratio, accounts receivable turnover, and the average collection period.

- **Current ratio** (current assets/current liabilities): The current ratio for Gian's Italian Cuisine is 2.63 for November and 3.15 for December. This indicates that in November, for every $1.00 of current liabilities, Gian's has $2.63 in current assets to cover these debts. The situation is even more favorable in December, when Gian's has $3.15 in current assets for each $1.00 it owes in current liabilities. Keep in mind that a company may have a current ratio that is too high, indicating that the company has too many dollars' worth of current assets that are not earning a return on investment.
- **Accounts receivable turnover** (total revenue/average accounts receivable): Gian's accounts receivable turnover ratio of 9.6 means that it is able to collect the receivables owed to the restaurant 9.6 times per month. A high accounts receivable turnover ratio is indicative of a high percentage of cash and credit card sales.
- **Average collection period** (31 days/accounts receivable turnover): This ratio measures, in number of days, the speed at which accounts receivables are turned into cash. Based on its Decem-

Gian's Italian Cuisine
Balance Sheets
As of November 30 and December 31, 2008

			Change
Cash	$ 9,000.00	$ 14,000.00	$ 5,000.00
Accounts Receivable	10,000.00	11,500.00	1,500.00
Food Inventory	4,000.00	3,538.00	(462.00)
Beverage Inventory	6,000.00	3,950.00	(2,050.00)
Prepaid Rent	18,000.00	20,000.00	2,000.00
Total Current Assets	47,000.00	52,988.00	5,988.00
Furniture, Fixture, and Equipment (FF&E)	7,500.00	9,870.00	$ 2,370.00
Accumulated Depreciation (FF&E)	(3,030.00)	(4,000.00)	(970.00)
Building	20,000.00	20,000.00	-
Long-term Investments	5,000.00	8,580.00	3,580.00
Long-term Assets	29,470.00	34,450.00	4,980.00
Total Assets	**$ 76,470.00**	**$ 87,438.00**	**$ 10,968.00**
Accounts Payable	$ 7,000.00	$ 6,790.00	$ (210.00)
Accrued Payroll	5,400.00	6,540.00	1,140.00
Accrued Taxes	5,500.00	3,500.00	(2,000.00)
Total Current Liabilities	17,900.00	16,830.00	(1,070.00)
Long-term Debt	10,000.00	12,000.00	2,000.00
Owner's Equity	39,000.00	40,620.00	1,620.00
Retained Earnings	9,570.00	17,988.00	8,418.00
Total Owner's Equity	48,570.00	58,608.00	10,038.00
Total Liabilities and Owner's Equity	**$ 76,470.00**	**$ 87,438.00**	**$ 10,968.00**

Other information
* Cash Flow from Operating Activities

Net Income	$ 4,645.20
Depreciation	500.00
Increase in Accounts Receivables	(1,500.00)
Decrease in Food Inventory	462.00
Decrease in Beverage Inventory	2,050.00
Increase in Prepaid Rent	(2,000.00)
Decrease in Accounts Payables	(210.00)
Increase in Accrued Payroll	1,140.00
Decrease in Accrued Taxes	2,000.00
	$ 7,087.20

Gian's Italian Cuisine
Income Statement
For the Month Ended Dec 31, 2xx8

		%
Revenues:		
Food	$ 78,000.00	75.58
Beverage	24,000.00	23.26
Other	1,200.00	1.16
Total Revenues	$ 103,200.00	100.00
Cost of Sales:		
Food	$ 24,960.00	32
Beverage	5,280.00	22
Other	660.00	55
Total Cost of Sales	$ 30,900.00	29.94
Gross Profit:		
Food	$ 53,040.00	68
Beverage	18,720.00	78
Other	540.00	45
Total Gross Profit	$ 72,300.00	70.06
Operating (Controllable) Expenses:		
Salaries and Wages	$ 29,870.00	28.94
Employee Benefits	7,467.50	7.24
Direct Operating Expenses	6,192.00	6.00
Marketing	3,612.00	3.50
Utilities	4,024.80	3.90
Administration and General	2,580.00	2.50
Repairs and Maintenance	1,857.60	1.80
Music and Entertainment	2,889.60	2.80
Total Operating Expenses	$ 58,493.50	56.68
Operating Income	$ 13,806.50	13.38
Other (Noncontrollable) Expenses:		
Rent	$ 7,000.00	6.78
Depreciation	500.00	0.48
Interest	500.00	0.48
Total Noncontrollable Expenses	$ 8,000.00	7.75
Income Before Income Taxes	$ 5,806.50	5.63
Less: Taxes	$ 1,161.30	1.13
Net Income	$ 4,645.20	4.50

ILLUSTRATION 3-5
Gian's Italian Cuisine Balance Sheets and Income Statement

Ratios analysis for Gian's Italian Cuisine

LIQUIDITY

Current ratio:
Current assets/current liabilities

November	47000/17900	2.63
December	52988/16830	3.15

Accounts receivable turnover:
total revenues/average accounts receivable

103200/[(10000+11500)/2]	9.60

Average collection period:
31 days / accounts receivable turnover

31/9.60	3.23

Operating cash to current liabilities:
operating cash average current liabilities

7087.2/[(17900+16830)/2]	
7087.2/17365	0.41

ACTIVITY

Food inventory turnover:
cost of food sold / average food inventory

24960/[(4000+3538)/2]	6.62

Beverage inventory turnover:
cost of beverage sold / average beverage inventory

5280/[(6000+3950)/2]	1.06

Fixed asset turnover:
total revenues / average net fixed assets

103200/[(29470+34450)/2]	3.23

Total asset turnover:
total revenues / average total assets

103200/[(76470+87438)/2]	1.26

PROFITABILITY

Profit margin:
net income / total revenues

4645.2/103200	4.50%

Return on assets:
net income / total assets

4645.2/87438	5.31%

Return on equity:
net income / total equity
or
cash flow / total equity

4645.2/58608	7.93%
4345.2+500/58608	8.78%

SOLVENCY

Operating cash to long-term debt:
operating cash average long-term debt

7087.2/[(10000+12000)/2]	0.64

Long-term debt to total capitalization:
total long-term liabilities / (total liabilities + total equity)

November	10000/76470	0.13
December	12000/87438	0.14

Debt-equity ratio:
total long-term liabilities / total equity

November	10000/48570	0.21
December	12000/58608	0.20

Times interest earned (TIE):
(net income + interest expense) / interest expense or
EBIT / interest expense

(4645.2+500)/500	10.29

Fixed charge coverage:
(net income + interest expense + rent expense) /
(interest expense + rent expense)

(4645.2+500+7000)/(500+7000)	1.62

OPERATING

Food cost percentage:
cost of food sold / food sales

24960/78000	32.00%

Beverage cost percentage:
cost of beverage inventory / beverage sales

5280/24000	22.00%

Labor cost percentage:
labor cost / total sales

(29870+7467.5)/103200	36.18%

ILLUSTRATION 3-6

Ratios Analysis for Gian's Italian Cuisine

ber financial statements, the average collection period for Gian's is only 3.32 days (31 days/9.6 times).

■ **Operating cash to current liabilities** (operating cash/average current liabilities): Gian's posted a ratio of 0.41, meaning that for $1.00 of current liabilities, Gian's has only $0.41 of cash to pay off current debt. This low ratio could be due to seasonality. If this ratio continues to fall under 1.0, ownership should examine closely the restaurant's management of cash and its cost control systems.

SOLVENCY RATIOS. Solvency ratios measure the relationship between operating cash flow to long-term debt, long-term debt to total capitalization, and total debt to total equity. Other solvency ratios include times interest expense earned and fixed charge coverage.

■ **Operating cash flow to long-term debt** (operating cash/average long-term debt): Gian's shows 0.64 for this ratio, meaning that it has $0.64 in operating cash for every $1.00 of its long-term debt. This number is higher than the $0.41 for operating cash to current liabilities, signifying that Gian's carries more current debt than long-term debt.

■ **Long-term debt to total capitalization** (long-term liabilities/[total liabilities + total equity]): Consistent with its low long-term debt ratio, Gian's long-term debt to total capitalization is 13% for November and 14% for December. Because Gian's does not carry a large amount of long-term debt, it is a very solvent operation.

■ **Debt-to-equity ratio** (total long-term liabilities/total equity): As expected, due to its low amount of long-term debt, Gian's debt-to-equity ratio is 21%. A low ratio indicates that the business is financed conservatively. You will learn later in the book, however, that by using more debt and less equity to finance your company, your return on the equity investment will be higher. This is called *financial leverage.*

■ **Times interest earned (TIE)** (earnings before interest expense and income tax [EBIT]/interest expense): While you want most solvency ratios to be low, you want TIE and the following solvency ratio to be high. TIE indicates the number of times an operation can cover its interest payments and is helpful to creditors in determining the solvency of a business. Gian's has a TIE of 10.29, meaning it can pay its interest expense more than ten times over.

■ **Fixed charge coverage** ([net income + interest expense + rent expense]/[interest expense + rent expense]): This ratio is similar to TIE, but it also includes expenses related to operating leases for property and equipment. Gian's has a fixed charge coverage of 1.62, which further indicates how conservatively it is capitalized.

ACTIVITY RATIOS. Activity ratios include food and beverage inventory turnover, fixed asset turnover, and total asset turnover.

■ **Food inventory turnover** (cost of food sold/average food inventory): Gian's has a food inventory turnover of 6.62, which means it sells its food inventory every four to five days (32 days/6.62 times), keeping its ingredients fresh for its customers.

■ **Beverage inventory turnover** (cost of beverage sold/average beverage inventory): Gian's 1.06 turnover rate indicates that it sells its beverage inventory in approximately one month's time and thus does not have a large amount of capital tied up in wines, beer, and liquors. A beverage inventory turnover ratio of 1.06 is very good for a restaurant operation like Gian's.

- **Fixed asset turnover** (total revenue/average net fixed assets): Gian's ratio of 3.23 means that for every $1.00 of fixed assets, it generates $3.32 of revenues per month. While this ratio is of some value for a hospitality asset, the more important ratios measure how much cash flow the fixed asset generates.

- **Total asset turnover** (total revenue/average total assets): If we focus on total assets, we find that $1.26 of Gian's revenue is generated for every dollar of total assets. Fixed asset and total asset turnover are used primarily in horizontal analysis to establish trends that may be taking place in the business.

OPERATING RATIOS. The key operating ratios focus on food, beverage, and labor cost.

- **Food cost percentage** (cost of food sold/food sales): A food cost of 32% means that for every $1.00 of food sold, Gian's spends $0.32 on the food ingredients. A food cost percent between 30% and 40% is common for most restaurants.

- **Beverage cost percentage** (cost of beverage sold/beverage sales): In Gian's case, for every $1.00 of beverage sales, it spends $0.22 on the cost of the product, thus generating a gross profit of $0.78. Beverage cost percentage varies depending on the mix of product sold but usually averages about 20% for a restaurant like Gian's.

- **Labor cost percentage** (labor cost/total sales): Gian's labor cost of 36.18% may appear a bit high to some restaurant operators, but it is representative of many midpriced family restaurants and includes not only salary and wages but also all employee benefits.

PROFITABILITY RATIOS. The primary profitability ratios are profit margin, return on assets, and return on investment.

- **Profit margin** (net income/total revenue): Gian's 4.5% profit margin for December is low for the restaurant industry. A profit margin of 10% or more is the target margin for most restaurants. Due to the financial risk involved with restaurants, equity investors seek returns in excess of 20% on their capital.

- **Return on assets** (net income/total assets): A return on assets of 5.31% means that each dollar in assets generates $0.05 in net income for Gian's. This is also low for the restaurant industry. A return of 10% or more is the target for most restaurant owners.

- **Return on investment (ROI) or Return on equity (ROE)** (cash flow/total equity) or (net income/total equity): This ratio is also known as return on equity. Gian's return on investment is 7.93%, which would not be looked upon favorably by most equity investors. An ROI of at least 15% is normally expected. This calculation appears in other ratios definitions you will find in any accounting text or the uniform systems. However, some investors view this in an alternate way by using cash flow rather than net income as the numerator. As an investor, some view the total cash generated, rather than simply the net income, as the preferred method. Since depreciation is a non-cash expense, therefore, cash flow, which is net income plus depreciation, is used. In this instance, the return on investment is 8.78%.

THE REAL DEAL

If you own stock in a company, regardless of whether it is one share or thousands of shares, you will receive an annual report from the company. In that report, you will see the entire set of financial statements. Many additional useful items are in the annual report as well. For example, the report includes a letter from the chairman summarizing the accomplishments of the company during the past year and projections for the following year. More importantly, it includes a letter from the auditing firm confirming that all information provided in the company's report is accurate and has been certified by independent accountants. Always pay attention to the section entitled "Notes to the Financial Statement." All the details, such as methods of inventory valuation used, methods of depreciation used, and even current or pending lawsuits and government regulations that have an impact on company operations, are discussed.

If you are not a stockholder but are interested in a certain company, how can you obtain a copy of its annual report? It's easy. Simply call the company's public relations office and ask for a copy. Alternatively, you can go to the EDGAR database at www.sec.gov/edgarhp.htm or to Yahoo's website at finance.yahoo.com. If all else fails, just enter the name of the company on the Internet. On the home page of most companies is a pull-down menu or a sidebar regarding financial information.

INDUSTRY AVERAGES AND NORMS

It is always wise to compare a business's actual operating results with its budget and prior-year results. There are, however, published industry averages and norms that can also be useful. The following are a few popular hospitality industry publications, together with links to their websites:

- Smith Travel Research Host Report for Lodging
  www.smithtravelresearch.com/smithtravelresearch/
- PKF Consulting Annual Lodging Trends and PKF Consulting Benchmarker Report for hotels
  www.pkfc.com/hrg/
- Ernst & Young Hotel Operating Trends
  www.ey.com/global/content.nsf/International/industry_-_REHC
- National Restaurant Association Annual Trends
  www.restaurant.org/research

Illustrations 3-7 and 3-8 present sample *Host* and *STAR* reports, both products of Smith Travel Research. The *Host Report,* which is published annually, is designed to allow a hotel to compare its operating results with those of other comparable hotels. Smith Travel Research

str

Smith Travel Research
Full-Service: Any Hotels

Date: 5/27/2006

Job #: 3338

Occupancy: 73.3%
ADR: $153.15
RevPAR: $120.15

Sample
Props: 7
Rooms: 7,326

REVENUE	Ratio to Sales * %	Amount Per Available Room $	Amount Per Occupied Room Night $
Rooms	58.6	41,239	153.16
Food	22.4	15,742	58.46
Beverage	5.4	3,782	14.05
Other Food & Beverage	4.1	2,873	10.67
Telecommunications	1.4	972	3.61
Other Operated Departments	5.4	3,834	14.24
Rentals & Other Income	2.4	1,715	6.37
Cancellation Fee	0.3	198	0.73
TOTAL REVENUE	100.0	70,355	261.29
DEPARTMENTAL EXPENSES			
Rooms	20.9	8,629	32.05
Food & Beverage	67.4	15,095	56.06
Telecommunications	69.4	675	2.51
Other Operated Depts & Rentals	3.8	2,657	9.87
TOTAL DEPARTMENTAL EXPENSES	38.5	27,056	100.49
DEPARTMENTAL PROFITS			
Rooms	79.1	32,610	121.11
Food & Beverage	32.6	7,302	27.12
Telecommunications	30.6	297	1.10
Other Operated Depts & Rentals	96.2	2,892	10.74
TOTAL DEPARTMENTAL PROFITS	61.5	43,299	160.80
UNDISTRIBUTED OPERATING EXPENSES			
Administrative & General	6.4	4,530	16.82
Marketing	5.4	3,805	14.13
Utility Costs	2.9	2,019	7.50
Property Operation & Maintenance	3.9	2,770	10.29
TOTAL UNDISTRIBUTED OPERATING EXPENSES	18.7	13,124	48.74
GROSS OPERATING PROFIT	42.8	30,175	112.06
Franchise Fees (Royalty)	0.2	156	0.58
Management Fees	4.6	3,223	11.97
INCOME BEFORE FIXED CHARGES	38.1	26,796	99.51
SELECTED FIXED CHARGES			
Property Taxes	3.6	2,534	9.41
Insurance	1.2	825	3.07
Reserve For Capital Replacement	3.7	2,594	9.63
AMOUNT AVAILABLE FOR DEBT **SERVICE & OTHER FIXED CHARGES ** **	29.6	20,843	77.40
SUPPLEMENTAL PAYROLL ANALYSIS * **			
Rooms	11.8	4,720	17.48
Total Food and Beverage	30.8	6,727	24.76
Telecommunications	47.4	415	1.55
Other Operated Departments	1.2	848	3.23
Administrative & General	3.3	2,193	8.04
Marketing	1.9	1,230	4.56
Property Operations & Maintenance	1.8	1,245	4.65
TOTAL PAYROLL & RELATED EXPENSES	26.1	17,802	65.82

ILLUSTRATION 3-7
Smith Travel Research Host Report: Compares Hotel Operating Results with Comparable Hotels

SUPPLEMENTAL FOOD & BEVERAGE INFORMATION ***			
Cost of Food Sales	35.5	5,134	19.08
Cost of Beverage Sales	22.7	817	3.04
Total Cost of F&B Sales	28.3	5,950	22.12
Food & Beverage Payroll	30.8	6,727	24.76
Food & Beverage Other Expenses	13.2	1,760	6.82

* Rooms, F&B, and Telecommunications expense ratios to sales for departmental expenses and profits are based on their respective departmental reveunes. All other expenses are based on total revenue.

** Other Fixed Charges include Depreciation and Amortization, Interest, Rent, and Equipment Leases.

*** Payroll and Costs of Sales are included in expenses. Amounts shown here are for additional detail only. Not all HOST participants provide detailed data on payroll and F&B costs; therefore, the following supplemental analyses provide the ratios for only these hotels in the samples that reported detailed information. Consequently, the amounts shown below may not tie to the departmental figures provided.

NOTE: Totals may not add due to rounding.

ILLUSTRATION 3-7
(*Continued*)

organizes the study, and presents the information, in a variety of ways, including sorting by hotel size, type, geographic location, and average room rate. While the sample size Smith Travel Research uses for its actual *Host Report* is much larger than the sample of seven properties containing 7,326 rooms shown in Illustration 3-7, the format of this sample report is the same as the actual *Host Report*. The sample *Host Report* shows that the seven hotels achieved a 73.3% occupancy with an average daily rate of $153.15 and RevPAR of $120.15. The Ratio to Sales column is an example of a common-size financial statement used for vertical analysis. Supplemental food and beverage information is also presented in the bottom part of the report.

The Smith Travel Research *STAR Report* is used by hotel owners and managers to compare their hotel's occupancy, average daily rate, and RevPAR with that of a customized set of hotels that compete with the subject hotel. The *STAR Report* is published monthly and has become the barometer by which almost all hotels in the United States are measured. In Illustration 3-8, we see that the *STAR Report* provides a trend analysis by month and year for the subject hotel and its competitive set, shows where the subject hotel ranks among its competitors with regard to occupancy, average daily rate, and RevPAR, and indexes the subject hotel's performance against the composite of the competitive set. For example, our test hotel achieved a 2005 year-to-date occupancy of 70.3%, while its competitors achieved an occupancy of 73.9%. Our hotel ranked fourth out of seven in occupancy, which computes to an index of 96.3. If our hotel had achieved an occupancy rate of 73.9%, its index would have been 100, reflecting that it achieved exactly the occupancy of its competitive set. Referring to Illustration 3-8, how did our test hotel fare against its competitors in terms of average daily rate? The *STAR Report* indicates that the test hotel's average daily rate of $114.45 was much higher than the $89.05 of the competitive

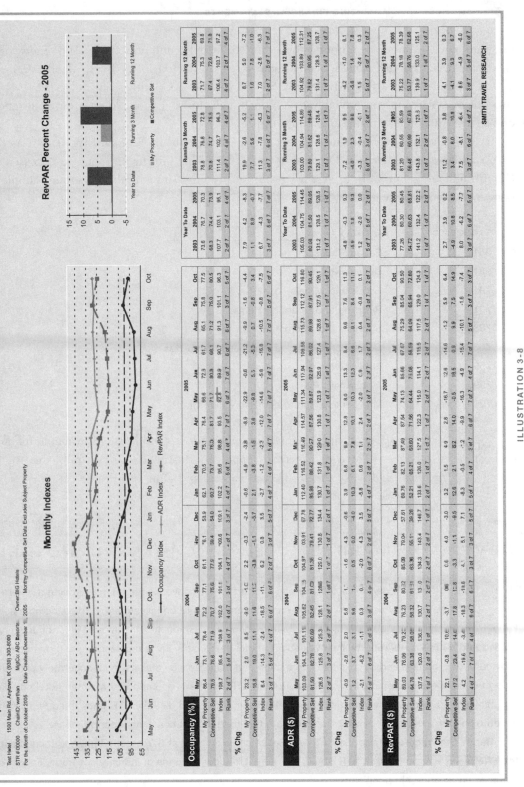

ILLUSTRATION 3-8

Smith Travel Research STAR Report: Trend Analysis by Month and Year for the Subject Hotel and its Competitive Set

set, ranking it number one among the other six, which computes to an ADR index of 128.5. Also note that the test hotel's higher room rate is reflected in its RevPAR of $80.45 for the period, compared to a RevPAR of only $65.81 for the competitive set and a RevPAR rank of two out of seven. As you probably have concluded, this is a valuable and powerful report, and one that all hospitality managers should utilize.

Hospitality managers should also become familiar with the Standard Industry Classification (SIC) codes assigned by the Department of Labor. This information can be accessed via the Department of Labor website at www.osha.gov/pls/imis/sicsearch.html. Some examples pertinent to the hospitality industry are:

SIC CODE	INDUSTRY
5812	Eating Places
5813	Drinking Places
7011	Hotels and Motels
7012	Rooming and Boarding Homes
7032	Sporting and Recreating Camps
7033	Recreational Vehicles Parks and Campsites
7992	Public Golf Course
7996	Amusement Parks
7997	Membership Sports and Recreation Clubs

Simply select a SIC code and explore the many industry publications available for your type of hospitality business. Three of the more popular industry reports are published by Robert Morris and Associates (RMA), the *Business Almanac,* and Dun and Bradstreet.

FEATURE STORY

RANDY SMITH—MAKING HOTEL BENCHMARKING POSSIBLE

Whether one is trying to determine if a city can support a new convention hotel, researching a hotel's ability to meet debt service payments and generate an acceptable return on investment, or developing a new marketing strategy to increase RevPAR, Smith Travel Research (STR) touches the lives of just about everyone in the lodging business. Its reports are invaluable to hotel developers, investors, lenders, and operators as they provide critical market and competitive information and help decision makers more accurately plan and execute their business strategies. In fact, the data from STR reports is so important to some hotel companies that they employ individuals whose sole job is to digest, slice, and dice the STR data. In addition, compensation plans for most hotel general managers are tied to their STR benchmark performance.

Randy Smith, cofounder of Smith Travel Research, is amazed at STR's contribution to the lodging industry. "We never envisioned that STR would be where it is today in terms of industry coverage, impact on the industry, and leadership position."

Twenty years ago, he and his wife, Carolyn, quit their jobs to build an industrywide database listing the name, address, and telephone number of every lodging establishment in the United States. Their original plan was to sell this database to vendors and suppliers. "My wife and I thought we could sell the data to vendors and suppliers. We soon discovered, however, that there was not enough depth to the market."

Realizing that their business model was flawed, Smith searched for a new target market. Having grown up in Memphis, he was well aware of a local company called Holiday Inns. In the process of researching this company, he became familiar with the lodging industry. Soon thereafter, he approached Holiday Inns and negotiated a contract with them to generate market share reports for the chain. Thus, in early 1987, the *Smith Travel Accommodation Report* (STAR) was born based on operating data supplied by approximately 10,000 participating hotels. With his first victory in hand, Smith was confident that other major hotel chains would soon follow Holiday Inns' lead. He wrote to other hotel companies, but received no response. Undeterred, he called on Hilton Hotels Corporation, where the management told Smith that it liked the idea but would not commit unless Smith could convince Sheraton to participate as well. Smith managed to convince Sheraton to join his program and, soon after, Hilton followed suit.

While the database and related software programs continued to expand, the business barely broke even. Smith's second break came in 1989, when Westin approached him with a proposal. While Westin's management was pleased with the existing data provided by the *STAR Report,* what they really wanted was to select the five or six hotels in the markets where their Westin Hotels were located and measure their hotel's performance against their competition. Smith's initial reaction was to say no because he was concerned he would not be able to control the data objectively. Even to this day, because STR's business is based on its customers providing sensitive financial information, confidentiality is very important to Smith. As he points out, "If our customers were to ever lose faith with us, they would cease providing the information we need to generate our reports." In any case, Westin persisted, and Smith ultimately gave in.

In hindsight, that small request from Westin turned out to be a godsend for Smith's research company. Once STR started rolling out their new competitive set reports, the STAR program really took off. Individual hotels around the United States could now select customized competitive sets to measure against their own results, yielding a much more accurate picture of how they stacked up against their competitors. It was a monumental improvement over the almost comical tactics used by many hotel managers in the past—counting cars in their competitors' parking lots and calling competing hotels—often in poorly disguised voices—to determine if their competitors were sold out or still had rooms to rent.

Smith's initial setback turned out to be a boon not only to STR but to the hotel industry as a whole. Today, Smith Travel Research tracks over 30,000 properties and has access to the operating results of every major chain in the industry. Its revolutionary benchmarking program provides a critical resource to the marketplace, which allows for better decision making and higher profits for U.S. hotels.

SOURCES

http://www.smithtravelresearch.com/SmithTravelResearch/About/AboutUsHistory.aspx.

"Looking Back with Randy Smith." http://www.lhonline.com/article/9124, July 2005.

"Newsmaker Interview: Randy Smith." http://www.hotel-online.com/SpecialReports1998/RandySmith.html, May 1998.

"STR Celebrates 20 Years of Hotel Industry Performance Benchmarking." http://www.hospitalitynet.org/news/ 4023433.search, June 2005.

"The Crowned Prince of Confirmation." http://www.hospitalitynet.org/news/4003749.search, November 1999.

"Rich Data Collection Gives Industry Key Talking Points." http://www.hotelmotel.com/hotelmotel/article/ articleDetail.jsp?id=183014, September 2005.

"The Date Game." http://www.hotelmotel.com/hotelmotel/article/articleDetail.jsp?id=183012, September 2005.

Management Decision Making

While reading, interpreting, and analyzing financial statements are important skills that hospitality managers must acquire, applying these skills to the overall decision-making process is also vital. Let us look at a few examples.

EMPLOYEE SCHEDULING

Decisions related to employee scheduling should be based on accurate revenue forecasts, productivity goals, and customer service levels. Because revenue forecasts are based on historical performance combined with the likelihood and timing of future events, the ability to analyze historical financial statements and other management reports is important in predicting the future.

The first step is to become confident that your forecasted number of occupied rooms and restaurant covers by day and meal period are accurate. Next, you need to establish labor guidelines based on your company's customer service standards, including housekeeping hours per occupied room and waitstaff hours per restaurant and banquet cover. Once you have these guidelines in place, employee scheduling becomes almost routine.

As we discussed in the preceding chapter, controlling labor hours and payroll cost on a daily basis is the mark of a good hospitality manager. A daily comparison of scheduled hours with actual hours, scheduled over time with actual overtime, budgeted payroll cost percent with actual payroll cost percent, and actual productivity statistics with productivity standards, sets the superior hospitality manager apart from the rest of the field. When each department in a hotel or restaurant is managed by a superior manager, favorable operating results are achieved and financial rewards are often forthcoming to all involved in the success of the operation.

FOOD AND BEVERAGE PRICING

The menu abstract shown and described in the previous chapter is an excellent tool to use in food and beverage pricing. Tracking the sales of each menu item and calculating their gross profitability over time can greatly assist the hospitality manager in setting menu prices and removing unprofitable items from the menu. Menu price and food cost, however, are only part of the equation. The storage cost of the product and the labor cost involved in preparing and serving the menu item must also be factored in. For example, a menu item may appear to be a profit leader based on its selling price and food cost percentage—but if it is a made-to-order dessert soufflé requiring thirty minutes of the chef's time to prepare, it may in reality be a loss leader rather than a profit leader. A financially oriented hospitality manager will take the time to estimate all the costs involved and include them in his pricing decision.

REVENUE MANAGEMENT

An exciting new area in lodging is revenue management. Revenue management is an outgrowth of yield management, the goal of which is to maximize RevPAR. The basic concept of revenue management is to tactfully close lower levels of pricing during times of high demand, open all pricing levels during times of low demand, and maximize cash flow as well as revenue for the hotel. A good revenue management system not only takes into consideration the room rate paid by the client but also considers the overall profitability of the business based on the timing of the meeting and the total amount of revenues and profits generated by the group.

The airlines were the first to develop sophisticated revenue management systems. Major hotel companies are now developing computerized systems of their own. A strategy common to all these new systems is to sell guest rooms at the higher rates first and then offer the lower rates later. Today, many hotel companies are also developing revenue management software that can assist revenue managers in making these critical pricing decisions.

The keys to a successful revenue management system are maintaining an accurate day-by-day forecast, twelve to twenty-four months out, for the subject hotel and the market as a whole; maintaining an accurate reconnaissance of what room rates competitors are charging and what groups they have booked in the past; ensuring the hotel general manager, director of marketing, and rooms division manager are committed to working together with the common goal of maximizing profit for the hotel as a whole in mind; and, of course, having a great revenue manager.

Once again, the more accurately a hospitality manager is involved in revenue management can read, interpret, and analyze the operating results of a business, and therefore forecast accurately, the more successful he or she will be.

PROFIT FLEXING

Profit flexing is a skill that is developed over time. It is almost an art. It is called into action when a hotel's actual revenues for the month fall behind budget. The trick is to try to adjust pricing for the balance of the month to maximize the remaining revenue opportunity and reduce expenses without impacting customer service. The goal is to minimize the negative impact on the bottom line for the month.

To become an effective profit flexer, a thorough knowledge of what revenues and expenses are recorded in each income statement account is prerequisite. Each budgeted line item must be reviewed to determine if there is an opportunity to increase sales or reduce cost by month end. Next, the profit flexer must possess a thorough knowledge of cost-volume-profit modeling (discussed in the next section of this chapter). The goal is to find ways to achieve budgeted profit at the less-than-budgeted level of sales now anticipated for the month. At a minimum, the profit flexer must find a way to maintain the budgeted profit percentage at the less-than-budgeted revenue level.

The key areas that a professional profit flexer focuses on are the following:

■ Occupancy: Can short-term business be attracted to the hotel for the month, even at a reduced price?

■ ADR: What incentive programs can be implemented to motivate the front desk staff to up sell walk-in guests to increase the average daily room rate for the balance of the month? What incentives can be offered to sales managers to sell more group business for the month?

■ Food and beverage revenue: What high-volume, high-profit food and beverage specials can be added to the current menu to increase food profit for the month?

■ Rooms profit: How can the housekeeping staff be motivated to clean one additional room per hour? How can the cost of guest supplies be reduced by 10% without impacting guest satisfaction?

■ Food and beverage profit: How can the chef find a way to shave a few percentage points off food cost? How can the beverage manager find a way to shave a few percentage points off beverage cost?

■ Labor cost: How can managers do a better job to eliminate overtime? Rather than eliminating positions, can members of the staff be persuaded to accept voluntary time off (VTO) to reduce labor cost for the month?

■ Other operating expenses: Can any budgeted operating expenses be deferred to the next month? Examples include administrative travel, employee recruiting programs, training programs, promotional parties, linen purchases, marketing brochures, sales trips, and repairs of nonessential furniture and equipment.

As you can see from the types of questions being asked, the key to successful profit flexing is to motivate the entire staff to work as a team to achieve the financial goals set by the general manager of the hotel.

COST-VOLUME-PROFIT ANALYSIS

Another name for **cost-volume-profit modeling** is *breakeven analysis*. By determining whether a cost is fixed, variable, or mixed, and by establishing what level of profit or return on investment is required by the owners, management can target the amount of revenue that must be achieved to attain the owner's goals. All of the cost information can be readily found on the income statement for the business. The formula for the breakeven level of sales is:

$$\text{breakeven volume} = \frac{\text{fixed costs}}{(\text{sales price} - \text{variable cost})}$$

For example, let's say that Jensen's Lodge sells its cabins during the ski season for $300 a night. The fixed cost to keep and maintain the lodge is $50,000 per month, while the labor cost to maintain each lodge unit (its only variable cost) is $60. How many room-nights does the Jensen's Lodge need to sell per month to at least break even?

According to the formula, the answer is 209 room-nights:

$$\text{breakeven volume} = \frac{\text{fixed costs}}{\text{sale price} - \text{variable cost}}$$

$$= \frac{50,000}{300 - 60}$$

$$= \frac{50,000}{240}$$

$$= 208.33, \text{ or } 209 \text{ rooms}$$

Let us look at this from a different angle. Assume that Jensen's has twenty rooms in its lodge. What occupancy percentage must it achieve in February to break even? Assuming that it is not a leap year and there are twenty-eight days in February, the breakeven occupancy percentage would be:

$$\text{occupancy } \% = \frac{\text{rooms sold}}{\text{rooms available for sale}}$$

$$= \frac{209}{28 \times 20}$$

$$= 37.32\%$$

Adding a desired profit level to the formula changes it as follows:

$$\text{desired volume} = \frac{\text{fixed costs} + \text{desired profits}}{\text{sale price} - \text{variable cost}}$$

If the desired monthly profit level is $25,000, then:

$$\text{desired volume} = \frac{50,000 + 25,000}{300 - 60}$$

$$= \frac{75,000}{240}$$

$$= 312.5, \text{ or } 313 \text{ rooms}$$

In terms of occupancy, this would convert to a 55.89% occupancy percentage if Jensen's Lodge wants to make a $25,000 profit for February.

$$\text{occupancy \%} = \frac{\text{rooms sold}}{\text{rooms available for sale}}$$

$$= \frac{313}{28 \times 20}$$

$$= 55.89\%$$

Cost-volume-profit skills are important to master if you want to be a successful hospitality manager.

Readers of Financial Statements Beware!

The Sarbanes-Oxley Act has focused attention on the credibility of a company's financial statements. Before we move on to the management of a company's working capital, let us spend a few more moments on the reading and interpretation of financial statements. While numbers don't lie, they *can* be manipulated. Therefore, when you read a company's financial statements, be aware of financial tricks that others may use to paint a false picture of their company's financial success. Here are a few ways that clever financial managers can make a company's financial position and operating results appear more favorable than they really are.

THE REAL DEAL

In terms of window dressing, certain infamous companies come to mind. A former partner of Arthur Andersen helped window-dress Enron's financial statements by inflating profits by over $400 million and then releasing the false statements at the appropriate time to give Enron a boost in stock price. The same man was also accused of masking $1 billion of losses in Enron's retail business by merging the accounting of various units. A former CEO of Sunbeam also had to pay the SEC $700,000 to settle charges of improper accounting. An example in the hospitality industry involved the Queens Moat Houses in England, whose profits were overstated for ten years, resulting in a £1 billion writeoff in 1993. How did this occur? A combination of false profit reports, deferred costs, and the overstatement of the value of certain hotels. Why did this happen? Only those involved know. What were the consequences? Fines and possible jail time. Don't risk your life and freedom by trying to accumulate personal wealth improperly.

WINDOW DRESSING

Artificially making a company's financial statement more favorable than it should be is known as **window dressing.** For example, one way to make a year-end balance sheet look better than it should look is for a company not to pay its outstanding invoices on time. Although the business will still show the same current ratio, the balance sheet will show more cash than it would if the invoices had been paid. If potential investors reviewing the balance sheet are not careful and simply look at the cash balance and not the whole picture, they could be misled about the current financial cash position of the business in which they are considering investing.

OFF-BALANCE-SHEET FINANCING

Off-balance-sheet financing is a clever method that is legal as long as you strictly follow the rules. Off-balance-sheet financing is used by some companies that do not want to show debt on their balance sheet associated with a real estate joint venture of which they own a percentage. GAAP allows a company to avoid showing its portion of the debt related to the investment as a liability on its balance sheet as long as it owns a "relatively" minor percentage of the joint venture. The company is allowed to book the investment as an asset and avoid depreciating it on its books. Here is how this type of financial window dressing works:

1. The amount of the joint venture the company owns is recorded as an asset.

2. No liability is recorded on the company's balance sheet, so the company's debt-to-equity ratio looks more favorable than it really is, which improves its credit rating.

3. The company's portion of net operating income generated by the joint venture is shown as revenue on the company's income statement, thus increasing its net operating income (NOI) and the perceived market value of its stock.

4. Depreciation expense for the company's portion of the asset is not shown on its income statement, which enhances its apparent NOI and further increases the perceived market value of its stock.

CAPITALIZE CURRENT OPERATING EXPENSES

Capitalizing current operating expenses is another financial trick to artificially reduce current expenses and increase profits. This is how a clever financial manager might try to window dress his company's financial statements:

1. Instead of booking a major expenditure as an expense, the financial manager could record it as a long-term asset. In this case, it would not appear as an expense on the company's income statement, which would result in a higher NOI. Concurrently, the total asset value shown on the balance sheet would be artificially inflated, making the business appear stronger than it should.

2. The financial manager would then depreciate the asset over a long period, thus artificially inflating current earnings and increasing the perceived market value of the company's stock.

IMPROPER REVENUE RECOGNITION

Improper revenue recognition occurs when revenues are recorded before they are actually earned. This financial trick, which violates the matching principle, is sometimes employed by savvy financial managers. Here's how the trick works:

1. The financial manager is informed that the company has signed a long-term contract to provide products or services to a customer.

2. Instead of following GAAP rules by recognizing revenues when they are earned, he records the full value of the contract as a current revenue. This, of course, is totally misleading and illegal. It grossly overstates sales and current net operating income and artificially increases the perceived value of the company's stock.

As you can see, as a businessperson, you must be on your guard when reading a company's financial statements. You must also be totally ethical yourself if you are involved in the preparation of a company's financial statements. No financial gain is worth the sad consequences that result when unethical dealings take place and are discovered. Short-term gains through unethical means inevitably result in long-term losses and personal disgrace.

THE REAL DEAL

The Sarbanes-Oxley Act has helped tighten financial controls in the hospitality industry. The temptations, however, are still there for those who insist on breaking the law. As a hospitality manager, don't fall into the trap of doing things the easy way. It will likely come back to haunt you. For example, some small businesses may not declare and report all its revenues and expenses accurately. By declaring less revenue than it should, such a business pays less income and sales tax. Other companies may hire illegal immigrants and therefore need money on the side to pay these workers off the books. Whenever employees sense that management is not following fair practices, they will likely not follow fair practices either and will try to steal from the company.

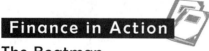

Finance in Action

The Boatman

The Boatman is a 290-room hotel located in a major metropolitan city near a medical center. Boatman, Inc. is an internationally franchised chain of midscale full-service hotels. This particular property focuses primarily on guests who visit the medical center for business purposes, but it also has limited meeting space that can accommodate a group of up to one hundred guests.

Ms. Teresa Sage, controller of the Boatman, is in the process of analyzing operations and is starting by conducting a horizontal analysis on the income statement for the previous two months.

QUESTIONS

1. When conducting a horizontal analysis, what numbers do you need to calculate?

    As seen in the shaded regions of the completed horizontal analysis for the Boatman Hotel, the change in dollar amounts and percent change must be calculated for each line item. All of the calculations are provided in the finished example.

Boatman Hotel

Horizontal Analysis

Income Statement

For the months ended March 31 and April 30, 2008

	March	April	$ change	$ change calculation	% change	% change calculation
Revenues:						
Rooms	$375,236	$425,105	$49,869	425,105 − 375,236	13.29	(49,869/375,236) × 100
Food and Beverage	186,253	176,523	(9,730)	176,523 − 186,253	(5.22)	(−9,730/186,253) × 100
Telecommunications	4,213	5,326	1,113	5,326 − 4,213	26.42	(1,113/4,213) × 100
Other Income	46,879	49,654	2,775	49,654 − 46,879	5.92	(2,775/46,879) × 100
Total Revenues	$612,581	$656,608	$44,027	656,608 − 612,581	7.19	(44,027/612,581) × 100
Departmental Expenses:						
Rooms	$130,256	$154,987	$24,731	154,987 − 130,256	18.99	(24,731/130,256) × 100
Food and Beverage	142,516	135,216	(7,300)	135,216 − 142,516	(5.12)	(−7,300/142,516) × 100
Telecommunications	(6,453)	(7,123)	(670)	(−6,453) − (−7,123)	10.38	(−670/−6,453) × 100
Other Operated Departments	35,648	41,213	5,565	41,213 − 35,648	15.61	(5,565/35,648) × 100
Total Departmental Expenses	$171,711	$169,306	$ (2,405)	169,306 − 171,711	(1.40)	(−2,405/171,711) × 100
Gross Operating Income	440,870	487,302	$46,432	487,302 − 440,870	10.53	(46,432/440,870) × 100
Undistributed Operating Expenses:						
Administrative and General	$ 11,605	$ 18,256	$ 6,651	18,256 − 11,605	57.31	(6,651/11,605) × 100
Marketing	41,219	44,362	3,143	44,362 − 41,219	7.63	(3,143/41,219) × 100
Franchise Fees	21,005	24,032	3,027	24,032 − 21,005	14.41	(3,027/21,005) × 100
Property Operations and Maintenance	37,456	38,612	1,156	38,612 − 37,456	3.09	(1,156/37,456) × 100
Utilities	32,156	36,459	4,303	36,459 − 32,156	13.38	(4,303/32,156) × 100
Total Undistributed Operating Expenses	$143,441	$161,721	$18,280	161,721 − 143,441	12.74	(18,280/143,441) × 100
Gross Operating Profit (House Profit)	297,429	325,581	$28,152	325,581 − 297,429	9.47	(28,152/297,429) × 100
Management Fee	6,145	6,425	$ 280	6,425 − 6,145	4.56	(280/6,145) × 100
Fixed Expenses						
Property Taxes	$ 25,613	$ 25,613	—	25,613 − 25,613	—	(0/25,613) × 100
Reserve for Capital Improvements	18,321	20,153	1,832	20,153 − 18,321	10.00	(1,832/18,321) × 100
Insurance	6,901	6,852	(49)	6,852 − 6,901	(0.71)	(−49/6,901) × 100
Interest Expense	75,004	78,450	3,446	78,450 − 75,004	4.59	(3,446/75,004) × 100
Total Fixed Charges	$125,839	$131,068	$ 5,229	131,068 − 125,839	4.16	(5,229/125,839) × 100
Net Operating Income (NOI)	$195,445	$188,088	$22,643		13.69	

2. First, determine if there were any major changes between the two reporting periods.

    The easiest way to identify major changes is to look at the percent change column. By looking at each line item, you can see there were significant increases in rooms revenue, telecommunications revenue, rooms expense, telecommunication expense, other operated departments expense, administrative and general expense, franchise fees, and utilities.

3. The next step is to analyze the data and put meaning to the numbers.

    ■   *In the previous answer, we noted a significant increase in rooms revenue (13.29%), which was matched with an increase in rooms expenses (18.99%).*

    ■   *As you go through the percent change column, you notice a decrease in food and beverage revenue (−5.22%), but there was also a matching decrease in food and beverage expense (−5.12%).*

■ *One other significant change was in telecommunications, which increased by 26.42% between March and April, but note that the actual dollar amount change was only $1,113. Revenue for telecommunications is very small compared to revenues for rooms or food and beverage. If rooms experienced a 26% increase, there would be a significant impact to the bottom line.*

■ *One area of particular interest is the increase in administrative and general expenses of 57.31%. Teresa must further investigate to determine why these expenditures increased $6,651 over one month. Franchise fees and utilities also increased over the period, causing total undistributed operating expenses to increase 12.74%.*

■ *Even though undistributed operating expenses and fixed expenses increased, there was still an increase of $22,643 (13.69%) in net operating income. This increase was achieved through higher rooms revenue and a slight drop in operating expenses.*

Overall, the property appears to be in good shape, but Teresa must conduct further analysis to determine why some of the expense accounts have increased. She could also perform a horizontal analysis on the changes in expenses as a percentage of departmental revenue.

WHERE WE'VE BEEN, WHERE WE'RE GOING

To fully understand what the numbers on a company's financial statements indicate and can really tell you requires that you develop excellent financial analysis skills. In this chapter, you read about vertical, horizontal, trend, and ratio analyses. You were also introduced to certain industry norms and standards to help you determine if your operation is on par with your competition. You are also now aware of financial tricks that can be played to purposely misrepresent financial data and mislead the readers of financial statements.

In the following chapter, we address two more important operational subjects: working capital and cash management. Without enough working capital, a company cannot sustain its operations; with too much working capital, assets sit idle, not generating a return on the owner's investment.

Key Points

➤ Vertical analysis, also known as *common-size analysis,* analyzes the relationship among assets, liabilities, equity, revenues, and expenses over a specified period. All accounts are expressed as a percentage of one base account.

➤ Horizontal analysis tracks the performance of a company over time and identifies meaningful trends in the accounts shown on both the balance sheet and the income statement. Horizontal analysis tracks both changes in dollar amounts and percentages.

> ➤ Trend analysis, an extension of horizontal analysis, compares the subject company's operating results with industry standards and norms.
>
> ➤ Ratio analysis compares one financial component with another. Ratio analyses are categorized as liquidity, solvency, activity, profitability, and operating ratios.
>
> ➤ Those reading and analyzing financial statements must be aware of certain financial tricks that financial managers may use to make a company's financial condition and operating performance appear more favorable than it should. These financial tricks are called *window dressing* and can include off-balance-sheet financing, capitalizing current expenses, and improper recognition of revenue.

Key Terms

VERTICAL OR COMMON-SIZE ANALYSIS: Analysis where all accounts on a financial statement are expressed as a percentage of one base account. When analyzing an income statement, all expenses are sized using revenue as the common base. In analyzing a balance sheet, total assets, total liabilities, or total equity serves as the base.

HORIZONTAL OR COMPARATIVE ANALYSIS: Tracks operating performance over a specified period, including dollar amount and percentage changes.

TREND ANALYSIS: Measures the effects or changes of accounts over time. Line graphs and bar charts are often used to graphically show the results of the analysis.

RATIO ANALYSIS: A ratio is an expression of one number divided by another. Ratios can be categorized as liquidity, solvency, activity, profitability, and operating ratios.

LIQUIDITY RATIO: Measures a business's ability to meet its short-term obligations (one year or less).

SOLVENCY RATIO: Measures a business's ability to meet long-term financial obligations (over one year).

ACTIVITY RATIO: Measures management's profit performance as compared to the management of the company's assets.

OPERATING RATIO: Assists management in determining how efficient an operation is

PROFITABILITY RATIO: Measures management's effectiveness in achieving profit margins and return on investment goals.

CURRENT RATIO (current assets divided by current liabilities): Measures the level of a company's working capital and the liquidity of a company.

ACCOUNTS RECEIVABLE TURNOVER (total revenue divided by average accounts receivable): Measures the speed at which a company collects its charge sales.

AVERAGE COLLECTION PERIOD: Measures the speed at which a company converts its accounts receivables to cash. It is expressed in number of days.

OPERATING CASH FLOWS TO CURRENT LIABILITIES: Cash flow from operations divided by average current liabilities.

OPERATING CASH FLOW TO LONG-TERM DEBT: Cash flow from operations divided by long-term debt.

LONG-TERM DEBT TO TOTAL CAPITALIZATION: Long-term debt divided by total liabilities and total equity.

DEBT-TO-EQUITY RATIO (total liabilities divided by total equity): Measures the amount of financial leverage a company is using to finance its growth.

TIMES INTEREST EARNED (TIE) (earnings before interest and tax [EBIT] divided by interest expense): Indicates the number of times a business can cover its interest payments.

FIXED CHARGE COVERAGE (net income plus interest expense and rent expense divided by the sum of interest expense and rent expense): Similar to TIE, but also includes expenses related to operating leases for property and equipment.

FOOD INVENTORY TURNOVER: Cost of food sold divided by the average food inventory.

BEVERAGE INVENTORY TURNOVER: Cost of beverages sold divided by the average beverage inventory.

FIXED ASSET TURNOVER: Total revenues divided by average net fixed assets.

TOTAL ASSET TURNOVER: Total revenues divided by average total assets.

FOOD COST PERCENTAGE: Cost of food sold divided by food sales.

BEVERAGE COST PERCENTAGE: Cost of beverages sold divided by total beverage sales.

LABOR COST PERCENTAGE: Labor cost divided by departmental or total sales.

PROFIT MARGIN (departmental or total income divided by total revenue): Measures the ability of a business to generate a profit.

RETURN ON ASSETS (net income divided by total assets): Measures the operation's ability to utilize assets to their maximum to generate income.

RETURN ON INVESTMENT OR EQUITY (cash flow divided by total equity): Measures the operation's ability to generate a return on the owners' capital investment.

PROFIT FLEXING: Maximizing revenues and minimizing costs at the same time to achieve the maximum profit level.

COST-VOLUME-PROFIT MODELING: Same as breakeven analysis. It is fixed costs divided by the contribution margin to obtain the volume of business needed to break even.

WINDOW DRESSING: Financial tricks used by financial managers to make a financial statement look better and more profitable than it should.

OFF-BALANCE-SHEET FINANCING: When a company records its portion of an investment as an asset with no liability being recorded on the company's balance sheet. As a result, the company's debt-to-equity ratio looks more favorable than it should, improving its credit rating. The company's portion of net operating income generated by the asset is shown as revenue on the company's income statement, which increases its NOI and the perceived market value of its stock. In addition, the depreciation expense for the company's portion of the asset is not shown on its income statement, which further increases the apparent NOI, which increases the perceived market value of its stock.

CAPITALIZING CURRENT OPERATING EXPENSES: A financial trick to artificially reduce current expenses by recording such expenses as long-term assets. Since expenses are reduced, profits increase.

IMPROPER REVENUE RECOGNITION: Record revenues before they are actually earned thereby inflating the revenues and thus profits of the business.

Application Exercises

Use the following sets of financial statements to complete Exercises 1 through 8:

The T Resort

Income Statement
For the year ended December 31, 2008

Revenues	$600,000.00
Cost of Goods Sold	192,000.00
Salaries and Wages	210,000.00
Employee Benefits	58,800.00
Other Expenses	118,520.00
Depreciation	2,000.00
Net Income	**$ 18,680.00**

The T Resort
Balance Sheets

As of December 31, 2007, and 2008

	2007	2008
Cash	$7,000.00	$12,980.00
Accounts Receivable	10,000.00	12,000.00
Marketable Securities	3,000.00	3,000.00
Inventory	8,000.00	9,500.00
Prepaid Rent	10,000.00	8,500.00
Total Current Asset	38,000.00	45,980.00
Furniture, Fixtures and Equipment (FF&E)	20,000.00	20,000.00
Accumulated Depreciation (FF&E)	(3,000.00)	(5,000.00)
Building	20,000.00	20,000.00
Long-term Investments	30,000.00	45,000.00
Long-term Assets	67,000.00	80,000.00
Total Assets	**$105,000.00**	**$125,980.00**

Accounts Payable	$ 14,000.00	$ 12,460.00
Accrued Payroll	9,450.00	8,000.00
Accrued Taxes	8,560.00	6,980.00
Total Current Liabilities	32,010.00	27,440.00
Long-term Debt	12,500.00	20,000.00
Owner's Equity	30,490.00	29,860.00
Retained Earnings	30,000.00	48,680.00
Total Owner's Equity	60,490.00	78,540.00
Total Liabilities and Owner's Equity	**$105,000.00**	**$125,980.00**

1. Perform a vertical analysis of the T Resort's 2008 income statement.
2. Perform a vertical analysis of the T Resort's December 31, 2007, balance sheet.
3. Perform a vertical analysis of the T Resort's December 31, 2008, balance sheet.
4. Perform a horizontal analysis of the T Resort's 2007 and 2008 balance sheets.
5. Is the T Resort too heavily in debt? How can you evaluate its debt structure?
6. What is the projected current ratio for the T Resort as of December 31, 2007, and 2008? Are the ratios favorable?
7. What are the projected profit margin, and return on equity for The T in 2008?
8. What will be the inventory turnover rate for The T in 2008?
9. **ETHICS** ✳ Macy, a friend of yours, started a small restaurant five years ago. She was doing well until last year. She is looking into selling the restaurant and would like your opinion on how she should prepare the restaurant's financial statements. You notice she has a large amount of current liabilities that are way overdue. She also shows a large cash balance on the books. Something tells you she is not being honest with you and is trying to make her statements look better than they should. What should you tell her?
10. **EXPLORING THE WEB** ✳ Search the Internet for information regarding SAS 99 or Statement on Auditing Standards No. 99. What is SAS 99, and how does it address the issues relating to window dressing?

Concept Check ✓

Larry's Luncheon Spot

Larry's Luncheon Spot is a chain of cafeteria-style restaurants geographically located in the southern sector of the United States. These restaurants concentrate on serving homestyle food such as meatloaf, fried chicken, mashed potatoes, barbecued foods, and apple pie at an affordable price. The primary clientele who frequent Larry's include retirees and young professionals who are on the go and enjoy the speed of cafeteria-style service.

Ms. Sarah Blackwell is a financial analyst who specializes in restaurant companies, and one of the companies in her portfolio is Larry's Luncheon Spot. Larry's is a public company, and analysts tend to keep a watchful eye on financial ratios to determine the strength of the company.

QUESTIONS

1. Utilizing the income statement and balance sheet provided, assist Ms. Blackwell with her analysis by calculating the following ratios for 2008.
   - Current ratio
   - Accounts receivable turnover
   - Average collection period
   - Food inventory turnover
   - Fixed asset turnover
   - Total asset turnover
   - Profit margin
   - Return on assets
   - Return on equity
   - Long-term debt to total capitalization
   - Debt-to-equity ratio
   - Time interest earned
   - Fixed charge coverage
   - Food cost percentage
   - Labor cost percentage

2. Utilizing the calculations in question 1, analyze the ratios for Larry's Luncheon Spot. Address any ratios that appear high or low, and explain why you think this is the case.

3. Based on your analysis, would you recommend that investors buy stock in this company? Please explain your answer.

Larry's Luncheon Spot

Income Statement

For the Month Ended September 30, 2008

		Percent
Revenues: Food	$412,000,000	100.0
Cost of Sales: Food	$101,352,000	24.6
Gross Profit	$310,648,000	75.4
Operating (Controllable) Expenses		
Salaries and Wages	$107,120,000	26.0
Employee Benefits	23,484,000	5.7

Direct Operating Expenses	76,045,230	18.5
Marketing	13,678,400	3.3
Utilities	12,318,800	3.0
Administrative and General	17,950,000	4.4
Repairs and Maintenance	5,850,400	1.4
Total Operating Expenses	$256,446,830	62.2
Operating Income	$ 54,201,170	13.2
Other (Noncontrollable) Expenses		
Rent	$ 22,660,000	5.5
Depreciation	16,502,000	4.0
Interest	8,450,000	2.1
Total Other Expenses	$ 47,612,000	11.6
Income Before Income Taxes	$ 6,589,170	1.6
Less: Income Taxes	$ 4,944,000	1.2
Net Income	$ 1,645,170	0.4

Larry's Luncheon Spot

Balance Sheets

As of Month Ended September 30, 2xx*

	2008	2007	Change
Cash	$ 1,502,153	$ 1,265,105	$ 237,048
Accounts Receivable	2,985,000	2,895,800	89,200
Short-term Investments	3,850,000	468,500	3,381,500
Food Inventory	2,034,000	1,810,000	224,000
Prepaid Rent	1,100,000	2,850,000	(1,750,000)
Total Current Assets	$ 11,471,153	$ 9,289,405	$ 2,181,748
Furniture, Fixtures, and Equipment (FF&E)	$ 120,300,000	$ 105,050,000	$ 15,250,000
Accumulated Depreciation (FF&E)	(160,000,000)	(158,600,000)	(1,400,000)
Buildings	190,290,000	195,890,000	(5,600,000)
Long-term Investments	495,600	637,000	(141,400)
Long-term Assets	$ 151,085,600	$ 142,977,000	$ 8,108,600
Total Assets	**$162,556,753**	**$152,266,405**	**$10,290,348**

Accounts Payable	$ 12,500,000	$ 14,500,000	$ (2,000,000)
Accrued Payroll	23,900,500	25,008,000	(1,107,500)
Accrued Taxes	118,050	173,000	(54,950)
Total Current Liabilities	$ 36,518,550	$ 39,681,000	$ (3,162,450)
Long-term Debt	$ 28,000,000	$ 21,000,000	$ 7,000,000
Shareholder's Equity	$ 8,771,000	$ 8,769,000	$ 2,000
Retained Earnings	89,267,203	82,816,405	6,450,798
Total Shareholder's Equity	$ 98,038,203	$ 91,585,405	$ 6,452,798
Total Liabilities and Shareholder's Equity	**$162,556,753**	**$152,266,405**	**$10,290,348**

Concept Check ✓

The Crescendo

The Crescendo is a full-service hotel located in a city with a population of 450,000. The hotel recently underwent a major renovation in which all of the guest rooms, the lobby, and meeting rooms were brought up to date. The owner of the property thought the renovation would boost the business, but so far the hotel is not meeting budgeted goals. The owner has challenged the current management to shape up, or he will find a new management company who can meet his expectations.

Ms. Beth Samuelson, the current general manager, is worried she may lose her job if she does not meet the projected goals, so she has turned to her fellow managers for help. The controller mentioned she should look into profit flexing and cost-volume-profit analysis.

QUESTIONS

1. Utilize the profit-flexing method to analyze the Crescendo Hotel's income statement provided. Explain how the company can reduce expenses or increase revenues to meet budgeted goals.

2. Utilize cost-volume-profit analysis to determine how many rooms you would need to sell to reach the budgeted revenue goal of $150 per room. Fixed costs for the hotel are $470,000 per room, and the labor cost to maintain each room is $40.

3. Now pretend you are Ms. Samuelson and the owner requests that you increase net operating profit to $300,000. Is this attainable if the Crescendo Hotel only has 125 rooms? (*Hint:* Use the desired volume calculation.)

Crescendo Hotel
Income Statement
January 20, 2009

	Actual	M-T-D Budget
Occupancy	75%	80%
Average Daily Room Rate	$ 125.00	$ 150.00
Revenue		
Rooms	$ 843,750	$ 1,080,000
Food	191,000	370,000
Beverage	141,000	185,000
Telephone	56,000	72,000
Other	20,000	30,000
Total Revenues	$1,251,750	$ 1,737,000
Departmental Expenses		
Rooms	$ 425,000	$ 375,000
Food and Beverage	265,000	280,000
Telephone	42,000	55,000
Other	12,000	5,000
Total Departmental Expenses	744,000	715,000
Departmental Profit	$ 507,750	$ 1,022,000
Unallocated Expenses		
Administrative and General	$ 180,000	$ 175,000
Marketing	65,000	125,000
Property Operations and Maintenance	30,000	98,000
Utilities	100,000	78,000
Total Unallocated Expenses	375,000	476,000
Gross Operating Profit	$ 132,750	$ 546,000
Fixed Costs		
Property Taxes	$ 300,000	$ 300,000
Building Insurance	50,000	50,000
Debt Service Payment	50,000	50,000
Reserve for Capital Improvements	—	70,000
Total Capital Expenses	400,000	470,000
Net Operating Profit (Loss)	($267,250)	$76,000

MANAGING WORKING CAPITAL AND CONTROLLING CASH

CHARLES WARCZAK: MOVING AHEAD WITH THE HELP OF RELATIONSHIPS AND NUMBERS

Charles Warczak is currently the chief financial officer for Sunburst Hospitality Corporation. How he rose to this position is an interesting story. Charles strongly believes in maintaining relationships and never burning bridges. After all, he says, "Aside from having a good grasp of the numbers, I have gotten to where I am today because of the mentors who guided me as I climbed up the corporate ladder."

While growing up in the Chicago area, Warczak worked part time for his father, who was a home builder. He also devoted his extra time to working in the hospitality industry during his high school and college years. His first job was as a busboy at the Drake Hotel in Oakbrook, Illinois. "That was where I learned how to get along and deal with people in all walks of life. I [also] found that if you just did things in a commonsense way, you could move ahead."

When he was promoted to room service waiter, a maître d' taught him how to take care of guests and earn big tips for superior service. Professional waiters also passed along other tricks of the trade.

Like many hourly workers in the hotel industry, Chuck's job was only a means to support himself while he studied accounting at Texas Christian University in Fort Worth, Texas. Upon graduation in 1970, the twenty-two-year-old Illinois native went to work for Arthur Young and Company as an auditor. This job marked a turning point in Warczak's business career. Although he liked the company, he didn't feel he really fit in. Basically, he was unhappy being an auditor. "I felt like people thought we were snoops. I longed to be back in the hospitality business."

Determined to make a career in hospitality, Chuck quit his well-paying job with Arthur Young and moved to Houston, Texas, where he enrolled in the Conrad Hilton School of Hotel and Restaurant Management at the University of Houston. While at the university, he met his first mentor, Donald Greenaway, a professor at the college and a former president of the National Restaurant Association. Upon Warczak's graduation in 1975, Professor Greenaway helped him find his first job by introducing him to Ernie Barker, the owner of a small hotel management company, Barker Enterprises, headquartered in Illinois. He stayed with Barker for eight years before moving on to AIRCOA Hospitality Services, a larger hotel management and investment company with over one hundred hotels and a wholly owned subsidiary, MHM.

At AIRCOA, Warczak met chief operating officer Don Landry, who became his second mentor. In 1992, when Landry moved to Manor Care Co., a healthcare company that also owned Choice Hotels International, Warczak followed him and assumed the role of vice president of finance. In 1997, Choice Hotels International was spun off from Manor Care and, shortly thereafter, Choice Hotels International spun off its real estate unit, Sunburst Hospitality Corporation. Landry became Sunburst Hospitality Corporation's CEO, and he took his protégé, Warczak, with him to the new company. Chuck's immediate task was to design new financial systems that would streamline the company's financial reporting process. To accomplish this, Chuck established centralized accounting, centralized staffing, and a new internal control system.

Many interesting things have happened to Warczak during his tenure with Sunburst Hospitality. He and fellow top executives at Sunburst took the company private by arranging a $370 million leveraged buyout in January 2001. As the senior vice president, chief financial officer, and treasurer, Warczak reduced the company's debt by selling its extended-stay properties and other non-core assets to the Blackstone Group for $100 million during the economic downturn following the 9/11 disaster. Between 2001 and 2004, Sunburst's debt to EBITDA (earnings before interest, tax, depreciation, and amortization) was reduced from over 6 to 1 to about 3.5 to 1 in spite of declining same-store revenues. Today, armed with a strong balance sheet and an improving economy, his company is aggressively pursuing opportunities as they arise. Recently, Sunburst added eleven self-storage facilities, four large apartment complexes, and fifteen hotels to its portfolio, making it one of the largest franchisees of Cendant Corporation. Sunburst is also developing a 225-unit condominium project and thirty townhomes in Arlington, Texas.

Throughout his thirty-year hospitality career, Warczak has relied on and applied the financial knowledge and skills he learned at Conrad N. Hilton College and the accounting experience he gained with Arthur Young. All of Chuck's positions in the hospitality industry have been in accounting, finance, and systems management. So what are his accounting and finance tips to aspiring hospitality managers and entrepreneurs?

Learn how the income statement and balance sheet relate to each other and how a change to one impacts the other. Also, understand the concept of return on investment and relate it to every financial decision you make in business and financial decisions in your personal life as well.

Even more importantly, he adds, "Build and maintain relationships. You accomplish things not through your own knowledge but by working with people collectively."

SOURCES

Warczak, Charles. Interview, 2006.

Cook, Lou. Feature Interview: "Technology and Teamwork: A Profile on Charles Warczak, CHAE, CPA, Vice President of Finance and Systems for Sunburst Hospitality." *The Bottomline* (August/September 2000).

"Sunburst Hospitality Completes Long-Term Disposition Plan, Reduces Debt, Improves Year-Over-Year RevPAR." http://www.hotel-online.com/News/PR2004_2nd/June04_SunburstPlan.html.

"Sunburst Hospitality Amends Bank Credit, Facility Pays Down Debt Early in Wake of Leveraged Buy-Out." http://www.hotel-online.com/News/PR2002_3rd/Sept02_Sunburst.html.

Learning Outcomes

1. Understand the concept of working capital and its importance to the success of a business.
2. Determine the level of working capital a business should maintain.
3. Understand the need for cash controls and cash management.
4. Understand the importance of a cash budget and its preparation.
5. Understand how credit cards are processed and the range of transaction fees charged.

Preview of Chapter 4

Managing working capital and controlling cash

1. WORKING CAPITAL

a. Definition of working capital
b. Factors impacting the amount of working capital required by a business
c. Ways to minimize the amount of working capital needed

2. CASH MANAGEMENT

a. Cash controls
b. Cash forecasts
c. Managing bank balances and services provided by banks
d. Credit card processing and transaction fees

MANAGING WORKING CAPITAL AND CONTROLLING CASH

ust because you project a nice profit for the year doesn't mean that profit will be automatically achieved. Even if you achieve your revenue goals, control your expenses, and reflect a favorable profit on your income statement, you still may not have enough cash to meet your financial obligations. It is critical, therefore, that you learn how to manage what is called *working capital*.

Working Capital

Most accounting and finance textbooks define **working capital** as the difference between current assets and current liabilities. Current assets include cash, accounts receivables, inventories, notes receivable, prepaid expenses, and any other assets that can easily be converted to cash within a year. Current liabilities are accounts payable and other monies owed that must be repaid during the current year. In the business world, the term *working capital* more commonly refers to the amount of cash required to operate a business. For the purposes of our discussion, we use this definition.

THE REAL DEAL

Most small businesses find it helpful to prepare a ninety-day rolling cash budget to better manage their cash inflows and outflows and to determine whether or not they will have enough working capital to meet their short-term financial obligations to vendors, suppliers, and staff. When preparing a cash forecast or budget, focus on the following issues:

1. Don't prepare the cash budget by yourself—consult your management team. Managers can sometimes sense the pattern of cash receipts and disbursements better than you can.

2. Negotiate with your suppliers to obtain favorable credit terms, and then factor the terms into your forecast of cash disbursements.

3. Be realistic and conservative when forecasting revenues. Remember that revenue is dependent on a variety of factors. While you can control some, you cannot control them all, including the economy and your competition. If your cash forecast looks good based on conservative revenue projections, it will look even better when you exceed your revenue goals.

It is your cash; take good care of it, or it will disappear before your very eyes.

As an astute hospitality manager, it is important you learn how to minimize the amount of working capital needed to operate your business. Any surplus cash not required to operate your business should be used for expansion, to fund projects that will generate additional cash flow, or simply be placed in a bank account that draws interest.

How Much Working Capital Is Needed?

The amount of working capital your business needs to operate is a function of several factors:

- *The mix of cash and credit sales:* The larger the percentage credit sales are of the total sales your business generates, the more working capital you may need.

- *The method used to process credit card transactions:* Some banks treat credit card sales as cash sales, with the cash payments being deposited in the business' bank account each day. Some credit card companies, however, record credit card sales as accounts receivables and pay only after the credit card transactions are processed by sending a check to the business.

- *The accounts receivable turnover ratio:* The longer you take to collect your accounts receivable, the more working capital you need.

- *The food and beverage turnover ratio:* The more food and beverage items your menu and wine list require you to stock and the slower your inventories turn over, the more working capital you need.

- *How quickly vendors and suppliers require their invoices to be paid:* The faster your vendors and suppliers require your business to pay its bills, the more working capital you need to maintain.

- *The pace at which the business is growing:* The faster your business grows, the more inventories you need to keep on hand to serve your customers and the more likely you are to add more staff. More sales means more accounts receivable, and more staff means a higher payroll. Because you need to pay your employees, suppliers, and vendors on a timely basis, rapid growth can cause a cash crunch.

Keys to Minimizing Working Capital

Your goal should be to minimize the amount of working capital you need to operate your business successfully. The less money you have tied up in non-interest-bearing bank accounts, uncollected accounts receivable, and inventories, the more money you will have available to invest in assets that generate cash flow for the owners of your business. Here are a few ways to keep your working capital requirements as low as possible:

- *Offer a discount on cash sales:* This saves your business the commission you would otherwise have to pay the credit card company and the expenses involved in collecting your other accounts receivable. Cash discounts are common in retailing. Why not offer them at hotels and restaurants as well?

THE REAL DEAL

For most hospitality companies, payroll is the largest expense. Should a hospitality business process its own payroll, or is it better to outsource the payroll function? Can this decision impact the cash picture of the business?

Many companies and banks offer payroll services that only take a few business days to process once the personnel documents are received and the system is set up. The payroll process is more than multiplying hours worked by the appropriate wage rates. It involves managing payroll records, calculating and deducting payroll taxes from employee checks, and maintaining employees' W-4 (tax) information. It also involves calculating the employer portion of taxes due, filing tax returns quarterly, and paying payroll taxes to the government. In addition to the regular weekly or biweekly payroll process, vacation and sick time must also be monitored and accrued. At the end of the year, businesses are required to generate W-2 forms for all employees to allow them to prepare and file their personal income tax returns. Some companies and banks provide small businesses with all of these services, including a payroll register, a direct deposit report, a 401K (retirement fund) report, a vacation and time off report, a tax report, an employee benefits profile, a workers compensation report, and even a tip credit report for foodservice employees. The cost? It depends on the number and type of services provided, the number of employees, and how often payroll checks are processed.

- *Turn your inventories over as quickly as possible:* As we discussed in chapter 3, stock only those products that are actually in demand. This converts your inventories into cash faster and reduces your need for working capital. Effective inventory management is a skill every hospitality manager should possess. Many restaurant operators are afraid to run out of a menu item and therefore overstock slow-moving items. Most customers like when a restaurant serves only fresh products, and they understand that a restaurant may occasionally run out of a menu item or two.

- *Establish a good credit rating with your suppliers and vendors:* This allows you to receive more favorable payment terms on your purchases, receive more frequent deliveries of product, and reduces your need for working capital. Many suppliers start a new account on a cash-on-delivery (COD) basis. Once the business is established and gains the trust of the supplier, more favorable credit terms are offered. Do the math: If your vendor delivers food to you on May 1 and invoices you at the end of the month, by the time you write him a check, he has actually financed your food purchase for thirty days. All during this time, your cash is earning you interest.

- *Manage your accounts payable effectively:* How and when you make your accounts payable payments can impact not only your need for working capital but also your reputation in the business community. Pay your suppliers on time, as they are your source of product, but use your credit to its maximum. For example, if your vendor allows you two weeks to pay your invoices, don't pay an invoice early just because you have the cash available. Pay suppliers on the last day the invoice is due to earn the most interest possible on your money.

■   *Track all transactions:* There will be times when you need to return merchandise or product because it was delivered incorrectly, was spoiled, or did not meet your specifications. Because an invoice will likely still be mailed to you, make sure you don't pay it until the corrections have been made. If you do not follow up, and your vendor is dishonest, you will have paid more for the product than you should have.

Cash

Cash is the most important asset a business can have. With cash, a business has both liquidity and buying power. As a hospitality manager, your job is to control cash. You should know how much cash you need to operate your business, plan your cash disbursements carefully, and prepare accurate cash forecasts at all times.

THE REAL DEAL

Effective October 28, 2004, a new federal law known as the Check Clearing for the Twenty-first Century Act—or, more commonly, Check 21—was passed to enable banks to process checks faster. Under this law, a bank or financial institution can convert a paper check into electronic form and submit it for payment instead of having to send paper checks to other banks to receive payment. The process saves banks time, resources, and money. Check 21 also allows banks to make substitute checks and, therefore, banks no longer need to keep a copy of the original check. If you have a checking account that returns cancelled checks, you may be able to receive your own checks, substitute checks, or combine these approaches. Substitute checks are special paper copies of the front and back of the original check. They are considered legal copy and can be used as proof of payment, just like the original check, and you are still fully protected. In fact, under both state and federal law, whether or not you receive any form of a cancelled check or an account statement, you are protected against errors the financial institution may make on your account. All Check 21 does is speed the processing time with new technology. But how does this affect your business? If you need to pay bills, make sure you have sufficient funds in your account. You can no longer play the float and hope the check will not clear for a few more days so you have the time to deposit funds in the bank to cover it. On the receiving end, you will be able to receive payments faster.

NEED FOR CASH CONTROLS

Cash is the one asset that is convertible into any other type of asset. It is liquid, often easily accessible to employees, and attractive to everyone that comes in contact with it. It is easier for your employees to steal cash from your business than to steal more concealable assets. Remember: Cash is not limited to currency; it includes checks, money orders, and marketable securities.

Having a sound internal control system with cash safeguards is a must for all successful businesses.

CASH FORECASTS

The best way to determine how much working capital a business needs is to develop a ninety-day rolling **cash forecast.** At the beginning of each month, estimate your cash inflows and project your cash needs for the ensuing ninety days. The forecast is, in essence, a cash budget.

Illustration 4-1 presents a ninety-day forecast for Theresa's Catering Company showing projected cash sales, credit sales, and the company's financial obligations for the upcoming period.

	A	B	C	D	E	F
1		November	December	January	February	March
2	Credit Sales	62,500.00	86,000.00	66,000.00	72,150.00	85,420.00
3	80% collected in next month	50,000.00	68,800.00	52,800.00	57,720.00	68,336.00
4	20% collected in two months	12,500.00	17,200.00	13,200.00	14,430.00	17,084.00
5	Cash Sales	12,500.00	16,390.00	15,080.00	13,520.00	15,280.00
6	Credit Purchases paid next month	22,500.00	28,675.00	29,860.00	25,877.00	29,640.00
7	Cash Purchases	3,080.00	2,793.00	2,985.00	3,288.00	3,762.00
8	Payroll 35% of total sales	26,250.00	35,836.50	28,378.00	29,984.50	35,245.00
9	Debt Service on mortgage per month	10,000.00				
10	Insurance prepaid every 3 months	3,000.00				
11	Property tax due in February	15,000.00				
12	Partner distribution paid every other month	12,500.00				
13						
14			Theresa's Catering			
15			90-day Cash Forecast			
16						
17		January	February	March		
18	**Beginning Cash Balance**	$ 3,000.00	$ 13,842.00	$ 9,229.50		
19						
20	Cash Receipts					
21	Cash sales	15,080.00	13,520.00	15,280.00		
22	Collection of accounts receivables next month	68,800.00	52,800.00	57,720.00		
23	Collection of accounts receivables 2 months	12,500.00	17,200.00	13,200.00		
24	Sales of fixed assets	-	-	-		
25						
26	Total Cash Available	99,380.00	97,362.00	95,429.50		
27						
28	Cash Disbursements					
29	Cash purchases	2,985.00	3,288.00	3,762.00		
30	Accounts payables	28,675.00	29,860.00	25,877.00		
31	Payroll	28,378.00	29,984.50	35,245.00		
32	Debt Service on mortgage	10,000.00	10,000.00	10,000.00		
33	Insurance premium	3,000.00	-	-		
34	Property taxes		15,000.00			
35	Partner cash distribution	12,500.00	-	12,500.00		
36						
37	Total Cash Disbursements	85,538.00	88,132.50	87,384.00		
38						
39	**Ending Cash Balance**	13,842.00	9,229.50	8,045.50		
40	Minimum Cash Balance	10,000.00	10,000.00	10,000.00		
41						
42	**Cash surplus / (deficit)**	$ 3,842.00	$ (770.50)	$ (1,954.50)		

ILLUSTRATION 4-1
90 Day Forecast for Theresa's Catering

As of January 1, the forecast begins with an initial cash balance of $3,000. Certain expenses are budgeted to occur sometime during the month, while others are forecasted to occur at specific times. Insurance is prepaid, and Theresa has agreed to pay her partner $12,500 every other month.

The forecast shows that, based on the company's need for $10,000 of working capital, there is a cash surplus for January. However, due to the $15,000 property tax payment due in February, cash available in February will be $9,229, which falls just below its minimum working capital balance. The $12,500 payment due to Theresa's partner in March will place an additional cash drain on her business.

CLARE SULLIVAN JACKSON ON RELATIONSHIPS, RISK, AND REWARD

Clare Sullivan Jackson believes that three *R*s have driven her career to where it is today: relationships, risk, and reward. Over the years, her relationships have led her to one opportunity after another. She constantly pushes herself to step outside her comfort zone because she believes that with greater risk comes greater reward. The risks she has taken to date have paid off handsomely to the point where she now has both the time and the money for her philanthropic efforts, which she loves. According to Clare, her real reward is her ability to give back to others. Through her philanthropic efforts, Clare has unintentionally increased Sullivan Group's visibility in the public eye.

Today, Jackson is the president and chief executive officer of Sullivan Group, a Houston-based meeting and event production company. Like many female entrepreneurs, the decision to strike out on her own was partly due to her desire to strike a work-life balance. "The hotel and hospitality industry has long been associated with long hours. After working in the industry for several years, I knew that I needed a change. . . . When I forgot my father's birthday, I definitely knew that something was wrong. There was no balance between career and family for me."

Clare founded her own company in 1989 with a small inheritance of $10,000 and a plethora of connections she had made during her years in school. The contacts she cultivated while at the University of Houston became both her role models and business associates. But, as do many start-up businesses, Jackson faced cash flow problems at the beginning. "There were a few months where I couldn't pay the rent, but my mother helped by moving in with me to do office tasks so I could get out and get my feet wet."

For aspiring managers and entrepreneurs, the importance of establishing relationships cannot be emphasized enough. If you have not yet begun to cultivate your relationships, start now and build on them.

Risk taking is another quality that defines an entrepreneur. What was the biggest risk Clare Jackson took in starting her business? "I really did not know how to run a business. I just knew the other side of things, how to work there."

Her lack of business experience did not deter her from following her dreams. It should not deter you either. If you have a good business plan, the passion to make things happen, and some understanding of the financial aspects of business, take the risk! At the Fall 2005 Career Fair Luncheon for Recruiters and Graduating Seniors at the Conrad N. Hilton College of Hotel and Restaurant Management, Ms. Jackson had this advice for the students about risk taking: To the degree one is willing to risk, the reward is far greater. "I'm always asking myself, what can I do today that might be a little bit risky? Who can I call that I might be a little intimidated about talking to? What am I avoiding? Step outside of your comfort zone and make something happen."

Finally, all aspiring entrepreneurs look forward to the day they can reap the rewards of their hard work and risk taking. When you have achieved your financial goals, you will have the resources to do the things that you could not afford to do earlier in your career, whether that means retiring early and traveling around the world or spending more time with your family. For Jackson, her success in the event and meeting planning business has given her the time and resources to do what she truly enjoys: volunteer work. She now spends 50% of her working hours doing volunteer work, including mentoring aspiring entrepreneurs at the Center for Entrepreneurship and Innovation at the University of Houston.

Take it from Clare: "Before you get to the fun part of reaping your financial rewards, work on your business plan, work on your networking, take some calculated risks, and take care of your numbers."

SOURCES

Jackson, Clare Sullivan. Keynote Speech, Conrad N. Hilton College Career Fair, October 20, 2005.

"Sullivan Group Management Team: Clare Sullivan Jackson, CSEP, President and CEO." http://www.sullivan-group.com/en/cms/?20.

Perin, M. "Special Event Planning Calls for Professional Expertise." *Houston Business Journal*, May 16, 1997.

"The Main Event Planner." *Houston Alumline*, March 2004.

The objective of a cash forecast is to alert management to probable cash shortages or surpluses in advance. If a cash shortage is forecasted, the business may need to take out a short-term business loan. If a cash surplus is forecasted, the business may have too much working capital on hand and should invest the surplus in a short-term interest-bearing account.

Illustration 4-2 shows how a cash budget can easily be prepared using an Excel spreadsheet. Excel allows the preparer to insert "what if" factors and obtain a clear picture of the business's probable future cash situation.

Illustration 4-3 presents a cash budget for the Sienna Resort, a hotel property. The top part of the cash budget is similar in format to the statement of cash flow discussed in chapter 2. This cash budget presents a detailed analysis of cash inflows and outflows from operations, financing activities, and investing activities. Schedule A focuses on cash flow from operations, including collections of accounts receivable. Schedule A also links with schedule C, which details cash sales, charge sales, and the accounts receivable aging process. Schedule B provides management with details related to cash disbursements from operations.

As you can see, cash budgets can be relatively simple, like the one shown in Illustration 4-1, or quite complicated, like the one shown in Illustration 4-3. The degree of sophistication is dictated by the type and size of the operation and the needs of management and ownership.

	A	B	C	D	E	F
1		November	December	January	February	March
2	Credit Sales	62500	86000	66000	72150	85420
3	80% collected in next month	=B2*0.8	=C2*0.8	=D2*0.8	=E2*0.8	=F2*0.8
4	20% collected in two months	=B2*0.2	=C2*0.2	=D2*0.2	=E2*0.2	=F2*0.2
5	Cash Sales	12500	16390	15080	13520	15280
6	Credit Purchases paid next month	22500	28675	29860	25877	29640
7	Cash Purchases	3080	2793	2985	3288	3762
8	Payroll 35% of total sales	=(B2+B5)*0.35	=(C2+C5)*0.35	=(D2+D5)*0.35	=(E2+E5)*0.35	=(F2+F5)*0.35
9	Service on mortgage per month	10000				
10	Insurance prepaid every 3 months	3000				
11	Property tax due in February	15000				
12	Partner distribution every other month	12500				
13						
14				Theresa's Catering		
15				90-day Cash Forecast		
16						
17			January	February	March	
18	Beginning Cash Balance		3000	=B39	=C39	
19						
20	Cash Receipts					
21	Cash sales		=D5	=E5	=F5	
22	Collection of accounts receivables next month		=C3	=D3	=E3	
23	Collection of accounts receivables 2 months		=B4	=C4	=D4	
24	Sales of fixed assets		0	0	0	
25						
26	Total Cash Available		=SUM(B18:B25)	=SUM(C18:C25)	=SUM(D18:D25)	
27						
28	Cash Disbursements					
29	Cash purchases		=D7	=E7	=F7	
30	Accounts payables		=C6	=D6	=E6	
31	Payroll		=D8	=E8	=F8	
32	Service on mortgage		=B9	=B9	=B9	
33	Insurance premium		=B10	0	0	
34	Property taxes			=B11		
35	Partner cash distribution		=B12	0	=B12	
36						
37	Total Cash Disbursements		=SUM(B29:B36)	=SUM(C29:C36)	=SUM(D29:D36)	
38						
39	Ending Cash Balance		=+B26-B37	=+C26-C37	=+D26-D37	
40	Minimum Cash Balance		10000	10000	10000	
41						
42	Cash overage / (shortage)		=B39-B40	=C39-C40	=D39-D40	

ILLUSTRATION 4-2

Preparing a Cash Budget Using an Excel Spreadsheet

BANK BALANCES AND SERVICES

Managing a business's bank accounts is also an important skill for the hospitality manager to learn. Many banks offer special services to help small businesses manage their cash more effectively. One service is called **account reconciliation,** whereby banks reconcile a business's cash accounts and create summary reconciliation reports. These reports are mailed to the business or can be accessed via the Internet. This reduces a small business's administrative cost and helps protect it against fraudulent activities such as unauthorized checks being posted to their accounts. This service is easy to use, but there is normally a set-up fee and a monthly charge.

Banks also offer what are called **sweep accounts,** which can generate additional interest income for a business. Here is how a sweep account would work for a small chain of restaurants:

1. The restaurant company first establishes a minimum cash balance that it wants to maintain in each local bank where the company has a restaurant.

2. Each day the restaurants make cash deposits to their local bank.

Sienna Beach Resort

Cash Flow Forecast
Prepared by:

	Budget Jan-09	Budget Feb-09	Budget Mar-09	Budget Apr-09	Budget May-09	Budget Jun-09	Budget Jul-09	Budget Aug-09	Budget Sep-09	Budget Oct-09	Budget Nov-09	Budget Dec-09	Budget Total

Beginning Cash Balance

Cash Flow from Operations
  Receipts:
    Cash from operations (schedule A)
    Other unique operational inflows (ex. Memberships)
    Total Receipts from Operations

  Disbursements
    Operations (schedule B)
    Management fee
    Sales taxes
    Audit fees
    Workers compensation insurance
    Other insurance
    Real estate and personal property taxes
    Other unique operational outflows
    Total Disbursements from Operations

  Net Cash Flow from Operations

Cash Flow from Financing & Reinvestment Activities
  Receipts:
    Owner contributions
    Loan proceeds
    Total Receipts from Financing Activities

  Disbursements:
    Owner disbursement
    Capital improvements (per 12 month schedule)
    Replacement reserve funding
    Total Disbursements from Financing Activities

  Net Cash Flow from Financing Activities

Net Cash Available for Debt Service

  Debt Service

Net Cash Flow for the Month

Ending Cash Balance for the Month

FF&E Reserve Account Balance
  Opening Balance
    Reserve contribution/funding
    Interest Income
    Disbursements
  Closing Balance

Schedule A
Cash From Operations

  Revenue
    Rooms
    Food & Beverage
    Other
    Total Revenue

  Receivable Changes:
    (Increase) Decrease in Guest Ledger balance:
    Less: Outgoing Accounts Receivable Billing (schedule C)
    Increase (Decrease) in Advanced Deposit ledger balance
    Total Receivable Changes

  A/R Collections:
    Add: Accounts Receivable Collections (schedule C)
    Add: Sales Tax Collections (schedule C)
    Total A/R Collections

  Net Cash Received From Operations

Schedule B
Disbursements

  Total operating expenses excluding payroll & beverage purchases
  Less:
    Bad debt provision
    Insurance
    Audit fees
    Depreciation/amortization
    Net Expenses

    Current month's payment of expenses (15%)
    Next month's payment of expenses (85%)
    Total Aged disbursements for the month

    Add: beverage purchases
    Add: cash payroll
    Add: payroll benefits excluding workers comp.

  Total Operating Disbursements

Schedule C
Accounts Receivable

  Total forecasted revenue
  Sales & occupancy tax based on above
  Total forecasted receipts

    Cash and credit card payments (10%)
    Accounts receivable billing (90%)

  Collections of A/R
    30 Days - 50%
    60 Days - 40%
    90 Days - 10%
    Total Accounts Receivable Collections

  Collections of Sales Tax
    30 Days - 50%
    60 Days - 40%
    90 Days - 10%
    Total Sales & Occ. Tax Collections

ILLUSTRATION 4-3
Cash Budget for Sienna Beach Resort

3. Each night, the central bank sweeps each local bank account, leaving only the minimum cash balance in each account.

4. The central bank then automatically invests the surplus cash in secure overnight investments on behalf of the restaurant company.

The interest earned is normally based on the federal funds traded rate, with the interest earned being credited to the restaurant company's central account daily. A monthly fee is usually charged for this service. If your business maintains large cash balances, a sweep account may be something you might want to pursue.

A **lockbox** is also recommended if you have a large number and amount of accounts receivable. Lockbox processing allows a business to collect and process payments quickly. Instead of having the payments mailed to your business and having your accounting department process and deposit them, your bank assigns your business a specially numbered post office (P.O.) box from which it collects and processes all payments for you on a daily basis. Using a P.O. box also protects the identity of your business. Today, with identity theft being so common, the use of a lockbox is another security feature your business may want to consider.

THE REAL DEAL

Are third-party credit card processing companies safe? They are if they are Cardholder Information Security Program (CISP) certified. Third-party credit card check processing is a big industry, and many reputable companies offer this service. To be in compliance, all merchants and service providers must follow the Payment Card Industry Data Security Standard (PCIDSS). This standard consists of six primary requirements:

1. Build and maintain a secure network.
2. Protect cardholder data.
3. Maintain a vulnerability management program.
4. Implement strong access control measures.
5. Regularly monitor and test networks.
6. Maintain an information security policy.

Safeguards are a must, as Internet fraud is so prevalent today. It is important for everyone to recognize that credit card information must be treated with the utmost care.

Banks also offer **zero balance accounts.** A zero balance account is a service whereby the balances of a business's cash accounts are consolidated into a single account, but separate checking account statements are provided. By consolidating cash balances, you eliminate the need to maintain cash balances in each account, thereby reducing the amount of working capital needed and also avoiding certain bank charges. Banks will also invest the excess funds on your behalf daily.

Local bankers can work with you to explore ways their bank resources can help you attain financial success. One suggestion: Don't be afraid to shop around, as some banks may offer better rates than others.

USE OF CREDIT CARDS

Credit card companies serve two groups of people: individual card users and merchants. These companies make their profit from the individual cardholder or the merchant—or in some cases, from both.

Some credit card companies, like American Express, charge their members an annual fee for the right to use the American Express card. They also expect full payment of the cardholder's charges each month. Other credit card companies provide charge cards to their customers on a no-fee basis. These companies anticipate that many of their cardholders will elect not to pay their monthly balance in full and, as a result, will incur a finance charge of up to 20%. This is one way the credit card company makes a profit.

All credit card companies charge the merchant a **credit card transaction fee.** This fee ranges from as low as 2% to as much as 6% of the transaction price. VISA and MasterCard normally charge fees at the low end of the range, while credit card companies like American Express charge fees at the high end of the range. The higher the average transaction price and the higher the credit card sales volume generated by the business, the lower the transaction fee. The actual percentage is negotiable. It is a good practice to meet with the sales representative of your credit card companies once a year to revisit the rates you are being charged. If your sales volume has increased during the year, you should be able to negotiate a more favorable transaction fee.

THE REAL DEAL

Due to the sensitivity of credit card data, the more progressive point-of-sale (POS) systems have programmed and reengineered their systems to be PCIDSS compliant. While this is a positive step, they still lack the ability to monitor reservations taken over the Internet that require a credit card to be used to hold the reservation. It is important to first secure your website and then work with your technology consultant to design a website that is secure. You might have visited websites that announce, "This is a secured site." Make sure you do the same for your company's website. Internet reservations and shopping are here to stay, and customers need to be confident that the information they are providing on your website is confidential!

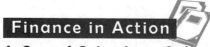

Finance in Action

A Cup of Colombian Coffee from Juancas Ltd.

Juancas Ltd., a Colombian coffee grower and producer of fine roasted coffees, has decided to open small cafés to feature their product. While they realize that many markets have already been saturated by major brands in the United States, they believe Juancas coffees have a better appeal because Colombia is known for producing high-quality coffee products.

Juan Carlos Sarmiento, the company's founder and current CEO, is evaluating financial projections for the first year of operations for a test location in the United States to determine how much working capital will be necessary to operate it. With his management team, Juan Carlos has determined cash inflows and outflows for the first ninety days of business:

- The test location will open in September to coincide with cooler weather and the hope that more people will be inclined to purchase hot coffee.

- During the first month, the company expects to earn $26,500 in credit sales and $13,500 in cash sales. It estimates that both of these figures will increase by 10% monthly from September to January. Another important note is that Juancas expects to collect 90% of credit card sales during the next month and 10% two months later.

- Credit purchases, which will be paid the following month, during September are $16,450. Cash purchases during this same period are estimated to be $2,345, and both credit and cash purchases are expected to increase 5% monthly from September through January.

- Another major expense considered is payroll, which will equal 32% of monthly credit and cash sales. Other expenses that must be considered are a monthly mortgage payment of $6,500 and a monthly insurance payment of $2,000.

- The company also wants to have a minimum cash balance of $15,000 in its account. Because the company is a large operation, this minimum balance can be subsidized the first couple of months of operation by cash flows from other divisions.

QUESTIONS

1. Utilizing the information provided by Juan Carlos, determine the monthly cash inflows and needs for the first Juancas Café.

   The following table provides a breakdown of the cash inflows and outflows for September through January. The September figures are provided, so all you have to do is place them in the correct row in the chart. Credit and cash sales are projected to grow at 10% each month, which can be calculated by simply multiplying the previous month's sales figure by 1.1 (26,500 × 1.1 = 29,150). The same calculation can be utilized for increased credit and cash purchases, but instead of multiplying by 1.1 you would multiply by 1.05 to account for the 5% increase.

	September	October	November	December	January
Credit Sales	$26,500	$29,150	$32,065	$35,272	$38,799
90% collected in next month	23,850	26,235	28,859	31,744	34,919
10% collected in two months	2,650	2,915	3,207	3,527	3,880
Cash Sales	13,500	14,850	16,335	17,969	19,765
Credit Purchases—paid next month	16,450	17,273	18,136	19,043	19,995

Cash Purchases	2,345	2,462	2,585	2,715	2,850
Payroll—32% of total sales	12,800	14,080	15,488	17,037	18,740
Service on Mortgage per Month	6,500	6,500	6,500	6,500	6,500
Monthly Insurance Payment	2,000	2,000	2,000	2,000	2,000

2. Develop a ninety-day cash forecast for Juancas Café during November, December, and January. Assume a beginning cash balance of $5,000 for November.

Use the example in the chapter for Theresa's Catering as a guide.

■ *The first item to consider is the beginning cash balance, which is $5,000 for Juancas Café.*

■ *The first major section in the ninety-day cash forecast is cash receipts. Input the amount of cash sales for November, credit sales for October that were collectable in one month, and credit sales for September that were collectable in two months, and add them to get total cash available.*

■ *The next section, which is cash disbursements, includes all of the cash outflows. This section includes cash purchases for November, credit purchases from October that were payable in one month, payroll expenses (32% of monthly sales), monthly debt service payment, and monthly insurance premium payment. Now, total the cash disbursements for November.*

■ *In order to determine the ending cash balance, simply subtract total cash disbursements from total cash available. Now you can do the same calculations for December and January.*

3. Analyze the forecasts and explain how Juancas Café is expected to perform.

The cash forecast looks optimistic, as the property is opening in September and expects to have an ending cash balance of over $6,000 after only two months of operation. If the forecast is accurate, Juancas Café will reach its proposed minimum cash balance of $15,000 in January.

Juancas Café
90-day Cash Forecast

	November	December	January
Beginning Cash Balance	$ 5,000.00	$ 6,374.14	$ 9,728.58
Cash Receipts			
Cash sales	16,335.00	17,968.50	19,765.35
Collection of accounts receivables—next month	26,235.00	28,858.50	31,744.35
Collection of accounts receivables—2 months	2,650.00	2,915.00	3,206.50
Total Cash Available	50,220.00	56,116.14	64,444.78

Cash Disbursements

Cash purchases	2,585.36	2,714.63	2,850.36
Accounts payables	17,272.50	18,136.13	19,042.93
Payroll	15,488.00	17,036.80	18,740.48
Service on mortgage	6,500.00	6,500.00	6,500.00
Insurance premium	2,000.00	2,000.00	2,000.00
Total Cash Disbursements	43,845.86	46,387.56	49,133.77
Ending Cash Balance	6,374.14	9,728.58	15,311.01
Minimum Cash Balance	15,000.00	15,000.00	15,000.00
Cash surplus/(deficit)	$ (8,625.86)	$ (5,271.42)	$ 311.01

WHERE WE'VE BEEN, WHERE WE'RE GOING

Forecasting a stagnant company's cash needs and managing its working capital is relatively easy. Forecasting a growth company's needs for cash and managing its working capital is much more difficult. Companies that don't grow usually go out of business fast. Annual growth in revenues and profits are expected by owners and demanded by top management. Growth is common to all successful companies. The next two chapters discuss the need for growth, the benefits of growth, alternative growth strategies, and ways to finance growth.

Key Points

➤ The effective management of working capital is critical to business success.

➤ Minimizing the need for working capital allows management to use available cash capital to expand the business and fund projects that generate cash flow.

➤ Managing a business's bank accounts can help the business maintain the appropriate amount of cash on hand while investing surplus funds in short-term interest-bearing accounts.

➤ A realistic and carefully prepared cash forecast alerts management to probable cash deficits and surpluses before they occur.

➤ Properly managing the use of credit cards can result in additional cash flow for the business.

Key Terms

WORKING CAPITAL: The numeric difference between current assets and current liabilities.

CASH FORECAST: A forecast of cash receipts and cash disbursements ninety days or more into the future.

ACCOUNT RECONCILIATION: A service provided by banks whereby banks reconcile a business's cash accounts and create summary reconciliation reports.

SWEEP ACCOUNTS: Accounts where banks automatically invest surplus cash balances in secure overnight accounts. Earnings are usually based on the federal funds traded rate, and the interest earned is credited daily.

LOCKBOX: A service whereby banks assign customers a specially numbered P.O. box and collect and process payments on a daily basis. This reduces the float time of payments.

ZERO BALANCE ACCOUNTS: A service whereby cash balances of all accounts are consolidated (or zeroed out) into a single account. Banks invest the surplus funds on behalf of the business.

CREDIT CARD TRANSACTION FEE: A fee that credit card companies charge to merchants for processing.

Application Exercises

1.   What are three key methods of minimizing the amount of working capital needed? Give an example of each.

2.   The cash sales and credit sales projected for Sarah's Kitchen are as follows:

	January	February	March	April	May
Cash	$17,000	$19,640	$16,200	$15,380	$17,390
Credit	40,000	42,000	48,000	50,000	49,500

   If collections of credit sales are 70% the first month and 30% the second month, what would be the cash receipts for March, April, and May?

3.   Using the same data as for Exercise 4-2, if Sarah's Kitchen has a 1% bad debt allowance and can collect only 29% of accounts receivable in the second month, what would be the cash receipts for March, April, and May?

4.   Discuss the zero balance accounts and lockbox services that most banks offer. List three advantages and three disadvantages of each service. Feel free to visit Internet sites for banks and other financial institutions as you determine your response.

5.   Ask your manager at work what credit card processing fees your hospitality operation is charged. Explain how credit card companies determine the transaction fee percentage charged to merchants.

6.   Search at least three websites regarding credit card fees and compile the range of transaction fees charged by these companies.

7.   You are the manager of the Potomac Inn. You would like to pay all your employees a Christmas bonus totaling $10,000. Your owner, Joseph, agrees with your incentive rewards but wants to make sure the Inn will generate enough cash flow in December to pay the $10,000 and still maintain a minimum $5,000 cash balance. Based on the following infor-

mation, prepare a cash budget to determine whether or not you can afford to pay your employees their Christmas bonus, which will be $10,000 in total:

	October	November	December
Credit Sales	$60,000.00	$80,000.00	$75,000.00
75% collected in next month			
25% collected in two months			
Cash Sales	12,500.00	16,390.00	20,590.00
Credit Purchases—paid next month	30,560.00	34,580.00	28,650.00
Cash Purchases	3,116.00	2,159.00	2,489.00
Payroll—35% of total sales	25,375.00	33,736.50	33,456.50
Service on mortgage per month	5,000.00		
Insurance—prepaid every 3 months	3,000.00		
Property tax—due in November		15,000.00	

What are three ways you can better manage your accounts payable? Please explain.

8. **ETHICS** ✳ Eugene did not prepare a cash budget and does not use the CP^3 system at his hotel. He finds himself short of cash and is about to play the float by sending in his accounts payable checks on their due date. By doing so, the payments will be in the mail and will take at least one additional day to reach his suppliers and then another day for them to process the checks. As of October 28, 2004, a new federal law, called Check 21, went into effect. Check 21 is designed to enable banks to process more checks through an electronic process rather than using paper checks. Electronic processing is more efficient and less costly. Do a search on the Internet on the Check 21 law. Is this a fair rule for the consumer? Is this a fair rule for businesses? Is Eugene being unethical in this particular case?

9. **EXPLORING THE WEB** ✳ Search the Web for bank services that can assist a business in managing its cash. Compile a comparison of at least three sources regarding the fees charged for such services and the minimum account balances required by each service.

Concept Check ✓

The Watree Lodge is struggling with cash flow and has been waiting until the last minute to pay its vendors. The Watree is a beautiful ski lodge located in a popular area, but during the summer months hotel guests become scarce and cash management becomes a major problem. Because the Watree is independently owned and operated, every once in a while the owners must provide additional funds to carry the business over.

Mr. Tom Broli has just been hired as the controller at the Watree and is in the process of analyzing all of its financial statements. The previous controller had to be replaced because he did not have an understanding of the business and knowledge of cash management. The general manager hired Mr. Broli because he heard that Tom was an experienced controller and very competent in financial management. Tom's first goal is to look at cash forecasts to help him determine where he can make improvements.

	May	June	July	August	September
Credit Sales	$65,500	$58,950	$53,055	$47,750	$52,524
70% collected in next month	45,850	41,265	37,139	33,425	36,767
30% collected in two months	19,650	17,685	15,917	14,325	15,757
Cash Sales	18,500	16,650	14,985	13,487	14,835
Credit Purchases—due in 30 days	24,500	24,990	25,490	26,000	26,520
Cash Purchases	4,100	4,141	4,182	4,224	4,266
Payroll—34% of total sales	28,560	25,704	23,134	20,820	22,902
Service on mortgage—Quarterly payments		15,450			15,450
Quarterly Insurance Payment		5,400			5,400
Partner distribution—due quarterly		10,000			10,000

Questions

1. From the information provided in the chart, determine available cash for the months of July, August, and September. Assume a beginning cash balance of $(10,000) in July.

2. How can this property better manage its working capital? Provide specific suggestions for Watree Lodge management.

Concept Check ✓

Managing Cash at the Greenville

The Greenville Restaurant, which is independently owned and operated by the Greenlee Family, is located in a small historical town frequented by antique shoppers and other tourists attempting to glimpse at American history. Mr. Anderson Greenlee, son of the owners, recently graduated from a hospitality program in which he focused his studies on finance and accounting. While Mr. Greenlee wants to continue the family business, he would also like to branch out and open restaurants in other locations, perhaps even franchising the Greenville Restaurant.

One of his first steps in this process is to evaluate the state of the restaurant's working capital. He needs to get the current restaurant into good financial shape before venturing out and opening additional stores. Even though Anderson's parents are good businesspeople, finance and accounting are not their strongest areas. Upon examining their records he notices the following:

■ The Greenlees currently manage two bank accounts for their restaurant. One account is for immediate access to pay bills and does not draw any interest. The second account is strictly for savings to pay for problems that may arise, such as an oven going out. This savings account has an average balance of $10,000 and receives 0.5% interest.

■ The restaurant does a significant amount of catering business for local companies and allows them to pay half the bill up front. A bill is sent for the remaining 50%, which is payable within 30 days. Approximately 80% of these customers mail in their payments.

■ The Greenville Restaurant accepts MasterCard, VISA, and American Express credit cards as a form of payment. American Express is currently charging the restaurant a 6% fee on all transactions, while MasterCard and VISA are charging 5.5%.

QUESTIONS

1. Evaluate Greenville Restaurant's banking situation. Can you give any tips to the restaurant to better manage their situation?

2. As the Greenlees open new restaurants what banking services are available to them?

3. How can the Greenlees better manage their credit card payments? How can they better manage fees as the business grows?

GROWING
THE BUSINESS

J.W. AND ALICE SHEETS MARRIOTT: FROM ROOT BEER STAND TO HOSPITALITY CONGLOMERATE

While today the Marriott brand stands for consistent high quality in numerous lodging concepts worldwide, did you know Marriott started out in the foodservice business?

In 1927, John Willard "J.W." Marriott, purchased an A&W root beer franchise for $1,000 and opened a nine-stool A&W root beer stand in Washington, D.C. His total capital outlay was $6,000: $1,500 of his own savings, $3,000 from his partner, Hugh Colton, and $1,500 of debt from a bank. After just three weeks of operation, J.W. returned to his Utah hometown to marry his college sweetheart, Alice Sheets. At the time, the couple had so little money that Alice's mother gave them four $50 bills to pay their way back to Washington, D.C.

Initially, Alice expected to be a stay-at-home wife. Before they married, she said to J.W., "You don't expect me to go back to Washington with you and sell root beer, do you?" But the bride soon found herself taking charge of the money and other aspects of the fledgling business. That year, business from the first stand was so good that the Marriotts opened a second stand. According to J.W., "Alice would count the money generated from the two stands and keep a record of the inflow and outflow of cash. As long as the receipts were more than the expenditures, we knew we were doing all right." When they suspected their waitresses were pocketing money, Mrs. Marriott would spy on them through a hole in the back door.

However, as fall approached, the cool weather caused their root beer sales to drop off. To divest the risk of this lost cash flow, J.W. negotiated a new clause in his franchise to allow his root beer stands to sell food as well. Chili, hot tamales, barbecued beef sandwiches, and hot dogs were added to the menu, and the Hot Shoppe concept was conceived. Soon, thereafter, the Marriotts renamed their root beer stands Hot Shoppes and grew the chain to over sixty-five restaurants.

In 1937, a Hot Shoppe manager at the Hoover Airport location observed that airline passengers would buy snacks and drinks from the restaurant to take with them on their flight. He told Mr. Marriott about this, and immediately the entrepreneur cleared a storeroom in the basement and converted it into a flight catering assembly room. The next day, he called the people at Eastern Air Transport and obtained his first catering contract, and the company's In-Flite catering division was born. In spite of World War II, this division quickly expanded into the foodservice management business, providing meals for thousands of workers in government and the private sector.

By 1952, the company's gross income had tripled from what it had been just seven years before. At the end of World War II, its income was over $19 million. Mr. Marriott was thus faced with a critical decision: Should he be conservative and grow the business slowly by reinvesting its cash flow, or raise a war chest for expansion and take the risk of going public? J.W. chose the latter. In 1953, Hot Shoppes, Inc., offered 229,880 shares of common stock to the public at $10.25 per share and 18,000 shares to its employees at $7.54 per share. The stock sold out in two hours of trading and raised close to $2.5 million. The flush of cash was used to further expand Hot Shoppes, in-flight catering, and the foodservice management businesses. The company then diversified into lodging with the construction and opening of the Marriott Twin Bridges in Arlington, Virginia. Other Marriott hotels soon followed in Washington, D.C., Dallas, and Philadelphia.

Even after officially relinquishing control to their eldest son, J.W. Marriott Jr., Mr. and Mrs. Marriott continued to shape the company's business until they passed away in 1985 and 2000 respectively. The phenomenal growth of their original root beer franchise into a worldwide hospitality conglomerate was no accident. As J.W. Marriott once said, "A man should keep on being constructive and do constructive things." He and his wife are certainly two great examples of this strong work ethic.

SOURCES

O'Brien, R. *Marriott: The J. Willard Marriott Story.* Salt Lake City: Deseret, 1997.

Marriott, J.W., Jr., and K.A. Brown. *The Spirit to Serve: Marriott's Way.* New York: HarperCollins, 1997.

"Company's Heritage: J. Willard Marriott." http://marriott.com/corporateinfo/culture/heritageJWillard-Marriott.mi.

"Company's Heritage: Alice Sheets Marriott." http://marriott.com/corporateinfo/culture/heritageAlice-SMarriott.mi.

"Marriott International, Inc.'s Investor Relations Center." http://ir.shareholder.com/mar/default.cfm.

"Alice S. Marriott, Company Co-Founder, Dies at 92." Marriott International news release. http://marriottschool.byu.edu/news/release.cfm?ID=42&format=print.

Learning Outcomes

1. Understand why a company must demonstrate consistent growth to be successful.

2. Understand the concept of shareholder value and how management strives to increase it.

3. Learn how to calculate earnings per share (EPS) and a company's stock multiple.

4. Learn what influences a company's stock multiple and, as a result, shareholder value.

5. Understand the concept of risk and return, and how to measure it.

6. Identify the benefits and advantages that growth offers a company.

7. Understand the growth strategies available to companies and the advantages and disadvantages of each.

Preview of Chapter 5

Growing the Business

1. THE NEED FOR GROWTH

2. SHAREHOLDER VALUE

a. Private company goals

b. Risk and reward

c. Public company goals

3. BENEFITS OF GROWTH

a. Provide career paths for employees

b. Attract new qualified employees

c. Increase market share

d. Limit new competition

e. Diversify to reduce risk

4. GROWTH STRATEGIES

a. Increase sales and productivity of existing properties

b. Expand physical facilities

c. Franchise brand rights

d. Secure additional management contracts

e. Merge with or acquire competitors

f. Go public

THE NEED FOR GROWTH

Regardless of whether you work for a public company, a private company, a large company, or small company, growing the business of your company is essential to its long-term success. Owners of private companies expect profits, cash flow, and ROI to increase each year. Stockholders of public companies expect the price of their stock to rise each year. To be considered a growth company, a company's earnings must increase by at least 15% each year. This is a major challenge for most companies and becomes even harder the larger the company becomes. The primary goal of management, therefore, is to increase **shareholder value.**

Shareholder Value

Shareholder value is the **market value** of the company. Shareholder value for a public company is the current market price of its common stock multiplied by the number of shares of common stock outstanding. Shareholder value for a private company is the price the company could be sold for on the open market.

PUBLIC COMPANY GOALS

The goals of a public company are to increase:

1. Earnings per share
2. The company's stock multiple
3. The market price of its common stock

Shareholder value for a public company is strongly influenced by analysts' estimates of the company's future **earnings per share** (EPS). Earnings per share is calculated by dividing the company's annual **EBITDA** (earnings before interest, income taxes, depreciation, and amortization) by the number of shares of its common stock outstanding. The relationship between earnings per share and the current market price of a company's common stock is referred to as its **multiple.**

The multiple is calculated by dividing the current market price of a company's common stock by its earnings per share. The higher the projected future earnings per share, the higher the multiple. If you were the chief financial officer of your company, would you want a high multiple or a low multiple? You would want a high multiple because for every dollar that earnings per share actually increases, the market value of its common stock should increase by a multiple of EPS. For example, if earnings per share increases by $1.00 and the company's stock multiple is 15, the current price of its stock should increase by $15.00.

Successful hospitality companies strive to increase shareholder value by increasing revenues and controlling or reducing expenses, which increases earnings per share. They also strive to increase shareholder value by managing investor expectations of future earnings per share and thus increasing the company's stock multiple.

The challenge they face, however, is the company's need for large quantities of capital to grow. The more capital a company requires for growth, the slower the growth rate, as raising capital takes time. The slower the company's growth, the slower its shareholder value increases.

Because shareholder value is a function of projected future earnings per share and the risks associated with achieving it, the higher the projected future earnings per share and the higher the probability of achieving them, the more investors will pay for the stock today and the higher the company's stock multiple. An important key to increasing shareholder value is to create the perception that earnings per share will grow steadily at a minimum of 15% per year. A high growth rate encourages investors to buy the company's stock, anticipating that the stock will be worth more in the future. Another key to increasing shareholder value is to make the perception reality by delivering the anticipated earnings. This makes for happy investors who will invest more capital in the company in the future. The more demand there is for a particular stock, the higher its market price. This is true because, in the short term, the number of shares of stock available for the public to purchase is fixed.

RISK AND REWARD

Because the element of risk is factored into a company's stock multiple, it is helpful to understand the basic concept of risk and reward. Investors are risk adverse to varying degrees. As a result, the greater the risk that future earnings may not be achieved, the higher the return on investment investors demand. The higher the return on investment demanded, the lower the stock multiple. It is therefore important for management to minimize the perceived risk associated with its future growth.

The degree of risk associated with an investment can be measured. If you have taken a class in statistics, you may remember that the probability of a return on investment can be shown by the normal bell-shaped curve where the variance and standard deviation (square root of variance) apply. The average or mean is the middle of the bell-shaped curve. A +1 to −1 standard deviation covers 68.3% of the bell-shaped curve. A +2 to −2 standard deviation covers 95.4%, and a +3 to −3 standard deviation covers 99.7% of the curve. The risk of an investment, therefore, can be measured by its standard deviation. The higher the standard deviation, the more the return varies from the mean—and the higher the risk.

Industry publications, such as *Value Line,* measure a company's market-related risk in terms of **beta.** The value of a company's beta is measured relative to the market. It is assumed that the market as a whole has a beta of 1.0. If a restaurant company's stock, for example, has a beta of exactly 1.0, it carries the same market risk as the market index and should offer the same return. In other words, it is likely that its stock price will closely track that of the market. If the market goes up by two points on a certain day, the price of the restaurant's company stock will likely go up by two points as well. Conversely, if the market as a whole goes down by three points, so will the restaurant company's stock.

If a resort company has a beta of 1.5 and the market goes down ten points, the price of the resort company's stock will likely decrease by 1.5 times ten or fifteen points. Conversely, if a hotel management company's stock has a beta of 0.5, the price of its stock will only react half as much to the market. The higher a stock's beta, the riskier investors perceive it to be and the more volatile the stock is in both an economic upturn and downturn.

PRIVATE COMPANY GOALS

The goals of a private company are similar to those of a public company, but they are less driven by the earnings estimates and risk measurements of others. A private company's primary goal is to increase cash flow and generate a favorable return on investment for its owners. Because private companies are not driven by shares held by the public, their metrics are normally not per share but rather the total value of the company. As cash flow increases, return on investment increases, as does the market value of the company.

FEATURE   STORY

LODGING BECOMES THE FACE OF MARRIOTT

J.W. Marriott Sr. handed over the corporate reins to his son J.W. Marriott Jr. in 1972. Under the leadership of Bill Jr., Marriott's lodging division became the company's public face. Bill focused the company's attention on the growth of hotels and originated the concept of brands within a brand, now known as *market segmentation.* The acquisition of Residence Inn, the creation of the Courtyard product, and the franchising of these brands and others led to explosive growth for the company. The Marriott conglomerate split into two companies on October 8, 1993: Host Marriott, which owned most of the real estate, and Marriott International, which owned the franchise rights to all the Marriott brands, the management contracts, and the franchise agreements. Marriott also spun off its food and concession services business in 1990.

The split was conceived to revive the original Marriott Corporation when it became mired in debt resulting from a hotel building frenzy followed by a period of economic recession. Suddenly, Bill Jr. was faced with crumbling stock prices, a takeover scare, and approximately $1 billion of unsold lodging property sitting on his company's balance sheet. Under the new structure, Host Marriott, the real estate arm, took over about two-thirds of the original corporation's $2.9 billion of debt, leaving its sister operating company, Marriott International, with a lighter balance sheet, strong earnings, and the flexibility to go after more management contracts. Without a real estate component, Marriott International was also better protected from the cyclical fluctuations of the economy. In addition to solving its immediate financial problems, the split also enabled

Marriott to return to what it did best: management and service. As Bill Jr. put it, "Marriott was (and is) not about debt, real estate ownership, and deals; we're about management and service."

Once again focused on management, Marriott International aggressively broadened its product offering by acquiring the Ritz-Carlton Hotel Company and the Renaissance Hotel Group. It also developed new franchisable lodging concepts such as Fairfield Inn and Spring Hill Suites. As a mega-chain, the company was able to leverage its operational expertise to provide a product for each market segment, which made it easier to cross-sell and provide referrals under one management system.

Marriott also diversified into related products such as vacation ownership and corporate housing by acquiring ExecuStay and expanding its vacation ownership portfolio. In both cases, the Marriott brand enhanced its product image and price points.

Bill Jr. also reembraced franchising to spur his company's growth. Marriott's previous attempt at franchising during the late 1960s failed due to the failure of top management to embrace the concept and the lack of suitable franchisable products. However, as Bill Jr. pushed for more product tiers, some of the concepts, such as Courtyard, Fairfield Inn, and Spring Hill Suites, that were relatively inexpensive to develop and easy to operate, proved to be ideal for franchising.

Even though the split was controversial at the time, Bill Jr.'s decision to go ahead in spite of the risk of lawsuits from unhappy bondholders proved, in hindsight, the right move. Since the split, the share price for Host Marriott has increased from $5.67 to $18.89, while the share price for Marriott International has skyrocketed from $11.77 to $67.02.

Today, Marriott International is a $14 billion company with over 2,600 lodging properties in sixty-six countries. It operates and franchises hotels under the Marriott, JW Marriott, Ritz-Carlton, Renaissance, Residence Inn, Courtyard, Towne Place Suites, Fairfield Inn, Spring Hill Suites, Ramada International, and Bulgari brand names; develops and operates vacation ownership resorts under the Marriott Vacation Club International, Horizons, Ritz-Carlton Club, and Marriott Grand Residence Club brands; and operates Marriott Executive Apartments. The company also provides furnished corporate housing and operates conference centers.

SOURCES

Marriott, J.W., Jr., and K.A. Brown. *The Spirit to Serve: Marriott's Way.* New York: HarperCollins, 1997.
"Company's Heritage: J.W. Marriott Jr." http://marriott.com/corporateinfo/culture/heritageJWMarriottJR.mi.
"Marriott International, Inc.'s Investor Relations Center." http://ir.shareholder.com/mar/default.cfm.
"About the Marriott Factbook." http://ir.shareholder.com/mar/downloads/factbook.pdf.

Other Benefits of Growth

In addition to the financial growth benefits that accrue to the owners of a business, sustained and steady growth provides other tangible benefits for the company as well.

PROVIDE CAREER PATHS FOR EMPLOYEES

Steady, sustained growth in the number of properties a company owns or manages provides clear career paths for its employees. As employees see their colleagues rewarded with promotions to more challenging and higher-paying positions, they are motivated to try harder to succeed. When employees can clearly see a promising career path ahead of them, they are also less likely to seek employment elsewhere. Because employee turnover is expensive for the company, it is important to maintain employee longevity.

ATTRACT NEW QUALIFIED EMPLOYEES

An expansion in the number of company properties can help attract qualified employees and managers currently employed by other companies who view your company as one that could provide them with a more lucrative career.

INCREASE MARKET SHARE

Growth, if managed properly, can increase a company's market share. Market share is the percentage of demand that a company captures within a defined market area. For example, a restaurant company may elect to grow by adding more stores in suburban areas of a large metropolitan region rather than expanding to new cities. By focusing its growth in one city, its market share in that city grows.

LIMIT NEW COMPETITION

Focused growth of business units in a particular market can limit new competition by making it more difficult for competitors to enter the market. As demand in a market grows, new supply is attracted to that market. If the new supply is provided by the existing brand, additional competition is not as threatening and the subject brand's market share grows.

An example of this occurred many years ago in the San Antonio airport area. La Quinta Hotels was enjoying a high occupancy at a favorable average rate at its airport property. The company's competitors viewed the market as desirable and wanted to expand into it. To prevent this, La Quinta decided to build a second La Quinta hotel right next door to the existing property. This strategic move limited new competition for several years and enabled La Quinta to continue as the market leader.

DIVERSIFICATION TO REDUCE RISK

Rather than focus on expansion in a single city, some companies elect to expand to new markets. The benefit of this type of growth is that it spreads the risk of expansion over several markets. If one market experiences economic problems, growth in earnings in the other markets may balance the overall profitability of the company. Some companies elect to reduce risk by diversifying into new products. The more diversified a company's product line, the less risk it is likely to incur if a particular product fails to achieve its profit goal. An example of a diversified company is Choice Hotels. Choice franchises numerous brands all across the world, as shown in Illustration 5-1.

Brands	Geographic Areas
Comfort Inn	Asia and Pacific (over 400)
Comfort Suites	Canada (over 200)
Quality	Central and South America (over 50)
Sleep Inn	Europe and Middle East (over 500)
Clarion	United States and Caribbean (over 3,000)
Clarion Collection	
Main Stay Suites	
Econo Lodge	
Rodeway Inn	

ILLUSTRATION 5-1
Brands and Geographic Areas of Choice Hotels International

THE REAL DEAL

Many have dined at a Wendy's and love the Wendy's choice of fries, baked potato, chili, garden salad, or Caesar salad with a combination meal. However, few may know that Wendy's also owns or partly owns Tim Hortons, Baja Fresh Mexican Grill, Café Express, and Pasta Pomodoro. Wendy's has successfully grown its business by merging with or purchasing other restaurants that complement its core mission. With over 6,600 Wendy's units, 2,700 Tim Hortons, 295 units of Baja Fresh, 19 units of Café Express, and 45 Pasta Pomodoros, Wendy's offers a lot of dining choices besides burgers. Visit Wendy's website at http://www.wendy-invest.com for more up-to-date information.

GROWTH STRATEGIES

Hospitality companies can elect to pursue a variety of strategies to achieve and sustain steady growth in earnings.

Increase Sales and Productivity of Existing Properties

A popular growth strategy is to attempt to generate more sales volume with the same number of stores (assets) while maintaining the business's current profit margin. As sales increase, earnings should grow as well. Higher sales volume can be achieved by either raising the price of products or by selling more products.

McDonald's Restaurants implemented a creative growth strategy many years ago when it began serving breakfast at all of its restaurants. With the addition of a new meal period, sales volume increased dramatically, as did profits. Today, breakfast is McDonald's highest-volume meal. A key benefit of this growth strategy is that it does not require new capital to achieve growth in earnings—and as you now know, capital, especially equity capital, can be expensive to secure.

McDonald's was able to utilize its existing stores and kitchen equipment to prepare and sell the new breakfast items. The only added expense was the cost of the new breakfast items, the labor to prepare and sell them, a little marketing expense to let customers know that McDonald's now served breakfast, and a few additional dollars for utilities. Another popular fast food growth strategy is to operate restaurants twenty-four hours a day, seven days a week. Once again, as long as the additional sales volume exceeds the additional variable cost, growth in earnings will be achieved.

REDUCE EXPENSES

When sales volume stops growing or stabilizes, companies look to cut costs to sustain earnings growth. The goal is to find ways to reduce expenses while maintaining the current level of sales. If this is accomplished, earnings grow even though sales remain static. An additional benefit of cost control is that for every dollar of cost reduction, 100% falls to the bottom line, while in the case of sales growth, expenses required to generate the new sales must be deducted from the increase in gross sales. A good example of how cost control may benefit the lodging industry is the occupancy versus average room rate debate. Which is more favorable, a 10% increase in occupancy or a 10% increase in the average daily rate (ADR) of the hotel? Although mathematically they achieve the same results in terms of revenue, if there is an increase in ADR, you are not selling any extra rooms and thus will not incur costs to clean and maintain those rooms. Therefore, by increasing revenues without increasing expenses, more profits go to the hotel's net income.

LABOR COST

In the hospitality industry, when costs must be cut, the first expense that gets management's attention is labor cost. Increasing labor productivity becomes management's short-term goal. Greater productivity can be achieved by improving employee scheduling, reducing expensive overtime, encouraging additional voluntary time off, reducing employee hours, eliminating employee positions, and using more advanced technology. Restaurants also focus on food cost and beverage cost to improve their bottom line. The cost control systems discussed in chapter 2 and chapter 4 can help reduce expenses and increase profits.

MARKETING EXPENSE

Unfortunately, another expense that is usually cut when costs must be reduced is sales and marketing. While the benefits of advertising and public relations are difficult to measure and a reduction in the amount of money spent in this area will increase profits, long-term harm to the property's profitability and long-term competitive position may result. Customers lured to a competitor are difficult to get back. Saving a few marketing dollars today can lose you hundreds or even thousands of dollars in the long run. We recommend that you carefully analyze the situation before you elect to reduce sales and marketing expense. There are usually better ways to prop up earnings.

CAPITAL IMPROVEMENTS

Another area to be cautious about when making arbitrary cost cuts is capital improvements. While it is sometimes tempting to get one more year out of old carpet, defer the replacement of television sets, or try to repair air conditioning units rather than buying new ones, once a property begins to deteriorate, it can go downhill fast. It is important to keep your hotel or restaurant looking clean and fresh. If guests perceive that your property is not being properly maintained, they will not hesitate to give your competition a chance to satisfy their needs. It does not take long for deferred maintenance to result in lower occupancy, lower average daily rate, and lower earnings.

ENERGY COST AND CREDIT CARD COMMISSIONS

Two areas that are often overlooked when expenses must be reduced are energy conservation and credit card commissions. An effective energy conservation program and the renegotiation of credit card rates can result in significant savings and an increase in profits.

HIGHER LODGING PROFITS

When sales plummeted following the 9/11 disaster, the lodging industry did an excellent job of increasing labor productivity, reducing expenses, and maintaining profit margins. Now that business volume is rebounding, profit margins are increasing dramatically, resulting in record profits for most hotel companies.

Expansion of Physical Facilities

Another popular growth strategy is to increase sales and profits by expanding existing properties, constructing new properties, and acquiring existing properties. As noted earlier, focus can either be on markets currently served by the company or on new markets. While this strategy can succeed in increasing earnings, it requires large quantities of new capital to finance the growth. In addition, management must make sure that the earnings generated by the additional assets are greater than the company's cost of capital. If the earnings from the new assets fail to cover a public company's cost of capital, earnings per share are **diluted,** which usually results in a decline in the company's stock price, which consequently reduces shareholder value.

Franchise Brand Rights

Once a company establishes the value of its brand in the marketplace and proves that its brand can travel, franchising the brand becomes another potential growth strategy. Numerous hotel and restaurant companies have learned that franchising can be very profitable. Franchising involves selling the rights to a company's brand in a specific location or market for a stated number of years. Franchise fees range from a few thousand dollars to $100,000 or more for a premium franchise. In addition, an ongoing franchise royalty is paid by the franchisee to the franchisor each month. The franchise royalty is calculated as a percentage of sales volume. The franchisor also charges the franchisee for ancillary services such as marketing, training, frequent guest programs, hotel reservations, and purchasing fees. Total franchise royalties and other fees charged by lodging brands range from 8% to 10% of rooms revenue. Total franchise royalties and other fees charged by restaurant brands range from 4% to 5% of total sales. For instance, McDonald's currently charges a 4% service fee, which is a monthly fee based on sales, and a monthly base rent or percentage rent that is a percentage of monthly sales. The fees paid to a hotel franchise company may include the following: franchise royalty (5% of rooms revenue), reservation fees ($5 to $10 per reservation, or around 2% of rooms revenue), national sales fee (2% of rooms revenue), and the frequent traveler program (1% to 2% of rooms revenue).

THE REAL DEAL

Franchising is an exciting opportunity, but it is not an easy process. Many hotel companies are user friendly, giving prospective franchisees valuable online information and providing an email address for further questions. Choice Hotels International has an elaborate website for its prospective franchisees, and Hilton Hotels and Cendant Hotels also offer useful information:

http://www.choicehotelsfranchise.com

http://www.hiltonfranchise.com

http://hotelfranchise.cendant.com

In addition to the financial rewards that franchising offers the owner of a particular brand, franchising also provides the following benefits to branded companies seeking growth:

1. Greater distribution system for both franchise and **company stores** (units owned and operated by the franchisor)

2. Rapid growth without the need for large amounts of capital

3. Higher profit margins, as the real estate is owned by the franchisee rather than the franchisor and no interest or depreciation expense is charged on the franchisor's income statement

The primary disadvantage of franchising, from the brand's perspective, is the risk of not being able to maintain brand standards or control the quality and consistency of the product and services. To minimize these problems, franchise companies inspect each franchise unit periodically and have the authority to de-franchise a unit if it does not meet brand standards or fails to achieve a passing score on customer satisfaction surveys.

Secure Additional Management Contracts

Another growth strategy, available primarily to lodging companies, is the expansion of management contracts to operate hotels for owners that do not have in-house management capabilities. In addition to the major hotel brands, over 100 independent hotel management companies offer hotel management services. Fees paid to the management company range from 3% to 5% of total sales plus an incentive fee based on a percentage of gross or net operating profit.

As in the case of franchising, securing contracts to manage hotels for other owners can be lucrative. A typical annual management fee for a 300-room full-service hotel ranges from $300,000 to $400,000 with no capital investment on the part of the management company. In addition, all costs associated with the management of the hotel, including employee wages and management salaries, are handled by the hotel owner, not the management company.

The primary disadvantage of growing a lodging company via management contracts is the risk of the contract being terminated. Many management contracts have a termination-on-sale provision that allows the owner to cancel the management contract if the property is sold.

THE REAL DEAL

While some businesses diversify in order to grow, McDonald's stays true to its original mission of providing high-quality food and thus guaranteeing customer satisfaction anywhere in the world. A McDonald's burger is of the same high quality whether someone purchases it in the United States, China, or Russia. Will McDonald's ever explore other ventures? This may be a question for the future. For now, McDonald's is using international connections such as basketball star Yao Ming of the Houston Rockets to do commercials that appeal to its Asian market, specifically China, Vietnam, and Korea. As the ad reads, "Trying to steal the ball from me is tough. Trying to steal my Chicken Selects is even tougher!"

Management contracts with the major hotel branded companies like Marriott, Hilton, and Starwood also include the franchise rights to their brand in addition to the management of the hotel. Management contracts with these companies, however, are normally for a minimum of ten years and often include the right to renew at the option of the brand. In addition, the termination rights of the hotel owner are limited.

Mergers and Acquisitions of Competitors

Once a public company reaches a certain size and has access to substantial amounts of capital, the merger and acquisition growth strategy becomes another option for the company to pursue. In the case of an acquisition, the purchasing company has the option of financing the purchase with debt, existing equity, selling new shares of stock to raise new capital, or using its stock as barter to acquire the company that is for sale.

Both the lodging industry and the foodservice industry have witnessed major mergers and acquisitions over the last several years. Illustration 5-2 highlights some of these transactions.

Going Public

The ultimate growth strategy, and the dream of most small business owners, is to go public someday and take part in an **initial public offering** (IPO) of its stock. As a company grows, becomes profitable, and requires more and more capital for growth, there comes a time when ownership must decide whether to take the company public or sell it to the highest private bidder. The decision of whether to take the company to the next level by going public, or simply cashing out, is not an easy one to make.

Parent Company	Mergers or Acquisitions
Blackstone	Wyndham and La Quinta
Diageo	Grand Metropolitan and Guinness
Harrah's	Caesars Entertainment
Hilton	British Hilton Group Plc.
Hilton	Promus
Landry's	Golden Nugget Las Vegas and Laughlin
Marriott	Ritz-Carlton and Renaissance
Starwood	Westin and Sheraton
Wendy's	Tim Hortons, Café Express, Baja Fresh, Pasta Pomodoro
Yum! Brands	A&W All-American Food, KFC, Long John Silver's, Pizza Hut, Taco Bell

ILLUSTRATION 5-2
Mergers and Acquisitions of Hospitality Companies

VALUING THE COMPANY

Before making this major decision, owners should first estimate how much they think they could sell the company for today and then compare that price with the company's potential value in a few years, assuming it goes public and accelerates its growth curve. If the difference is significant and the owners believe they are up to the challenge, an IPO should be seriously considered.

One of the biggest misconceptions people have about going public is that you do so to cash out. All investment bankers will tell you just the opposite. If you are fortunate enough to be in this position someday and are looking to cash out, simply sell your company privately. The purpose of taking a company public is to raise a large amount of new capital to accelerate future growth. If you want to cash out, you should not attempt to go public.

If a company is private, it can command a sales price that is normally based on a multiple of its annual cash flow. The multiple varies based on the type of business but usually ranges from nine to twelve. For example, if a company's annual cash flow is $1 million, it would sell for between $9 and $12 million. On the other hand, if the owners are patient, management dedicates itself to growth, and an experienced investment banker is hired to orchestrate the public offering, the value of the company could, in a few years, be worth several times more than it is today.

THE IPO PROCESS

While going public sounds exciting and can be lucrative to everyone involved, owning and managing a public company is much different than owning and managing a private company. A public company is just what the term implies—*public*. Everything from management salaries to the company's profitability to lawsuits filed against the company is available for public viewing.

Here is how the process of going public works:

1. The company hires an investment banking firm. The firm manages the process of going public and charges approximately 5% of the amount of capital raised as their fee.

2. Next, a law firm is hired to help write the prospectus. The prospectus tells the company's story. It clearly describes the corporate business plan and growth strategy, and it explains why an investor should buy its stock versus the other stocks available. This is what's referred to as an *out-of-pocket expense*. The company is obligated to pay the law firm's fee before the new capital is raised.

3. Next, the company hires an accounting firm to prepare certified audits for the company's prior three years of operation. This too is an out-of-pocket expense. Nobody said that going public was inexpensive. In fact, a company normally ends up spending up to 10% of the capital raised in out-of-pocket expenses.

4. Once the prospectus is drafted, it's time to plan the road show. A road show is a coast-to-coast whirlwind journey with the investment banker, chief executive officer, and chief financial officer to meet prospective institutional investors and retail stockbrokers to sell them on the merits of the public offering. In many cases, the CEO and CFO have only ten minutes to tell the company's story and get the prospective buyer excited about buying the stock.

5. After the road show, it's time to price the offering and finalize how much of the company the existing owners are willing to sell to the public. The investment banker helps make this important decision based on feedback from the institutional investors during the road show.

6. Once the stock is priced, the owners meet with the management of the stock exchange selected to make a market for the stock.

7. When the bell rings, signifying that the stock exchange is open for business, the company has officially gone public.

WORKING WITH AN INVESTMENT BANKER

The role of an investment banker in the IPO process is twofold. First, the banker helps value the company, establishes a price for the stock, and manages the selling process. The selling process includes preparing the prospectus, making sure it is in compliance with all the security regulations and laws; marketing the prospectus to potential buyers; and arranging for a syndication of investment bankers to expand the marketing effort, if required. The second duty of the investment banker, and probably the most important one, is to maintain a market for the company's stock once it is offered for sale so the stock not only gets off to a good start but enjoys a steady rise in price over time. The investment banker accomplishes this by promoting the company's stock to its clients and by purchasing stock for his or her own account when trading activity is low. Generally, the higher the daily trading volume of a stock, the more likely it is the stock will increase in price.

BEING A PUBLIC COMPANY

Once a company is public, everything management does or does not do is open to public scrutiny, praise, and criticism. As a public company, management is required to file extensive quarterly and annual reports with the SEC. Management is also required to deal regularly, sometimes several times a day, with Wall Street research analysts who follow the company's stock and attempt to predict how many cents per share of EBITDA the company's next quarter will yield to public shareholders. Management is also now required to report to a board of directors at least four times a year and hold an annual stockholder's meeting to answer any questions shareholders may have, even if they own only one share of the company's stock.

Managing a public company is significantly different than managing a small start-up company. As the chief executive officer of a public company, you have one goal and one goal only: to increase shareholder value. If management is successful in achieving this goal and can meet or exceed Wall Street analysts' projections of the company's EBITDA each quarter, the rewards will be significant.

THE SECURITIES AND EXCHANGE COMMISSION

All public companies are regulated by the SEC and therefore must comply with its rules and regulations. The SEC was established in 1934 to enforce the Securities Act of 1933 and the Securities Exchange Act of 1934. These laws were designed to restore investor confidence in the capital markets by providing more structure and government oversight after the stock market crash of 1929. The first chairman of the SEC was Joseph P. Kennedy, the father of President John F. Kennedy.

EQUITY MARKETS

Equity markets are stock exchanges where the public can buy and sell shares of stock. Although the markets discussed below also deal with public debt securities, the discussion in this section focuses strictly on equity issues. The two main public equity markets in the United States are the New York Stock Exchange (NYSE) and NASDAQ.

The most notable stock exchange in the United States is the NYSE. It is a corporation managed by a board of directors that monitors and oversees the activities of the stock exchange, its members, and the companies whose stock is traded on the exchange. The NYSE was founded in 1792 and originally comprised twenty-four securities brokers. A fixed commission was charged by each broker whenever a stock was bought or sold. In 1850, a seat on the NYSE cost $1,000. Today that same seat costs about $2.2 million. Only those who have a seat on the exchange can do business and trade. The NYSE has created a market for securities trading. This market comprises listed companies, individual investors, institutional investors, and member firms. It is a place where buyers and sellers meet and conduct business in an organized fashion under the rules of the SEC. On average, over 1.4 billion shares of stock are traded daily at a value of over $45 billion.

NASDAQ was founded in 1971 and originally stood for National Association of Securities Dealers Automated Quotation. Today, SDAQ is its official name. Although the business and goals of NASDAQ are basically the same as those of the NYSE, all of NASDAQ's transactions are transmitted over a telecommunications network. There is no physical address for NASDAQ. Today, NASDAQ is the largest electronic market in the United States, processing about 1.8 million transactions per day.

Finance in Action

Analyzing Goldtown

Mr. Perry Silverton is a financial analyst who specializes in the casino segment of the hospitality industry. Forty-eight states currently allow various types of gaming, such as riverboat casinos, Native American casinos, lottery, bingo, and pari-mutuel gambling. Mr. Silverton is specifically interested in publicly traded land-based and riverboat casino operations. Only a few major players operate in the world because the industry has undergone a period of many mergers and acquisitions.

People depend on Mr. Silverton's analysis of the casino market on a daily basis to determine whether they should buy or sell stocks in any particular company. One of the unique features of casino operations is that the majority of revenue is generated on the casino floor and not from rooms or food and beverage. This also means that casinos have to operate with a great deal of working capital because the nature of their business is dealing in cash.

Mr. Silverton is currently analyzing one of the smaller casino companies, Goldtown Casinos, Inc., which operates riverboat casinos in four states and has slightly over 10,000 employees. Goldtown Casinos, Inc., has 25.34 million shares of outstanding common stock, a current sales price of $22.55, an annual EBITDA of $204,345,000, and a beta of 9.5.

QUESTIONS

1. Calculate Goldtown's shareholder value, earnings per share, and multiple.

    Shareholder Value = Current Market Price of Common Stock × Number of Outstanding Shares of Common Stock

    OR

    $ 620,830,000 = $22.55 × 25,340,000

    Earnings per Share = EBITDA ÷ Number of Outstanding Shares of Common Stock

    OR

    $ 8.06 = $204,345,000 ÷ 25,340,000

    Multiple = Current Market Price ÷ Earnings per Share

    OR

    2.8 = $22.55 ÷ 8.06

2. If the overall casino industry has an EPS of $1.5, how does Goldtown Casinos' EPS compare?
    Because Goldtown Casinos has an EPS of $8.06, it is faring better than the overall industry and can produce $8.06 in earnings per share of common stock, while the industry is only able to produce $1.50 per each share of common stock.

3.   Analyze Goldtown's beta and what this number means to a potential investor.

Goldtown has a relatively high beta of 9.5, which indicates an overall higher risk than the market. If the market goes down 1 point, Goldtown is likely to go down 9.5 points; however, on the upside, if the market goes up, then Goldtown's stock should increase 9.5 points.

WHERE WE'VE BEEN, WHERE WE'RE GOING

Growing the business is a must for any operation to continue to be successful. Growth provides financial rewards to its shareholders and other benefits and advantages to its management and employees. Growth in the hospitality industry can be achieved through expansion of physical facilities, franchising, management contracts, or a combination of these strategies. The key is to select the strategy or combined strategies best suited to your business. Once you select a growth strategy, your next step is to secure the capital required to finance the growth. Should you invest more of your personal equity, borrow the funds, or raise additional equity from outside investors? We examine these options and the costs associated with each one in the next chapter.

Key Points

➤   A company must demonstrate consistent growth to be successful. It does so by increasing the wealth of its shareholders.

➤   The goals of a public company are to increase current earnings per share, to increase the company's stock multiple, to increase projected earnings per share, and to increase the market price of the common stock. The goals of a private company are similar because they are also profit driven. Private companies look at the total value of the company in terms of increasing profits, increasing cash flow, and increasing its return on investment. All these increases cause the company's market value to increase as well.

➤   The relationship between earnings per share (EPS) and the current market price of a company's common stock is referred to as its multiple. The multiple is calculated by dividing the current market price of a company's common stock by its earnings per share. The higher the earnings per share, the higher the multiple.

➤   The benefits and advantages of growth in a company include providing career paths for employees, increasing market share, limiting new competition, and diversifying in an effort to reduce risk.

➤   The growth strategies available to companies include increased sales and productivity, expanding physical facilities, franchising brand rights, securing additional management contracts, merging or acquiring companies, and going public. Each of these strategies has advantages and disadvantages.

Key Terms

SHAREHOLDER VALUE: For a public company, the current market price of its common stock multiplied by the number of shares of common stock outstanding; for a private company, the price the company could be sold for on the open market.

MARKET VALUE: The number of shares of common stock outstanding multiplied by the current market price of one share of a company's common stock.

EBITDA: Earnings before interest, income taxes, depreciation, and amortization.

EARNINGS PER SHARE: EBITDA divided by the number of shares of common stock outstanding.

MULTIPLE: The current market price of a company's common stock divided by its EPS.

BETA: Indicates the risk of an investment relative to the risk of the market.

DILUTED: Reduced earnings per share.

COMPANY STORES: Units owned and operated by a franchisor.

INITIAL PUBLIC OFFERING (IPO): Where stocks of a company are sold to the public for the first time.

Application Exercises

1. Compare and contrast the goals of a pubic company with those of a private company.

2. Name two incentives for companies to grow their business rather than maintaining the status quo.

3. Define the term *risk* and explain why a company needs to balance risk and return.

4. This chapter discusses six strategies for increasing sales and productivity in order for a company to grow. Describe three of the six strategies and comment on the pros and cons of each one.

5. Consider franchising versus mergers and acquisitions. Which is a better strategy for growth? Please explain.

6. What are management contracts, and how would they help a company grow? Is this a risky proposition?

7. List the steps required when a company goes public.

8. How can an investment banker help or obstruct the process of taking a company public?

9. **ETHICS** ✳ One of the major expenses in the hospitality industry is the cost of energy. At one point in the last few years, a surcharge was added to hotel folios to cover the increase in energy cost. Do you think this is an ethical or sound business practice? What would you do if you were the manager of a 400-room spa resort? Propose three strategies to combat increased energy cost without passing the cost to the guests in the form of surcharges.

10. **EXPLORING THE WEB** ✳ Based on the websites mentioned in this chapter and on other websites you may find, choose one company you would want to open a franchise with and explain the financial rationale behind your choice.

Concept Check ✔

The Case of Expansion for Brownstone

The Fillis Bistro, operated by Brownstone Restaurants, Inc., is a fine dining restaurant that caters to those with discerning taste. The executive chef was trained in France and only uses the highest-quality organic ingredients. He even grows his own herbs in a garden behind the restaurant so he can serve the freshest food possible.

Restaurant sales for the Fillis Bistro have leveled off over the last couple of years, and Brownstone is trying to determine the best method for expanding the business. Management has discussed several ideas for expansion, including increasing off-premise catering sales, opening a second operation, and scrutinizing costs to cut back expense, but they cannot agree on anything.

Brownstone Restaurants, Inc. owns and operates over 20 restaurants on the east coast of the United States. These restaurants include The Fillis Bistro, 6 Mexican restaurants, 5 Chinese restaurants, and 8 Greek restaurants. All of the restaurants are operating at optimal levels and reaching budgeted financial projections.

QUESTIONS

1. Utilizing the information covered in this chapter, list all growth options available to Brownstone Restaurants, Inc.

2. Analyze each expansion option and discuss the positive or negative impacts they could have on the restaurant's operations.

3. Which expansion option would you recommend to Brownstone Restaurants, Inc. and why?

Concept Check ✔

Private or Public for Tranquil Hotels

Tranquil Hotels Co. specializes in developing resorts and spas for busy people who are always on the go and need to relax. Each location is specially chosen for the beauty of its setting, the ambiance of the city, and the ease of arrival for its guests. Tranquil Hotels are located all over the world in countries like France, Brazil, Greece, Italy, and many other locations. The company's mission is to "provide our guests with the most relaxing experience that they would find at any place in the world."

Tranquil Hotels Co. has hired a consultant to analyze its business and determine if the company should remain privately held or go public. The company has experienced an influx of business from U.S. travelers over the last couple of years. U.S. employees tend to work very hard, so when they have time off to relax, they want to get away from everything, and Tranquil

Hotels is the perfect place. Management believes there is a big market for their resorts and the best option for expansion is through an IPO. Last year, the company's cash flow reached nearly $7.5 million. Overall the company has been enjoying annual cash flow increases of 5%.

QUESTIONS

1. What price range would you currently assign to Tranquil Hotels Co. if you were to sell it as a private operation?
2. Describe the IPO process the owners would need to go through if they decided to take the company public.
3. If you were an owner, would you go public? Why or why not?
4. If the owner is considering getting out of the business, should he or she take the company public? Why or why not?

CHAPTER 6

FINANCING GROWTH

BARRY STERNLICHT—A DEALMAKER'S DEALMAKER

One of the biggest hotel news stories in 2003 was the unexpected announcement by Barry Sternlicht, chairman and CEO of Starwood Hotels and Resorts Worldwide, that he would be stepping down from the helm as soon as a replacement could be found. Just two years later, the renowned dealmaker is orchestrating yet another big deal that could shake the hotel world and will pit him head to head with his previous company, which he built into one of the world's largest lodging companies.

The son of the president of a small manufacturing company located in Stamford, Connecticut, Sternlicht joined JMB Realty Corporation shortly after graduating from the Harvard Business School. At age twenty-seven, fresh out of college, he was immediately assigned the $400 million acquisition of a real estate development company, Arvida Corporation, by the Walt Disney Company. In 1991, just four years after joining JMB, he lost $425 million for his employer when the British property company, Randsworth Trust PLC, which he had acquired on behalf of JMB, collapsed following the British real estate market crash. For a young dealmaker, that was a lot of money to lose in a single transaction, and it should have ended Sternlicht's dealmaking career. Instead, it marked the beginning of his illustrious run in the lodging business.

Following his costly mistake, Sternlicht left JMB and struck out on his own. In 1991, the U.S. commercial real estate market was still depressed after its bubble burst in 1986. Many commercial buildings were available for sale at deeply discounted prices, much lower than their replacement cost. Like many, Sternlicht saw an opportunity to make a lot of money. He shared his ambitious vision with many well-heeled individuals and persuaded the likes of the Ziff publishing family and the Pritzker (Hyatt) family to invest a total of $60 million in his new company, Starwood Capital Group LLC.

Sternlicht's investors' faith in him proved well justified. Between 1991 and 1997, Barry rewarded them with returns averaging more than 50% per year. One of his first deals was a $52 million acquisition of multifamily apartments, priced extremely low, at a Resolution Trust Corporation auction, which he then exchanged for a 20% stake in Zell's Equity Residential Property Trust. When Zell went public in 1993, his stake was valued at $180 million. At that time, Sternlicht was among the first to acquire nonperforming hotels at prices deeply discounted from their replacement cost. His strategy was to buy hotels located in urban markets where building costs were high and selling prices were low. He then operated them until the market turned around and, eventually, sold them when their value increased and stabilized.

A key to his early success in outbidding others for these targeted hotel assets was his 1995 acquisition of Hotel Investors Trust, a troubled real estate investment trust (REIT) with a grandfathered paired-share structure. Although Congress had outlawed this structure in 1984, it grandfathered five small existing REITs, one of which was Hotel Investors Trust. As a paired-share REIT, Sternlicht's new financial vehicle, Starwood Lodging Trust, linked a hotel real estate investment trust that was exempt from income taxes at the corporate level with a hotel operating company, Starwood Lodging Corporation, which was able to not only earn rental income from its properties, like other equity REITs, but also earn operating profits as well. The shares of each company were paired to trade together as one unit. Unlike other hotel REITs, which were required to lease their assets to a management company and pay the company a management fee, this business structure enabled Sternlicht to both acquire and manage hotels. It also helped him avoid the corporate income taxes that burdened conventional hotel companies. As a result, his company could afford to pay more for an asset than its competitors and still achieve its investors' hurdle rate, a luxury other bidders did not enjoy.

Perhaps Sternlicht's greatest coup was his back-to-back acquisition of Westin Hotels and Resorts and the Sheraton hotel chain in 1998. These major acquisitions established his Starwood Lodging Trust as the largest hotel operator in the world—overnight. During the Sheraton negotiations, Sternlicht took on Hilton Hotel's CEO Steve Bollenbach, who had launched a $10.5 billion hostile takeover of the company. In the end, Sternlicht's REIT was able to outbid Hilton and paid $14.6 billion for the company. As a result of these transactions, Starwood was established as the owner of the Westin, Sheraton, St. Regis, and Four Points brands in addition to the hotel assets the Westin and Sheraton companies owned around the world.

Following these two transactions, other lodging companies put tremendous pressure on the government to outlaw the paired-share REIT structure enjoyed by Starwood, claiming it gave Starwood an unfair tax-driven advantage over its corporate lodging chain competitors in both acquiring and operating hotels. The pressure proved successful, as the government enacted legislature in August 1998 forbidding further expansion by paired-share REITs, with the penalty loss of their REIT status. As a result, the trust dissolved its paired-share REIT structure in favor of a C-corporation.

In 2003, Sternlicht surprised everyone when he resigned as chief executive of the giant hotel company he had created and then resigned as chairman and sold a large portion of his Starwood stock. Recently, he positioned himself to compete head to head with Starwood Hotels and Resorts when he acquired thirty-two hotels from London-based Le Meridian Hotels and Resorts and Société du Louvre, which owned the venerable Crillon Hotel in Paris. His plan is to expand the Crillon into a luxury hotel chain with locations in major gateway cities and resort destinations. His goal: "We are going to make each hotel obscenely rich and obscenely beautiful and position them at the top of their markets."

Sternlicht also envisions introducing a number of new brands to the lodging market. His company, Starwood Capital Group, is considering revamping a budget brand owned by Société du Louvre as well as developing a new mid-tier brand. While it is still too early to tell how successful Sternlicht's latest venture will be, based on his past record, it will likely be a winner.

SOURCES

Deady, Tim. "Hotel Investors to Merge with Eastern Partnership—Hotel Investors Corp. and Hotel Investors Trust; Starwood Capital Group L.P." *Los Angeles Business Journal,* June 20, 1994.

Morris, K., and K. Felcyn. "Fast, Smart, 'Dangerous': Dealmaker Barry Sternlicht Is Eyeing All of Westin's Hotels." *Business Week,* Finance, April 7, 1997.

Grover, R., and J.M. Laderman. "The Unhappy Campers at ITT: Shareholders Are Losing Patience as It Tries to Elude Hilton." *Business Week,* News: Analysis and Commentary, June 23, 1997.

Sheridan, D., and B. Johnson. "Starwood's ITT Deal May Be the Start of Another Hot Year." *National Real Estate Investor,* December 1, 1997.

"Barry Sternlicht Steps Down." http://www.hotelinteractive.com/index.asp?page_id=5000&article_id=2869, October 30, 2003.

Sanders, P. "Former Chief of Starwood Launches Rival." *Wall Street Journal,* Marketplace, B1, B4, January 23, 2006.

Learning Outcomes

1. Understand how to finance the growth of a company.
2. Become familiar with the two types of capital: debt and equity.
3. Understand the cost of debt and equity.
4. Learn how to determine the best mix of capital for a company.
5. Understand the concept of weighted cost of capital (WACC) and how to calculate it.
6. Define *financial leverage* and understand how it can increase ROI.
7. Identify the types of debt and equity and their sources.
8. Determine how restaurant financing parameters differ from hotel parameters.
9. Learn how hotels were financed during the 1970s and 1980s.
10. Identify the latest schemes to finance hotels.

Preview of Chapter 6

Financing Growth

THE NEED FOR CAPITAL

Because companies in the hospitality industry rely heavily on real estate to house their businesses, the hospitality industry is deemed capital intensive. Therefore, in order to grow, most hospitality companies require substantial amounts of capital to fund their expansion. Knowing how and where to seek capital is important to the success of a hospitality company. This chapter discusses the types of capital, their relative costs, advantages, disadvantages, and sources, and popular financial schemes hospitality companies use to finance their growth. Chapters 10 and 11 focus on how to prepare a professional investment package and successfully secure the capital needed for growth.

Capital

Capital is money, or the equivalent of money, that is loaned to, or invested in, a business. While capital is often equated with cash, it can also take the form of land, a building, or anything else of value.

TYPES OF CAPITAL

There are two types of capital: debt and equity. **Debt** is a fixed obligation or liability of the business that must be paid back, with interest, over a specified period. **Equity** is ownership in the business that does not require immediate repayment, but a return on the capital invested is expected.

A business must secure a commitment for a certain amount of equity before approaching a lender for a loan because a lender will not loan 100% of the project cost. Lenders require the borrower to have some money at risk. The percentage of equity required depends on the perceived risk of the project. The greater the perceived risk, the larger the amount of equity a lender will require a borrower to provide in order to secure the loan.

THE COST OF CAPITAL

The **cost of capital** can be divided into two parts: The **cost of debt** is the interest expense the borrower is obligated to pay the lender, and the **cost of equity** is the portion of cash flow the sponsor of the deal agrees to allocate to the new investor in return for the equity provided. The cost of debt and equity is usually stated as a percentage and is calculated by dividing the projected annual payment to the lender or investor by the amount of capital it provides.

As seen in Illustration 6-1, a restaurateur projects an annual cash flow of $50,000, borrows $100,000 from a bank, and agrees to pay interest expense of $10,000 per year. She also raises $100,000 of equity from an investor in exchange for 50% ownership in the restaurant.

The cost of debt is calculated by dividing interest expense by the loan amount ($10,000 divided by $100,000), which yields a 10% cost of debt. If you know the interest rate the financial institution charges, then the interest rate charged is the actual cost of debt. In some investment analyses, however, debt service is also known as the cost of debt. The cost of equity is calculated by dividing the investor's portion of the cash flow (after debt service) by the amount of equity invested ([$50,000 less $16,000] multiplied by 50% divided by $100,000), yielding a cost of 17%. Thus, in this case, the cost of debt is 10% and the cost of equity is 17%.

WEIGHTED AVERAGE COST OF CAPITAL (WACC)

In real life, the cost of capital is a little more complicated. The mix of debt and equity is not always 50-50, and the total cost of capital is not always the average of the two individual costs.

A restaurateur provides you with the following information for you to calculate the cost of debt and equity for her business venture:

1. She borrows $100,000 from a bank and agrees to pay the bank interest expense of $10,000 per year.

2. She raises another $100,000 of equity from an investor and agrees to give him a 50% ownership position in her restaurant.

3. Projected annual cash flow before debt service is $50,000.

What is the projected cost of debt and cost of equity?

The annual cost of debt is 10% and is calculated as follows:

$10,000 (interest expense) divided by $100,000 (loan principal) = 10%

The annual cost of equity is 17% and is calculated as follows:

$50,000 (annual cash flow before debt service) less $16,000 (debt service) = $34,000

$34,000 × 50% (investor ownership) = $17,000 (net cash flow to your investor)

$17,000 (net cash flow to your investor) divided by $100,000 (equity invested) = 17%

ILLUSTRATION 6-1
Cost of Debt and Equity

Also, in the United States, the interest portion of debt service that businesses pay on loans is treated as an expense for tax purposes. The amount of interest expense reduces taxable income and thus the amount of income tax owed. This reduction in income tax owed is called a **tax effect.**

To calculate the true cost of capital, the **weighted average cost of capital** (WACC) method is used as shown below:

$\text{WACC} = w_d\, k_d\, (1 - T) + w_e\, k_e$, and

Weight of debt $= w_d$

Cost of debt $= k_d\, (1 - T)$

Tax rate of business $= T$

Tax effect $= (1 - T)$

Weighted cost of debt $= w_d\, k_d\, (1 - T)$

Weight of equity $= w_e$

Cost of equity $= k_e$

Weighted cost of equity $= w_e\, k_e$

Let us use some of the information provided in Illustration 6-1 to complete the calculation of the weighted average cost of capital. Because the restaurant entrepreneur used $100,000 of debt and another $100,000 of equity, the weight of each is 50%. However, if she raised $80,000 in debt and $120,000 in equity, the weight of debt would be 40% and the weight of equity would be 60% as shown in Illustration 6-2.

To continue the weighted cost of capital calculation, assuming the tax rate is 20%, the weight of debt is 40%, and the weight of equity is 60%, the weighted cost of capital would be 15.2%, as shown in Illustration 6-3.

FINANCIAL LEVERAGE

Why borrow money in the first place? The answer to this question is easy: You borrow money because your cost of debt is almost always less than your cost of equity. This is true because equity investors demand a greater return on their capital than lenders due to the greater risk involved for the investors. With this in mind, when raising capital, you should strive to maximize the amount of debt you can borrow and minimize the amount of equity you need. The more debt you borrow, the less equity you need and the greater the return on investment you will achieve for both you and your investor. This is called **financial leverage,** or leveraging your equity.

If debt is less expensive than equity, why not use 100% debt to avoid having to bring on an equity investor? The answer is that no lender today will loan you 100% of your project cost; therefore, you need an equity investor to bridge the gap between the amount you can borrow and the total amount of capital you need for your project. Depending on how risky a lender perceives your business opportunity to be, he may loan you as little as 10% to 20% of your total capital requirement—or nothing at all.

Total capitalization = $200,000

If debt and equity are each $100,000, the weights would be:

Weight of debt = $100,000/$200,000 = 0.5 or 50%

Weight of equity = $100,000/$200,000 = 0.5 or 50%

If the entrepreneur put together a financing plan calling for $80,000 of debt and $120,000 of equity, then the weights would be:

Weight of debt = $80,000/$200,000 = 0.4 or 40%

Weight of equity = $120,000/$200,000 = 0.6 or 60%

ILLUSTRATION 6-2
Weights of Debt and Equity

ILLUSTRATION 6-3
Weighted Average Cost of Capital

Weight of debt = 0.4

Cost of debt = 10% (1–0.2)

Tax rate of business = 0.2

Tax effect = 0.8

Weighted cost of debt = (0.4)(10%)(0.8)

Weight of equity = 0.6

Cost of equity = 20%

Weighted cost of equity = (0.6)(20%)

WACC = (0.4)(10%)(0.8) + (0.6)(20%)

= 3.2% + 12%

= 15.2%

An outside equity investor can also be of value to you if he agrees to personally guarantee the bank loan, provide additional collateral for your loan, or place unencumbered cash deposits in the bank that is making your loan.

In the end, remember that the mix of capital that is best for you depends on your projected cash flow, how comfortable your lender is with your deal, and how big a risk taker you are. The more debt you can borrow, the less equity you will need, and the higher your **return on investment** (ROI) will be. On the other hand, an aggressive use of debt results in a larger debt service obligation. This is fine as long as your business generates enough cash flow to pay your debt service. However, even when revenues decline, debt service still must be paid. Using debt is a good thing, but using too much debt can be risky. The more debt you obligate your company to service, the greater risk you run of having your creditors force you into bankruptcy. **Bankruptcy** occurs when your liabilities exceed your assets and you are unable to meet your current financial obligations. A conservative mix of debt and equity for a start-up business is strongly recommended.

COST AND MIX OF CAPITAL FOR HOTELS AND RESTAURANTS

Real estate lenders view hotels and restaurants more as businesses than real estate. Therefore, they tend to perceive them as riskier than other types of real estate loans. This perceived higher risk translates into a higher interest rate that is charged to hotels and restaurants than to office buildings, shopping centers, and other traditional types of real estate. The added perceived risk also impacts the mix of capital for a hospitality project. Today, lenders require between 40% and 50% of a hotel's project cost to be financed with equity, and even more for a restaurant.

This translates into a higher WACC for the sponsor of the project. The more you can apply financial leverage to your deal and skew the mix to debt versus equity, the lower your WACC and the higher your ROI.

ADVANTAGES OF DEBT FINANCING

The advantages of debt far outweigh the disadvantages. Because the cost of debt is almost always lower than equity, applying financial leverage to a deal can significantly increase its ROI. As noted earlier in this chapter, financial leverage is the degree to which a business utilizes debt to finance growth. Illustration 6-4 illustrates how the use of financial leverage can increase ROI.

Another benefit associated with debt is its income tax effect. The government classifies interest as an expense of business. As a result, businesses can deduct all the interest associated with loans to reduce their taxable income. Recalling the weighted average cost of capital discussion highlighted in Illustration 6-3, the tax effect reduced the cost of debt from 10% to 8% ($10\% \times (1 - 20\%)$), as the tax rate was 20%.

If your company's interest expense for the year was $100,000 and your company is in the 20% income tax bracket, its cost of debt would be reduced by 20% of $100,000, or $20,000.

Illustration 6-5 compares two companies. Company A is financed with 100% equity, and Company B is financed with 100% debt. Company A has no debt and therefore no interest payments. This essentially increases earnings before taxes and, as a result, more income tax is levied. You might think that the 100% equity-financed Company A is better off than Company B, as it has $210,000 of net income versus Company B's $140,000. However, while Company A has no significant debt, it has many outside equity investors who share the $210,000. On the

---

If you require $100,000 of capital and you project annual cash flow of $10,000:

1. What would your ROI be if you raise 100% of the capital as equity?

2. What would your ROI be if you raised 50% of the capital as equity, 50% of the capital as debt, and your annual debt service payment was 5% of your loan?

100% Equity

• $10,000 of cash flow divided by $100,000 of equity = ROI of 10%

50% Equity & 50% Debt

• $10,000 of gross cash flow less $2,500 of debt service = $7,500 of net cash flow

• $7,500 of net cash flow divided by $50,000 of equity = ROI of 15%

ILLUSTRATION 6-4
Use of Leverage

	Financed with 100% equity	Financed with 100% debt
Revenues	$600,000	$600,000
All costs	300,000	300,000
Interest	0	100,000
Earnings before income tax	300,000	200,000
Income Tax (30%)	90,000	60,000
Net Income	$210,000	$140,000
Tax savings is $90,000 – $60,000 = $30,000		

ILLUSTRATION 6-5
Tax Savings with Interest Payments

other hand, after paying its debt service, Company B is left with the entire $140,000 for the founder of the company.

Another advantage of debt financing is that it is normally easier to obtain than equity, and there are more potential sources to approach. As long as the borrower perseveres and is not afraid of rejection, she can approach many lenders seeking sound, financially feasible projects for investment of their funds.

Using debt also does not dilute ownership like equity does. When a business raises capital using the equity option, it is selling part of the business to the new investors.

ADVANTAGES OF EQUITY FINANCING

While the cost of equity is higher than the cost of debt and is harder to raise than debt, there are advantages to equity financing. As much as the owners of a business may not want to take on a new partner and dilute the business's cash flow, there are advantages to having an equity partner rather than a major creditor. Creditors demand their debt service payments be made on time, while partners are usually more patient. If, for some reason, a business is not doing well and unable to make its debt service payments on time, the lender may foreclose on the loan or take other actions against the company. Owners, on the other hand, are partners. If business is poor, they may not receive their portion of the cash flow for a few months, but they cannot close down the business. Partners can also add experience, knowledge, and expertise to the business. In some cases, finding one or more partners may be the only way to get the deal financed if the perceived risk of the venture is high.

EFFECTIVE COST OF DEBT

Business owners can use debt to their advantage and retain a larger percentage of their business's profits for themselves. Be aware, however, of **variable rate loans,** which start out with a low interest rate that escalates over time. While the low initial rate may look attractive, remember that as interest rates increase, your business's cash flow must grow at a higher rate than the increase in the interest rate over time in order for you to stay ahead of the game. Also, be careful of hidden charges that may be attached to a loan agreement. Always look at the **effective borrowing rate** rather than the stated interest rate. Some lenders charge a fee to make the loan and deduct the fee from the loan proceeds. This raises your effective rate of interest and reduces the amount of money you actually receive.

Loan Terminology

As a hospitality manager, you should be familiar with the types of loans available to your company, understand their characteristics, and know where to go to borrow money. As you advance professionally within a company or form a company of your own, the more you will need to know about debt and how to secure it. First, let us define basic loan terms.

PRINCIPAL, TERM, INTEREST, AND AMORTIZATION RATE

The **principal** is the amount of money you borrow, **term** means the number of months or years you are given to repay the loan, and **interest** is the amount you pay to the lender. Interest is often expressed as a percentage of the principal. **Principal repayment** is the portion of your debt service payment that reduces the amount of money you owe to your lender. The remainder of your debt service payment is also known as the *interest*. The **amortization rate** is the number of years on which your debt service payment calculation is based. Illustration 6-6 shows a loan of $100,000 with an annual interest of 10% paid over a three-year period and over a five-year period.

As you can see in Illustration 6-6, the longer the amount of time you have to pay back a loan, the lower your debt service payment will be. In the three-year scenario, the debt service payment is $40,211 per year, whereas the debt service payment on the five-year schedule is $26,379 per year. Note that even though it will take you longer to repay your loan in the five-year scenario, the lower debt service payment is more than worth it. An annual debt service of $26,000 versus $40,000 is much preferred, especially if your are just starting a new business.

COLLATERAL AND PERSONAL GUARANTEE

Most real estate loans require collateral. **Collateral** is an asset that is offered to the lender as loan insurance. If you fail to make your regular debt service payments, the lender has the right to foreclose on the loan and take ownership of the collateral. At times, a personal guarantee is also required by your lender. A **personal guarantee** is a written promise that if your business fails to make regular debt service payments, the signatory agrees to use his or her personal funds to make the debt service payments.

Loan compounded for 3 years				
Year	Payment	Principal	Interest	Balance
1	40,211.48	30,211.48	10,000.00	69,788.52
2	40,211.48	33,232.63	6,978.85	36,555.89
3	40,211.48	36,555.89	3,655.59	0.00
Total	120,634.44	100,000.00	20,634.44	
Loan compounded for 5 years				
Year	Payment	Principal	Interest	Balance
1	26,379.75	16,379.75	10,000.00	83,620.25
2	26,379.75	18,017.72	8,362.03	65,602.53
3	26,379.75	19,819.50	6,560.25	45,783.03
4	26,379.75	20,801.45	4,578.30	23,981.59
5	26,379.75	23,981.59	2,398.16	0.00
Total	131,898.75	100,000.00	31,898.75	

ILLUSTRATION 6-6
Loan Payment or Amortization Schedule

PREPAYMENT PENALTY, BULLET LOAN, AND BALLOON PAYMENT

What if interest rates fall and you want to refinance your loan? Some loan documents contain a **prepayment penalty** requiring the borrower to pay the total amount of interest that would be owed to the lender for the full term of the loan, even if the loan is paid off early. This penalty discourages you from prepaying your loan and assures the lender that even if you do, he will receive the equivalent of the amount of interest that you would have paid him over the full term of the loan.

Because hotels, restaurants, and clubs are largely real estate in nature, let us focus on a few types of real estate loans. Today, the lengths of hospitality loans are short term but offer long-term amortization rates. For example, if the amortization rate is twenty-five years on a five-year loan, debt service is based on a twenty-five-year repayment schedule. However, at the end of five years, you are required to repay or refinance 100% of the outstanding loan balance. This type of loan is called a **bullet loan.** Your lender figuratively holds a gun to your head.

Finally, have you ever heard the term **balloon payment?** A balloon payment is the payment due at the end of the term of the loan that is equal to the balance of the principal still owed. Balloon payments occur when the amortization rate is longer than the term of the loan. This is usually a large sum, as the debt service payments of a short-term loan are composed primarily of interest. This type of loan is attractive to businesses that ramp up slowly and have limited amounts of cash flow during the first few years of business.

Types of Loans

Depending on your capital need, a wide variety of loan types is available to your company, including business, construction, mini-perm, permanent, mezzanine, convertible, SBA, CDC (504) program, and even leases.

BUSINESS LOAN

A **business loan** is used to start a company or to expand it. It is based primarily on the personal merits of the borrower, the merits of the business plan, and the financial strength of the borrower. Normally, no specific collateral is involved other than the assets of the company. Also, the more the owners of the business are willing and able to deposit unencumbered cash in the bank lending the money, the more favorable the loan terms offered will be.

CONSTRUCTION LOAN

A **construction loan** is a one- to two-year interest-only loan used to build, expand, acquire, or renovate a physical facility. A construction loan is a form of mortgage loan whereby the asset being constructed, acquired, or renovated is provided as collateral for the loan. The asset is said to be mortgaged.

Today, the amount of a construction loan is usually about 60% of the total project cost and therefore requires 40% as equity. The mortgaged asset is the collateral for the loan. A personal guarantee from the borrower is almost always required.

Prior to funding a construction loan, the construction lender requires a **take-out commitment** from the take-out lender, who agrees to provide the permanent financing once the project is successfully completed. This is a written promise from the take-out lender that he will repay the construction loan at the end of its term as long as the project meets the specifications the borrower and construction lender agree to in advance of the funding of the loan.

A construction lender can also serve as the permanent lender. In this case, the construction loan is said to roll into the permanent loan when the project is completed. The interest rate on the construction loan is usually slightly higher than the interest rate on the permanent loan, as the construction lender assumes the risk that the project may not be completed.

PERMANENT AND MINI-PERM LOANS

Today, a **permanent loan** is not really permanent. Thirty years ago, the term *permanent loan* was based on the useful life of the asset. Today the length or term of what is still called a *permanent loan* is about ten years. A hybrid of a permanent loan is a **mini-perm** loan. As you might surmise, the term of a mini-perm loan is shorter than the term of a permanent loan. The average term of a mini-perm loan is about five years.

The only differences between a mini-perm and a permanent loan are the term and, occasionally, the interest rate if it is fixed rather than floating. A **fixed interest rate** remains constant during the term of the loan, while a **floating rate** fluctuates with the market rate of interest. You can control the fluctuation by negotiating a **ceiling** and a **floor,** or the maximum and minimum amount the interest rate can move up or down during the term of the loan.

A permanent loan sometimes carries a slightly higher interest rate than a mini-perm to compensate the lender for a possible rise in market interest rates during the longer term of the loan. Both mini-perm and permanent loans repay or take-out construction loans, have amortization rates of between fifteen and twenty-five years, use the subject asset as collateral, and often have prepayment penalties. These loans also usually do not require the personal guarantee of the borrower and are therefore called non-recourse loans. A **non-recourse loan** limits the lender's repayment options to the assets of the business and the collateral at risk, as opposed to a **recourse loan,** which allows the lender to also seek repayment from the borrower's personal assets.

MEZZANINE LOAN

A **mezzanine loan** is a second layer of debt that fills the gap between the total project cost, the amount of the first mortgage loan, and the equity capital to be invested. The mezzanine lender, with the permission of the first mortgage lender, may receive the second right to the first mortgage lender's collateral in the event of a loan default. More commonly, however, the borrower's equity or ownership interest in the deal serves as the mezzanine lender's only recourse should a default on the mezzanine loan occur. For example, if the borrower defaults on the first mortgage, the mezzanine lender will also want the right to **cure** the default or pay the debt service on the first mortgage on the borrower's behalf and assume ownership of the deal and the responsibility for the first mortgage.

Because the risk of a mezzanine loan is much higher than the risk of a first mortgage loan, the associated interest rate is also much higher. In fact, the cost of a mezzanine loan is usually equal to the return on investment or hurdle rate that an equity investor demands. Today, this rate is between 15% and 20%, depending on the perceived risk of the investment.

What often happens, however, is the mezzanine lender agrees to accept a **coupon rate,** or lower interest rate, for the first few years of the loan, or until the project generates a sufficient cash flow to pay the full interest rate due. Once an adequate level of cash flow is generated to service the full amount of interest, the mezzanine lender is paid the difference between the interest he should have received during the first few years of the loan and the coupon rate actually paid.

The term of a mezzanine loan runs concurrently with the term of the mini-perm or permanent loan and does not contain a prepayment penalty. In fact, a borrower's strategy is often to pay off the mezzanine loan as soon as possible.

THE REAL DEAL

Why mezzanine financing? Since the 1980s, hotel lenders have become more sophisticated, take fewer risks, and lend a smaller percentage of the total project cost. In today's economy, most loans range between 50% to 60% of the total project cost, leaving a significant gap to be filled by equity. By using mezzanine loans with terms of three to seven years, entrepreneurs are able to finance projects and generate favorable financial returns for the owners. *Note:* Mezzanine debt is more expensive than regular debt, as mezzanine lenders want a higher return on the money they provide. Thus, mezzanine loans serve an important role in hospitality financing today.

Source: Gose, J. "Why Borrowers Are Flocking to Mezz Debt." National Real Estate Investor, p. 46–49, March 2004.

CONVERTIBLE LOAN

A **convertible loan** is a hybrid of debt and equity. It is a loan that can be converted to equity at certain points at the request of the source providing the capital. The purpose of a convertible loan is to limit the short-term risk for the capital source while providing the source with the ability to convert the loan to equity once the project begins generating a favorable cash flow.

Convertible loans are often used to encourage potential equity investors to provide capital for deals they normally would perceive as too risky. Convertible loans are essentially loans that will likely be converted to equity in the future.

THE REAL DEAL

SBA loans are for small businesses. If the government reduces the SBA's budget, who would be impacted? Small restaurateurs, of course, but also hoteliers, especially those who own limited-service hotels. Associations such as the American Hotel and Lodging Association (AH&LA) and the Asian American Hotel Owners Association (AAHOA) have worked with hotel franchise companies to lobby Washington lawmakers to look out for the interests of small business owners. Visit the websites of the AH&LA and AAHOA and see what they do to protect the interests of entrepreneurs.

SMALL BUSINESS ADMINISTRATION (SBA 7(A)) LOANS

A **Small Business Administration loan (SBA 7(a))** provides funding for start-up ventures as well as existing businesses. The maximum amount of a SBA 7(a) loan is $2 million. The borrower can use the proceeds for working capital, expansion, renovation, purchase of real estate, purchase of equipment, new construction, or the acquisition of an existing business. SBA 7(a) loans can be either short term or long term and offer a below-market interest rate, as a large portion of the money is loaned to the local bank by the federal government at a very low interest rate. Private SBA-licensed companies fund the remaining portion of the loan.

CERTIFIED DEVELOPMENT COMPANY (504) LOAN PROGRAM

A **CDC (504)** or federal 504 loan is backed by a loan program created to help small businesses finance the purchase of fixed assets such as land, buildings, and equipment. A major advantage of a federal 504 loan is that the borrower is required to provide only 10% of the total project cost in equity. This is possible due to partnerships between the federal government and local commercial banks. The federal government provides 40% of the total project cost, while the local commercial bank provides 50% of the cost. The interest rate is below market due to the favorable rate charged by the federal government. To qualify for a federal 504 loan, your company must have a net worth under $7 million and average annual earnings for the prior two years of under $3 million.

LEASES

While technically not a loan, the leasing of physical facilities and equipment is a form of debt financing. **Leases** require a fixed or variable monthly lease payment, which is the equivalent of debt service. The leased asset or improvements made to the facility serve as collateral. A lease is normally for a fixed term with options to renew. Equipment leases also offer the lessee the opportunity to purchase the equipment at the end of the lease term for the equipment's estimated salvage value.

Sources of Loans

While most lenders provide a variety of loans, most tend to specialize in one or two types. The following are the primary sources for hospitality loans:

- ■ Local and national banks
- ■ Small business investment companies
- ■ Business and industrial development organizations
- ■ Insurance companies
- ■ Pension funds
- ■ Private credit companies

- Individuals
- Venture capitalists

LOCAL AND NATIONAL BANKS

When people think about borrowing money, their local bank is usually the first lending source on their list. Local banks specialize in short-term loans, including construction and business loans. National banks focus more on longer-term loans, including mini-perms and permanent real estate loans.

SMALL BUSINESS INVESTMENT COMPANIES

Small Business Investment Companies (SBIC) are entities licensed by the Small Business Administration to grant SBA 7(a) loans to small business entrepreneurs. These are privately organized and privately managed investment firms. They serve as partners with the federal government and private lenders to provide financing opportunities.

BUSINESS AND INDUSTRIAL DEVELOPMENT ORGANIZATIONS

Business and Industrial Development Corporations, or BIDCOs, fund CDC(504) loans. These companies obtain the money they lend by selling bonds to investors in the private capital market. BIDCOs may also make mezzanine loans.

INSURANCE COMPANIES

While many people don't think of insurance companies as sources of financing, the money insurance companies receive as premiums must be wisely invested to generate funds to pay insurance claims. Some insurance companies provide construction loans, but most specialize in mini-perm and permanent real estate loans.

PENSION FUNDS

Much like insurance companies, pension funds also need to invest the money employees contribute so that when the individuals retire, there is sufficient money to provide for their retirement. Like insurance companies, pension funds specialize in mini-perm and permanent loans.

PRIVATE CREDIT COMPANIES

Private credit companies specialize in mini-perm, permanent, mezzanine, and convertible loans. Some private credit companies also have a leasing division, although their interest rates are often quite high.

INDIVIDUALS

High-net-worth individuals look for favorable returns on their money; therefore, they are another source for loans. Family, friends, associates, and relations are often approached to provide loans for start-up ventures.

VENTURE CAPITALISTS

Venture capital funds focus on start-up business ventures with significant upside potential. Normally, a group of wealthy investors is assembled by an investment banker to form a venture capital fund. The fund is managed by the investment banker, who decides where to invest the money. While most venture capital funds are equity oriented, some provide convertible loans.

See Illustration 6-7 for a summary of the various sources hospitality companies can approach for loans.

Sources/Loans	Business	Con-struction	Mini-Perm	Perm.	Mezza-nine	Conver-tible	SBA 7(a)	CDC (504)
Local Banks	X	X	X					
National Banks			X	X				
Small Business Investment Companies							X	
Business and Industrial Development Organizations					X			X
Insurance Companies			X	X		X		
Pension Funds			X	X		X		
Private Credit Companies			X	X	X	X		
Individuals			X	X		X		
Venture Capitalists						X		

ILLUSTRATION 6-7
Sources of Loans

Equity

There are several other important things you need to know about equity. First, equity must be raised before debt. Your lender will not loan money to a business without strong assurance that you have an adequate amount of equity committed to fund your project. Second, equity is harder to raise than debt, and more costly. With this in mind, if at all possible, leverage your project as much as you can until you reach the optimal level of debt. Third, treat your outside equity partners well. If you do, they will be there when you need them on your next project. Last, but not least, invest your equity wisely. A good track record is critical to your future success and your ability to raise capital for your next project.

TYPES OF EQUITY

Cash is the most common type of equity, but there are several other forms that your lender will view as equity when evaluating a loan request.

CASH. Some amount of cash equity is necessary to open and operate a business. Therefore, lenders examine the amount of cash equity a business has committed or invested before evaluating a loan request. Remember, cash is and always will be king.

LAND. Land is often the single most expensive item in a project budget. Sometimes owners agree to contribute land in return for an equity position in the project. If a business is seeking equity and a landowner agrees to contribute land as equity for the project, this could be a win-win opportunity for both the business and the landowner. The amount of equity invested by the landowner is based on the market value of the land.

THE REAL DEAL

Leasing is a good financing option for restaurateurs, especially for equipment financing. As of 2003, under IRS Section 179, a company can write off up to $100,000 in income when entering into a lease agreement. Major issues to consider when entering into a lease agreement are the terms, option to buy, tax effects, advance payment requirements, and financial limits. It is also prudent to research the terms of several leasing companies in order to obtain the best package for your business. In addition, the servicing agreement is an important item. You do not want to end up with a piece of equipment that will cost too much to service.

Source: Tyrell, L. A. "Finance Sources." *Restaurant Finance Monitor* 15(5) (May 20, 2004): 4.

LEASES. A popular equity financing strategy for restaurateurs is a building lease. If the restaurateur is willing to sign a long-term lease, she may be able to negotiate several months of free rent from the landlord and a build-out allowance to renovate the facility if the landlord really

ILLUSTRATION 6-8
Investing Land as Equity

values her as a tenant. Sometimes lenders count the value of these concessions as equity for loan purposes.

EXISTING BUILDINGS. An existing building can be a form of equity. For example, if a business is contemplating acquiring a building in need of major renovation, the owner of the building might agree to contribute the building in its existing condition to the business in return for an ownership position in the deal if the business agrees to finance the renovation. As in the case of contributed land, the amount of equity is based on the market value of the building.

GOVERNMENT SUBSIDIES. The government can provide financial assistance to a new project that a lender considers as equity. A **government subsidy** can take the form of tax abatements, training grants, or project infrastructure. A **tax abatement** is a written authorization given to a developer by a local taxing authority that exempts the property from having to pay property or other taxes for a specified period. By avoiding the payment of these taxes, the cash flow from the project increases, and more money is available for debt service. A **training grant** is a cash contribution from a governmental authority to a developer for the training of certain members of the local community for positions in the new enterprise. The grant is usually restricted to training local citizens who live within a certain distance from the project and consists of a fixed sum of money per person trained. **Project infrastructure** is construction needed to connect a new building with existing public facilities and/or utilities. It can also be related to the construction of a new highway exit, a new curb cut, a new sidewalk, or a new parking structure. When a local government authority funds these projects, the cost is often treated as equity by a lender analyzing a particular loan.

SOURCES OF EQUITY

Equity can be raised from a variety of sources. The most common are individuals, venture capital funds, insurance companies, pension funds, existing owners of assets, government, construction companies, and management companies.

INDIVIDUALS. Just as you can ask family, friends, and acquaintances to lend money to your business, you can also ask them to become owners of your venture. Some wealthy individuals may want to limit their risk and will elect to provide debt financing, but those who are less risk averse may want to share in the business's upside potential and elect to provide equity in the business.

INSURANCE COMPANIES AND PENSION FUNDS. While insurance companies and pension funds make loans, they also invest equity. These companies seek opportunities where they can be owners and achieve a higher return on their investment.

VENTURE CAPITALISTS. While venture capital funds occasionally provide debt financing, equity investments in businesses are their primary objective. Venture capitalists are risk-takers and will support projects that offer high ROIs.

GOVERNMENT. More and more, both state and local governments are becoming equity partners in hotel projects. Many cities are either redeveloping or rehabilitating their downtown areas to attract new residents and tourists. They are building convention hotels and convention centers to attract conventions, corporate meetings, and the incentive travel market. These local and state governments are providing not only tax incentives and subsidies but also cash and other forms of equity to motivate developers to build new hotels in their cities.

EXISTING OWNERS OF ASSETS. Although existing owners of assets may not be ideal partners, they can be a valuable source of equity for hospitality companies. This is especially true when dealing with owners of land or buildings. Depending on the owner's financial needs, there may be an opportunity to persuade him to become a partner in the business instead of having to use valuable capital to buy his land or building.

THE REAL DEAL

As surprising as it may sound, one can obtain equity capital from the Salvation Army. A 124-suite hotel bearing the Homewood Suites brand will be built in Salt Lake City in partnership with the Salvation Army. The land on which the hotel will be built was the location of a soup kitchen and thrift store. Both were relocated, leaving a parcel of land for the project. In return for contributing the land, the Salvation Army will own 55% of the cash flow generated by the hotel. The money will be used to support the Salvation Army's homeless and family services in the Salt Lake City area. This is a project that wins on all counts—Homewood Suites has a new hotel, Salt Lake City's downtown area can be redeveloped, tourists have another lodging option in the downtown area, and the Salvation Army has cash flow to fund its much-needed projects.

Source: "Unique Agreement with Non-profit Salvation Army Allows for Construction of Homewood Suites by Hilton in Salt Lake City." http://www.hotel-online.com/News/PR2004_2nd/June04_HomewoodSLC.html.

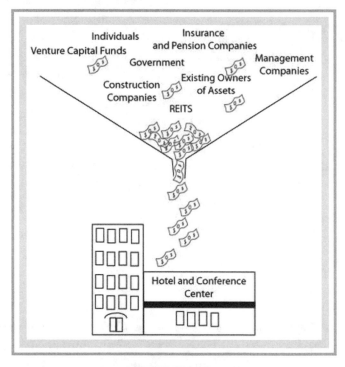

ILLUSTRATION 6-9
Sources of Debt and Equity Capital

CONSTRUCTION AND MANAGEMENT COMPANIES. Although you may consider construction and management companies as companies you pay to build or manage your hotel, they can, in some cases, become your equity partners as well. Construction and management companies are often providers of what is known as **sliver equity.** Sliver equity is a relatively small amount of equity that companies agree to invest in return for being selected as the contractor or the manager of the hotel.

INVESTMENT BANKS. Investment banks are companies that work with businesses to raise both debt and equity capital. Wall Street investment bankers normally deal only with large transactions of $100 million or more and therefore are not a primary source of capital for small businesses. There are, however, regional investment banking firms that work on smaller capital transactions.

FEATURE STORY

KEMMONS WILSON

Kemmons Wilson was Memphis' most famous entrepreneur. A builder, developer, super-salesman, and wheeler-dealer, he built the first Holiday Inn in 1952 on Highway 70, just outside of Memphis. Although he promised his wife, Dorothy, that he would build 400 Holiday Inns, he accomplished much more.

Kemmons was a master when it came to raising capital. John Martin, his first attorney, liked to joke that "Kemmons Wilson is the biggest borrower in history." Indeed, according to Kemmons, he borrowed more than $1 billion during his career—and paid it all back including interest.

His first Holiday Inn was financed with a first-mortgage take-out commitment from National General Life, an insurance company based in Galveston, Texas. With that commitment, he was able to secure a $325,000 construction loan from First Tennessee Bank to build the hotel.

To reach his goal of developing 400 Holiday Inns, Kemmons needed a large source of equity capital. Utilizing his excellent selling skills, he convinced Wallace Johnson to help him market Holiday Inn franchises to members of the National Home Builders Association, of which Wallace was the vice president. While this strategy proved less successful than anticipated, it provided Kemmons with valuable experience in raising equity from wealthy doctors, lawyers, and investors, which was an important key to Holiday Inns' explosive growth.

In 1957, with approximately fifty Holiday Inns in his chain, Kemmons took his lodging company public. By the fifth year, Kemmons fulfilled his 400-Inn promise with the opening of a Holiday Inn in Vincennes, Indiana. By the time he retired from Holiday Inns in 1979, the company's annual revenues exceeded $1 billion, with 1,759 Holiday Inns in more than fifty countries. This amounted to twice as many rooms as its closest competitor.

Here are Kemmons Wilson's Twenty Tips for Success:

1. Work only half a day. It makes no difference which half—it can be either the first twelve hours or the last twelve hours.
2. Work is the master key that opens the door to all opportunities.
3. Mental attitude plays a far more important role in a person's success or failure than mental capacity.
4. Remember that we all climb the ladder of success one step at a time.
5. There are two ways to get to the top of an oak tree. One way is to sit on an acorn and wait; the other is to climb it.
6. Do not be afraid of taking a chance. Remember that a broken watch is exactly right at least twice every twenty-four hours.
7. The secret to success is not in doing what one likes but in liking what one does.
8. Eliminate from your vocabulary the words "I don't think I can" and substitute, "I know I can."
9. In evaluating a career, put opportunity ahead of security.
10. Remember that success requires half luck and half brains.
11. A person has to take risks to achieve.
12. People who never do more than they are paid for never get paid for anything more than they do.
13. No job is too hard as long as you are smart enough to find someone else to do it for you.
14. Opportunity comes often. It knocks as often as you have an ear trained to hear it, an eye trained to see it, a hand trained to grasp it, and a head trained to use it.
15. You cannot procrastinate—in two days, tomorrow will be yesterday.
16. Sell your wristwatch and buy an alarm clock.
17. A successful person realizes his personal responsibility for self-motivation. He starts himself because he possesses the key to his own ignition switch.
18. Don't worry. You can't change the past, but you sure can ruin the present by worrying over the future. Remember that half the things we worry about never happen, and the other half are going to happen anyway. So why worry?
19. It is not how much you have but how much you enjoy that creates happiness.
20. Believe in God and obey the Ten Commandments.

SOURCE

Wilson, K., and R. Kerr. *Half Luck and Half Brain*, 1st ed. Nashville, Tenn.: Hambleton-Hill, 1996.

HOTEL FINANCING TRENDS AND SCHEMES

Before we move on to learning about investment analysis and how to procure favorable debt and equity financing, let us review how hotels were financed during the 1970s and 1980s and explore a few new innovative hospitality financing vehicles.

The Golden Age of Hotel Financing

The period between 1975 and 1986 was a boom time for hotel real estate developers. The nation was coming out of a recession, the economy was beginning to grow again, and business in general was getting better. Financing for new hotel projects was plentiful, as both lenders and investors sensed that the real estate cycle was taking a turn for the better. Lenders were anxious to make loans, and investors were equally anxious to provide equity for developers to build new projects.

Hotel developers were literally wooed by lenders and investors and were able to choose between competing capital sources for their financing. Because loans, in those days, were solely based on a percentage of value, determined by an appraisal with little consideration of cost, developers were often able to secure debt financing in excess of the project's actual cost. This excess funding, of course, went directly into the pockets of the developers.

Savings and Loans

To fuel the financing fires even more, the savings and loan industry convinced the federal government it should be allowed to make commercial real estate loans in addition to residential loans and should also be allowed to own commercial real estate. This provided a boost to the economy and another means for real estate developers to secure funds, and it further increased the availability of financing for new hotel projects. While members of the savings and loan industry were somewhat knowledgeable about commercial lending, they knew little about real estate and therefore did not understand the cyclical nature of the real estate industry.

Investment Tax Credits

The federal government, in an effort to kick-start the economic recovery, offered investment tax credits to those who agreed to develop new real estate projects as part of the Economic Stimulus Bill of 1982. The tax credits, which were calculated as a percentage of the total development cost, could be directly deducted from the amount of personal income tax owners of the real estate owed the federal government. This made equity capital even more available, as many individuals looked for projects in which to invest their money in an effort to reduce the amount of the personal income tax they owed.

Influx of Foreign Capital

During the late 1980s, certain international financial markets were not performing well. As a result, investors began to look for alternate opportunities to invest their funds. U.S. hotels became attractive to many international investors, as their projected return on investment was higher than investment opportunities overseas. Japan, in particular, became a major player during this buying spree of hotel assets in the United States.

Accelerated Depreciation

Next, the federal government allowed real estate developers to use accelerated depreciation methods to calculate taxable income. The faster the real estate assets were depreciated, the more paper or non-cash losses were created. It became legal for these non-cash losses to be directly passed on to the owners of the real estate. This dramatically reduced the amount of the personal income tax they owed to the federal government.

Real Estate Tax Shelters

As clever businesspeople quickly realized that these new investment tax credits and paper losses had significant value to wealthy individuals in high income tax brackets, they began to create limited partnerships to develop new hotels. The deal sponsor packaged a new hotel project, found a savings and loan or traditional commercial lender to provide as much as 100% non-recourse financing for the project, and then sold partnership units to wealthy individuals to shelter their taxable personal income. These limited partnerships were called **tax shelters.**

Some creative businesspeople even opened their own savings and loans to provide debt and equity financing for their projects. New real estate was being developed at a frantic pace due to the vast amounts of debt and equity capital available rather than in response to market demand.

The Tax Reform Act of 1986

The Tax Reform Act of 1986 brought new real estate development to a screeching halt. The act effectively eliminated tax shelters, accelerated depreciation, and prohibited savings and loans from owning real estate. It stated that in order for limited partners to apply non-cash or paper losses against their personal taxable income, they must personally guarantee the real estate loan.

What ensued was an unprecedented, monumental financial crisis in the United States. The crisis was a result of the thousands of real estate projects that went bankrupt because they were not economically feasible in the first place. Savings and loans and other commercial lenders began foreclosing on these loans by the thousands.

Because these assets were not generating cash flow, they had little economic value and could not be sold for anywhere near the face value of their mortgages. In addition, because savings and loans were now prohibited from owning real estate, they were forced to attempt to sell their foreclosed assets in a market that had a glut of non-cash-flowing real estate. As a result, the entire savings and loan industry collapsed.

The Resolution Trust Corporation (RTC)

In 1986, the federal government had no choice but to step into the crisis and bail out the savings and loan industry. A federal government agency named the Resolution Trust Corporation (RTC) was formed for this purpose. The task of the RTC was to assume ownership of all failed savings and loans, sell the loans to commercial banks and other investment groups, sell the foreclosed assets to investors, and recoup some of the money U.S. citizens had lost by placing cash deposits, and, in many cases, their life savings, in the coffers of the savings and loans.

While the RTC was successful in selling most of the loans and foreclosed assets, they were sold for a very small percentage of their original value. To facilitate the sale of these assets, and to motivate potential buyers to acquire them, the RTC even provided loans up to 90% of the purchase price at below-market interest rates. Ironically, many of the original developers of these assets ended up buying them back for pennies on the dollar with favorable federal government financing.

New Financing Schemes

More recently, several new financing schemes have become popular, including real estate investment conduits, hotel REITs, timeshares, condominium hotels, and mixed-use developments.

REAL ESTATE MORTGAGE INVESTMENT CONDUITS

As you might surmise, for many years after 1986, little new real estate was developed. Investors who wanted to own real estate could acquire underperforming real estate assets for far less money than the cost of constructing new ones.

Their strategy was to acquire the assets for as little as 25% of replacement cost, renovate them, reposition them, turn them into profitable, cash-flowing assets, and then sell them at huge profits. Thus, a demand was created for debt financing to acquire these underperforming, non-RTC assets

Wall Street investment banking firms seized the opportunity and created **real estate mortgage investment conduits,** or REMICs. REMICs made mortgage loans and sold them as **commercial mortgage-backed securities** (CMBS) primarily to financial institutions that formerly made real estate loans directly to real estate developers

Here's how the conduits worked:

1. Wall Street investment banking firms provided the initial seed capital to form the conduit.
2. Local and regional U.S. lenders and mortgage brokers originated the mortgage loans. In other words, they identified companies that needed debt to acquire real estate assets.
3. The Wall Street firms analyzed each loan request and funded those they deemed worthy of investment.
4. Once a pool of mortgages was accumulated, the Wall Street firm hired an outside rating agency to evaluate and rate each loan based on its risk of default.
5. The loans were then placed in packages and sold to investors in the form of commercial mortgage-backed securities.
6. After the loans closed, local firms serviced or monitored them on behalf of the owners of the CMBS.

Illustration 6-10 shows this process and illustrates how companies benefited from these mortgage-backed securities.

The advantage to the purchasers of the securities was that instead of making one loan and assuming 100% of the risk of that loan, for the same cash outlay they could purchase a small percentage of several loans and spread their risk.

The economics of the conduit worked like this:

1. The originator made a fee for identifying the borrower.
2. The borrower received financing from the investment banking firm.
3. The rating agency made a fee for rating each loan.
4. The servicing agent made a fee for monitoring the loan.
5. The institution that purchased the CMBS received interest on its investment and its investment back at the end of the term of the loan.

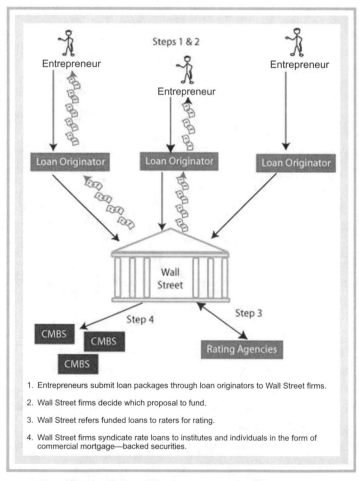

ILLUSTRATION 6-10
The Benefits of Mortgage-Backed Securities

6. The investment banking firm earned the difference between the interest rate paid by the borrower and the interest rate paid to the owners of the CMBSs.

The conduit system became popular during the 1990s and was relatively successful until it fell prey to the international financial crisis that hit the world markets in 1998 and the economic recession that followed. The banking crisis, caused by the financial problems in Russia, Brazil, and Asia, impacted the major U.S. financial institutions that had made investments in these countries.

A substantial number of these loans defaulted, which forced these institutions to curtail most of their lending activity. The lenders who remained in the market reduced the percentage they would loan for a project to between 50% and 60% of its actual cost. This placed an extra premium on equity and increased the need for mezzanine financing.

REAL ESTATE INVESTMENT TRUST (REIT)

The **real estate investment trust** (REIT) dates to the early 1880s. At that time, a REIT enabled individual investors to pool their capital, invest in commercial real estate, and avoid double taxation. In addition, a REIT provided investors with a professionally managed entity, a tradable liquid investment, and limited liability. The REIT law was revoked in the 1930s, which made all passive investments taxed first at the corporate level and also at the individual income level. The Real Estate Investment Trust Tax Provision of 1960 reestablished REITs and restored their special tax considerations. REITs once again became pass-through entities. The Tax Reform Act of 1986 allowed most REITs to directly manage their properties. Up to this time, a REIT was required to lease its property to a third party to manage. Hotels, however, were considered businesses and therefore did not qualify for this benefit. In 1993, REIT laws were modified to allow pension funds to invest in REITs. This set the stage for the significant growth REITs enjoyed during the mid- to late 1990s.

There are three categories of REITs:

- **Equity REITs,** which invest in and own properties. Their revenues are derived primarily from rental income.
- **Mortgage REITs,** which invest in mortgages and mortgage-related securities. Mortgage REITs derive their revenues from interest income.
- **Hybrid REITs,** which invest in both commercial properties and mortgages.

Approximately 96% of all REITs are equity REITs.

To qualify as a REIT and gain the favorable tax benefits offered by the REIT structure, an entity must comply with the following Internal Revenue Code provisions:

- It must be structured as a corporation or business trust.
- It must be managed by a board of directors or trustees.
- Shares must be fully transferable.
- It must have a minimum of 100 shareholders.

- Ninety-five percent of taxable income must be paid to shareholders as dividends.
- No more than 50% of shares outstanding may be held by fewer than five individuals.
- A minimum of 75% of the REIT's total assets must be in real estate.
- No more than 30% of annual gross income may be derived from the sale of real property held for less than four years.

Hotel equity REITs became popular in the early to mid-1990s. Their popularity was driven by Wall Street's discovery that a large number of hotels developed in the 1980s could be acquired at well below their replacement cost. These hotels often required renovation, better management, and market repositioning. After making the necessary capital improvements, rebranding the hotel, and obtaining qualified management, significant increases in profits and value could be achieved. Wall Street's strategy was to identify a small portfolio of hotels that could be acquired, create new companies structured as REITs to purchase these portfolios, orchestrate initial public offerings to raise equity from their largest institutional and high-net-worth clients, and lease the hotels to a qualified management company, often owned by the sponsor of the REIT. Because the hotels were financed by 100% equity, the REITs would then establish large lines of credit from major banks, acquire additional hotel portfolios and large individual hotels, lease these hotels to the affiliated or third-party management company, and raise additional public equity to pay off the debt. This process was then repeated, allowing the REITs to grow rapidly, and it worked very well as long as the REITs could acquire hotels at well below their replacement cost and raise new equity from public markets.

The first two hotel equity REITs to enter the hotel business were RFS Investors, Inc., and Starwood Lodging. RFS was created in August 1994 with a small portfolio of limited-service hotels and an initial public offering of $30 million. It began as a small, regional, limited-service hotel REIT based in Memphis, Tennessee. By 2001, RFS had grown to sixty hotels with over 9,000 rooms in twenty-four states and had upgraded its portfolio to include not only limited-service hotels but also Sheratons, Courtyards, and Residence Inns. Due to RFS's success, many other limited-service REITs were formed and enjoyed similar success. These included Equity Inns, Winston Hotels, and Jameson Inns.

Starwood Lodging's history dates all the way to 1969, when it was originally organized as Hotel Investors Trust, which was a hybrid REIT. In 1980, Hotel Investors Trust and its affiliated operating corporation were paired, allowing the two companies to trade as one. This structure allowed the paired-share REIT to earn profits not only from the leasing of its hotels but also from the management of its properties. The Internal Revenue Code has prohibited the pairing of shares between a REIT and a management company since 1983. This rule, however, did not apply to Hotel Investors Trust and a few other select REITs that existed prior to 1983.

Hotel Investors Trust was purchased in 1994 by Starwood Capital Group and became known as Starwood Lodging. Starwood's paired-share structure, the oversupply of full-service hotels that could be purchased at well below replacement cost, and savvy management propelled Starwood's growth into the world's largest lodging company by the end of 1997. It was also the largest REIT, with over $16 billion in assets. Included in its portfolio were the Sheraton and Westin

ILLUSTRATION 6-11
Hotel REITs

Boykin Lodging
Equity Inns
Felcor Lodging
Hospitality Properties Trust
Host Marriott
Humphrey Trust
Innkeepers USA
InnSuites Hospitality Trust
Jameson Inns, Inc.
LaSalle Hotel Properties
Meristar Hospitality Corp
RFS Hotel Investors
Sunstone Hotel Investors
Winston Hotels

chains and Caesar's World casinos. Starwood's success prompted other full-service REITs to form, including Patriot American Hospitality, Felcor, and American General Hospitality.

As the value of hotels rose, there were fewer opportunities to acquire existing hotels below their replacement cost, and a·slowing in profit growth occurred. Wall Street became disenchanted with the hotel industry in the late 1990s. This disenchantment caused hotel company stock prices to decline significantly, making it difficult to raise new equity for REIT growth. On a positive note, the REIT Modernization Act of 1999, which went into effect in 2001, now allows hotel REITs to manage their own hotels through a corporate taxable subsidiary much like the former paired-share REIT structure. Today there are fourteen hotel REITs, which are listed in Illustration 6-11.

THE REAL DEAL

As the real estate market has been trending upward since the latter half of 2003, there has been a resurgence of REITs in the hotel industry. Both Ashford Hospitality Trust and Highland Hospitality have raised several hundred million dollars for investment in hotels. According to a REIT report poll conducted by *Hotel Business* magazine, 71.4% of the lodging REITs saw themselves as net buyers of hotel properties in 2004. Only 14.3% saw themselves as net sellers. The $342.3 million raised by Highland Hospitality was used to acquire 100% interest in three hotels—a Renaissance hotel and conference center, a Hilton Garden Inn in Virginia, and a Marriott hotel and conference center in Texas—totaling $70.7 million.

Source: Billing, M. "Hotel REITs Are Again Demonstrating Appeal as Worthwhile Investment Vehicles." *Hotel Business*, (January 21–February 6, 2004): 34–35.

TIMESHARE

Timeshare is a financing strategy used primarily by developers of leisure-oriented hospitality properties. The concept is to sell the rights to a guest room or suite on a weekly basis for approximately thirty years or for the life of the property at a retail price. If the cost to develop the hotel or resort is $100,000 per key, the selling price per key, based on the sale of fifty-two weeks, is approximately $200,000 or more. The difference between the selling price for each week and the cost represents the profit for the timeshare developer.

The timeshare concept allows the developer of the project to receive its profit up front rather than having to wait for the project to generate positive cash flows and a favorable return on investment over time. The key to the success of a timeshare project is to sell the units as quickly as possible and not incur heavy marketing costs. It is not unusual for a timeshare project to spend up to 50% on the marketing of the units.

CONDOMINIUM HOTELS

While condominium hotels have been around for quite some time, they are definitely in vogue today. The financing scheme for a condominium hotel is similar to the timeshare concept, except that each hotel room is sold as an investment rather than as a right to use. The investor does not intend to utilize the guest room, as in a timeshare; instead, he is investing in the guest room to make a return on his investment over time. As in timesharing, the developer makes his profit up front, with future profits, if any, accruing to the owners of the condominium units. Condominium hotels are popular in Florida and other leisure markets and are usually sold to the same buyers who purchase timeshare units.

HOTEL MIXED-USE DEVELOPMENT

The hotel mixed-use concept was pioneered by Millennium Partners, which was founded in New York in 1990 by Christopher Jeffries, Philip Aarons, and Philip Lovett. Millennium Partners has developed over $5 billion of mixed-use projects in less than fourteen years. With Four Seasons and Ritz-Carlton as their hotel partners, Millennium's strategy has been to create large, mixed-use complexes featuring luxury hotels, luxury residential condominiums, entertainment venues, health club facilities, and upscale retail space in center city locations. Some of Millennium Partners' most recent projects are shown in Illustration 6-12.

The Millennium approach to mixed-use development is to offer a range of products, all of which capitalize on a luxury brand to create synergies that provide a tremendous premium to their real estate.

In addition to the usual key to a successful real estate project—location—three keys to a successful mixed-use project are as follows:

1. The ability of the mixed-use developer to sense and anticipate a market for a combination of products before the market for these products is recognized by its competitors.
2. The ability of the developer to effectively sell the story to investors, lenders, and potential customers.
3. The ability of the developer to attract high-quality operating partners to lend their brand names to the project.

Name of Project	Project Description	Estimated Cost
Ritz-Carlton Hotel and Residences, Washington, D.C.		$260 million
	300-room hotel	
	98,000 sq. ft. fitness facility	
	25,000 sq. ft. retail/restaurant space	
	162 luxury condominiums; 700 parking spaces	
Ritz-Carlton Hotel and Residences, NYC, NY		$205 million
	311-room hotel	
	122 luxury residential condominiums	
	New York's Skyscraper Museum	
Four Seasons Hotel and Residences, San Francisco		$500 million
	277-room hotel	
	142 luxury residential condominiums	
	100,000 sq. ft. fitness facility	
Ritz-Carlton Hotel and Residence, NYC, NY		$500 million
	292-room hotel	
	11 luxury residential condominiums	
Ritz-Carlton Hotel and Towers, Boston Common		$500 million
	191-room hotel	
	270 luxury residential condominiums	
	85 rental apartments	
	100,000 sq. ft. fitness facility	
	4,700-seat theatre	
	50,000 sq. ft. retail space	
	1,100 parking spaces	
Ritz-Carlton Hotel and Residences, Georgetown		$150 million
	93-room hotel	
	15 luxury residential condominiums	
	3,000 sq. ft. theatre	
	13,000 sq. ft. retail space	
	600 parking spaces	
Four Seasons Hotel and Tower, Miami		$359 million
	222-room hotel	
	56 interval ownership units	
	162 luxury residential condominiums	
	55,000 sq. ft. spa and fitness facility	
	200,000 sq. ft. office space	
	6,000 sq. ft. retail space	
	1,015 parking spaces	

ILLUSTRATION 6-12
Hotel Mixed-Use Development

Mixed-use projects offer several advantages over traditional single-purpose development projects, including:

1. The opportunity to leverage the brand name of one component with the other components of the project to generate additional demand and command premium pricing.

2. A distinct point of difference versus the project's more conventional competition.

3. A larger pool of investors and lenders to draw from. Some investors and lenders who would never do a hotel deal are attracted to mixed-use projects that include a hotel.

4. A lower blended interest rate created by lower interest rates offered by lenders on the non-hotel components of the project.

5. A higher internal rate of return driven by the lower cost of capital and the premium pricing.

While mixed-use development offers advantages, it brings with it certain additional requirements and challenges, including:

1. The need for a more complex and sophisticated market study to fully understand and present the economics of each project component.

2. Substantially more capital to fund the project based on the number of components involved.

3. Fewer potential markets and sites to select from due to the uniqueness of such projects.

4. More time required to complete a project due to its complexity.

5. More up-front seed money and soft costs to raise before actual construction begins.

Finance in Action

Purchasing an Oceanfront Restaurant

Cary Cruz, an experienced restaurant operator and owner of Brownbark Restaurants, has been presented with the opportunity to purchase an oceanfront seafood restaurant in a prominent area. The restaurant is currently in distress and can be purchased for only $120,000. Mr. Cruz would want to renovate the property and convert it to a Brownbark Restaurant, which is a family-friendly gourmet hamburger restaurant. The most popular items on the menu include the grilled salmon burger and blue cheese Kobe beef burger. The typical Brownbark Restaurant earns an annual gross cash flow of $70,000.

Even though it will only cost $120,000 to purchase this prime piece of property, several costs are involved in renovating and remarketing a restaurant. These costs include the renovation itself, marketing, licenses, legal fees, and working capital. The following chart provides a breakdown of the total cost:

Purchase of restaurant	$120,000
Licenses	$50,000
Renovation	$190,000
Marketing	$10,000
Legal fees	$10,000
Working Capital	$30,000
Total	**$410,000**

Mr. Cruz has two options to fund this opportunity. He currently has $200,000 of his own money available to invest in the project; therefore, he needs to raise only an additional $210,000. He could either find additional equity investors or take out a loan. Upon further investigation, he is able to determine that debt service on a five-year loan of $210,000, with an interest rate of 12% and amortized over twenty years, would be $28,115.

QUESTIONS:

1. Calculate the return on investment if Mr. Cruz funds the project entirely with equity.

    $70,000 of cash flow divided by $410,000 of equity = ROI of 17.1%

2. Calculate the ROI if a combination of debt and equity is utilized.

    $70,000 of gross cash flow less $28,115 of debt service = $41,855 of net cash flow

    $41,855 of net cash flow divided by $200,000 of equity = ROI of 20.9%

3. Should Mr. Cruz maximize the amount of debt or equity used in this project? Why?

    Mr. Cruz should maximize the amount of debt for this project. Based on the ROI calculations, it is evident that Mr. Cruz will receive a higher return if he utilizes debt to fund the additional $210,000 needed to purchase and renovate the restaurant. Also, debt is almost always less than the cost of equity because equity investors require a higher return, as they are exposed to a greater risk than lenders.

4. What type of loan has a five-year term but payments based on a twenty-year repayment schedule? What would Mr. Cruz's options be after the five-year term has ended?

    The loan described in this case is a bullet loan, and Mr. Cruz would have two options at the end of the five years. He could pay the remaining principal or refinance 100% of the outstanding loan balance. If Mr. Cruz chooses to pay the balance of the principal, still owed, this is called a balloon payment.

WHERE WE'VE BEEN, WHERE WE'RE GOING

While growth is financed with debt, equity, or a combination of both, you have learned in this chapter that the types and sources of hospitality financing are extensive. The new mixed-use development, condominium hotel, and timeshare financing schemes are just a few you can expect to surface. Regardless of what type of financing you elect to pursue, it is important that you understand the time value of money concept and the investment analysis tools associated with it. It is also important to factor risk and reward elements into your investment analysis and understand how a new venture can create value for investors.

Chapter 7 introduces you to the time value of money concept and the basic calculation methods associated with it. Chapters 8 and 9 expand on the time value of money concept and apply it to the hospitality industry. Together, these next three chapters provide you with a good working knowledge of financial decision making.

Key Points

➤   The two main types of capital are debt and equity.

➤   The cost of debt is calculated by dividing the amount of your interest expense payment by the amount of your loan, while the cost of equity is the amount of cash flow that the equity investor is projected to receive divided by the amount of equity he is investing.

➤   Key debt terms are *principal, term, interest rate,* and *amortization rate.*

➤   Depending on your particular capital need, a variety of loans is available, including business, construction, mini-perm, permanent, mezzanine, convertible, SBA7(a), CDC (504) program, and leases.

➤   Sources for loans include local and national banks, insurance companies, pension funds, small business investment companies, business and industrial development organizations, private credit companies, individuals, and venture capitalists.

➤   Debt is less expensive than equity, is easier to obtain, carries an income tax incentive, and does not dilute the ownership of a business. Thus, utilizing financial leverage can increase the return on investment.

➤   With equity financing, there is no set payment schedule, and equity partners cannot foreclose on their investment. During economic downturns, equity markets are more stable and provide a good source of funding for entrepreneurs.

➤   Equity partners can share their expertise, which can be good for the overall success of the business.

➤   The five types of equity are cash, land, leases, existing buildings and government subsidies.

➤   Equity capital can be obtained from individuals, venture capital funds, insurance companies, pension funds, real estate investment trusts (REITs), existing owners of assets for sale, government, construction companies, and management companies.

➤   The 1970s and 1980s were the Golden Age of hotel financing.

➤   Real estate investment conduits, REITs, timeshares, condominium hotels, and hotel mixed-use developments are examples of current hotel financing schemes.

Key Terms

CAPITAL: Funds needed for any investment project.

DEBT: Borrowed funds.

EQUITY: Invested funds; represents ownership.

COST OF CAPITAL: The amount of cash flow allocated to the provider of the capital divided by the amount of capital provided.

COST OF DEBT: Annual interest expense divided by the amount of the loan.

COST OF EQUITY: The amount of cash flow allocated to the provider of equity divided by the amount of equity provided.

TAX EFFECT: The reduction in income tax owed. The interest portion of debt service that businesses pay on loans is treated as an expense for tax purposes. Thus, interest expense reduces taxable income and the amount of income tax owed.

WEIGHTED AVERAGE COST OF CAPITAL (WACC): The amount of debt service and cash flow allotted to equity investors divided by the amount of capital provided.

FINANCIAL LEVERAGE: Degree to which the entrepreneur is utilizing debt to increase ROI.

RETURN ON INVESTMENT (ROI): Net income divided by the amount invested.

BANKRUPTCY: Occurs when liabilities exceed assets and the business is unable to meet its current financial obligations.

VARIABLE-RATE LOAN: Loan that starts out with a low interest rate that escalates over time.

EFFECTIVE BORROWING RATE: The true rate rather than the stated interest rate. Due to compounding periods and other hidden fees and charges, the effective borrowing rate is higher than the stated interest rate.

PRINCIPAL: The amount of money borrowed.

TERM: Number of months or years given to repay a loan.

INTEREST: The amount paid to the lender for lending the funds, often expressed as a percentage of the principal.

PRINCIPAL REPAYMENT: The portion of the debt service payment that reduces the amount of money owed to the lender.

AMORTIZATION RATE: The number of years the debt service payment calculation is based on.

COLLATERAL: An asset offered to the lender as loan insurance.

PERSONAL GUARANTEE: A promise to pay debt service regardless of the ability of the company to do so.

PREPAYMENT PENALTY: When the borrower pays the total amount of interest owed to the lender had the loan not been paid off early.

BULLET LOAN: A short-term loan with long-term amortization rates. For example, if the amortization rate is twenty-five years on a five-year loan, the debt service is based on a twenty-five-year repayment schedule. At the end of five years, the lender is required to repay or refinance 100% of the outstanding loan balance.

BALLOON PAYMENT: The balance of the principal on a loan owed the lender at the end of the term of the loan. This is often a large sum due to the lower principal paid back in the early part of the loan.

BUSINESS LOAN: Used to start or expand a company. It is based primarily on the personal merits of the borrower, the merits of the business plan, and the financial strength of the borrower.

CONSTRUCTION LOAN: A one- to two-year interest-only loan used to build, expand, acquire, or renovate a physical facility. It is a form of mortgage loan whereby the asset being constructed, acquired, or renovated is provided as collateral for the loan.

TAKE-OUT COMMITMENT: A written promise from the take-out lender that he will repay the construction loan at the end of its term as long as the project meets the specifications the borrower and construction lender agree to in advance of the funding of the loan.

PERMANENT LOAN: The length or term of what is still called a permanent loan is about ten years.

MINI-PERM: A hybrid of a permanent loan where the term is shorter than a permanent loan, with an average of about five years.

FIXED INTEREST RATE: An interest rate that remains constant during the term of the loan.

FLOATING RATE: An interest rate that fluctuates with the market rate of interest. You can control the fluctuation by negotiating a ceiling and a floor.

CEILING: Maximum amount the interest rate can move up during the term of the loan.

FLOOR: Minimum amount the interest rate can move down during the term of the loan.

NON-RECOURSE LOAN: A loan that limits the lender's repayment options to the assets of the business and the collateral at risk, as opposed to a recourse loan, which allows the lender to also seek repayment from the borrower's personal assets.

RECOURSE LOAN: A loan which allows the lender to seek repayment from the borrower's personal assets.

MEZZANINE LOAN: A second layer of debt that fills the gap between the total project cost, the amount of the first mortgage loan, and the equity capital to be invested. The mezzanine lender, with the permission of the first mortgage lender, may receive the second right to the first mortgage lender's collateral in the event of a loan default.

CURE: Payment of the debt service on a first mortgage on the borrower's behalf and assumption of ownership of the deal and the responsibility for the first mortgage.

COUPON RATE: The annual pay rate on a mezzanine loan.

CONVERTIBLE LOAN: A hybrid of debt and equity. It is a loan that can be converted to equity at certain points at the request of the source providing the capital.

SBA 7(a): Provides funding for start-up ventures as well as existing businesses. The maximum amount of a SBA 7(a) loan is $2 million. SBA 7(a) loans can be either short term or long term and offer a below-market interest rate.

CDC (504): Certified Development Company (504) Loan Program created to help small businesses finance the purchase of fixed assets such as land, buildings, and equipment. A major advantage of a federal 504 loan is that the borrower is required to provide only 10% of the total project cost in equity.

LEASE: A means to acquire physical facilities and equipment and requires a fixed or variable monthly payment, which is equivalent to debt service.

BUSINESS AND INDUSTRIAL DEVELOPMENT CORPORATIONS (BIDCOs): These companies fund the CDC(504) loans and obtain money they lend by selling bonds to investors in the private capital market.

VENTURE CAPITAL: Funds available for start-up business ventures with great potential.

GOVERNMENT SUBSIDIES: Financial assistance provided by the government to a new project that a lender will often recognize as equity. A government subsidy can take the form of a tax abatement, a training grant, or project infrastructure.

TAX ABATEMENT: An agreement with the government to forego the payment of property and other taxes.

TRAINING GRANT: A subsidy offered by the government to a hotel developer to train local residents for employment positions.

PROJECT INFRASTRUCTURE: Construction cost provided by the government related to curb cuts, exit ramps, and connections to utilities.

SLIVER EQUITY: A small amount of equity provided by construction companies and/or management companies.

INVESTMENT BANKERS/BANKS: Companies that work with businesses to raise funds for projects.

TAX SHELTERS: Means where individuals can invest and defer paying taxes until later, thereby "sheltering" their tax liabilities to the government.

REAL ESTATE MORTGAGE INVESTMENT CONDUITS (REMICs): These conduits made mortgage loans and sold them as commercial mortgage-backed securities primarily to financial institutions that formerly made real estate loans directly to real estate developers.

COMMERCIAL MORTGAGE-BACKED SECURITIES (CMBSs): Securities created by real estate mortgage investment conduits, or REMICs. They are essentially mortgage loans.

REAL ESTATE INVESTMENT TRUSTS (REITs): Tax-exempt corporations that own real estate.

EQUITY REITs: REITs that invest in and own properties. Their revenues are derived primarily from rental income. Approximately 96% of all REITs are equity REITs.

MORTGAGE REITs: REITs that invest in mortgages and mortgage-related securities. Mortgage REITs derive their revenues from interest income.

HYBRID REITs: REITs that invest in both commercial properties and mortgages.

Application Exercises

1. Sarah Scott borrowed $200,000 from a bank to start a catering business and has agreed to pay the bank $15,000 per year in interest expense. What is the cost of debt for Sarah?

2. If Sarah raises another $100,000 of equity from her sister Allison, agrees to give her a 25% ownership position in her catering business, and projects annual cash flow before debt to be $50,000, what is Sarah's cost of equity?

3. What is the weight of debt for Sarah's catering business?

4. What is the weight of equity for Sarah's catering business?

5. If Sarah's business falls in the 30% tax bracket, what is her cost of debt after tax?

6. What is the weighted average cost of capital for Sarah?

7. Define *business loans, permanent loans,* and *mezzanine loans.*

8. What sources can provide convertible loans and mini-perms?

9. Compare and contrast venture capital and SBICs.

10. **ETHICS** ✳ To qualify for financial assistance from the SBA, Jim realizes his application must have positive credit merits. One of the criteria is the relationship between the business's debt and equity. In order to satisfy this criterion, Jim asks his best friend, D.J., for a loan of $20,000, which he promises to repay in six months. Jim then deposits the money from his friend in his own bank and states on the application form that he himself has invested $20,000 in the business as equity. Has Jim violated any ethical principle?

11. **EXPLORING THE WEB** ✳ Using the Small Business Administration website (www.sba.gov), research the options of the SBA 7(a) program and the Certified Development Company (504) programs.

12. Besides cash, what are three forms of financing that lenders often consider as equity when making a loan? Explain.

13. Identify and describe the three major forms of government subsidies that can be viewed by lenders as equity.

14. What is a REIT? What are the two major classifications of REITs?

15. What type of equity financing is prevalent in restaurant projects, especially in major cities?

16. Name and describe three sources of equity financing.

17. Explain why venture capitalists prefer investing in equity rather than debt.

18. Explain the role of construction and management companies in providing equity capital in the hospitality industry.

19. **ETHICS** ✳ Patrick Clark is a young entrepreneur who wants to open a restaurant in San Francisco, California. Because real estate prices are very high, he is not able to secure enough equity to present to lenders to convince them of the viability of his project. A friend of his, Jack Rosse, owns an auto parts store and the land where the store is located. Jack tells Patrick he will write a note for him to take to the bank that states that he is going to close his store, contribute the land to Patrick, and become a part owner of Patrick's new restaurant. Jack, however, really has no intention of closing his store and contributing the land to Jack's restaurant project. Can Jack still write the note for Patrick to bring to the bank? Should Patrick use this letter? What may be some of the consequences?

20. **EXPLORING THE WEB** ✳ Using the Hotel-Online website (www.hotel-online.com), search for five recent hotel development articles and comment on how the debt and equity components were arranged. Besides the major benchmarking companies mentioned in chapter 3, others provide news information on condominium hotels, timeshare, and mixed-used development. For example, you can type in "condo hotel development" and gain access to a number of useful sites. Some examples:

    www.lodging-econometrics.com

    www.multi-housingnews.com

    www.hotelnewsresource.com

    www.nreionline.com

    www.hospitalitynet.org

Concept Check ✓

A Bank to a Hotel

The Williams Bennett Hotel Development Co. has identified a historic bank building that could be converted into a hotel. The location is in the heart of downtown Smithton, a densely populated metropolitan city. The structure was designed by an acclaimed architect and built in 1913. The fifteen-story building will be transformed into a chic boutique hotel with the hotel lobby, meeting rooms, café, and fitness area on the first two floors. The remaining thirteen floors will contain 130 guest rooms.

The entire project will cost $35,000,000. Sixty percent of the project cost ($21,000,000) will be financed through debt, and $14,000,000 is being provided by equity investors. The lender is offering a favorable 12% interest rate on the $21,000,000, and the equity investors are requiring a return of 18% on their investment. The current business tax rate is 25%.

Because the structure is historic, the Williams Bennett Hotel Development Co. has been in discussions with the city government to determine if there are any public incentives for redeveloping this property. The development company knows the hotel supply in Smithton is underserved and that the city needs additional rooms to attract larger convention groups. The city would also gain from additional jobs, which would lower the unemployment rate. There are obvious benefits for both the City of Smithton and the Williams Bennett Hotel Development Co.

QUESTIONS

1. Calculate the WACC and show step-by-step calculations for the weight of debt, cost of debt, tax effect, weighted cost of debt, weight of equity, cost of equity, and weighted cost of equity.
2. Explain the tax effect and its relation to the interest portion of debt service.
3. What subsidies can the government provide to the development company?
4. In this case, the city government offered Williams Bennett a tax abatement in the amount of $1,000,000, spread evenly over the first five years of operations. Explain how the tax abatement impacts the company's ability to pay debt service.

Concept Check ✓

Equity and Loans

Frank Douglas, a real estate developer, just finalized a major deal with Turner County to develop a major hotel/luxury condominium/golf/conference center/residential mixed-use development on land owned by Turner County.

The development is proposed to include a 150-room five-star hotel, 75 luxury 2,500 sq. ft. condominium units, an eighteen-hole championship golf course, and 360 residential golf course lots. The total development cost, exclusive of the cost of land and financing expenses, is projected to be $250,000 per room for the hotel, $200 per square foot for the luxury condominium units, $6 million for the golf course, and 10% of the current selling price of $500,000 for each residential lot.

The county has agreed to contribute the land to Mr. Douglas, the developer, at no cost. The county's justification for this contribution is the new jobs, taxes, and new visitors to the area generated by the mixed-use development.

QUESTIONS

1. Calculate the total project cost for this mixed-use development from the information provided.

2. If lenders are willing to provide 55% of the project cost in the form of debt, calculate the dollar amount of debt and equity that Frank Douglas must raise.

3. What sources of loans are available to Mr. Douglas? What sources of equity are available? Which sources of loans and equity are the best options for this development, and why?

THE TIME VALUE

OF MONEY

FEATURE STORY

RAY KROC: HOW MUCH GOLD ARE THE GOLDEN ARCHES WORTH?

In 1965, McDonald's went public with its first stock offering. If you purchased 100 shares of stock at that time, they would have cost you $2,250. Today, your initial investment would have a value of well over $2.2 million.

McDonald's success was founded on the entrepreneurial zeal of Ray Kroc, who used his almost evangelical ability to motivate nearly everyone he encountered. These qualities enabled Kroc to build the largest and most successful restaurant franchise company in the world. His fair and balanced franchise partnership is said to be his greatest legacy.

Ray's operating credo of "Quality, Service, Cleanliness, and Value" became the mantra for all McDonald's owners and established a permanent benchmark for the entire foodservice industry. His exacting mandates for uniformity and product consistency made it possible for a customer to get an identical Big Mac® and fries in Houston or in Moscow. To underscore his own commitment to "taking the hamburger business more seriously than anyone else," he established Hamburger University and demonstrated his willingness to invest in the training and education of McDonald's people. McDonald's Golden Arches are said to be the second most widely recognized trademark in the world. It has been said that 96% of all Americans have eaten at a McDonald's restaurant on at least one occasion. Today, McDonald's is one of the largest restaurant brands in the world, with more than 30,000 local restaurants serving nearly 50 million customers in more than 119 countries each day. How much do you think those original 100 shares of stock will be worth in another fifty years?

SOURCES

http://www.mcdonalds.com/corp/news/corppr/2005/cpr_04152005.html.

http://www.hoovers.com/mcdonald's/—ID_10974—/free-co-factsheet.xhtml.

"Ray Kroc. 1996 Hall of Honor Inductee of the Hospitality Industry Hall of Honor." http://www.hrm.uh.edu/home.asp?PageID=191.

Robbins, T. "Ray Kroc Did It All for You." *Esquire,* 100, pp. 340–342, 344 (December, 1983).

Learning Outcomes

1. Define the concept of time value of money.
2. Understand the concept of market value.
3. Identify the factors that impact market value.
4. Learn the basic mathematics of time value of money.
5. Understand how to perform the basic time value of money calculations using a business calculator or an Excel spreadsheet.

Preview of Chapter 7

Time Value of Money

1. THE CONCEPT OF TIME VALUE OF MONEY (TVM)

   a. The value of a dollar today
   b. The future value of a dollar invested today
   c. The present value of a dollar to be received in the future

2. THE MARKET VALUE CONCEPT

   a. The sum of projected future cash flows to be generated by the investment
   b. The factors that influence the market value of an investment
      i.   Amount of cash flow projected to be generated
      ii. The timing of the cash flow
      iii. The risk of projected cash flow not being achieved
      iv. The mix of capital to be used to finance the investment

3. TVM CALCULATIONS

a. The business calculator

b. Future value of a single lump sum

c. Present value of a single lump sum

d. Future value of an annuity

e. Present value of an annuity

f. Future value of an annuity due

g. Present value of an annuity due

h. Present value of a perpetuity

i. Future value of an uneven stream of cash flow

j. Present value of an uneven stream of cash flow

k. Time period and compounding

l. Loan amortization

CONCEPT OF TIME VALUE OF MONEY

Before you learn to perform the basic time value of money calculations, it's important that you have a clear understanding of the time value of money concept, the concept of market value, and the factors that influence both.

Time Value of Money

The **time value of money** concept (TVM) is the cornerstone of investment analysis. The decision-making skills regarding investments that you will learn in chapters 8 and 9 are based on the concept of the time value of money. It is one of the most difficult concepts for a hospitality manager to grasp.

The TVM concept is based on the premise that the value of money is not only its face value but also the interest or profit that can be earned by investing it wisely. For example, if today you placed $1.00 in a **certificate of deposit** (CD) that pays an annual interest of 10%, at the end of the year your $1.00 investment would be worth $1.10. If you left your money in the CD for another year, at the end of year two your investment would be worth $1.21.

If someone wanted to sell you an I.O.U. for $1.21 that was payable two years from now, how much would you pay for it today? The answer is no more than $1.00 if you believe you can earn at least a 10% annual return on your money. Whoever owns money wants to invest it and make a return on it, either in the form of interest income or a profit. If you have to wait two years to receive payment of the I.O.U., you would have lost two years' worth of investment income. The value of the I.O.U., therefore, is the face value of the I.O.U ($1.00) less the twenty-one cents you could have earned on the $1.00 over the two years.

In time value of money terminology, the $1.00 is the asset's **present value** (PV) and the $1.21 is the asset's **future value** (FV). We discuss these terms more fully later in the chapter.

Market Value

The concept of **market value** is an extension of the time value of money concept. An asset's market value is deemed to be the sum of the future cash flow it is likely to generate over its life. Market value takes the following into consideration:

- The amount of the cash flow
- The timing of the cash flow
- The risk of the cash flow not being generated
- How the cash-flowing asset is to be financed

In TVM terms, market value is the present value of the asset.

AMOUNT OF CASH FLOW

We are sure you would agree that the more cash flow an asset is likely to generate in the future, the more you would pay to acquire it today. Therefore, the higher the amount of cash flow to be generated, the higher the asset's present or market value. With this in mind, it's clear that the more cash flow an asset is generating at the end of five years, the more an investor would pay to acquire it at that time. Therefore, the more you could sell the asset for in the future, the more the asset is worth today and the higher its present or market value. In other words, the present value of an asset is a function of its future cash flow, including its terminal selling price.

TIMING OF THE CASH FLOW

Intuitively, if we told you we would give you $100 in five years or $100 in ten years, you would choose the five-year payday. This, as we learned earlier, is the basis for the time value of money concept. In other words, one dollar received today is worth more than one dollar to be received in the future. The sooner you receive the money, the more value it has today and the higher its present value.

Consider purchasing a U.S. savings bond. You could purchase a $100 bond today for less than $100 because you won't receive your $100 until sometime in the future. The actual purchase price depends on how long you have to wait to receive your $100. The longer you have to wait to receive your money, the less the bond is worth today.

RISK OF NOT RECEIVING THE PROJECTED CASH FLOW

The final factor that impacts an asset's present or market value is risk. Consider the expression "The greater the risk, the greater the reward." Translated into time value of money terms, the riskier the investment, the lower the asset's present or market value. From an equity investor's perspective, the greater the perceived risk of the projected levels of cash flow being achieved, the higher return on investment (ROI) he will demand.

If an investor is presented with two acquisition opportunities projected to generate the same amount of cash flow over a five-year period, but investment A has twice the perceived risk of investment B, which of the two would you pay your money to acquire? Of course, opportunity B, the one with the lower risk. Therefore, which one has the higher present value? If you responded that B has the higher present value due to its lower risk, you are correct. As the risk of a potential investment increases, its present value decreases. Conversely, as the risk of a potential investment decreases, its present value increases.

HOW THE ASSET IS TO BE FINANCED

As you learned in chapter 6, capital has a cost. The cost of debt is debt service divided by the amount of the loan. The cost of equity is the investor's **hurdle rate.** The mix of capital used to finance the asset determines the **weighted average cost of capital** (WACC). The more equity required to finance the deal, the higher the WACC. The higher the WACC, the lower the asset's present or market value. The lower the present or market value, the less an investor will likely pay to acquire the asset.

IMPORTANCE TO THE HOSPITALITY MANAGER

As a hospitality manager, understanding the time value of money concept, the concept of market value, and learning the **investment analysis** skills based on these concepts is important to your success. Investment analysis skills also come in handy when you need to request capital for a new project such as an additional meeting room for the hotel where you work, a guest room expansion, a new restaurant concept, or purchasing new computer equipment. When requesting capital, you must demonstrate that the money you are asking for will generate a favorable return on investment for your company. This is critical whether you are requesting capital from your general manager, owner, lender, or public shareholders.

FEATURE STORY

TOM CORCORAN—A CREATOR OF SHAREHOLDER VALUE

Tom Corcoran's involvement in the hospitality industry began at age fourteen, when he was a dishwasher. After working in a variety of kitchen positions during his school years, he joined the U.S. Army during the Vietnam War. Upon his return, he attended law school at Washington University in Kansas City, Missouri. After graduation, he accepted a position with Brock Hotel Corporation as a developer in Topeka, Kansas. During the next eleven years, Mr. Corcoran held positions with Brock in their mergers and acquisitions, financial planning, and project development departments. The investment analysis skills he learned in college served him well in these real estate–related positions. He later served as the president and CEO of Brock Hotel Corporation and as a board member for Chuck E. Cheese Entertainment, Inc. (formerly ShowBiz Pizza Time, Inc.).

In 1991, Tom decided it was time to fulfill his lifetime dream of owning his own company. Together with his good friend, Hervey Feldman, Tom signed a contract to purchase a Holiday Inn hotel, located near the Dallas–Fort Worth Airport from the Resolution Trust Corporation, for $9.0 million. Tom and Hervey each contributed $500,000 of equity to the deal and worked hard to secure the remaining $8 million of financing to purchase the hotel. Given the level of volatility in the hospitality industry and poor economic conditions at the time, it was difficult for Tom and Hervey to obtain their financing. However, Mr. Corcoran's assertiveness and outstanding business experience, combined with his partner's reputation as a hospitality mogul and experience as the first president of Embassy Suites Hotels, enabled them to convince a lender that the deal had significant upside value. They secured a loan of $6 million. Business associates provided the remaining $2 million of equity to close the deal.

Since its inception, Corcoran and Feldman's company has focused exclusively on upscale, full-service hotels and suites, and has become the world's largest owner of Embassy Suites hotels. In 1994, Mr. Corcoran saw the opportunity to take his six-hotel company public and make it debt free. It went public under the name FelCor Suite Hotels, Inc., with a market capitalization of approximately $120 million.

By 2004, FelCor owned 154 hotels located in thirty-three states and Canada, and had a market capitalization of approximately $3 billion. Today, it is the nation's second-largest lodging real estate investment trust (REIT) and the nation's largest owner of full-service, all-suite hotels.

Over the years, FelCor has demonstrated growth higher than the industry average and established a favorable track record for acquiring, renovating, redeveloping, and rebranding hotels. FelCor is the only lodging REIT with a diversified portfolio of nationally branded, upscale, full-service hotels managed by brand owners. These brands include Hilton, InterContinental, and Starwood.

Today, through Mr. Corcoran's leadership, FelCor continues to improve the financial performance of its existing hotels, acquire additional hotels, and increase shareholder value.

SOURCES

Corcoran, Thomas J., Jr. Interview, 2004.
https://secure.twst.com/notes/articles/nas618.html.
http://www.smhm.unt.edu/governors/hosp_gov/Corcoran_Thomas.htm.
http://www.travelcomexpo.com/speaker_bios.asp?reqEvent=6&ID=1667.

Calculating Time Value of Money

The analysis of time value of money has changed dramatically over time. Years ago, complicated mathematical formulas were used to analyze financial transactions. More recently, shorter formulas using interest tables were developed. Over the last twenty years, the business calculator has become the most popular method of analyzing investment opportunities. Computer spreadsheets such as Lotus and Excel have also become popular, as they offer special functions to make financial modeling easier. Instead of using long algorithms, an Excel spreadsheet's function wizard assists the user, who simply selects the variables required to perform the investment analysis.

This section of the chapter presents time value of money calculations using a business calculator and a computer spreadsheet. While the Texas Instrument BAII Plus business calculator and Microsoft's Excel are featured, other business calculators and computer spreadsheets are available in the marketplace. While the operation of all business calculators and computer spreadsheets is not exactly the same, each is similar enough for you to understand and calculate using your particular business calculator and computer spreadsheet.

THE BUSINESS CALCULATOR

The main difference between a business calculator and a regular calculator is the additional functions it performs. In addition to basic math, a business calculator includes a set of function keys that allow the user to calculate future value and present value. As a hospitality manager, you need to familiarize yourself with the five basic function keys of a business calculator and learn how to perform each function.

The five basic function keys are:

- N = number of years
- I/Y = interest or **discount rate**
- PV = present value
- PMT = annuity payment
- FV = future value

There is also a second set of functions whose keys are directly above these five basic function keys. For example, above the N key is xP/Y, which stands for number of compounding periods per year. Above the I/Y key is P/Y, which stands for the number of payments per year. To invoke any of these functions, you must use the 2nd key, which is found between the CPT key and the N key. We discuss these keys further in a moment.

As some business calculators are equipped with default settings from the manufacturer, always check the settings before using the calculator. For example, the BAII Plus calculator comes with a factory setting for two decimal places. When working with percentages, two decimal places are usually fine. Some calculations, however, require four decimal places.

Before you perform the calculations presented is this chapter, please check your calculator to make sure it is set for annual compounding and four decimal positions. Here are the steps to follow:

1. The 2nd key lets you perform the function printed above each of the other keys.
2. For example, the function description above the . key says *FORMAT.*
3. To format the calculator for decimals, press the 2nd key and the . key.

4.   Once these two keys are pressed, your calculator will display DEC = 2.00.

5.   Now enter *4* and press *ENTER*.

This tells the calculator you want four decimal places calculated rather than two. As soon as you press the *ENTER* key, the display will change to DEC = 4.0000, showing four decimal places. To exit and return to normal calculations, press the *2ⁿᵈ* key and the *CPT* key to quit the function. The quit function is above the *CPT* key. Now, all you see on the display is 0.0000.

Another factory setting you must change is the number of compounding periods per year. While we do some monthly compounding, most calculations we ask you to do are on an annual basis. Because the factory default for most calculators is set at twelve compounding periods per year, you need to set your calculator for annual calculations. Remember, the *P/Y* function directly above the *I/Y* key? *P/Y* stands for the number of compounding periods per year. In order to see the number of compounding periods per year, you will need to:

1.   Press *2nd* and *I/Y*. By pressing these two keys, you are letting the calculator know you want to access the *P/Y* function to look at the number of compounding periods per year. If your calculator is a new one from the factory, it will display P/Y = 12.

2.   Set your calculator for annual compounding; thus, you need to press the *1* key and the *ENTER* key, which is on the top row of your calculator. The display will show P/Y = 1.00.

3.   Press *2ⁿᵈ* and *CPT* (QUIT) to exit.

Now that your calculator is set correctly, the last step before we perform some calculations is to clear it of any previous calculations. The calculator is a storage device; therefore, if you have not cleared a previous calculation, the information is still stored in the calculator. It is always good practice to clear the calculator before starting a new calculation. There are two clear keys on your calculator. Above the *FV* key is the *CLR TVM*, which stands for "clear time value of money calculations." The other clear key is on the lower left-hand corner above the *CE/C* key, which says *CLR WORK*. This key clears any work you have recently performed other than time value of money calculations.

THE REAL DEAL

A certificate of deposit (CD) with a bank is a good example of present/future value of money. An individual purchases a CD with $5,000 and selects a set period for his investment such as six months, one year, three years, etc. If he chooses a longer period, the bank normally gives him a slightly higher interest rate because he has committed to having his money with them longer. Small local and regional banks offer slightly higher interest rates than larger institutions because there is a perceived risk with smaller institutions. Next time, before you open a CD account, look at a newspaper or shop on the Internet before you deposit your money. You may never know what you might have missed in terms of interest rates.

1.   To clear all previous time value of money calculations, press 2nd and *FV*.

2.   To clear all other calculations, press 2nd and *CE/C*.

Now that you've prepared your calculator correctly, let's work some problems.

SINGLE SUM

A **single sum** investment is the most basic form of a time value of money calculation. For example, if you invested $100 today and it yields a 10% annual interest, at the end of one year you would have $100 plus $10 of interest earned, or a total value of $110. The present value is $100, the future value is $110, the compounding period is one year, and the interest rate is 10.0%.

FUTURE VALUE OF A SINGLE SUM

To make this example a little more interesting, let us assume the present value is $1,000, the compounding period is five years, the interest rate is 12%, and the future value is what the investment will be worth at the end of the five years, with the principal and interest added together.

THE REAL DEAL

According to the Consumer Price Index Inflation Calculator posted on the U.S. Department of Labor Bureau of Statistics website, $100 in 1985, when most of today's college-age students were born, would have been worth $177.42 in December 2004. For the baby boomers, or those who were born in 1955, $100 in 1955 would have been worth $712.31 in 2004. How can that be? Compounding is the key! If you input $100 as the present value of an investment, $712.31 as the future value, and 49 years as the compounding period, you would have earned an interest rate of 4.09% per year. This means, on the average, the inflation rate for the last forty-nine years has been 4.09%. Of course, there have been years when the inflation rate has been higher, sometimes in double digits, and years when the inflation rate has been very low. Regardless, this means our parents' or grandparents' investments should have earned at least 4.09% during the last forty-nine years just to maintain their buying power. Otherwise, their investments have not even kept up with the rate of inflation. This is why you should not put your money away in a shoebox and hide it under your bed!

When calculating time value of money problems, it is helpful to list all the particulars of the problem on a timeline:

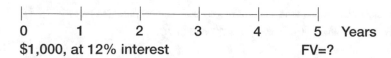

0   1   2   3   4   5   Years

$1,000, at 12% interest   FV=?

You may remember that you can calculate time value of money problems using the formula and table method, a business calculator, or a spreadsheet. Illustration 7-1 shows how this future value calculation is performed using a formula and the interest factor table respectively.

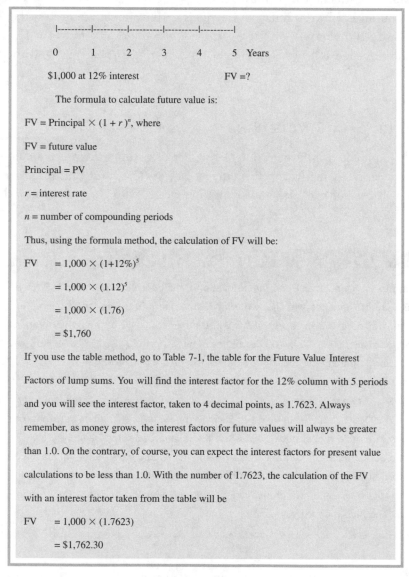

|----------|----------|----------|----------|----------|

0   1   2   3   4   5   Years

$1,000 at 12% interest   FV =?

The formula to calculate future value is:

$FV = \text{Principal} \times (1 + r)^n$, where

FV = future value

Principal = PV

r = interest rate

n = number of compounding periods

Thus, using the formula method, the calculation of FV will be:

$$FV = 1,000 \times (1+12\%)^5$$

$$= 1,000 \times (1.12)^5$$

$$= 1,000 \times (1.76)$$

$$= \$1,760$$

If you use the table method, go to Table 7-1, the table for the Future Value Interest Factors of lump sums. You will find the interest factor for the 12% column with 5 periods and you will see the interest factor, taken to 4 decimal points, as 1.7623. Always remember, as money grows, the interest factors for future values will always be greater than 1.0. On the contrary, of course, you can expect the interest factors for present value calculations to be less than 1.0. With the number of 1.7623, the calculation of the FV with an interest factor taken from the table will be

$$FV = 1,000 \times (1.7623)$$

$$= \$1,762.30$$

ILLUSTRATION 7-1

Future Value of a Lump Sum Calculation Using the Formula and Table Methods

TABLE 7-1
Table of Compound Factors

NUMBER OF PERIODS	COMPOUNDING RATE											
	1%	2%	3%	4%	5%	6%	7%	8%	9%	10%	11%	12%
1	1.0100	1.0200	1.0300	1.0400	1.0500	1.0600	1.0700	1.0800	1.0900	1.1000	1.1100	1.1200
2	1.0201	1.0404	1.0609	1.0816	1.1025	1.1236	1.1449	1.1664	1.1881	1.2100	1.2321	1.2544
3	1.0303	1.0612	1.0927	1.1249	1.1576	1.1910	1.2250	1.2597	1.2950	1.3310	1.3676	1.4049
4	1.0406	1.0824	1.1255	1.1699	1.2155	1.2625	1.3108	1.3605	1.4116	1.4641	1.5181	1.5735
5	1.0510	1.1041	1.1593	1.2167	1.2763	1.3382	1.4026	1.4693	1.5386	1.6105	1.6851	1.7623
6	1.0615	1.1262	1.1941	1.2653	1.3401	1.4185	1.5007	1.5869	1.6771	1.7716	1.8704	1.9738
7	1.0721	1.1487	1.2299	1.3159	1.4071	1.5036	1.6058	1.7138	1.8280	1.9487	2.0762	2.2107
8	1.0829	1.1717	1.2668	1.3686	1.4775	1.5938	1.7182	1.8509	1.9926	2.1436	2.3045	2.4760
9	1.0937	1.1951	1.3048	1.4233	1.5513	1.6895	1.8385	1.9990	2.1719	2.3579	2.5580	2.7731
10	1.1046	1.2190	1.3439	1.4802	1.6289	1.7908	1.9672	2.1589	2.3674	2.5937	2.8394	3.1058
11	1.1157	1.2434	1.3842	1.5395	1.7103	1.8983	2.1049	2.3316	2.5804	2.8531	3.1518	3.4785
12	1.1268	1.2682	1.4258	1.6010	1.7959	2.0122	2.2522	2.5182	2.8127	3.1384	3.4985	3.8960
13	1.1381	1.2936	1.4685	1.6651	1.8856	2.1329	2.4098	2.7196	3.0658	3.4523	3.8833	4.3635
14	1.1495	1.3195	1.5126	1.7317	1.9799	2.2609	2.5785	2.9372	3.3417	3.7975	4.3104	4.8871
15	1.1610	1.3459	1.5580	1.8009	2.0789	2.3966	2.7590	3.1722	3.6425	4.1772	4.7846	5.4736
16	1.1726	1.3728	1.6047	1.8730	2.1829	2.5404	2.9522	3.4259	3.9703	4.5950	5.3109	6.1304
17	1.1843	1.4002	1.6528	1.9479	2.2920	2.6928	3.1588	3.7000	4.3276	5.0545	5.8951	6.8660
18	1.1961	1.4282	1.7024	2.0258	2.4066	2.8543	3.3799	3.9960	4.7171	5.5599	6.5436	7.6900
19	1.2081	1.4568	1.7535	2.1068	2.5270	3.0256	3.6165	4.3157	5.1417	6.1159	7.2633	8.6128
20	1.2202	1.4859	1.8061	2.1911	2.6533	3.2071	3.8697	4.6610	5.6044	6.7275	8.0623	9.6463
21	1.2324	1.5157	1.8603	2.2788	2.7860	3.3996	4.1406	5.0338	6.1088	7.4002	8.9492	10.8038
22	1.2447	1.5460	1.9161	2.3699	2.9253	3.6035	4.4304	5.4365	6.6586	8.1403	9.9336	12.1003
23	1.2572	1.5769	1.9736	2.4647	3.0715	3.8197	4.7405	5.8715	7.2579	8.9543	11.0263	13.5523
24	1.2697	1.6084	2.0328	2.5633	3.2251	4.0489	5.0724	6.3412	7.9111	9.8497	12.2392	15.1786
25	1.2824	1.6406	2.0938	2.6658	3.3864	4.2919	5.4274	6.8485	8.6231	10.8347	13.5855	17.0001
26	1.2953	1.6734	2.1566	2.7725	3.5557	4.5494	5.8074	7.3964	9.3992	11.9182	15.0799	19.0401
27	1.3082	1.7069	2.2213	2.8834	3.7335	4.8223	6.2139	7.9881	10.2451	13.1100	16.7386	21.3249
28	1.3213	1.7410	2.2879	2.9987	3.9201	5.1117	6.6488	8.6271	11.1671	14.4210	18.5799	23.8839
29	1.3345	1.7758	2.3566	3.1187	4.1161	5.4184	7.1143	9.3173	12.1722	15.8631	20.6237	26.7499
30	1.3478	1.8114	2.4273	3.2434	4.3219	5.7435	7.6123	10.0627	13.2677	17.4494	22.8923	29.9599

To see how to calculate future value using the business calculator and Excel, please take a look at Illustration 7-2.

Once you master the use of a business calculator or Excel, you will not want to even think about using the old-fashioned formula and table method.

PRESENT VALUE OF A SINGLE SUM

The earlier scenario can also be considered from the present value perspective. The timeline is much the same, except that now the future value is known and you need to calculate how much the money to be received at the end of five years is worth today:

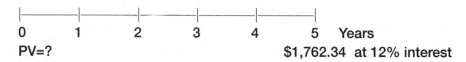

In this example, the value of the money at the end of five years is $1,762.34 and the market rate of interest is 12%. Your task is to calculate how much the $1,762.34 is worth today—that is, how much you would need to invest today at a 12% rate of interest to have $1,762.34 in five years.

To see how to calculate the present value using the formula and table method, please take a look at Illustration 7-3.

Again, it is more practical and accurate to perform these calculations using a business calculator or a spreadsheet such as Excel. The steps to accomplish this are listed in Illustration 7-4.

ANNUITY

An **annuity** can be either a regular annuity or an annuity due. A **regular annuity** is a fixed amount of money received or paid at the end of each compounding period for a set time. Consider the following timeline, where $600 is to be received at the end of each year for five years at a 12% interest rate:

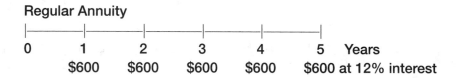

An **annuity due** is the same as a regular annuity, except the money is received or paid at the beginning of each period.

PV = –$1,000
N = 5
I/Y = 12
And you will be computing for FV
CPT FV
FV as calculated is $1,762.34

Steps on calculator:
1. Check default to make sure it is on annual compounding.
    [2nd] [I/Y], display should show P/Y = 1.0000
    [2nd] [CPT] to exit
    If you are sure your calculator is set correctly, this step can be omitted.
2. Clear all previous entries.
    [2nd] [CE/C] [2nd] [FV]
3. Enter the following:
    1000 [+/–] [PV] (by entering the [+/–] key, the value of the 1,000 will show as
        PV=–1,000 on the display.
    5 [N]
    12 [I/Y]
    [CPT] [FV]
    Display will show FV = 1,762.3417*
4. To exit and start another calculation:
    [2nd] [CPT]
5. To clear all previous entries to get it ready for the next calculation.
    [2nd] [CE/C] [2nd] [FV]

Note: Some calculators require you to enter a negative sign for the present value for the calculation; otherwise, it will give you a wrong answer or an error message. This is because in the logical mind of a calculator, it looks at an investment or loan from two ends. If one pays out today and invests, it is a negative cash flow; thus, a negative sign is associated with the PV. As such, the FV will be a positive number. Although the BAII Plus does not require its user to enter a negative sign, it is advisable to do so. In this case, we can all keep track of the flow of money.

Steps on Excel
Note: **Type only the symbols or letters within the bracket [ ] and not the bracket itself.**
1. Type [=] to invoke an equation calculation.
2. Type [fv] to invoke the future value function.
3. Type the open bracket [(]. As soon as [(] is typed, EXCEL displays:
    FV(**rate**,nper,pmt,[pv],[type]); the word rate is bolded to prompt you to enter the rate.
4. Enter rate in decimal form and type a comma[,], **nper** will then be highlighted.
    0.12,
5. Enter number of years and type a comma [,], **pmt** will then be highlighted.
    5,
6. Because we are calculating FV using a PV, pmt will not be applicable for this calculation, so, enter a [,] and now **pv** will be highlighted.
7. Enter 1000 and then close the calculation by typing [)]. As soon as you press enter, the amount $1762.34 will show in the cell.
8. To recap, for the entire calculation, type the following, then hit the enter key:
    =fv(0.12,5,,1000)

ILLUSTRATION 7-2
Future Value of a Lump Sum Calculation Using the Calculator and Spreadsheet Methods

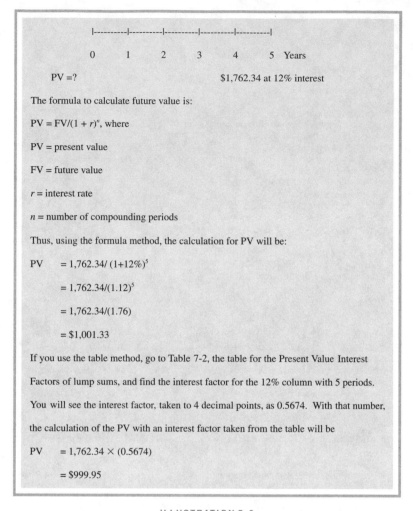

|----------|----------|----------|----------|----------|

0   1   2   3   4   5   Years

PV =? $1,762.34 at 12% interest

The formula to calculate future value is:

$PV = FV/(1 + r)^n$, where

PV = present value

FV = future value

r = interest rate

n = number of compounding periods

Thus, using the formula method, the calculation for PV will be:

$$PV = 1,762.34/ (1+12\%)^5$$

$$= 1,762.34/(1.12)^5$$

$$= 1,762.34/(1.76)$$

$$= \$1,001.33$$

If you use the table method, go to Table 7-2, the table for the Present Value Interest Factors of lump sums, and find the interest factor for the 12% column with 5 periods. You will see the interest factor, taken to 4 decimal points, as 0.5674. With that number, the calculation of the PV with an interest factor taken from the table will be

$$PV = 1,762.34 \times (0.5674)$$

$$= \$999.95$$

ILLUSTRATION 7-3

Present Value of a Lump Sum Calculation Using the Formula and Table Methods

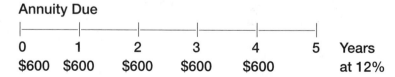

Annuity Due

|———|———|———|———|———|

0   1   2   3   4   5   Years

$600 $600 $600 $600 $600   at 12%

Annuity calculations are similar to lump sum calculations, except now you are dealing with multiple sums of the same amount.

FUTURE VALUE OF AN ANNUITY

Consider the following timeline, where $600 is to be received at the end of each year for five years at a 12% interest rate:

TABLE 7-2
Table of Discount Factors

NUMBER OF PERIODS	DISCOUNT RATE											
	1%	2%	3%	4%	5%	6%	7%	8%	9%	10%	11%	12%
1	0.9901	0.9804	0.9709	0.9615	0.9524	0.9434	0.9346	0.9259	0.9174	0.9091	0.9009	0.8929
2	0.9803	0.9612	0.9426	0.9246	0.9070	0.8900	0.8734	0.8573	0.8417	0.8264	0.8116	0.7972
3	0.9706	0.9423	0.9151	0.8890	0.8638	0.8396	0.8163	0.7938	0.7722	0.7513	0.7312	0.7118
4	0.9610	0.9238	0.8885	0.8548	0.8227	0.7921	0.7629	0.7350	0.7084	0.6830	0.6587	0.6355
5	0.9515	0.9057	0.8626	0.8219	0.7835	0.7473	0.7130	0.6806	0.6499	0.6209	0.5935	0.5674
6	0.9420	0.8880	0.8375	0.7903	0.7462	0.7050	0.6663	0.6302	0.5963	0.5645	0.5346	0.5066
7	0.9327	0.8706	0.8131	0.7599	0.7107	0.6651	0.6227	0.5835	0.5470	0.5132	0.4817	0.4523
8	0.9235	0.8535	0.7894	0.7307	0.6768	0.6274	0.5820	0.5403	0.5019	0.4665	0.4339	0.4039
9	0.9143	0.8368	0.7664	0.7026	0.6446	0.5919	0.5439	0.5002	0.4604	0.4241	0.3909	0.3606
10	0.9053	0.8203	0.7441	0.6756	0.6139	0.5584	0.5083	0.4632	0.4224	0.3855	0.3522	0.3220
11	0.8963	0.8043	0.7224	0.6496	0.5847	0.5268	0.4751	0.4289	0.3875	0.3505	0.3173	0.2875
12	0.8874	0.7885	0.7014	0.6246	0.5568	0.4970	0.4440	0.3971	0.3555	0.3186	0.2858	0.2567
13	0.8787	0.7730	0.6810	0.6006	0.5303	0.4688	0.4150	0.3677	0.3262	0.2897	0.2575	0.2292
14	0.8700	0.7579	0.6611	0.5775	0.5051	0.4423	0.3878	0.3405	0.2992	0.2633	0.2320	0.2046
15	0.8613	0.7430	0.6419	0.5553	0.4810	0.4173	0.3624	0.3152	0.2745	0.2394	0.2090	0.1827
16	0.8528	0.7284	0.6232	0.5339	0.4581	0.3936	0.3387	0.2919	0.2519	0.2176	0.1883	0.1631
17	0.8444	0.7142	0.6050	0.5134	0.4363	0.3714	0.3166	0.2703	0.2311	0.1978	0.1696	0.1456
18	0.8360	0.7002	0.5874	0.4936	0.4155	0.3503	0.2959	0.2502	0.2120	0.1799	0.1528	0.1300
19	0.8277	0.6864	0.5703	0.4746	0.3957	0.3305	0.2765	0.2317	0.1945	0.1635	0.1377	0.1161
20	0.8195	0.6730	0.5537	0.4564	0.3769	0.3118	0.2584	0.2145	0.1784	0.1486	0.1240	0.1037
21	0.8114	0.6598	0.5375	0.4388	0.3589	0.2942	0.2415	0.1987	0.1637	0.1351	0.1117	0.0926
22	0.8034	0.6468	0.5219	0.4220	0.3418	0.2775	0.2257	0.1839	0.1502	0.1228	0.1007	0.0826
23	0.7954	0.6342	0.5067	0.4057	0.3256	0.2618	0.2109	0.1703	0.1378	0.1117	0.0907	0.0738
24	0.7876	0.6217	0.4919	0.3901	0.3101	0.2470	0.1971	0.1577	0.1264	0.1015	0.0817	0.0659
25	0.7798	0.6095	0.4776	0.3751	0.2953	0.2330	0.1842	0.1460	0.1160	0.0923	0.0736	0.0588
26	0.7720	0.5976	0.4637	0.3607	0.2812	0.2198	0.1722	0.1352	0.1064	0.0839	0.0663	0.0525
27	0.7644	0.5859	0.4502	0.3468	0.2678	0.2074	0.1609	0.1252	0.0976	0.0763	0.0597	0.0469
28	0.7568	0.5744	0.4371	0.3335	0.2551	0.1956	0.1504	0.1159	0.0895	0.0693	0.0538	0.0419
29	0.7493	0.5631	0.4243	0.3207	0.2429	0.1846	0.1406	0.1073	0.0822	0.0630	0.0485	0.0374
30	0.7419	0.5521	0.4120	0.3083	0.2314	0.1741	0.1314	0.0994	0.0754	0.0573	0.0437	0.0334

FV = $1,762.34
N = 5
I/Y = 12
And you will be computing for PV
CPT   PV
PV as calculated is $1,000.00

Steps on calculator:
1. Check default to make sure it is on annual compounding.
    [2nd] [I/Y], display should show P/Y = 1.0000
    [2nd] [CPT] to exit
    If you are sure your calculator is set correctly, this step can be omitted.
2. Clear all previous entries.
    [2nd] [CE/C] [2nd] [FV]
3. Enter the following:
    1762.34 [FV]
    5 [N]
    12 [I/Y]
    [CPT] [PV]
    Display will show PV = −999.9990*
4. To exit and start another calculation:
    [2nd] [CPT]
5. To clear all previous entries to get it ready for the next calculation.
    [2nd] [CE/C] [2nd] [FV]

Note 1: The PV will be shown as a negative number, as it is logical for the calculator to assume that someone has to "give out" (−) $999.9990* today in order to be able to "receive" (+) $1,762.34 at the end of the fifth year.

Note 2: Some calculators may have a compute button such as *CPT*. Some more sophisticated models may let you simply push the particular button, in this case the PV button, as soon as three of the variables have been entered.

Steps on Excel
Note: **Type only the symbols or letters within the bracket [ ] and not the bracket itself.**
1. Type [=] to invoke an equation calculation.
2. Type [pv] to invoke the present value function.
3. Type the open bracket [(]. As soon as [(] is typed, EXCEL displays:
    PV(**rate**,nper,pmt,[fv],[type]); the word rate is bolded to prompt you to enter the rate.
4. Enter rate in decimal form and type a comma[,], **nper** will then be highlighted.
    0.12,
5. Enter number of years and type a comma [,], **pmt** will then be highlighted.
    5,
6. Because we are calculating PV using a FV, pmt will not be applicable for this calculation, so, enter a [,] and now **fv** will be highlighted.
7. Enter 1762.34 and then close the calculation by typing [)]. As soon as you press enter, the amount $1,000 will show in the cell.
8. To recap, for the entire calculation, type the following, then hit the enter key:
    =pv(0.12,5,,1762.34)

ILLUSTRATION 7-4

Present Value of a Lump Sum Using the Calculator and Spreadsheet Methods

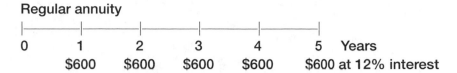

Regular annuity

0	1	2	3	4	5 Years
	$600	$600	$600	$600	$600 at 12% interest

Using this timeline and the other information provided, let us calculate the future value of this annuity. The calculations using the formula and table method are shown in Illustration 7-5.

The calculations using a business calculator or an Excel spreadsheet are detailed in Illustration 7-6. This calculation indicates that an investment of $600 per year with a 12% interest rate yields a total value of $3,811.71 in five years.

THE REAL DEAL

We all express our feelings at one time or another, positively or negatively, regarding the amount of money the government takes from us in the form of taxes, although we do receive some of our taxes back later in our lives as Social Security. We all contribute a percentage of our income to Social Security now so that when we retire we will have an annuity coming back to us from the government. Whether one should rely solely on Social Security for retirement is debatable, and the health and stability of Social Security has been in the news headlines and a major topic of debate with politicians. However, it is a fact that saving now to obtain an annuity in the future is a must if we are to have an enjoyable retirement!

PRESENT VALUE OF AN ANNUITY

Let's refer to Illustrations 7-5 and 7-6 once again. Consider that you have won a small lottery and now have the choice of receiving $600 per year for five years or a lump sum payment today. The lump sum payment today would represent the present value of the five-year $600 annuity using a 12% rate of interest. To calculate the present value of an annuity using the formula and table method, see Illustration 7-7.

The present value of an annuity can be calculated using the *PV*, *N*, *I/Y*, and *PMT* keys on a business calculator. Illustration 7-8 shows the timeline of the payments and the interest rate, and takes you through the calculations using both the business calculator and the Excel spreadsheet.

FUTURE VALUE OF AN ANNUITY DUE

As mentioned earlier, the difference between an annuity and an annuity due is the timing of the cash flow. While the cash flow for a regular annuity is received or paid at the end of each period, the cash flow for an annuity due occurs at the beginning of each period.

```
|----------|----------|----------|----------|----------|
0          1          2          3          4          5   Years
          $600       $600       $600       $600       $600 at 12% interest
```

Using this timeline, this annuity can be an example that a manager of a country club has asked its controller to set aside $600 for some small equipment replacement to take place in five years' time. If the club can find a bank or a financial institution giving a 12% return per year, how much will these five $600 deposits be worth in five years' time?

The formula to calculate the future value of an annuity, written out in long form, is:

$$FVA_5 = \$600 \times (1 + .12)^4 + \$600 \times (1 + .12)^3 + \$600 \times (1 + .12)^2 + \$600 \times (1 + .12)^1 + \$600 \times (1 + .12)^0$$

where

FVA = future value of an annuity

FVA = 944.11 + 842.96 + 752.64 + 672 + 600

        = \$3,811.71

At the same time, this can be done via a formula:

$$FVA_n = PMT \times [(1 + r)^n - 1/r]$$

Where PMT = payment or the annuity amount.

Thus, using the formula method, the calculation of FV will be:

$$FVA_5 = 600 \times [1.12^5 - 1/0.12]$$

$$= 600 \times [6.35]$$

$$= \$3,810$$

If you use the table method, go to Table 7-3, the table for the Future Value Annuity Interest Factors, and find the interest factor for the 12% column with 5 periods. You will see the interest factor, taken to 4 decimal points, as 6.3528. Again, because money grows, the interest factors for future values will always be greater than 1.0. With the number of 6.3528, the calculation of the FVA with an interest factor taken from the table will be

$$FVA_5 = 600 \times (6.3528)$$

$$= \$3,811.68$$

ILLUSTRATION 7-5

Future Value of an Annuity Calculation Using the Formula and Table Methods

TABLE 7-3
Table of Factors for the Future Value of a $1 Annuity

NUMBER OF CASH FLOWS	COMPOUNDING RATE											
	1%	2%	3%	4%	5%	6%	7%	8%	9%	10%	11%	12%
1	1.0000	1.0000	1.0000	1.0000	1.0000	1.0000	1.0000	1.0000	1.0000	1.0000	1.0000	1.0000
2	2.0100	2.0200	2.0300	2.0400	2.0500	2.0600	2.0700	2.0800	2.0900	2.1000	2.1100	2.1200
3	3.0301	3.0604	3.0909	3.1216	3.1525	3.1836	3.2149	3.2464	3.2781	3.3100	3.3421	3.3744
4	4.0604	4.1216	4.1836	4.2465	4.3101	4.3746	4.4399	4.5061	4.5731	4.6410	4.7097	4.7793
5	5.1010	5.2040	5.3091	5.4163	5.5256	5.6371	5.7507	5.8666	5.9847	6.1051	6.2278	6.3528
6	6.1520	6.3081	6.4684	6.6330	6.8019	6.9753	7.1533	7.3359	7.5233	7.7156	7.9129	8.1152
7	7.2135	7.4343	7.6625	7.8983	8.1420	8.3938	8.6540	8.9228	9.2004	9.4872	9.7833	10.0890
8	8.2857	8.5830	8.8923	9.2142	9.5491	9.8975	10.2598	10.6366	11.0285	11.4359	11.8594	12.2997
9	9.3685	9.7546	10.1591	10.5828	11.0266	11.4913	11.9780	12.4876	13.0210	13.5795	14.1640	14.7757
10	10.4622	10.9497	11.4639	12.0061	12.5779	13.1808	13.8164	14.4866	15.1929	15.9374	16.7220	17.5487
11	11.5668	12.1687	12.8078	13.4864	14.2068	14.9716	15.7836	16.6455	17.5603	18.5312	19.5614	20.6546
12	12.6825	13.4121	14.1920	15.0258	15.9171	16.8699	17.8885	18.9771	20.1407	21.3843	22.7132	24.1331
13	13.8093	14.6803	15.6178	16.6268	17.7130	18.8821	20.1406	21.4953	22.9534	24.5227	26.2116	28.0291
14	14.9474	15.9739	17.0863	18.2919	19.5986	21.0151	22.5505	24.2149	26.0192	27.9750	30.0949	32.3926
15	16.0969	17.2934	18.5989	20.0236	21.5786	23.2760	25.1290	27.1521	29.3609	31.7725	34.4054	37.2797
16	17.2579	18.6393	20.1569	21.8245	23.6575	25.6725	27.8881	30.3243	33.0034	35.9497	39.1899	42.7533
17	18.4304	20.0121	21.7616	23.6975	25.8404	28.2129	30.8402	33.7502	36.9737	40.5447	44.5008	48.8837
18	19.6147	21.4123	23.4144	25.6454	28.1324	30.9057	33.9990	37.4502	41.3013	45.5992	50.3959	55.7497
19	20.8109	22.8406	25.1169	27.6712	30.5390	33.7600	37.3790	41.4463	46.0185	51.1591	56.9395	63.4397
20	22.0190	24.2974	26.8704	29.7781	33.0660	36.7856	40.9955	45.7620	51.1601	57.2750	64.2028	72.0524
21	23.2392	25.7833	28.6765	31.9692	35.7193	39.9927	44.8652	50.4229	56.7645	64.0025	72.2651	81.6987
22	24.4716	27.2990	30.5368	34.2480	38.5052	43.3923	49.0057	55.4568	62.8733	71.4027	81.2143	92.5026
23	25.7163	28.8450	32.4529	36.6179	41.4305	46.9958	53.4361	60.8933	69.5319	79.5430	91.1479	104.6029
24	26.9735	30.4219	34.4265	39.0826	44.5020	50.8156	58.1767	66.7648	76.7898	88.4973	102.1742	118.1552
25	28.2432	32.0303	36.4593	41.6459	47.7271	54.8645	63.2490	73.1059	84.7009	98.3471	114.4133	133.3339
26	29.5256	33.6709	38.5530	44.3117	51.1135	59.1564	68.6765	79.9544	93.3240	109.1818	127.9988	150.3339
27	30.8209	35.3443	40.7096	47.0842	54.6691	63.7058	74.4838	87.3508	102.7231	121.0999	143.0786	169.3740
28	32.1291	37.0512	42.9309	49.9676	58.4026	68.5281	80.6977	95.3388	112.9682	134.2099	159.8173	190.6989
29	33.4504	38.7922	45.2189	52.9663	62.3227	73.6398	87.3465	103.9659	124.1354	148.6309	178.3972	214.5828
30	34.7849	40.5681	47.5754	56.0849	66.4388	79.0582	94.4608	113.2832	136.3075	164.4940	199.0209	241.3327

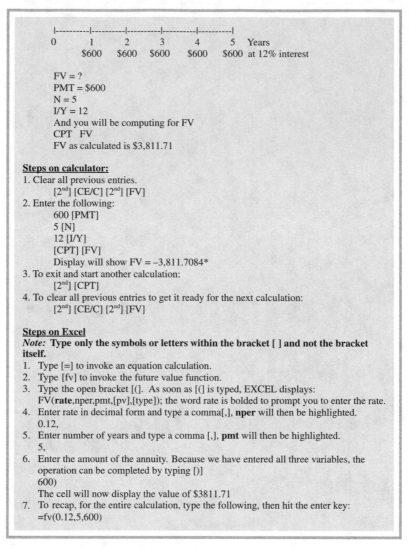

```
|----------|----------|----------|----------|----------|
0          1          2          3          4          5   Years
          $600       $600       $600       $600       $600 at 12% interest
```

FV = ?
PMT = $600
N = 5
I/Y = 12
And you will be computing for FV
CPT   FV
FV as calculated is $3,811.71

Steps on calculator:
1. Clear all previous entries.
　　[2nd] [CE/C] [2nd] [FV]
2. Enter the following:
　　600 [PMT]
　　5 [N]
　　12 [I/Y]
　　[CPT] [FV]
　　Display will show FV = –3,811.7084*
3. To exit and start another calculation:
　　[2nd] [CPT]
4. To clear all previous entries to get it ready for the next calculation:
　　[2nd] [CE/C] [2nd] [FV]

Steps on Excel
Note: **Type only the symbols or letters within the bracket [ ] and not the bracket itself.**
1. Type [=] to invoke an equation calculation.
2. Type [fv] to invoke the future value function.
3. Type the open bracket [(]. As soon as [(] is typed, EXCEL displays:
　　FV(**rate**,nper,pmt,[pv],[type]); the word rate is bolded to prompt you to enter the rate.
4. Enter rate in decimal form and type a comma[,], **nper** will then be highlighted.
　　0.12,
5. Enter number of years and type a comma [,], **pmt** will then be highlighted.
　　5,
6. Enter the amount of the annuity. Because we have entered all three variables, the operation can be completed by typing [)]
　　600)
　　The cell will now display the value of $3811.71
7. To recap, for the entire calculation, type the following, then hit the enter key:
　　=fv(0.12,5,600)

ILLUSTRATION 7-6
Future Value of an Annuity Calculation Using the Calculator and Spreadsheet Methods

Annuity Due

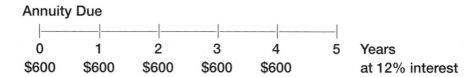

```
|----------|----------|----------|----------|----------|
0          1          2          3          4          5   Years
$600       $600       $600       $600       $600           at 12% interest
```

The formula and table method used to calculate the future value of an annuity due can be found in Illustration 7-9.

```
|----------|----------|----------|----------|----------|
0          1          2          3          4          5   Years
        $600       $600       $600       $600       $600  at 12% interest
PV-?
```

The formula to calculate the present value of an annuity (PVA), written out in long form, is:

$$PVA_5 = \frac{\$600}{(1+.12)^1} + \frac{\$600}{(1+.12)^2} + \frac{\$600}{(1+.12)^3} + \frac{\$600}{(1+.12)^4} + \frac{\$600}{(1+.12)^5}$$

$$= 535.71 + 480 + 428.57 + 382.17 + 340.91$$

$$= \$2,167.36$$

Notice this is like doing the present value calculation five different times. At the same time, this can be done via a formula:

$$PVA_n = PMT \times \frac{[1-\{1/(1+r)^n\}]}{r}$$

Where PMT = payment or the annuity amount.

Thus, using the formula method, the calculation of PVA will be:

$$PVA_5 = 600 \times \frac{[1-\{1/(1+0.12)^5\}]}{0.12}$$
$$= 600 \times 3.6047$$

$$= \$2,162.80$$

If you use the table method, go to Table 7-4, the table for the Present Value Annuity Interest Factors, and find the interest factor for the 12% column with 5 periods. You will see the interest factor, taken to 4 decimal points, as 3.6048. With the number of 3.6048, the calculation of the PVA with an interest factor taken from the table will be:

$$PVA = 600 \times (3.6048)$$

$$= \$2,162.88$$

ILLUSTRATION 7-7

Future Value of an Annuity Calculation Using the Formula and Table Methods

Please note that in order to perform annuity due calculations, business calculators have a button that says *Begin* or *BGN*. Once your calculator is in the *BGN* mode, simply enter the same information as you would for a regular annuity, and the calculator will provide you with answers for an annuity due. Once these calculations are made, you will see that while the future value of a regular annuity was $3,811.71, the future value of an annuity due would be $4,269.11.

TABLE 7-4
Table of Factors for the Present Value of a $1 Annuity

NUMBER OF CASH FLOWS	1%	2%	3%	4%	5%	6%	7%	8%	9%	10%	11%	12%
1	0.9901	0.9804	0.9709	0.9615	0.9524	0.9434	0.9346	0.9259	0.9174	0.9091	0.9009	0.8929
2	1.9704	1.9416	1.9135	1.8861	1.8594	1.8334	1.8080	1.7833	1.7591	1.7355	1.7125	1.6901
3	2.9410	2.8839	2.8286	2.7751	2.7232	2.6730	2.6243	2.5771	2.5313	2.4869	2.4437	2.4018
4	3.9020	3.8077	3.7171	3.6299	3.5460	3.4651	3.3872	3.3121	3.2397	3.1699	3.1024	3.0373
5	4.8534	4.7135	4.5797	4.4518	4.3295	4.2124	4.1002	3.9927	3.8897	3.7908	3.6959	3.6048
6	5.7955	5.6014	5.4172	5.2421	5.0757	4.9173	4.7665	4.6229	4.4859	4.3553	4.2305	4.1114
7	6.7282	6.4720	6.2303	6.0021	5.7864	5.5824	5.3893	5.2064	5.0330	4.8684	4.7122	4.5638
8	7.6517	7.3255	7.0197	6.7327	6.4632	6.2098	5.9713	5.7466	5.5348	5.3349	5.1461	4.9676
9	8.5660	8.1622	7.7861	7.4353	7.1078	6.8017	6.5152	6.2469	5.9952	5.7590	5.5370	5.3282
10	9.4713	8.9826	8.5302	8.1109	7.7217	7.3601	7.0236	6.7101	6.4177	6.1446	5.8892	5.6502
11	10.3676	9.7868	9.2526	8.7605	8.3064	7.8869	7.4987	7.1390	6.8052	6.4951	6.2065	5.9377
12	11.2551	10.5753	9.9540	9.3851	8.8633	8.3838	7.9427	7.5361	7.1607	6.8137	6.4924	6.1944
13	12.1337	11.3484	10.6350	9.9856	9.3936	8.8527	8.3577	7.9038	7.4869	7.1034	6.7499	6.4235
14	13.0037	12.1062	11.2961	10.5631	9.8986	9.2950	8.7455	8.2442	7.7862	7.3667	6.9819	6.6282
15	13.8651	12.8493	11.9379	11.1184	10.3797	9.7122	9.1079	8.5595	8.0607	7.6061	7.1909	6.8109
16	14.7179	13.5777	12.5611	11.6523	10.8378	10.1059	9.4466	8.8514	8.3126	7.8237	7.3792	6.9740
17	15.5623	14.2919	13.1661	12.1657	11.2741	10.4773	9.7632	9.1216	8.5436	8.0216	7.5488	7.1196
18	16.3983	14.9920	13.7535	12.6593	11.6896	10.8276	10.0591	9.3719	8.7556	8.2014	7.7016	7.2497
19	17.2260	15.6785	14.3238	13.1339	12.0853	11.1581	10.3356	9.6036	8.9501	8.3649	7.8393	7.3658
20	18.0456	16.3514	14.8775	13.5903	12.4622	11.4699	10.5940	9.8181	9.1285	8.5136	7.9633	7.4694
21	18.8570	17.0112	15.4150	14.0292	12.8212	11.7641	10.8355	10.0168	9.2922	8.6487	8.0751	7.5620
22	19.6604	17.6580	15.9369	14.4511	13.1630	12.0416	11.0612	10.2007	9.4424	8.7715	8.1757	7.6446
23	20.4558	18.2922	16.4436	14.8568	13.4886	12.3034	11.2722	10.3711	9.5802	8.8832	8.2664	7.7184
24	21.2434	18.9139	16.9355	15.2470	13.7986	12.5504	11.4693	10.5288	9.7066	8.9847	8.3481	7.7843
25	22.0232	19.5235	17.4131	15.6221	14.0939	12.7834	11.6536	10.6748	9.8226	9.0770	8.4217	7.8431
26	22.7952	20.1210	17.8768	15.9828	14.3752	13.0032	11.8258	10.8100	9.9290	9.1609	8.4881	7.8957
27	23.5596	20.7069	18.3270	16.3296	14.6430	13.2105	11.9867	10.9352	10.0266	9.2372	8.5478	7.9426
28	24.3164	21.2813	18.7641	16.6631	14.8981	13.4062	12.1371	11.0511	10.1161	9.3066	8.6016	7.9844
29	25.0658	21.8444	19.1885	16.9837	15.1411	13.5907	12.2777	11.1584	10.1983	9.3696	8.6501	8.0218
30	25.8077	22.3965	19.6004	17.2920	15.3725	13.7648	12.4090	11.2578	10.2737	9.4269	8.6938	8.0552

```
|----------|----------|----------|----------|----------|
0          1          2          3          4          5    Years
         $600       $600       $600       $600       $600  at 12% interest


PV=?
PMT = $600
N = 5
I/Y = 12
And you will be computing for PV
CPT  PV
PV as calculated is $2,162.87
```

Steps on calculator:
1. Clear all previous entries.
    $[2^{nd}]$ [CE/C] $[2^{nd}]$ [FV]
2. Enter the following:
    600 [PMT]
    5 [N]
    12 [I/Y]
    [CPT] [PV]
    Display will show PV = −2,162.87
3. To exit and start another calculation:
    $[2^{nd}]$ [CPT]
4. To clear all previous entries to get it ready for the next calculation:
    $[2^{nd}]$ [CE/C] $[2^{nd}]$ [FV]

Steps on Excel
Note: **Type only the symbols or letters within the bracket [ ] and not the bracket itself.**
1. Type [=] to invoke an equation calculation.
2. Type [fv] to invoke the future value function.
3. Type the open bracket [(]. As soon as [(] is typed, EXCEL displays:
    PV(**rate**,nper,pmt,[pv],[type]); the word rate is bolded to prompt you to enter the rate.
4. Enter rate in decimal form and type a comma[,], **nper** will then be highlighted.
    0.12,
5. Enter number of years and type a comma [,], **pmt** will then be highlighted.
    5,
6. Enter the amount of the annuity. Since we have entered all 3 variables, the operation can be completed by typing [)]
    600)
    The cell will now display the value of $2,162.87,
7. To recap, for the entire calculation, type the following, then hit the enter key:
    =pv(0.12,5,600)

ILLUSTRATION 7-8
Present Value of an Annuity Calculation Using the Calculator and Spreadsheet Methods

PRESENT VALUE OF AN ANNUITY DUE

In financial management, present value is used to evaluate investment opportunities. The formula and table method is shown in Illustration 7-11.

Let us now calculate the present value of this annuity due using a business calculator or Excel. In this case, while the regular annuity yielded a present value of $2,162.87, the present value is now $2,422.41. Because an annuity due is received or paid at the beginning of the period, as opposed to the end, the present value of an annuity due will always be more than the present value of a regular annuity.

Annuity Due

```
|----------|----------|----------|----------|----------|
0          1          2          3          4          5    Years
$600       $600       $600       $600       $600            at 12% interest
```

The formula to calculate the future value of an annuity due, written out in long form, is:

$$FVAD_5 = \$600 \times (1 + .12)^5 + \$600 \times (1 + .12)^4 + \$600 \times (1 + .12)^3 +$$

$$\$600 \times (1 + .12)^2 + \$600 \times (1 + .12)^1$$

where

FVAD = future value of an annuity due

FVAD = 1,057.41 + 944.11 + 842.96 + 752.64 + 672

    = $4,269.12

At the same time, this can be done via a formula:

$$FVAD_n = PMT \times [(1 + r)^n - 1/r] \times (1+r)$$

Where PMT = payment or the annuity amount.

Thus, using the formula method, the calculation of FV will be:

$$FVAD_5 = 600 \times [1.12^5 - 1/ 0.12] \times (1.12)$$

$$= 600 \times [6.35] \times (1.12)$$

$$= \$4,267.20$$

If you use the table method, go to Table 7-3, the table for the Future Value Annuity Interest Factors, and find the interest factor for the 12% column with 5 periods. You will see the interest factor, taken to 4 decimal points, as 6.3528. However, to get to annuity due, you are compounding it for one more period, so you will multiply by another $(1+r)$ or, in this case $(1 + 0.12)$. With the number of 6.3528, the calculation of the FVAD with an interest factor taken from the table will be:

$$FVAD_5 = 600 \times (6.3528) \times 1.12$$

$$= \$4,269.08$$

ILLUSTRATION 7-9

Future Value of an Annuity Due Calculation Using the Formula and Table Methods

Annuity Due

```
|----------|----------|----------|----------|----------|
    0          1          2          3          4          5    Years
  $600       $600       $600       $600       $600              at 12% interest
```

Future Value of an Annuity Due
    PMT = $600
    N = 5
    I/Y = 12
    And you will be computing for FV
    CPT FV
    FV as calculated is $4,269.11

Steps on calculator:
1. Change to annuity due mode:
    [2nd] [PMT]
    If display shows the word END, then enter:
    [2nd] [ENTER] which will invoke the SET function above the [ENTER] key.
    The display will now show BGN in big letters and also SET and BGN in small letters.
2. Enter [2nd] [CPT] to exit to get ready for calculation.
    The display will now show the smaller letters BGN on top of the value 0.0000
3. Enter the following:
    600 [PMT]
    5 [N]
    12 [I/Y]
    [CPT] FV]
    Display will show FV = −4,269.1134*
4. To exit and start another calculation:
    [2nd] [CPT]
5. To clear all previous entries to get it ready for the next calculation:
    [2nd] [CE/C] [2nd] [FV]
6. To change calculator back to the END mode:
    [2nd] [PMT] [2nd] [ENTER] [2nd] [CPT]

Steps on Excel
Note: **Type only the symbols or letters within the bracket [ ] and not the bracket itself.**
1. Type [=] to invoke an equation calculation.
2. Type [fv] to invoke the future value function.
3. Type the open bracket [(]. As soon as [(] is typed, EXCEL displays:
    FV(**rate**,nper,pmt,[pv],[type]); the word rate is bolded to prompt you to enter the rate.
4. Enter rate in decimal form and type a comma[,], **nper** will then be highlighted.
    0.12,
5. Enter number of years and type a comma [,], **pmt** will then be highlighted.
    5,
6. Enter the amount of the annuity and type a comma [,], **[pv]** will then be highlighted.
    Because we are calculating FV using PMT, PV is not needed, so we can type another comma [,], **[type]** will then be highlighted.
    600,,
7. To signify an annuity due, type [1], close the bracket [)], and hit enter.
    1)
8. The cell will now display 4,269.11
9. To recap the entire calculation, type the following, then hit the enter key:
    =fv(0.12,5,600,,1)

ILLUSTRATION 7-10
Future Value of an Annuity Due Calculation Using the Business Calculator and Spreadsheet Methods

To calculate the present value of an annuity due (PVAD), written in long form:

$$PVAD_5 = \$600 + \frac{\$600}{(1+.12)^1} + \frac{\$600}{(1+.12)^2} + \frac{\$600}{(1+.12)^3} + \frac{\$600}{(1+.12)^4}$$

$$= 600 + 535.71 + 480 + 428.57 + 382.17$$

$$= \$2,424.45$$

At the same time, this can be done via a formula:

$$PVAD_n = PMT \times \frac{[1-\{1/(1+r)^n\}]}{r} \times (1+r)$$

Where PMT = payment or the annuity amount.

Thus, using the formula method, the calculation of PVAD will be:

$$PVAD_5 = 600 \times \frac{[1-\{1/(1+0.12)^5\}]}{0.12} \times 1.12$$

$$= 600 \times 3.6047 \times 1.12$$

$$= \$2,422.34$$

If you use the table method, go to Table 7-4, the table for the Present Value Annuity

Interest Factors, and find the interest factor for the 12% column with 5 periods. You will

see the interest factor, taken to 4 decimal points, as 3.6047. However, to get to annuity

due, you are compounding it for one more period, so you will multiply by another $(1+r)$,

or, in this case $(1+0.12)$. With the number of 3.6047, the calculation of the PVAD with

an interest factor taken from the table will be:

$$PVAD_5 = 600 \times (3.6047) \times 1.13$$

$$= \$2,422.34$$

ILLUSTRATION 7-11

Present Value of an Annuity Due Calculation Using the Formula and Table Method

Using Excel, an annuity due is signified in the formula under [type]. Simply enter the number [1] to signify that your calculation is an annuity due. As detailed in Illustration 7-12, an investment of $600 per year yields a present value of $2,422.41.

PERPETUITY

A **perpetuity** is a special type of annuity that pays or receives cash with no time limit. One method of valuation, known as the *capitalization method,* uses the basics of a perpetuity. The cap rate method of valuation is an investment analysis tool that will be discussed in the next chapter. The formula for a perpetuity is simple:

Regular Annuity

```
|---------|---------|---------|---------|---------|
0         1         2         3         4         5   Years
          $600      $600      $600      $600      $600  at 12% interest
```

Annuity Due

```
|---------|---------|---------|---------|---------|
0         1         2         3         4         5   Years
$600      $600      $600      $600      $600          at 12% interest
```

Present Value of an Annuity Due

    PMT = $600
    N = 5
    I/Y = 12
    And you will be computing for PV
    CPT   PV
    PV as calculated is $2,422.41

Steps on calculator:

1. Change to annuity due mode:
    [2nd] [PMT]
    If display shows the word END, then enter
    [2nd] [ENTER] which will invoke the SET function above the [ENTER] key.
    The display will now show BGN in big letters and also SET and BGN in small letters.
2. Enter [2nd] [CPT] to exit to get ready for calculation.
    The display will now show the smaller letters BGN on top of the value 0.0000
3. Enter the following:
    600 [PMT]
    5 [N]
    12 [I/Y]
    [CPT] [PV]
    Display will show PV = –2,422.4096*
4. To exit and start another calculation:
    [2nd] [CPT]
5. To clear all previous entries to get it ready for the next calculation:
    [2nd] [CE/C] [2nd] [FV]
6. To change calculator back to the END mode:
    [2nd] [PMT] [2nd] [ENTER] [2nd] [CPT]

Steps in Excel

Note: **Type only the symbols or letters within the bracket [ ] and not the bracket itself.**

1. Type [=] to invoke an equation calculation.
2. Type [pv] to invoke the future value function.
3. Type the open bracket [(]. As soon as [(] is typed EXCEL displays:
    PV(**rate**,nper,pmt,[fv],[type]); the word rate is bolded to prompt you to enter the rate.
4. Enter rate in decimal form and type a comma[,], **nper** will then be highlighted.
    0.12,
5. Enter number of years and type a comma [,], **pmt** will then be highlighted
    5,
6. Enter the amount of the annuity and type a comma [,], **[fv]** will then be highlighted.
    Because we are calculating PV using PMT, FV is not needed, so we can type another comma [,], **[type]** will then be highlighted.
    600,,
7. To signify an annuity due, type [1], close the bracket [)], and hit enter.
    1)
8. The cell will now display 2,422.41.
9. To recap the entire calculation, type the following, then hit the enter key:
    =pv(0.12,5,600,,1)

ILLUSTRATION 7-12

Present Value of an Annuity Due Calculation Using the Business Calculator and Spreadsheet Methods

THE REAL DEAL

How much do you need to put away on a monthly basis if you want to be a millionaire when you retire? It depends on several variables. It depends on how old you are now, the age at which you want to retire, and the average annual rate of return you think you can earn on your investment from now until your retirement. For example, a college student at age twenty who wants to retire at age sixty has forty years or 480 months (40 years × 12 months a year) to save. If she can earn a 12% annual return on her investment, or 1% per month, all she needs to save and invest is $85.00 per month. If you are very conservative and just want to open a savings account in a bank or put your savings into a certificate of deposit, which earns roughly 3% per year, you must put away $1,079.84 per month. Many people invest in some sort of mutual fund and earn about 8% per year, which translates into $286.45 a month. If you wait until you are thirty, you will only have thirty years or 360 months to save. If you can earn 12% interest on your money, your monthly investment must be $286.13 rather than $85.00—a big difference! The secret? Save early and often!

$$PV \text{ perpetuity} = \frac{PMT}{r}, \text{ where}$$

$$PMT = \text{annuity payment}$$

$$r = \text{interest rate}$$

You don't necessarily need to use a business calculator or Excel to calculate the value of a perpetuity. Simply divide the annuity payment by the interest or cap rate. To prove the formula, select a hypothetical annuity payment and calculate its present value using a large N of 1,000. You will find that your answer is exactly the same as you calculated by dividing the payment by the cap rate.

THE REAL DEAL

Is a car loan an annuity or an uneven cash flow? While the car loan may be an annuity, the entire car purchase transaction is more like an uneven cash flow, especially if you are leasing a car with a purchase option and have a balloon payment to make at the end of the lease. The initial down payment and the one large balloon payment at the end make the entire purchase an uneven stream of cash flow. Much of the advertising on the radio and on television stresses low monthly payments. While this may be the case, do not jump into signing papers until you absolutely understand how much you need to pay now and what the balloon payment is that you must pay in the future. Some balloon payments may be thousands of dollars and, at times, 40% to 50% of the total value of the car. Now that you know the mathematics of finance, make sure you do your own calculations rather than just taking the word of the advertisers.

UNEVEN STREAM OF CASH FLOW

Now that you have a working knowledge of the basic mathematics of finance, let's apply this knowledge to simple investment analysis. In the real world, not everything comes in neat packages. For example, the cash flow for a particular business is not usually the same each month or each year. Thus, the concept of an **uneven stream of cash flow** mirrors reality much better than an annuity does.

PRESENT VALUE OF AN UNEVEN CASH FLOW

Illustration 7-13 presents an uneven stream of cash flow a hospitality manager has projected for his business over a five-year period. In this example, he expects business to be a little slow during the initial years. He expects business to pick up a bit in the second year, really take off in Year 3, and then stabilize and earn around $300 annually thereafter. Based on the projections, how much is this stream of cash flow worth today?

One approach is to calculate the present value of each year's cash flow individually and add them together, as shown in Option 1. This option takes a little longer but will result in the correct answer of $760.49. Alternatively, you can use the *cash flow* function key on your business calculator, enter each year's cash flow as instructed, and compute the present value a little faster.

Illustration 7-13 details the steps you should take if using a Texas Instrument BAII Plus business calculator. Using this calculator for cash flow calculations may be daunting the first time you try; however, you need to learn this method because you will use it to calculate net present value and internal rate of return a little later in the text. Learning the steps, practicing them a few times, and mastering them will save you a lot of time and headaches later.

FUTURE VALUE OF AN UNEVEN CASH FLOW

Because the cash flow [CF] functions only work with net present value [NPV] and internal rate of return [IRR], to compute the future value [FV] of an uneven cash flow stream, you must first compute its present value [PV] and then compute its future value. In this case, the present value [PV] was calculated to be $760.49. To calculate its future value, enter the present value as calculated, the interest rate, and 5 as the period. The future value is $1,224.78.

Time Period and Compounding

In terms of debt financing, a monthly versus annual compounding period favors the lender over the borrower because interest expense is accrued or paid monthly. Thus, compounding can make a big difference when calculating debt service payments. Let us look at how compounding can change results. Using the example shown earlier in Illustration 7-2, we will use the same variables but change the compounding period from annual to monthly and see what happens.

```
|----------|----------|----------|----------|----------|
0          1          2          3          4          5    Years
          $50        $100       $300       $305       $320  I/Y at 10%
```

Option 1 Using Lump Sum Calculations   Steps on calculator
FV = 50   50 [FV]
N = 1   1 [N]
I/Y = 10   10 [I/Y]
CPT PV = −$45.45   [CPT] [PV]

FV = 100   100 [FV]
N = 2   2 [N]
I/Y = 10   10 [I/Y]
CPT PV = −$82.64   [CPT] [PV]

FV = 300   300 [FV]
N = 3   3 [N]
I/Y = 10   10 [I/Y]
CPT PV = −$225.39   [CPT] [PV]

FV = 305   305 [FV]
N = 4   4 [N]
I/Y = 10   10 [I/Y]
CPT PV = −$208.32   [CPT] [PV]

FV = 320   320 [FV]
N = 5   4 [N]
I/Y = 10   10 [I/Y]
CPT PV = −$198.69   [CPT] [PV]

*The five individual amounts will have to be totaled manually to obtain the aggregate PV of $760.49.

Option 2 Using the cash flow function in a business calculator
The [CF] button is right above the [I/Y] button on the calculator. Next to the [CF] button are two important function buttons: [NPV] and [IRR].

Steps on calculator
1. Enter into the cash flow function:
        [CF]   Display will show CFo = 0.0000 with the word ENTER and the down
                arrow [↓] and up arrow [↑] keys as your prompters.
2. Clear all previous entries in this worksheet (in case the calculator has been used to
    perform another cash flow calculation and has not been cleared).
        [2nd] [CE/C]
3. Enter the cash flows given, and their frequencies, year by year. On the display, the
    notation C0 means cash flow and the 1, 2, etc., stand for the year. In other words, C01
    means the cash flow for the first year. Similarly, F0 stands for the frequency. Thus
    F01 stands for the number of times C01 can be found consecutively. In this example,
    as all cash flows are different, the frequencies will all be 1. If the first year and
    second year cash flows are both the same, then F01 will be 2 instead.
        When entered [CF] in step one, display shows CFo= 0.0000
        After clearing the worksheet with [2nd] [CE/C], use the down arrow key:
        [↓]   Display shows C01   0.0000 with no equal sign "="
        50 [ENTER]   Display shows C01= 50.0000
        [↓]   Display shows F01=   1.0000, since this is true that we only have
                      C01 one time, we can simply accept this by entering the down
                      arrow key again
        [↓]   Display shows C02   0.0000 with no equal sign "="
        100 [ENTER]   Display shows C02= 100.000
        [↓]   Display shows F02=   1.0000, since this is true that we only have
                      C02 one time, we can simply accept this by entering the down

ILLUSTRATION 7-13
Present Value of an Uneven Cash Flow Stream

```
                        arrow key again
          [↓]           Display shows C03   0.0000 with no equal sign "="
          300 [ENTER]   Display shows C03= 300.0000
          [↓]           Display shows F03=     1.0000, since this is true that we only have
                        C03 one time, we can simply accept this by entering the down
                        arrow key again
          [↓]           Display shows C04   0.0000 with no equal sign "="
          305 [ENTER]   Display shows C04= 305.0000
          [↓]           Display shows F04=     1.0000, since this is true that we only have
                        C04 one time, we can simply accept this by entering the down
                        arrow key again
          [↓]           Display shows C05   0.0000 with no equal sign "="
          320 [ENTER]   Display shows C05= 320.0000
          [↓]           Display shows F05=     1.0000, since this is true that we only have
                        C04 one time, we can simply accept this by entering the down
                        arrow key again
          [↓]           Display shows C06  0.000 with no equal sign "=". Now that all
                        cash flows have been entered, you can compute
          [CPT] [NPV]   Display shows I = 0.0000, prompting you to enter the interest
          10 [ENTER]
          [CPT] [NPV]   Display shows I = 10.0000, now you can do the final steps
          [↓]           Display shows NPV =  0.0000
          [CPT]         Display shows 760.5075*
```

*There is a slight difference due to rounding.

ILLUSTRATION 7-13
(*Continued*)

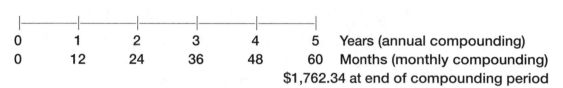

0	1	2	3	4	5	Years (annual compounding)
0	12	24	36	48	60	Months (monthly compounding)

$1,762.34 at end of compounding period

Because there are twelve months in a year, a five-year compounding period now becomes sixty periods (5 years × 12 months per year), and the interest rate associated with each month's payment (compounding period) is now 1% (12% ÷ 12 months per year). If money is compounded semiannually, we would have to multiply the time by two (5 years × 2 halves per year = 10 compounding periods) and divide the rate by two (12% ÷ 2 = 6%). If the loan were compounded quarterly, the compounding period would become twenty (5 years × 4 quarters per year) and the interest rate 3% (12% ÷ 4 quarters per year). Illustration 7-14 shows the effects on present value if the compounding period changes from annual to monthly. In this case, the PV is $970.08 when the money is compounded monthly, which is less than the $1,000 when money is compounded annually.

LOAN AMORTIZATION

Earlier in the book, we discussed loan terms such as principal, length of loan, interest rate, and amortization rate. Recall that in one illustration, a loan of $100,000 that charged a 10% annual interest rate was calculated for both a three-year and five-year period, compounded annually.

Annual Compounding
FV = $1,762.34
N = 5
I/Y = 12
And you will be computing for PV
CPT   PV
PV as calculated is $1,000.00

Monthly Compounding
FV = $1,762.34
N = 5 X 12 = 60
I/Y = 12 / 12 = 1
CPT PV
PV as calculated is $970.0794*

Steps on calculator:
1. Clear all previous entries
        [2nd] [CE/C] [2nd] [FV]
2. Enter the following:
        1762.34 [FV]
        60 [N]
        1 [I/Y]
        [CPT] [PV]
        Display will show PV = –970.0794*
3. To exit and start another calculation:
        [2nd] [CPT]
4. To clear all previous entries to get it ready for the next calculation:
        [2nd] [CE/C] [2nd] [FV]

Steps on Excel
Note: **Type only the symbols or letters within the bracket [ ] and not the bracket itself.**
1. Type [=] to invoke an equation calculation.
2. Type [pv] to invoke the present value function.
3. Type the open bracket [(]. As soon as [(] is typed, EXCEL displays:
    PV(**rate**,nper,pmt,[fv],[type]); the word rate is bolded to prompt you to enter the rate.
4. The rate has now changed to 1%. Enter rate in decimal form and type a comma[,],
    nper will then be highlighted.
    0.01,
5. The number of compounding periods has now changed to 60. Enter the number of
    compounding periods and type a comma [,], **pmt** will then be highlighted.
    60,
6. Because we are calculating PV using a FV, pmt will not be applicable for this
    calculation, so, enter a [,] and now **fv** will be highlighted.
    ,
7. Enter 1762.34 and then close the calculation by typing [)]. As soon as you press
    enter, the amount $1,000 will show in the cell.
    1762.34)
8. To recap, for the entire calculation, type the following, then hit the enter key:
    =pv(0.01,60,,1762.34)

ILLUSTRATION 7-14

Compounding Period for a Lump Sum: Annual Compounding to Monthly Compounding

LOAN COMPOUNDED FOR 3 YEARS

YEAR	PAYMENT	PRINCIPAL	INTEREST	BALANCE
1	40,211.48	30,211.48	10,000.00	69,788.52
2	40,211.48	33,232.63	6,978.85	36,555.89
3	40,211.48	36,555.89	3,655.59	0.00
Total	120,634.44	100,000.00	20,634.44	

LOAN COMPOUNDED FOR 5 YEARS

YEAR	PAYMENT	PRINCIPAL	INTEREST	BALANCE
1	26,379.75	16,379.75	10,000.00	83,620.25
2	26,379.75	18,017.72	8,362.03	65,602.53
3	26,379.75	19,819.50	6,560.25	45,783.03
4	26,379.75	20,801.45	4,578.30	23,981.59
5	26,379.75	23,981.59	2,398.16	0.00
Total	131,898.75	100,000.00	31,898.75	

Now that you know the basic time value of money calculations, the debt service calculation for a loan is easy. It's an annuity calculation where:

PV = loan amount

N = number of compounding periods

I/Y = interest per compounding period

With three variables, you can compute the fourth—PMT, in this case—the debt service payment you need to make each period. Illustration 7-15 provides the steps necessary to calculate PMT using a business calculator and Excel.

LOAN AMORTIZATION SCHEDULE

Preparing a loan amortization schedule that includes years, payment, principal, interest, and balance is easy to do using your calculator. Using a three-year loan as an example, here are the steps involved:

YEAR 1

1. Calculate the interest amount:

   $100,000 × 10% = $10,000

2. Calculate the principal paid: Payment − interest

   = $40,211.48 − $10,000

   = $30,211.48

3. Calculate the balance: Balance from last payment − principal

   = $100,000 − $30,211.48

   = $69,788.52

3-Year Loan
```
    |-----------|-----------|-----------|
    0           1           2           3    Years
                                        at 10%
```
PV=100,000
            PMT?   PMT?   PMT?

5-Year Loan
```
    |-----------|-----------|-----------|-----------|-----------|
    0           1           2           3           4           5    Years
                                                                at 10%
```
PV=100,000
            PMT?   PMT?   PMT?   PMT?   PMT?

Given:
3-Year Loan
    PV = $100,000
    N = 3
    I/Y = 10
    And you will be computing for PMT
    CPT PMT
    PMT as calculated is $40,211.48

5-Year Loan
    PV = $100,000
    N = 5
    I/Y = 10
    And you will be computing for PMT
    CPT PMT
    PMT as calculated is $26,379.75

Steps on calculator:
1. Clear all previous entries.
    $[2^{nd}]$ [CE/C] $[2^{nd}]$ [FV]
2. Enter the following:
    100,000 [PV]
    3 [N]
    10 [I/Y]
    [CPT] [PMT]
    Display will show PMT = –40,211.4804*

To calculate for the 5-year loan, simply change the 3 to a 5.

Steps in Excel
Note: **Type only the symbols or letters within the bracket [ ] and not the bracket itself.**
1. Type [=] to invoke an equation calculation.
2. Type [pmt] to invoke the future value function.
3. Type the open bracket [(]. As soon as [(] is typed, EXCEL displays:
    PMT(**rate**,nper,pv,[fv],[type]); the word rate is bolded to prompt you to enter the rate.
4. Enter rate in decimal form and type a comma[,], **nper** will then be highlighted
    0.1,
5. Enter number of years and type a comma [,], **pv** will then be highlighted.
    3,
6. Enter the amount of the loan or present value. Because we have entered all three
    variables, the operation can be completed by typing [)]
    100,000).
    The cell will now display the value of $40,211.48.
7. To recap, for the entire calculation, type the following, then hit the enter key:
    =pmt(0.1,5,100000)

To calculate for the 5-year loan, simply change the 3 to a 5.

ILLUSTRATION 7-15
Loan Payment Calculation

YEAR 2 (REPEAT STEPS)

1. Calculate the interest amount

    $69,788.52 × 10% = $6,978.55

2. Calculate the principal paid: Payment − interest

    = $40,211.48 − $6,978.85

    = $33,232.63

3. Calculate the balance: Balance from last payment − principal

    = $69788.52 − $33,232.63

    = $36,555,89

YEAR 3 (REPEAT STEPS)

1. Calculate the interest amount

    $36,555.89 × 10% = $3,655.59

2. Calculate the principal paid: Payment − interest

    = $40,211.48 − $3,655.59

    = $36,555.89

3. Calculate the balance: Balance from last payment − principal

    = $36,555.89 − $36,555.89

    = $0, as it should be, as this is the end of the loan

THE REAL DEAL

Always know how to calculate an annuity! Ever wonder if you can afford that brand-new luxury car that costs $50,000 when you graduate from college and land your first full-time job? At $50,000, with no down payment, a six-year note at 8% interest equates to a monthly payment of $876.66. Considering that most undergraduate hospitality students receive a starting salary of $40,000, your take-home pay per month would be approximately $2,500. A luxury-type car would probably also carry a huge insurance premium. With gas prices at $3.00 per gallon, you would require over $1,000 per month to drive that car. This does not even include maintenance work such as oil changes. So, before you shop for a brand-new car, consider a used vehicle and perhaps one that is more a middle-of-the-road model. What you need is a dependable set of wheels to get you to work. Once you arrive at your place of work, whether a hotel, restaurant, or club, the type of car you drive does not affect your job performance!

The second level of your business calculator makes it even easier to prepare an amortization schedule. Above the PV button you will see the word *Amort*. Illustration 7-16 shows how an amortization schedule can be generated.

3-Year Loan
|-----------|-----------|-----------|
   0   1   2   3   Years
                                 at 10%

PV=100,000

              PMT?   PMT?   PMT?

Steps on calculator:
1. Clear all previous entries.
    [2nd] [CE/C] [2nd] [FV]
2. Calculate the loan payment:
    100,000 [PV]
    3 [N]
    10 [I/Y]
    [CPT] [PMT]
    Display will show PMT = –40,211.4804*
3. Once this is calculated, the calculator now has this loan component stored. As soon as the PMT is shown, enter:
    [2nd][PV] to invoke the amortization function
4. P1 = 1.000 will now be displayed. P1 stands for the beginning of a period and P2 stands for the end of a period. With the display showing P1, this means the calculator is looking at the beginning of period 1, in this case, Year 1. You will also notice three choices on the display: "ENTER" "↓" and "↑". We would want to start with the first year, so we can go ahead and enter the down arrow:
    [↓]
5. P2 = 1.000 will now be displayed. This means we are looking at the end of the first period, in this case, first year. Again, we can enter the down arrow to go to the next screen:
    [↓]
6. The display now shows the balance of after the first year at $69,788.5196. Again enter the down arrow:
    [↓]
7. The display now shows the principal of $30,311.4804. Enter down arrow one more time:
    [↓]
8. The display now shows the interest of $10,000.
9. When the down arrow is entered again, P1 = 1.000 will come up. To go to the second year, enter the following to change the 1.000 to 2.000:
    2 [ENTER] [↓]
10. P2 = 1.000 will come up. You also want to change that to the second year:
    2 [ENTER] [↓]
11. When you enter the [↓] again, you will see the balance, principal, and interest for the second year.
12. To obtain the numbers for the third year, when the calculator wraps back showing P1 = 2.000, then enter the following to change it to three years' time:
    3 [ENTER] [↓]
13. Follow the same steps, and you will be able to obtain all the numbers for the amortization table.

ILLUSTRATION 7-16
Loan Amortization

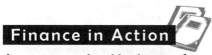

Finance in Action

Acquiring the Underperforming Urban Hotel

The Clover Hotel Company has an opportunity to acquire an underperforming hotel below market value in a great market with high barriers to entry. Clover specializes in purchasing properties of this type, turning them around, and then selling them for a profit. The asking price is $10 million, and Clover has projected the following annual cash flows:

Year	Cash Flow
1	$750,000
2	$1,000,000
3 forward	$1,250,000

This opportunity offers a major challenge in that Clover Hotel Company only has thirty days to secure financing and close the deal. Luckily, the company has a good reputation with several lenders and is able to secure the two financing scenarios listed below.

1. Sherman Bank has offered an $8 million loan at a 7% annual interest rate with a twenty-year term.

2. The second lender, Clayton Bank, has also offered an $8 million loan with a twenty-year term, but with a 6% interest rate compounded monthly.

In both scenarios, Clover Hotel Company will provide the additional $2 million required to fund the deal.

QUESTIONS

1. Compute debt service payments for each scenario. Compare total annual payments owed in each scenario.

   The first step necessary in answering this question is to identify the variables needed for the payment calculation:

   present value [PV]

   number of compounding periods [N]

   interest per compounding period [I/Y]

   Let's look at Scenario #1, Sherman Bank, first.

   present value is $8,000,000

compounding periods are 20

interest rate of 7% per compounding period

The second scenario, for Clayton Bank, is slightly more complicated because this lender requires monthly payments with a monthly compounding interest rate.

Again, the present value is $8,000,000

number of compounding periods is 240 (20 × 12)

monthly interest rate of 0.5% (6% ÷ 12)

Now that you have the input variables, simply enter them into your finance calculator or Excel spreadsheet to calculate debt service payments. Annual debt service payments for Sherman Bank equal $755,143 and for Clayton Bank total $687,774 ($57,314 × 12). Simply looking at the numbers, annual debt service payments would be less for Clayton Bank than for Sherman Bank.

2. Based on your calculations, for each of the financing scenarios, what amount of net cash flow would the company receive each year?

As stated in the case, cash flows are $750,000 for Year 1, $1,000,000 for Year 2, and $1,250,000 for Year 3. To determine net cash flow, simply subtract annual debt service payments from the projected cash flows. The following tables detail the two scenarios.

Scenario #1: Sherman Bank

Year	Cash Flow	Debt Service Payments	Net Cash Flows
1	$750,000	($755,143)	($5,143)
2	$1,000,000	($755,143)	$244,856
3	$1,250,000	($755,143)	$494,856

Scenario #2: Clayton Bank

Year	Cash Flow	Debt Service Payments	Net Cash Flows
1	$750,000	($687,774)	$62,226
2	$1,000,000	($687,774)	$312,226
3	$1,250,000	($687,774)	$562,226

3. Which of the two financing scenarios would you recommend Clover pursue, and why?

Clearly, Clayton Bank is offering a better option for the Clover Hotel Company. As can be seen in the calculations, choosing Sherman Bank would leave Clover with negative net cash flows of $5,143 in Year 1, whereas the Clayton Bank option would provide positive net cash flows of $62,226.

WHERE WE'VE BEEN, WHERE WE'RE GOING

You should now have a basic understanding of the time value of money concept, the market value concept, the factors that impact present or market value, and how to perform the basic time value of money calculations. Chapters 8 and 9 apply these concepts and calculations to investment analysis techniques and hospitality industry scenarios. First, however, please remember the old adage "practice makes perfect" and work through the mini case studies and exercises that follow to gain a better command of the basic time value of money calculations before moving on to the next chapter.

Key Points

- ➤ When analyzing an investment opportunity, the key value is an asset's present or market value.
- ➤ An asset's present or market value is based on the amount of future cash flow the asset is projected to generate, the timing of the cash flow, the risk of the cash flow being generated, and the mix of capital used to finance the cash flowing asset.
- ➤ As the risk of receiving projected future cash flow increases, the investor's hurdle rate increases, WACC increases, and the present or market value of the asset decreases. The reverse is also true—that is, as risk decreases, present or market value increases.
- ➤ Present or market value can also be defined as the current value of an asset's projected cash flows discounted back to the present, using WACC as the discount rate.
- ➤ Future value is the value that accumulates from an initial amount of money placed in an investment that earns interest income or a profit over time. Factors affecting present values similarly affect future values.
- ➤ Cash flow can be a single sum, a fixed stream (annuity), or an uneven stream. In reality, most cash flows generated by investments come in the form of an uneven cash flow stream.
- ➤ The concept of an annuity can be applied to loan payments. The schedule of payments is called a *loan amortization schedule*.

Key Terms

TIME VALUE OF MONEY (TVM): The cornerstone of investment analysis. This concept is based on the premise that the value of money is not only its face value but also the interest or profit that can be earned by investing it wisely.

CERTIFICATE OF DEPOSIT: Also known as a CD, a savings vehicle that gives the purchaser or bearer of the certificate the right to receive interest. A CD has a fixed interest rate and maturity date. If the bearer withdraws the funds before the maturity date, a penalty is normally assessed.

PRESENT VALUE (PV): The current value of a cash-flowing asset based on the amount and timing of its projected cash flows.

FUTURE VALUE (FV): The value of a cash-flowing asset some time in the future, assuming a compounded rate of interest.

MARKET VALUE: The present value of a cash-flowing asset based on its projected future cash flow, factoring in the timing of the cash flow, the risk of the cash flow being generated, and the mix of capital used to finance the deal.

HURDLE RATE: An investor's ROI target.

WACC: Weighted average cost of capital—that is, the blended cost of the debt and the equity used to finance a deal.

INVESTMENT ANALYSIS: A process of estimating an asset's current market value, which can then be compared with its cost to acquire or develop.

DISCOUNT RATE: The weighted average cost of capital used, as the I/Y in present value calculations.

SINGLE SUM (LUMP SUM): A time value of money concept where only a single sum of money is involved in the calculation.

ANNUITY: A fixed amount of money received or paid each compounding period for a set period.

REGULAR ANNUITY: Fixed amount of money received or paid at the end of each compounding period for a set time.

ANNUITY DUE: Same as a regular annuity except the payments occur at the beginning of the compounding period rather than at the end.

PERPETUITY: An annuity that yields the same cash flow forever.

UNEVEN STREAM OF CASH FLOW: A stream of cash flow where the payments are not the same in all compounding periods.

Application Exercises

1. Which is better, a present value of $100 or a future value of $100? Please explain.

2. Define and explain two factors that affect the present value of an asset.

3. In five years, what is the future value of $4,000 if the interest rate is 10% and money is compounded monthly? What is the future value if money is compounded semiannually?

4. Clark has an investment proposal that invites him to invest $1,000 a year for ten years in a hotel and promises to pay him a return of 11% per year. If Clark agrees, how much will his investment be worth at the end of ten years?

5. What is the maximum amount of money you should pay for an investment today that is projected to yield $8,000 in four years if the market rate of interest is 12% and the money is compounded semiannually? What would be the present value if the money is compounded monthly?

6. Milton is trying to convince you to invest in his restaurant deal and make ten annual payments of $500, with the first payment due today. If the market rate of interest is 6%, how much will this investment be worth at the end of ten years?

7. An investment banker is offering a fixed-income investment that guarantees an 8% interest rate. It requires you to make monthly payments, with the first payment due today. If your goal is to have $10,000 in ten years, how much would you need to invest monthly to reach your goal? If you made annual payments with the first payment due today, what would your annual payment need to be for this investment to be worth $10,000 at the end of the ten-year period?

8. Your restaurant needs some kitchen remodeling, and the proposal for a new dishwasher is $55,000. Your banker will make you a loan at 8% interest compounded monthly over the next five years. What would be your monthly debt service payment to the bank? If your banker required a 10% down payment, how would this affect your monthly payment to the bank?

9. How much would you pay for an investment that promises you $1,500 each year for ten years if the going interest rate in the market is at 6.5%?

10. **ETHICS** ✳ Joseph just finished talking to five different bankers regarding a loan for his limited-service hotel. He needs $100,000 for a renovation project. However, with his current credit rating, he can only secure a loan of $75,000. Knowing that he has future contracts coming in with a few long-time corporate customers, he hopes he will be able to achieve higher sales next year. With that in mind, he is thinking about increasing his sales numbers to make his cash flow look better. Of course, in time value of money calculations, higher cash flows yield a higher present value, which would allow him to borrow more money. Is Joseph right in doing this?

Concept Check ✓

Addition of a Spa at a Resort Hotel

Powell Hospitality Ltd. is proposing the redevelopment of the spa at its Whispering Winds Resort. Currently the spa space is leased to a spa management company, but Powell Hospitality Ltd. wants to bring the operation in-house to have more control. The spa facility will also be expanded from its current 5,000 square feet to 10,000 square feet, with 8,000 square feet of indoor space and 2,000 square feet of outdoor treatment space.

Powell Hospitality Ltd. believes it is time to expand its facility because the health and fitness industry has experienced rapid growth due to increasing health awareness. The goal of the spa facility will be to offer guests of the resort, visitors to the area, members, and people living and working nearby the opportunity to experience a world-class spa facility.

The spa will provide an additional revenue stream for the resort and should increase occupancy during the slow periods by offering spa conference packages. On average, it is estimated that 180 guests will visit the facility throughout the day. The spa will offer services including massage, herbal wraps, facials, mind/body programs, fitness activities, and alternative health treatments. Here are some financial projections for the spa:

WHISTLING WINDS RESORT SPA PROFORMA

Year	Year 1	Year 2	Year 3	Year 4	Year 5
Spa Occupancy	29%	50%	55%	60%	65%
Spa Services Rendered	33,271	58,269	64,096	69,923	75,749
Revenue					
Spa Services	$ 1,760,000	$3,167,075	$3,577,022	$4,003,922	$4,447,775
Beauty Services	$ 832,000	$1,497,163	$1,690,957	$1,892,763	$2,102,585
Health and Fitness Services	$ 32,000	$ 57,582	$ 65,035	$ 72,797	$ 80,867
Other Revenue	$ 576,000	$1,036,497	$1,170,663	$1,310,375	$1,455,637
Total Spa Revenue	$ 3,200,000	$5,758,317	$6,503,677	$7,279,858	$8,086,863
Cost of Goods Sold	$ 160,000	$ 287,915	$ 325,183	$ 363,992	$ 404,343
Payroll	$ 2,304,000	$3,278,150	$3,559,542	$3,901,888	$4,256,566
Operating Expenses	$ 896,000	$1,111,380	$1,197,812	$1,297,296	$1,404,492
Gross Operating Income	$ (160,000)	$1,080,872	$1,421,140	$1,716,681	$2,021,462

QUESTIONS

1. Based on the projections, how much is this stream of uneven cash flows worth today if the discount rate is 10%? First, compute the present value of each year's cash flow individually and add the results. Then, check your answer utilizing the cash flow function.

2. Given the present value calculated in question 1, what will this be worth in 4 years' time?

Concept Check ✓

New Fast Casual Restaurant

Austin Anderson, a development manager for a fast casual restaurant chain, has chosen the geographic area where he would like to locate the next company restaurant. Based on competition and local market demand, he has made several sales projections for best- and worst-case scenarios. He has also determined that start-up cost will be about $125,000, which includes renovation of the leased site, equipment, marketing, and other start-up costs.

1. Using the following information, determine operating profit for the first year of operation based on the three scenarios provided:

	Best Case	Expected	Worst Case
Daily F&B Sales	$2,054.80	$1,643.84	$1,232.88
Annual F&B Sales*			
Cost of Sales	32.6%	32.6%	32.6%
Operating Expenses	60.7%	60.7%	60.7%
Operating Profit (Loss)			

*Based on 365 days per year.

Now that Mr. Anderson has the financial projections, he needs to secure financing to develop the restaurant. Luckily, he has already found an equity investor who will provide $50,000 in exchange for 40% ownership of the project. This leaves Mr. Anderson with another $75,000 that he needs to secure from a lender. He has talked to two lenders, and the terms they have offered are below.

Lender A

Loan Amount: $75,000

Annual Interest Rate: 7%

Term: 4 years

2. Calculate the annual debt service payment and complete the following amortization schedule.

Year	Payment	Principal	Interest	Balance
1				
2				
3				
4				
Total				

Lender B

Loan Amount: $75,000

Annual Interest Rate: 6%

Term: 7 years

3. Calculate the annual debt service payment, and complete the following amortization schedule.

Year	Payment	Principal	Interest	Balance
1				
2				
3				

4	
5	
6	
7	
Total	

4. Evaluate the lender options and determine which lender Mr. Anderson should choose for his company and why.

INVESTMENT ANALYSIS

MICHAEL A. LEVEN—THE MASTER OF USING OTHER PEOPLE'S MONEY

Mike Leven had spent his entire career learning the hotel business from the ground up, analyzing investment opportunities for the companies he managed, convincing lenders and equity investors to finance the growth of the hotel chains with which he was associated, and selling franchises as well, if not better than, anyone who had come before him. He was now the number-two person at one of the largest international lodging companies. What would make him leave his cushy corporate career with Holiday Inns Worldwide to start his own company? This is what he said:

1. Autonomy. "The ultimate freedom is being your own boss."
2. To control his own destiny. "Most of my career has been turning around somebody else's mess. This time, I have a chance to create my own."

3. The desire to make a real difference. "I knew that no matter what I did, [Holiday Inn] would survive and go on. I was just a cog in the wheel."

Yet, reasons and circumstances alone are sometimes not enough to convince yourself to make such a life-changing decision. Opportunity is the other ingredient. For Leven, his opportunity came when his nephew, Neal Aronson, who was in the business of acquiring companies, approached him with the idea of forming a franchise company. Leven suggested Microtel, a new budget hotel brand. The next thing he knew, Aronson had put the deal together. So, Leven resigned from Holiday Inns Worldwide, and US Franchise System (USFS) was launched in October 1995.

Aronson and Leven raised $94 million of equity in three phases—a private placement, an initial public offering, and a secondary public offering. They also acquired two additional hotel brands to franchise: Hawthorne Suites, an extended-stay hotel concept, and Best Inn and Suites, a midlevel economy chain. To finance the acquisition, they sold seventeen of the Best Inn and Suites hotels to a private investment partnership for $84 million.

In spite of this growth, the company's stock performed poorly and failed to reach the price expectations envisioned by Mr. Leven. To continue to grow his franchise company, Leven took the company private in 2000 by convincing the Pritzker family, which owns Hyatt Hotels and Hyatt International, to acquire USFS for $50 million.

Leven's strategy was to continue to franchise the three concepts using the franchisee's money to finance the growth of USFS. His strategy proved successful, as all three brands demonstrated significant growth. For Leven, the franchise model was ideal. He had made his mark in the franchise world from 1985 to 1990, when he led Atlanta-based Days Inn through a reorganization that resulted in the company growing from a 225-unit regional chain into a national chain with more than 1,000 hotels. During his tenure with Days Inn, he also started a diversity program to attract Asian American franchisees to USFS and helped found the Asian American Hotel Owners Association. The goodwill, alliances, and relationships he formed with these franchisees over the years played a major role in USFS's ability to grow into a 500-unit company with hotels in Africa, Argentina, Canada, Honduras, India, Israel, Mexico, Philippines, and the United States.

SOURCES

Gibbs, Melanie F. "At USFS, Leven Brings New Meaning to 'Franchise'." *National Real Estate Investor.* http://www.findarticles.com/p/articles/mi_m3208/is_n3_v39/ai_19239029#continue, March 1997.

Larson, Mary J. "Bucking Conventional Wisdom Pays Off for Dealmaker." *Franchise Times.* http://www.roarkcapital.com/franchisetimes.pdf, March 2001.

Poole, Shelia M. "Atlanta-based Hotel Franchiser Becomes Major Player at CEO's Hands." *Hotel Online.* http://www.hotel-online.com/Neo/News/1999_Jul_25/k.ATH.933026431.html, July 25, 1999.

http://www.usfsi.com/usfsstory/.

Learning Outcomes

1. Learn how to apply the time value of money and market value concepts and skills to investment analysis.

2. Review and understand the concepts of weighted average cost of capital (WACC), discount rate, and capitalization method of valuation as they apply to investment analysis.

3. Understand and apply payback period, net present value (NPV), internal rate of return (IRR), and modified internal rate of return (MIRR) techniques to potential investments and analyze investment opportunities.

4. Perform investment analyses calculations using a business calculator and an Excel spreadsheet.

5. Learn how lenders and equity investors use net present value and internal rate of return techniques to make wise investment decisions.

Preview of Chapter 8

Investment Analysis

1. THE APPLICATION OF TIME VALUE OF MONEY AND MARKET VALUE CONCEPTS AND SKILLS TO INVESTMENT ANALYSIS

2. REVIEW OF WACC, DISCOUNT RATE, AND THE CAPITALIZATION METHOD OF VALUATION AS THEY APPLY TO INVESTMENT ANALYSIS

   a. Weighted average cost of capital (WACC)

   b. Discount rate

   c. Capitalization method of valuation

3. INVESTMENT ANALYSIS TOOLS

   a. Payback period

   b. Net present value (NPV)

   c. Internal rate of return (IRR)

   d. Modified internal rate of return (MIRR)

4. INVESTMENT CALCULATIONS USING

   a. A business calculator

   b. An Excel spreadsheet

5. FACTORS IMPACTING INVESTMENT ANALYSIS CALCULATIONS

   a. The cost of capital (WACC)

   b. The cap rate used to calculate the terminal sales price

   c. The amount and timing of annual cash flow projected

   d. The acquisition price or development cost of the subject asset

INVESTMENT ANALYSIS

N ow that you understand the time value of money concept and the market value concept, and know how to solve time value of money problems, you are ready to learn how to apply your new knowledge and skills to investment analysis opportunities.

As a hospitality manager, you will experience occasions when you need to request capital to grow the business unit for which you are responsible. You may need capital for the renovation of a hotel restaurant, the renovation of guest rooms, a new membership management and billing system for a country club, or even to finance a new start-up business. Your challenge will be to convince your capital source that the project or venture you are proposing will generate a favorable return on investment, meets your investor's hurdle rate with minimal risk, and merits funding.

All decisions related to a capital expenditure warrant an investment analysis. To convince your general manager, regional vice president, owner, lender, or potential equity investor to provide additional capital, you must present your investment story in a professional manner. The better you understand the financial analysis methods, techniques, and skills your capital provider uses to analyze and evaluate investment opportunities, the better your chances of securing the approval for, and the funding of, your capital request. The time value of money skills and math you learned in chapter 7 provide the foundation for the investment analysis methodology the providers of capital use and rely on.

Three important components of investment analysis are the **weighted average cost of capital** (WACC), the **discount rate,** and the **capitalization method of valuation.** Once you understand them and know how they are derived or calculated, you are ready to move on and learn how to analyze investment opportunities.

Weighted Average Cost of Capital (WACC)

As we learned in chapter 7, the mix of debt and equity, the cost of each, and the income tax rate of the business drive WACC. When computing the present value of an investment, the rate used to discount future cash flows is the investor's WACC. The following formula represents the WACC of a company where $WACC = w_d k_d (1 - T) + w_e k_e$, and:

Weight of debt = w_d

Cost of debt = $k_d (1 - T)$

Tax rate of business = T

Tax effect = $(1 - T)$

Weighted cost of debt = $w_d k_d (1 - T)$

Weight of equity = w_e

Cost of equity = k_e

Weighted cost of equity = $w_e k_e$

We noted earlier in the text that the mix of debt and equity depends on how much the company can comfortably borrow and still meet its monthly debt service obligations, and how much additional equity capital the project requires to cover the balance of the project cost. Because the cost of debt is always less than the cost of equity, most companies try to apply financial leverage as much as possible, using debt to finance the project and thus minimize the need for large amounts of equity. On the other hand, lenders don't usually lend a business 100%

A business proposal presents the following financing plan:

Debt $750,000

Equity   250,000

Total $1,000,000

The interest rate on the loan is 12%, and the equity investor requires a 16% return on investment. It is expected that the business will fall within the 20% tax bracket.

Calculations:

Weight of debt = 750,000/1,000,000 = 0.75

Cost of debt = 12%

Tax rate of business = 0.2

Tax effect = (1–0.2) = 0.8

Weighted cost of debt = (0.75)(12%)(0.8) = 7.0%

Weight of equity = 250,000/1,000,000 = 0.25

Cost of equity = 16%

Weighted cost of equity = (0.25)(16%) = 4.0%

WACC = 7.0 + 4.0 = 11.0%

ILLUSTRATION 8-1
Weighted Average Cost of Capital (WACC)

of the project cost. Lenders most often insist that there be some amount of equity in the deal to reduce the lender's risk and to make certain the borrower is sufficiently committed to the deal.

The weighted average cost of capital—or, more simply put, the cost of capital—significantly influences the present value of an investment opportunity. As you learned in the previous chapter, as the discount rate increases, the present value of the investment decreases. The higher the risk, the more lenders and investors want to be compensated for their capital, and the higher the cost of capital. The higher the cost of capital, the lower the present value of the deal.

Discount Rate

The discount rate is the long-term WACC of the company. It includes not only the cost of debt but also the investor's required ROI. A discount rate is like an interest rate in reverse. It is used to calculate the present value of a cash flowing asset by discounting or reducing each year's projected cash flow by the discount rate, with the sum of the discounted cash flows equaling the asset's present value.

Capitalization Method of Valuation

When calculating the present value of a potential investment, an important component of investment value is the **terminal selling price.** The terminal selling price is the estimated price for which the asset could be sold at the end of the analysis period. The terminal selling price captures the asset's future value without having to project future cash flows for ensuing years. The terminal selling price is then discounted back to the present, using WACC as the discount rate to calculate the present value of the investment. The method used to capture this terminal value is called the *capitalization rate method of value* (cap rate approach to value).

The cap rate approach to value capitalizes or values the asset's prior twelve months' cash flow by dividing the cash flow by the market cap rate to arrive at the asset's approximate market value. The market cap rate is the short-term WACC that a sophisticated investor would use to establish the approximate sales price to acquire the asset. The formula is as follows:

X = estimated current market value

CR = cap rate (or WACC)

CF = prior or trailing twelve months of cash flow

CR (X) = CF   or   X = CF/CR

As seen in Illustration 8-2, if the asset's trailing twelve-month cash flow was $50,000 and the market cap was 10%, the approximate selling price of the asset would be $500,000 ($50,000 ÷ 10%). An even faster way to make the calculation is to divide the cap rate into 1.00 (1.00 ÷ 10%) and multiply your answer by the trailing twelve-month cash flow.

As the cap rate increases, the market value decreases. The converse is also true. Think of it this way: As the risk of a deal increases, the investor's targeted ROI (hurdle rate) increases. As the hurdle rate increases, so does WACC.

Trailing 12-month cash flow = $50,000

WACC = 10%

Estimated current market value = $\dfrac{\text{Prior 12 months cash flow}}{\text{Cap rate (or WACC)}}$

Estimated current market value = $50,000/0.10 = $500,000

ILLUSTRATION 8-2
Capitalization Method of Valuation

Which of the following two scenarios yields the higher current market value?

Scenario A: CF = $10,000 and CR = 10%
Scenario B: CF = $10,000 and CR = 20%

Scenario A is the correct answer, as $10,000 divided by 0.10 equals $100,000, while Scenario's B value is $10,000 divided by 0.20, or $50,000.

Investment Analysis Tools

Both lenders and equity investors use payback period, net present value (NPV), internal rate of return (IRR), and modified internal rate of return (MIRR) to make investment decisions. Each method has advantages and disadvantages. A study published in 2003 reported that the internal rate of return method was preferred by lodging companies when analyzing potential new investment opportunities. The study also reported that the payback method was used more in replacement-type situations. Let's take a look at each method.

PAYBACK PERIOD

The **payback period** is simply the amount of time a project requires to pay back the initial equity investment. For example, if a company has a 2.5-year payback period for new spas, any project that takes more than 2.5 years to pay back its initial investment is rejected.

The primary advantage of the payback period method is that it is easy to calculate and understand. A company sets a threshold of so many years, and any project that does not meet that threshold is rejected. It is simple to use, clear, and concise. Consider the example of an existing pizzeria. The cost to renovate the pizzeria is $25,000. The estimated life of the renovated asset is five years. The renovated pizzeria is projected to generate an incremental cash flow of $10,000 per year for the next five years.

The payback calculation divides the initial investment by the annual cash flow:

$$\text{Payback} = \frac{\text{cost}}{\text{Incremental cash flow}}$$

$$= \frac{\$25,000}{\$10,000}$$

$$= 2.5 \text{ years}$$

If the pizzeria's targeted payback period is two years, then this project does not meet its criterion and ownership will reject this capital request.

Consider, however, the following proposal:

YEAR	CASH FLOWS
0	$(25,000)
1	5,000
2	15,000
3	15,000
4	25,000
5	25,000

Project cost = $25,000

cash flow 1	5,000
	20,000
cash flow 2	15,000
	5,000
cash flow 3	15,000

More than is needed

Cash flow in Year 3 is $15,000, which is more than enough to cover the remaining $5,000 payback; therefore the project meets the payback period requirement:

$$\frac{\$5,000}{\$15,000} = 0.33$$

In other words, it would take 2.33 years for the project to pay back the initial investment.

THE REAL DEAL

How should a hospitality manager set the maximum allowable payback period to help with the financial analysis and decision-making process? Is there any rule of thumb? A 2004 study shows the maximum allowable payback period for an asset depends on the expected number of years the asset will last. For assets with three or fewer years of life expectancy, the median maximum amount is one year. This threshold increases to 2.25 years and 3.5 years for assets that have five or seven years of life expectancy respectively. Assets of ten years garner a five-year median, while assets with fifteen years' life have a six-year maximum and assets with a twenty-year life expectancy have a ten-year maximum. One may say that the rule of thumb for setting time limits for payback is normally half or less than half of an asset's expected life.

Source: Damitio, J. W., and R. D. Schmidgall. "Budgeting for Capital Expenditures: Results to a Survey Studying the Capital Budget Practices of Major Lodging Chains." *The Bottomline* 18(5): 15–19.

While the payback period method has its advantages, it also has its disadvantages. A project that generates a favorable ROI in the long term is often rejected because it does not meet the company's payback period standard. The payback method ignores the cash flow generated after the required payback period. Second, the payback method does not take into consideration the time value of money, which is a basic concept of finance. By considering the amount of cash flow alone, rather than both the amount and timing of the cash flow, the analysis is flawed.

Although the payback method has its shortcomings, it is often used because of its simplicity and because it provides the decision maker with a quick and easy way to analyze an investment opportunity. In most cases, however, it is used in conjunction with another tool for analysis, such as net present value or internal rate of return.

F E A T U R E   S T O R Y

JOSEPH L. JACKSON–OUTBACK AS A PARTNER

Joseph L. Jackson is a twenty-eight-year veteran of the restaurant industry and a graduate of the Conrad N. Hilton College. He has worked as a general manager for Steak and Ale Restaurants, Bennigan's Restaurants, and Olive Garden Italian Restaurants before branching out as the owner and managing partner of Outback Steakhouse, located in San Antonio, Texas. Today Mr. Jackson is a vice president with Outback Steakhouse, Inc.

His story of how he came to own the San Antonio Outback Steakhouse and reap the financial rewards of ownership is an interesting one. According to Jackson, as a restaurant manager, he was expected to act like an owner. This helped him when he became the managing partner of the Outback Steakhouse—and the owner. His dream had turned into reality. Jackson particularly liked the freedom to make decisions without interference from upper management. "You are more flexible as an owner. You make decisions each day that you are held accountable for."

From a staffing perspective, he realized he was able to build a better team as an owner-manager because employees knew he was not going to be transferred any time soon. "Employees love consistency. We had one of the lowest employee turnover rates in the entire chain."

For most aspiring entrepreneurs, securing the necessary capital to open a new business is a daunting task. For Jackson, however, financing was relatively easy. Only a small financial investment was required on his part to open the Outback Steakhouse. As managing partner, he invested $25,000 of his own money and oversaw the day-to-day operations of the restaurant. His financial partners in the deal were Outback Steakhouse, Inc., and a private equity investor. According to Jackson, his partnership with Outback Steakhouse, Inc., was typical of other partnerships around the United States that enabled Outback Steakhouse to grow the chain.

The financial rewards Jackson reaped were significant. In return for his $25,000 investment, he received a 10% ownership position in the restaurant, a monthly salary, and stock options in the public company, Outback Steakhouse, Inc. There was also a buyout arrangement that allowed him to sell his ownership position back to Outback Steakhouse, Inc., at the end of five years. According to Mr. Jackson, buyouts normally range from $100,000 to $300,000 based on the profitability of the particular restaurant.

Because the average Outback Steakhouse generates over $200,000 a year in profit, according to the company's 2004 annual report, managing partners like Jackson earn, on average, $20,000 a year on their initial $25,000 investment, which is an 80% ROI. In five years, the initial capital investment normally yields a $300,000 payback, assuming a buyout price of $200,000. If you have $25,000 and decided to play it safe and put it in a savings account, how long do you think it would take your $25,000 to grow to $300,000? The answer is over fifty years, assuming the bank pays a compound interest of 5%. Think about that!

Jackson provides would-be entrepreneurs with one other piece of advice: "As a restaurant owner, you can't be absent and be successful. Successful owners need to interact daily with their employees and their customers."

SOURCES

Jackson, Joseph L. Interview, 2005.
Outback Steakhouse 2004 Annual Report.

NET PRESENT VALUE (NPV)

As its name indicates, **net present value** calculates the net, or difference, between an asset's present value and its purchase price or development cost. If the present value of an asset is greater than its cost, net present value is positive and the investment is deemed favorable. In other words, the asset's projected annual cash flow more than covers the investor's WACC. As you now know, WACC includes both the cost of the debt placed on the asset and the investor's targeted ROI. If the asset's present value is less than its cost, the investment is deemed unfavorable, as it will not cover debt service and achieve the investor's targeted ROI. If net present value is zero, the investment is considered favorable, but it barely covers the cost of capital. The concept of NPV is outlined in Illustration 8-3.

In chapter 7, you read about the time value of money concept and learned to make time value of money calculations. Now that you understand the math, the calculation of net present value should be easy. In fact, you have already calculated it, as shown in Illustration 7-13. The only difference is that in Illustration 7-13 there is no cash outflow in Year 0, so there is nothing to net the present value of the cash flows against to calculate net present value.

Let us refer to Illustration 7-13, but now add the assumption that the initial cost of the project is $800. Should you invest in this deal? You know that its present value, as shown in the illustration, is approximately $760, and if you net that value against the cash outflow of $800, your net present value would be a negative $40. Because this is a negative number, you would not invest in the deal. Illustration 8-4 shows you how to add one more step to your earlier calculation to arrive at your answer of ($40).

The Microsoft Excel formula to calculate NPV is "= − initial investment +NPV (rate, values)," where rate is the weighted average cost of capital (WACC) and the values are the cash flows in the correct time sequence, not including the initial investment. In this example, because the formula is, " = − initial investment," you need to type in $800 rather than −$800. Illustration 8-5 presents the Excel calculation.

In less than a minute, or as fast as you can type, you have calculated NPV. If any of the cash flows change, including the cash outflow (for example, $600), you need change one value

---

Scenario

You are looking to invest in a deal and are considering several investment alternatives. Seller A approaches you with a new hotel/condominium opportunity with a development cost of $150 million. The present value of the development's projected cash flow is $135 million. Using the net present value method of investment analysis, is this a favorable investment? If the present value of the project were $175 million, would the investment decision be different? How?

Analysis

Scenario 1

Present value of the project: $135 million

Development cost: $150 million

Net present value: $135 million less $150 million = ($15 million), therefore the NPV is negative and the investment is deemed unfavorable.

Scenario 2

Present value of the project: $175 million

Development cost: $150 million

Net present value: $175 million less $150 million = $25 million, therefore the NPV is positive and the investment is deemed favorable.

ILLUSTRATION 8-3
Net Present Value Concept

only, and the formula will automatically update the net present value for you. As you can see, with the advancements in technology, there is no reason why every hospitality manager should not use a business calculator or a program like Excel to assist in the investment decision-making process.

The NPV method is superior to the payback method in that it takes into account all cash flows, not just those that occur before the set time criterion. NPV also takes the time value of money into consideration, while the payback method does not. While many prefer using the NPV method of investment analysis, it does have shortcomings when used to analyze multiple investment opportunities of varying dollar amounts. While it can indicate whether or not a project meets the company's investment standard, it is not able to accurately rank one investment against another unless both investments require the same amount of capital.

```
        |---------|---------|---------|---------|---------|
        0         1         2         3         4         5   Years
                  50       100       300       305       320  I/Y at 10%
    -800
```

Steps on calculator:

[CF]	Display shows CFo= 0.0000

After clearing the worksheet with [2nd] [CE/C], use the down arrow key, enter

800[+/-] [ENTER]	Display shows CFo= -800.0000
[↓]	Display shows C01 0.0000 with no equal sign "="
50 [ENTER]	Display shows C01= 50.0000
[↓]	Display shows F01= 1.0000, since we only have C01 one time, we can simply accept this by entering the down arrow key again
[↓]	Display shows C02 0.0000 with no equal sign "="
100 [ENTER]	Display shows C02= 100.000
[↓]	Display shows F02= 1.0000, since we only have C02 one time, we can simply accept this by entering the down arrow key again
[↓]	Display shows C03 0.0000 with no equal sign "="
300 [ENTER]	Display shows C03= 300.0000
[↓]	Display shows F03= 1.0000, since we only have C03 one time, we can simply accept this by entering the down arrow key again
[↓]	Display shows C04 0.0000 with no equal sign "="
305 [ENTER]	Display shows C04= 305.0000
[↓]	Display shows F04= 1.0000, since we only have C04 one time, we can simply accept this by entering the down arrow key again
[↓]	Display shows C05 0.0000 with no equal sign "="
320 [ENTER]	Display shows C05= 320.0000
[↓]	Display shows F05= 1.0000, since we only have C05 one time, we can simply accept this by entering the down arrow key again
[↓]	Display shows C06 0.000 with no equal sign "=". Now that all cash flows have been entered, you can compute
[CPT] [NPV]	Display shows I = 0.0000, prompting you to enter the interest
10 [ENTER]	
[CPT] [NPV]	Display shows I = 10.0000, now you can do the final steps
[↓]	Display shows NPV = 0.0000
[CPT]	Display shows -39.49

ILLUSTRATION 8-4
Net Present Value

INTERNAL RATE OF RETURN (IRR)

While NPV is a good investment analysis tool for a single investment opportunity, in the business world, most financial managers use the **internal rate of return** method to analyze multiple investment opportunities.

The technical definition of *internal rate of return* is the discount rate that makes the net present value of an investment equal to zero. For example, if the equity investor's goal is to achieve at least a 20% IRR on his investment, and your investment package has a projected IRR of 25%, your investor would like your deal a lot. On the other hand, if you projected an IRR of 15%, the equity investor would not likely be a candidate to provide the equity for your deal. An advantage of the IRR method of investment analysis is that it allows you to compare deals with different sales prices and costs.

```
|----------|----------|----------|----------|----------|
   0        1         2         3         4         5     Years
 (800)      50        100       300       305       320   I/Y at 10%
```

Steps in Excel
Note: **Type only the symbols or letters within the bracket [ ] and not the bracket itself.**

1. Type all cash flows, from "−800" to "320" in the correct sequence. It does not matter whether you are typing them in a row or column
2. Type [=] to invoke an equation calculation
3. Type [−] and then highlight the cell that has the cash outflow, or the −800. If you did enter −800, then you can skip this step
4. Type [+] and then [npv]the open bracket [(]. As soon as [(] is typed, EXCEL displays: npv(**rate**,value1, value2,…); the word rate is bolded to prompt you to enter the rate
5. Enter rate in decimal form and type a comma[,], value1 will then be highlighted 0.1,
6. Simply highlight all the values from 50 to 320. Because we have entered all variables, the operation can be completed by typing [)], then hit the enter key
   The cell will now display the value of −$39.49.

ILLUSTRATION 8-5
NPV Calculation Using EXCEL

Using the business calculator, the calculation of an investment's IRR is similar to that of its NPV. All you need to do is to enter the projected annual cash flows into the calculator and ask it to compute the IRR. Illustration 8-6 details the steps involved in this calculation. In this example, Siu Ling needs to invest $130,000 to start her catering business. The projected cash flow, including the projected terminal sales price of $160,000 at the end of the fifth year, is as follows:

YEAR	CASH FLOW
1	$10,000
2	12,500
3	14,000
4	18,550
5	21,250 + 160,000

If she invests $130,000 of equity, what is her IRR?

Using IRR methodology on your business calculator or Excel, the correct answer is 14.60%.

As you can see, the steps are exactly the same as the NPV calculation except that once all cash flows are entered, you direct the calculator to compute IRR instead of NPV. In most cases, you will want to calculate both the IRR and the NPV. To do so, first follow the steps to calculate NPV; then, without clearing the calculator, press [IRR] and [CPT]. The display will show IRR = 14.5995*. It is as simple as that.

Siu Ling is paying $130,000 to start her catering business. The cash flows she projects for the next 5 years are:

Year	Cash Flow
1	10,000
2	12,500
3	14,000
4	18,550
5	21,250 + 160,000

What is this project earning her in terms of an interest rate?

Option 1 Using the cash flow function in a business calculator

Steps on calculator

[CF]   Display shows CFo= 0.0000
              After clearing the worksheet with [2ⁿᵈ] [CE/C], use the down arrow key, enter
              130000[+/–] [ENTER]   Display shows CFo= –130000.0000
[↓]   Display shows C01   0.0000 with no equal sign "="
10000 [ENTER]   Display shows C01= 10000.0000
[↓]   Display shows F01=   1.0000, since we only have C01 one time,
              we can simply accept this by entering the down arrow key again
[↓]   Display shows C02   0.0000 with no equal sign "="
12500 [ENTER] Display shows C02= 12500.0000
[↓]   Display shows F02=   1.0000, since we only have C02 one time,
              we can simply accept this by entering the down arrow key again
[↓]   Display shows C03   0.0000 with no equal sign "="
14000 [ENTER]   Display shows C03= 14000.0000
[↓]   Display shows F03=   1.0000, since we only have C03 one
              time, we can simply accept this by entering the down arrow key
              again
[↓]   Display shows C04   0.0000 with no equal sign "="
18550 [ENTER]   Display shows C04= 18550.0000
[↓]   Display shows F04=   1.0000, since we only have C04 one time,
              we can simply accept this by entering the down arrow key again
[↓]   Display shows C05   0.0000 with no equal sign "="
181,250 [ENTER]   Display shows C05= 181250.0000
[↓]   Display shows F05=   1.0000, since we only have C05 one time,
              we can simply accept this by entering the down arrow key again
[↓]   Display shows C06 0.000 with no equal sign "=". Now that all
              cash flows have been entered, you can compute
[CPT] [IRR]   Display shows IRR = 14.5995*

The internal rate of return is calculated as 14.5995*%

Option 2 Steps in Excel
Note: **Type only the symbols or letters within the bracket [ ] and not the bracket itself.**

1. Type all cash flows, from "–130000" to "181250" in the correct sequence. It does not matter whether you are typing them in a row or column.
2. Type [=] to invoke an equation calculation.
3. Type [irr] and then the open bracket [(]. As soon as [(] is typed, Excel displays: =irr(**values**, [guess]); the word values is bolded to prompt you to enter the values
4. Use your cursor, highlight all the cash flows, from "–130000" to "181250" and type a comma[,], **guess** will then be highlighted.
5. Excel needs a guess, any guess will do, in the form of a rate, so that it can begin to compute. You may want to use 10% or 0.1 as a rule, but any rate will work. 0.1,
6. The operation can be completed by typing [)], then hit the enter key.
7. The cell will now display the value of 14.60%

ILLUSTRATION 8-6
Internal Rate of Return Calculation

Unfortunately, the IRR method also has its shortcomings. For starters, it assumes that cash flows generated by the project can be reinvested at the IRR rate calculated. This may not be realistic if the IRR of the subject project is substantially higher than the company's normal ROI. Also, due to its mathematical equation, in situations where a project's cash flow goes from positive to negative and then back to positive, it is possible to calculate multiple IRRs for the same project. However, this is usually not a problem, as most hospitality deals have normal cash flow patterns.

$$O = CF_0 \frac{CF_1}{(1 + r)^1} + \frac{CF_2}{(1 + r)^2} + \frac{CF_3}{(1 + r)^3} + \frac{CF_n}{(1 + r)^n}$$

CF = cash flows for the specified period of 1, 2, 3, to n

$IRR = r$, to be calculated as the discount rate that forces the present value of cash flows to equal the cost of the investment, making the net present value zero

CONFLICTS BETWEEN NPV AND IRR

In most cases, both NPV and IRR calculations indicate the same accept or reject decision. It is possible, however, for the IRR and NPV methods to produce different accept or reject decisions. For example, assume that Project A costs $4,000,000 to build and has a present value of $5,000,000 and therefore a NPV of $1,000,000. Project B costs $11,000,000 and has a present value of $12,000,000 and an NPV of $1,000,000. If we compare the deals based on NPV, they would rank the same. However, the IRR of Project A is much higher than that of Project B. For Project A, only $4,000,000 is needed to yield $1,000,000, while Project B will tie up $11,000,000 of capital to yield the same dollar return.

Based on this example, it would appear that the IRR method, rather than NPV, should always be used when evaluating two or more investment opportunities. This is not necessarily true, however, as mathematics can be deceiving. Let us explain: If you are analyzing independent projects such as buying a new property management system or upgrading your guest rooms, where the acceptance or rejection decision of one project does not affect the acceptance or rejection decision of another, both IRR and NPV will provide the same accept or reject answers. However, if you are looking at two mutually exclusive projects, such as two different property management systems, where selecting one system means you automatically reject the other, IRR and NPV decisions may conflict.

What follows may sound a little confusing, so read carefully: As the discount rate increases, the NPV of a project decreases. Each project, therefore, has a profile that can be plotted. If there are two mutually exclusive projects, there will be two profiles on the graph. The point where the two profiles intersect is known as the **crossover rate.** As long as the discount rate or cost of capital is above the crossover rate, there is no conflict between NPV and IRR. The conflict arises when the discount rate or cost of capital is below the crossover rate. In this case, the NPV method indicates that one project will be more lucrative, while the IRR method indicates the other as the better investment choice. Therefore, when the IRR answer conflicts with the NPV answer, always go with the NPV answer.

MODIFIED INTERNAL RATE OF RETURN (MIRR)

Due to the reinvestment rate issue, the finance community created another investment analysis tool, known as **modified internal rate of return.** Although it has been around for quite some time, it is not as widely used and recognized as the payback, NPV, and IRR methods. Nonetheless, a brief description of the method follows for those who are interested in learning about it.

MIRR differs from IRR in that it assumes the cash flow generated by the project is reinvested at the company's cost of capital (WACC) rather than the calculated IRR. Modified internal rate of return discounts all negative cash flows to the present at year zero and grows all positive cash flows to the future at the WACC rate. At the end of the project's life, it computes the rate earned as the modified internal rate of return.

The MIRR calculation is somewhat more time-consuming than the others, but it can easily be computed on a calculator or computer spreadsheet. Refer to Illustration 8-7. In this example, the numbers are similar to those shown in Illustration 8-6, except the cost is now $100,000 rather than $130,000, making this proposal more attractive. In this case, IRR is computed to be 21.92%. If the company's WACC is 20%, a rate of 21.92% is favorable.

Now, let's calculate the MIRR using the business calculator (see Illustration 8-6). Because there is only one negative cash flow and it is in year zero, no calculation is needed. There are five positive annual cash flows, so we need to compute the future values of each at the end of Year 5 and total them. The total is $266,006, assuming a 20% cost of capital. With a present value of −$100,000 and a future value of $266,006, (I/Y) computes to be 21.61%. Comparing the MIRR of 21.61% to the IRR of 21.92%, the difference seems slight. However, 0.3% can sometimes make or break a deal. You can also see that MIRR is more conservative than IRR.

Calculating MIRR on an Excel spreadsheet is really simple. As seen in Illustration 8-7, the function can be invoked by "=mirr(". The formula will prompt you for the values, the finance rate, and the reinvestment rate.

Factors Affecting Tools of Investment Decisions

When you become more familiar and comfortable with NPV, IRR, and MIRR, they can help you sell your corporate management, lenders, and equity investors on the merits of your proposed projects. Remember that when a lender applies its loan-to-value (LTV) formula to the present value of your project, the higher the present value, the more money it will likely allow you to borrow.

For example, if the present value of a business venture is $15 million and the bank has a 75% loan-to-value limit, then the most the bank will lend is $12.5 million. However, if the

Year	Cash Flow
0	(100,000)
1	10,000
2	12,500
3	14,000
4	18,550
5	21,250 + 160,000

IRR Using the cash flow function in a business calculator

Steps on calculator

[CF]   Display shows CFo= 0.0000
After clearing the worksheet with [2ⁿᵈ] [CE/C], use the down arrow key, enter
100000[+/−] [ENTER]   Display shows CFo= −100000.0000
[↓]   Display shows C01 0.0000 with no equal sign "="
10000 [ENTER]   Display shows C01= 10000.0000
[↓]   Display shows F01=   1.0000, since we only have C01 one time, we can simply accept this by entering the down arrow key again.
[↓]   Display shows C02 0.0000 with no equal sign "="
12500 [ENTER] Display shows C02= 12500.0000
[↓]   Display shows F02=   1.0000, since we only have C02 one time, we can simply accept this by entering the down arrow key again.
[↓]   Display shows C03 0.0000 with no equal sign "="
14000 [ENTER]   Display shows C03= 14000.0000
[↓]   Display shows F03=   1.0000, since we only have C03 one time, we can simply accept this by entering the down arrow key again.
[↓]   Display shows C04 0.0000 with no equal sign "="
18550 [ENTER]   Display shows C04= 18550.0000
[↓]   Display shows F04=   1.0000, since we only have C04 one time, we can simply accept this by entering the down arrow key again.
[↓]   Display shows C05 0.0000 with no equal sign "="
181,250 [ENTER]   Display shows C05= 181250.0000
[↓]   Display shows F05=   1.0000, since we only have C05 one time, we can simply accept this by entering the down arrow key again.
[↓]   Display shows C06 0.000 with no equal sign "=". Now that all cash flows have been entered, you can compute
[CPT] [IRR]   Display shows IRR = 21.9243*

The internal rate of return is calculated as 21.9243*%.

MIRR Option 1 Using the cash flow function in a business calculator

```
|-------------|-------------|-------------|-------------|-------------|
     0            1             2             3             4             5        Years
 (100,000)    10,000        12,500        14,000        18,550        181,250     at 20%
```

All negative cash   All positive cash
flows to year 0   flows to year 5

 (100,000)   181,250
                                        ↓⇨⇨ 22,260 (1 year, 20%)
                              ↓⇨⇨⇨⇨⇨⇨ 20,160 (2 years, 20%)
                         ↓⇨⇨⇨⇨⇨⇨⇨⇨⇨⇨ 21,600 (3 years, 20%)
 _____   ↓⇨⇨⇨⇨⇨⇨⇨⇨⇨⇨⇨⇨⇨⇨ 20,736 (4 years, 20%)
 (100,000)   266,006
   PV   FV
```
|-------------|-------------|-------------|-------------|-------------|
     0            1             2             3             4             5
```

ILLUSTRATION 8-7
Modified Internal Rate of Return Calculation

PV = –100,000
FV = 266,006
N = 5
CPT I/Y
= 21.61%

MIRR Option 2 Steps in Excel
Note: **Type only the symbols or letters within the bracket [ ] and not the bracket itself.**

1. Type all cash flows, from "–100000" to "181250" in the correct sequence. It does not matter whether you are typing them in a row or column.
2. Type [=] to invoke an equation calculation.
3. Type [mirr] and then the open bracket [(]. As soon as [(] is typed, Excel displays: =mirr(**values**, finance_rate, reinvest_rate); the word values is bolded to prompt you to enter the values.
4. Use your cursor, highlight all the cash flows, from "–100000" to "181250" and type a comma[,], **finance_rate** will then be highlighted.
5. Finance rate is your cost of capital, thus enter 20% or 0.2, and then the [,], **reinvest_rate** will then be highlighted.
   0.2,
6. Reinvest rate is the rate at which the cash flow that you receive will be invested in. It is the same rate as the finance rate, so you will enter the same information, 20%. The operation can be completed by typing [)], then hit the enter key.
   0.2) enter
7. The cell will now display the value of 21.61%

ILLUSTRATION 8-7
(*Continued*)

present value of the business venture is $20 million, you may receive a loan of up to $15 million. The present value of a business venture is very important in borrowing money. Who would not want to be able to borrow more funds rather than having to raise additional, more expensive equity?

Four factors impact the present value, net present value, internal rate of return, and the modified internal rate of return of a project:

1. The cost of capital (WACC)
2. The cap rate used to calculate the assumed sale price at the end of the analysis period
3. The amount and timing of annual cash flow projected
4. The acquisition price or development cost of the subject asset

COST OF CAPITAL

Let's look first at the cost of capital. The more you use financial leverage, the lower your cost of capital will be. The lower your cost of capital, the lower your discount rate will be. The lower your discount rate, the higher the present value of your deal and the higher your NPV. The higher your NPV, the more lenders and equity investors will like your deal. On the other hand, if someone is trying to sell you a deal, you will need to reverse this line of thinking to check the validity of the numbers.

CAP RATE

The second factor is the cap rate. The lower the cap rate used to calculate the terminal sales price of the asset at the end of the analysis period, the higher the sales price and the higher the PV, NPV, and IRR. The higher the cap rate used, the lower the PV, NPV, and IRR (see Illustration 8-8).

TIMING OF CASH FLOW

The third factor that affects the present value, net present value, and internal rate of return of a deal is the amount and timing of the cash flows projected. The more cash flow projected in the early years, the higher the PV, NPV, and IRR will be.

ACQUISITION PRICE OR PROJECT COST

Finally, the lower the acquisition price of the asset—or, in the case of a new development, the total project cost—the higher the NPV and IRR. Therefore, don't be afraid to sharpen your

---

Scenario A

Given: Annual cash flow projected for the final year of the analysis period = $120,000

Assumed cap rate = 12%

Estimated sale price: $120,000 divided by 12% = $1,000,000

Scenario B

Given: Annual cash flow projected for the final year of the analysis period = $120,000

Assumed cap rate = 10%

Estimated sale price: $120,000 divided by 10% = $1,200,000

Point

The discounted present value of $1.2 million is greater than the discounted present value of $1.0; therefore, the lower the cap rate, the higher the resulting PV, NPV, and IRR.

ILLUSTRATION 8-8
The Effect of Capitalization Rate on the Assumed Sales Price of an Asset

pencil and see if you can get the seller to lower the asking price. In the case of a new development, if your NPV and IRR don't look favorable enough, you may need to modify your architectural plans to reduce your project cost or convince members of your development team to lower their prices and fees. The lower your total project cost, the higher your NPV and IRR will be.

Finance in Action

The Investment for Balcones

The Balcones Hotel Company is looking to acquire a 100-room independent hotel in need of renovation and convert it to a national brand. The decade-old company currently owns and operates a mix of eight branded full-service and limited-service hotels in major U.S. metropolitan areas.

The hotel can be acquired for $3,000,000 and requires another $2,000,000 of renovation and conversion costs. The hotel has not undergone a renovation in the past ten years, and the $2,000,000 will allow for renovations to meet brand standards.

The hotel is currently breaking even, but Balcones Hotel Company management believes the property has much greater potential as a national brand. After the renovation and conversion, the hotel company estimates it can generate the following cash flows:

YEAR	CASH FLOW
1	$250,000
2	$500,000
3	$750,000

After Year 3, the Balcones Hotel Company plans on selling the property when it has increased cash flow and created additional value to the property. Company management projects the market cap rate to be 10% in Year 3, and the company's WACC is 12%.

QUESTIONS:

1. Utilizing the cap rate method, what will be the sale price for the hotel in year three?

   If we look at the capitalization method of valuation section at the beginning of this chapter, it says that sale price can be determined by dividing the prior or trailing twelve months' cash flow by the market cap rate to arrive at the asset's approximate market value. We must identify the variables in the calculation, which are the cap rate (10%) and the prior twelve months' cash flow ($750,000). Now the calculation is simple. Divide $750,000 by 10%, and the sale price, as determined by the cap rate approach, would be $7,500,000 in year 3.

2. Calculate the hotel's present value, net present value, and IRR.

First, look at the present value of this project. We know from chapter 7 that the present value of a project is the current value of a cash-flowing asset based on the amount and timing of its projected cash flows, which, in this case, include the terminal selling price for year 3 calculated in question 1.

Now we need to discount the cash flows for years 1 through 3 and add them to determine the present value of the investment.

To calculate present value, you need the number of compounding periods [N], interest rate [I/Y], and future value [PV]. The following chart presents the inputs needed to calculate present value for years 1 through 3:

Year	Compounding Periods [N]	Interest Rate [I/Y]	Future Value [FV]	Present Value [CPT] [PV]
1	1	12%	$250,000	$223,214
2	2	12%	$500,000	$398,597
3	3	12%	$8,250,000	$5,872,187

After computing the present value for each year, simply add the present value calculations; the total equals $6,493,998.

The next step is to calculate net present value. In this case, there are two ways to compute the answer. Because we know that net present value is the present value of an asset less the asset's initial cost, you can simply subtract $5,000,000 (the cost of acquisition and renovation/conversion of the project) from the calculated present value of $6,493,998 to reach the answer of $1,493,998. You can also calculate the NPV by entering the cash flows, including the initial acquisition and renovation/conversion expense, as a negative at time zero, along with the discount rate of 12%, into your calculator or Excel spreadsheet. You should arrive at the same answer of $1,493,998.

The third part of the question requires you to compute the internal rate of return (IRR) for this project. If you already input the cash flows while calculating NPV, you are a step ahead. If not, enter the cash flows into your calculator or Excel spreadsheet, as seen below:

Year	Cash Flow
0	−$5,000,000
1	$250,000
2	$500,000
3	$8,250,000

Now, all you have to do is compute the IRR by utilizing the functions on either your calculator or Excel spreadsheet. In either case, the internal rate of return should be 22.72%.

WHERE WE'VE BEEN, WHERE WE'RE GOING

While chapter 7 provides the alphabets, chapter 8 offers you the sentence structure so you can begin to compose a more meaningful picture of finance. The payback, net present value, internal rate of return, and modified internal rate of return are used in the hospitality business to help financial managers make sound financial decisions to support operations. In the next chapter, we present various applications of these financial analysis tools that relate to finance in the hospitality industry.

Key Points

➤ The time value of money concept and the associated skills and calculations are the foundation of investment analysis.

➤ The weighted average cost of capital, the discount rate, and the capitalization method of valuation are important ingredients of investment analysis.

➤ The payback period, net present value (NPV), and internal rate of return (IRR) techniques are the three most popular methods used to analyze an investment opportunity.

➤ An investor accepts a project when its:

   a. Payback period is less than the minimum allowable time period.

   b. NPV is equal to or greater than zero.

   c. IRR is more than the investor's cost of capital (WACC).

➤ Conversely, an investor rejects a project when its

   a. Payback period is longer than the targeted time period.

   b. NPV is less than zero, or negative.

   c. IRR is less than the investor's cost of capital.

➤ Four factors impact the present value, net present value, and internal rate of return of an investment opportunity.

   a. The lower the cost of capital (WACC), the lower the discount rate and the higher the NPV.

   b. The lower the cap rate used to calculate the terminal sale price of the asset at the end of the analysis period, the higher the sale price and the higher the PV, NPV, and IRR.

   c. The more cash flow projected in the early years, the higher the PV, NPV, and IRR.

   d. The lower the acquisition price of the asset—or, in the case of a new development, the total project cost—the higher the NPV and IRR.

Key Terms

WEIGHTED AVERAGE COST OF CAPITAL (WACC): The blended cost of debt and equity, taking into account the income tax bracket of the entity, the percentage mix of debt and equity, and the cost of each.

DISCOUNT RATE: Also known as the long-term WACC. It includes the cost of debt and the investor's required ROI. It is used to calculate the present value of a cash flowing asset by discounting, or reducing, each year's projected cash flow by the discount rate, with the sum of the discounted cash flows equaling the asset's present value.

TERMINAL SELLING PRICE: Estimated price for which the asset could be sold at the end of the analysis period.

CAPITALIZATION RATE (CAP RATE): Used to estimate the current market value of a cash flowing asset by dividing the amount of the prior twelve months' cash flow by the rate. The cap rate is the investor's short-term WACC.

PAYBACK PERIOD: The amount of time a project needs to pay back or cover its initial investment.

NET PRESENT VALUE (NPV): The present value of an asset less its initial cost.

INTERNAL RATE OF RETURN (IRR): The discount rate that makes the present value of a cash flowing asset equal to its acquisition price or project cost—for example, NPV = 0.

CROSSOVER RATE: As the discount rate increases, the NPV of a project decreases. Each project, therefore, has a profile that can be plotted. If there are two mutually exclusive projects, there will be two profiles on the graph. The point where the two profiles intersect is known as the *crossover rate.*

MODIFIED INTERNAL RATE OF RETURN (MIRR): A rate of return assuming all cash flows are reinvested at the firm's cost of capital rather than at the internal rate of return, thus making the MIRR more conservative.

Application Exercises

1. Define and explain the components of the weighted average cost of capital.
2. If the cost of debt increases by 5%, the cost of equity decreases by 5%, and the deal is composed of 50% debt and 50% equity, how is the cost of capital affected? Does it go up or down, or does it remain the same?
3. Define *payback period,* and explain how lenders and investors make investment decisions using this tool.
4. Define *net present value,* and explain how lenders and investors make investment decisions using this tool.
5. Define *internal rate of return,* and explain how lenders and investors make investment decisions using this financial analysis tool.
6. Define *modified internal rate of return,* and explain how lenders and investors make investment decisions using this financial analysis tool.
7. How does the capitalization rate used to calculate the terminal sale price affect a project's net present value, internal rate of return, or modified internal rate of return?
8. If the market cap rate for a hotel is 10% and the sale price of the hotel is $600,000, what was its trailing twelve months' cash flow? What would the cash flow have been if the market cap rate were 20%?

9. Explain how the timing of a stream of cash flows can affect the internal rate of return of an investment.

10. Naomi has always wanted to open a cyber coffee shop and has made her cash flow projections. She estimates that it will cost her $225,000 to develop the project, and the cash flows for the next six years will be $45,000, $69,000, $125,000, $185,000, $189,000, and $200,000 respectively. If her cost of capital is 9.5%, what is the net present value and internal rate of return of her project? Should she accept or reject this investment?

11. What would be the payback period for Naomi's proposal in the preceding question? If the maximum allowable time is 2.5 years, should Naomi accept this project?

12. Bernard has been approached about a hotel investment proposal by a young entrepreneur named Winston. The young man seems to have done his homework and presents Bernard with a five-year pro forma showing cash flows of $128,000, $138,900, $141,250, $142,870, and $146,780 respectively. Bernard knows he can earn an 8% return if he puts his money in a mutual fund. Winston is asking for $500,000. What is the internal rate of return of this project? Should Bernard invest in this project? If you assume 8% as the cost of capital, compute net present value.

13. What would be the MIRR of Bernard's proposal in the preceding question?

14. **ETHICS** ✳ Irene has a hospitality degree and has taken a few finance courses. Her friend, June, is putting together a proposal for a sports bar, to be reviewed by a banker. The NPV she calculates is negative. The IRR is also calculated to be less than June's cost of capital. Knowing that Irene understands finance and the factors that affect the NPV and IRR of an investment, June asks Irene to make things look better so the banker will give June the loan. Is there anything Irene can do to help June without being unethical in this situation?

15. **EXPLORING THE WEB** ✳ Visit www.money.cnn.com. Aside from regular news and financial news, this site also offers a glossary of all financial terms and a calculator under "Financial Tools." While a business calculator and an Excel worksheet offer quick, easy, and accurate means of calculating the value of money, many sites such as CNN also offer financial tools to educate the public.

Concept Check ✓

Restaurant Purchasing a POS System

Nance's Restaurant, a local independent restaurant, is evaluating new point-of-sale (POS) systems and must determine if a new installation is feasible. A new POS installation would include both software and hardware, with a total cost of $20,000.

Nance's Restaurant is currently operating without a point-of-sale system and utilizes a chit system with carbon copy papers that allow the waitstaff to provide a copy to the kitchen and the customer while retaining a copy for accounting purposes. Management is aware that this is an archaic system and that a POS system will create efficiencies, but they are not sure it is worth the cost.

Through analysis, management has determined that a POS system would allow the waitstaff to turn tables quicker, therefore increasing the number of guests serviced and the sales volume. Another advantage of the POS system is that it provides reports to management, allowing them to better analyze their business. Taking all of these factors into consideration, Nance's management forecasts incremental increases in profit over the next three years of $8,000, $9,000, and $10,000.

QUESTIONS

1. Determine the payback period, present value, and net present value of this project for the three-year period, utilizing an 8% discount rate.

2. Management has received an offer from another POS vendor with installation costs of $25,000. The second vendor is offering increased functionality in the form of additional cost control reports, which would allow the restaurant to realize an additional $500 in incremental profits per year for a total of $8,500, $9,500, and $10,500. Financially, does this option fit Nance's Restaurant's criteria? Please explain your answer.

Concept Check ✓

Golf Course installing a new Automatic Sprinkler System

The eighteen-hole Redwood Golf Course is in need of a new sprinkler system, which is estimated to cost $1 million. The Golf Course Superintendent, who is in charge of maintaining the golf course, has advised the members that the system must be replaced within the next year because the system is beginning to fail. The board of directors has known about this problem for several years but has been putting off the repair due to the cost.

The members, however, have been complaining because the condition of the course is deteriorating. After looking into the matter further, the Board estimates that the property has lost nearly $250,000 in incremental profits over the past year alone due to membership terminations and lower guest fees and golf shop sales. If this problem is not solved quickly, more members will leave and revenues will continue to decrease.

Mr. Hans Tripler, general manager of Redwood, has requested a loan for $1 million from a local bank. The bank has offered to grant the loan at a 6.5% interest rate for a term of ten years.

QUESTIONS

1. Calculate the annual payment on the loan.

2. Calculate the payback period on the project based on the amount of revenues currently being lost by the golf operation.

3. The golf professional believes that with the installation of the new sprinkler system the club will see new members joining and golf shop revenues increasing. He estimates the club will enjoy the following incremental profits, which level off in year 5.

    Incremental Profits

1	$ 150,000
2	$ 175,000
3	$ 200,000
4	$ 225,000
5	$ 250,000

    Based on the incremental profits in the table and a discount rate of 9%, calculate the PV, NPV, and IRR of the irrigation project, assuming the sprinkler system has a ten-year useful life with no salvage value at the end of ten years.

HOSPITALITY INDUSTRY APPLICATIONS OF TIME VALUE OF MONEY CONCEPTS AND SKILLS

FEATURE STORY

BILL KIMPTON AND TOM LATOUR— THE DREAM TEAM

In 30 seconds, I knew he was the guy. **Bill Kimpton, 2000**
When we met, we clicked instantly. **Tom LaTour, 2000**

This defining moment in 1983 brought together the two men instrumental for growing regional Kimpton Hotels into a national boutique hotel chain with several successful restaurant concepts.

Kimpton's first hotel was the Clarion Bedford, located in San Francisco. The hotel nearly failed. He purchased it for $6.9 million in 1980 and invested another $1.1 million on renovations. It was an all-equity deal. Working as an investment banker in his earlier life, he knew that shrewd investors diversify their portfolios and place only a small percentage of their investments in high-risk, high-yield ventures such as his. He also, however, knew many high-net-worth individuals from his investment banking days. Using his investment analysis skills, he presented his deal to potential equity investors, raised $7.5 million, and put his $500,000 life savings into the deal as well. Just as the hotel was ready to reopen, however, in 1981 the U.S. dollar spiked and killed the international tourist market on which San Francisco hotels heavily depended. Revenues plunged 60% as occupancy fell below 30%. In danger of losing the property, Kimpton began making cold calls to corporate customers, pitching the hotel's low rates. It worked! Within a year, occupancy increased to 75% and the hotel began to generate cash flow.

By now, Kimpton was keenly aware that he lacked the operational skills needed to take his hotel business to the next level. Enter Tom LaTour, the missing link. LaTour began his hospitality career as a dishwasher at age fourteen at the Michigan State University dining facility. In 1966, he received his degree in hotel and restaurant management from the same university. Prior to meeting Kimpton, he worked for Amfac Hotels as its senior vice president of administration. Before that, he worked for the Sky Chef division of American Airlines. His immediate responsibility, upon joining Kimpton, was to develop a growth strategy, a corporate management structure, and operating systems to manage future Kimpton hotels more effectively. The partnership ensured that the needs of the guests and investors were balanced, which resulted in successful hotels and a favorable return of investment for the equity investors.

Their growth strategy was to find distressed properties, buy them at a bargain price, renovate them, turn them around, and then refinance them. They added one hotel per year for the next four years, then two a year until 1998. Kimpton continued to use equity as their main source of financing, as the hotel deals were high-risk endeavors. Payback occurred when the assets were refinanced, the equity returned to the investors, and the additional profits divided among Kimpton, LaTour, and their outside investors.

One of Kimpton's keys to success was to eliminate expensive ballrooms, room service, expensive amenities, and unnecessary overhead. This allowed Kimpton hotels to charge lower room rates than their fancier competition and achieve a higher profit margin than their more conventional competitors. In addition, by attaching new creative signature restaurants to their hotels and leasing them to well-known local chefs, they created the perception of being a full-service hotel without the costs associated with one. The restaurants became so popular that dining customers who wanted to ensure a reservation would book a room at the hotel, as only hotel guests were guaranteed a restaurant reservation.

> *Restaurants, ballrooms, meeting rooms—that stuff is outrageously expensive from a real-estate perspective of hotels. . . . We have restaurants next door that make money because . . . locals won't walk through a hotel lobby unless they absolutely have to, so having the restaurant next door gives you the best of both worlds.* **Bill Kimpton, 1998.**

When Kimpton passed away in 2001 from leukemia, LaTour took over as chairman and chief executive officer. The year was especially difficult for the company in light of Kimpton's passing, the dot.com bust, and repercussions from the events of 9/11. LaTour forged ahead, drawing on lessons that he had learned from

Bill. "[Kimpton] helped me tap into my latent entrepreneurial personality. . . . As we grew . . . every step of the way he helped me learn what I needed to learn to get to the next level. Ultimately, what he's given me has been the confidence I now have to manage the company's operations and the expansion of our new boutique lodging brands."

While LaTour still shares his friend and mentor's vision of creating a comfortable and distinctive lodging facility for travelers and generating comfortable returns for its shareholders, he has made geographic diversification a priority since 2001. In 2005, LaTour announced a national expansion program with the goal of becoming the next Four Seasons. Under LaTour's leadership, many experts think Kimpton Hotels has a good chance of just that.

SOURCES

LaTour, Tom. Interview, 2005.

http://www.kimptonhotels.com/pdfs/LaTour_CEO_bio.pdf.

http://www.inc.com/magazine/20050401/26-latour.html.

Cebrzynski, G. "William Kimpton: Hotel Head Rolls Out the Welcome Mat to Restaurants." *Nation's Restaurant News* (January 2000): 106–107.

Higley, Jeff. "Kimpton Group Broadens Its Horizon." *Hotel and Motel Management* 213(13): 4–5.

King, Paul. "Hotel Restaurant Pioneer Kimpton Dies of Leukemia." *Nation's Restaurant News* (April 2001): 1–4.

Machan, D., and F. Meeks. "We Sell Sleep." *Forbes* 150(6): 421–423.

Tate, Ryan. "Kimpton Hotels Remakes Its Beds: CEO Checks In with National Expansion, Major Rebranding." *San Francisco Business Times,* January 28, 2005.

Learning Outcomes

1. Utilize time value of money calculations in preparing a loan application and negotiating a loan.
2. Utilize time value of money calculations in crafting a deal with an equity investor, factoring in issues such as a preferred return, a carried interest, a promoted interest, and an equity kicker.
3. Analyze potential investment opportunities using NPV and IRR.
4. Apply NPV to lease versus purchase decisions.
5. Understand how an appraiser uses time value of money calculations to estimate the current market value of a hospitality asset.
6. Analyze multiple investment opportunities using NPV and IRR.

Preview of Chapter 9

Applications of time value of money concepts

1. QUESTIONS TO CONSIDER WHEN SECURING A LOAN:

a. What is the maximum amount I can borrow?

b. What is the maximum rate of interest I can afford?

c. What will my debt service payment be?

    d. What amortization rate do I need to negotiate?

2. QUESTIONS TO CONSIDER WHEN RAISING EQUITY:

    a. How much equity can I raise based on my cash flow projections?

    b. What is the equity investor's IRR?

    c. How much ownership do I need to offer my equity investor to satisfy his investment goals?

3. SENSITIVITY ANALYSIS TO MEET LENDERS' AND EQUITY INVESTORS' FINANCIAL TESTS AND STANDARDS

4. FINANCE IN ACTION CASE STUDIES

    a. Loan amortization schedule

    b. A hotel appraisal using the income approach to value

    c. The lease versus purchase decision

    d. The analysis of multiple investment opportunities using ROI, NPV, and IRR

TIME VALUE OF MONEY APPLICATIONS

Time value of money skills can be useful when seeking capital to grow a business or embark on a new venture. Once you fully understand the time value of money concepts and have mastered the use of the investment analysis tools presented in chapters 7 and 8, you are ready to apply your new skills to real-world situations. Your new skills can help you negotiate debt and equity agreements and structure successful deals.

Loan Questions

All loans have the following components: **principal**—the amount of money being borrowed; **debt service**—the amount of the regular fixed payments to the bank in repayment of the loan; **interest rate**—the percentage of the loan balance the lender charges the borrower for the use of the money; and **amortization rate**—the number of years the debt service payment is based on. As you learned in chapters 7 and 8, if you know three of the four components or variables in time value of money calculations, you can solve for the fourth.

Calculations of this nature can be helpful when negotiating a loan. They can, for example, answer questions like:

1. What is the maximum amount of money I can borrow?
2. What is the maximum interest rate I can afford to pay?
3. How much will my annual debt service payment be?
4. What amortization rate do I need to ask for?

As you learned in earlier chapters, the cost of debt is almost always less than the cost of equity; therefore, debt is usually the preferred financing source, especially when interest rates are low. The amount of principal a bank will lend is largely dependent on:

1. Cash flow projections of the borrower
2. The estimated present value of the business or new venture calculated by discounting projected future cash flows back to the present
3. Loan-to-value, loan-to-cost, and debt service coverage ratios of the lender

Let's start by defining the ratios a lender uses to analyze a loan request. Once you have estimated the value of your business or venture, multiply it by your lender's **loan-to-value ratio** (LTV). Your answer will be the maximum amount of money your lender is likely to lend you. As you may remember, the loan-to-value ratio is the percentage of a venture's estimated value a lender will loan out. For example, if the value of your new venture is estimated at $1.0 million and your lender's LTV is 60%, the maximum he will lend you is about $600,000. We discuss how to estimate the value of a business or venture later in this chapter.

A further limiting factor on the amount your lender will lend is his **loan-to-cost ratio** (LTC). The loan-to-cost ratio is the same as loan to value, with the cost of the project substituted for value in the calculation. If your lender's LTV is 60%, his loan-to-cost ratio is usually 60% as well. Therefore, if 60% of your new venture's value is more than 60% of your total project budget, your lender will be favorably impressed but will lend you only up to 60% of your total project cost.

Another limiting factor is your lender's **debt service coverage (DSC) ratio** (cash flow divided by debt service). Most hospitality lenders today require a debt service coverage ratio between 1.25 and 1.50; therefore, if your cash flow projections do not meet this test, the maximum amount you can borrow will be reduced. Illustration 9-1 provides examples of these ratios.

MAXIMUM AMOUNT OF DEBT

While your lender's LTV, LTC, and DSC ratios will limit the amount you can borrow, an important question to ask yourself is, "How much can I borrow based on how much cash flow I am comfortable in committing to debt service?" Once you answer this question and know the interest rate and amortization rate your lender is prepared to offer you, you can calculate the maximum amount of money you will be able to borrow.

For example, if you believe your lender will likely offer you an interest rate of 7.5% and a twenty-year amortization rate, and you are comfortable committing $10,000 each year to debt service, the maximum amount you can borrow is $101,945, as shown on Illustration 9-2. This is the present value of an annuity calculation you learned in chapter 7. The 7.5% interest rate

Loan-to-value ratio

The value of the restaurant building that you are mortgaging: $350,000

Lender's loan-to-value ratio: 65%

Maximum possible loan from lender:

$350,000 × 65% = $227,500

If you need a loan of $300,000, what loan-to-value ratio do you need to find in a lender?

$300,000 / $350,000 = 86%

Debt service coverage ratio

The annual debt service from your loan to purchase a new fleet of golf carts is $125,000, and your annual cash flow is $400,000. What is your debt service coverage ratio? If you are about to seek a loan and know that most hospitality lenders today require a debt service coverage ratio of between 1.25 and 1.50, would you be able to obtain a loan?

Debt service coverage ratio	=	Cash flow / Debt service
	=	$400,000 / $125,000
	=	3.20

You are well above the 1.25 to 1.50 range, so obtaining a loan should not be a problem.

ILLUSTRATION 9-1
Loan Ratios

I/Y = 7.5
N = 20
PMT = 10,000
CPT PV

PV = –$101,945

ILLUSTRATION 9-2
The Maximum Amount You Should Borrow

is the (I/Y), the twenty-year amortization rate is the (N), and the $10,000 of debt service is the (PMT).

If you need to borrow more than $101,945 and are not comfortable committing more than $10,000 per year to debt service, what are your alternatives? One alternative is to raise more equity. This may not, however, be your best move, as the cost of equity is higher than the cost of debt and raising more equity will lower your deal's IRR. A better alternative is to try to negotiate a lower interest rate or a longer amortization period.

INTEREST RATE AND AMORTIZATION RATE CALCULATIONS

Let's try another loan time value of money calculation. Let's assume you need to borrow $110,000 based on the amount of equity you believe you can raise. Based on annual debt service of $10,000 and a twenty-year amortization rate, what interest rate would you need to negotiate? The answer is 6.52%, as shown on Illustration 9-3. Note how this also applies what you learned in chapter 7 to the real world of finance. The $110,000 loan amount is the present value (PV), the $10,000 annual debt service is the payment (PMT), and the twenty-year amortization rate the debt service payment is based on is the (N).

THE REAL DEAL

Software to calculate the time value of money and loan amortization can be purchased at stores or on the Internet. Are these products useful? It depends on your purpose, the complexity of the calculation, and your degree of comfort when using spreadsheets and/or a business calculator. Software is also available to calculate mortgages, loans, leases, adjustable interest rates, and other features. The software ranges in price from $10 to a few hundred dollars. Some products even come with a subscription and upgrades. There are also free Internet sites that can help you calculate loans and print amortization schedules. For the most part, a spreadsheet or a business calculator should be sufficient. Do shop diligently and wisely before spending your money. Remember, money has value!

Conversely, if you doubt your lender will lower his interest rate below 7.5%, what amortization rate would you need to negotiate in order to borrow $110,000 at an interest rate of 7.5%?

PV = –$110,000
PMT = $10,000
N = 20
CPT I/Y

I/Y = 6.52%

ILLUSTRATION 9-3
The Interest Rate to Negotiate

PV = –$110,000
PMT = $10,000
I/Y = 7.5%
CPT N

N = 24.1 years

ILLUSTRATION 9-4
Finding the Optimal Amortization Rate

In this case, the amortization rate you need to solve for is (N). Thus, 7.5% is the (I/Y), $10,000 is the (PMT), and $110,000 is the (PV). Your answer is 24.1 years, as shown in Illustration 9-4.

In other words, if you borrow $110,000 and agree to pay your lender an interest rate of 7.5%, and your lender agrees to a twenty-five-year amortization period, your annual debt service payment would be approximately $10,000.

DEBT SERVICE CALCULATION

Given the amount of the loan, the interest rate, and the amortization rate, you can calculate what the loan's debt service payment would be. A debt service payment is a form of annuity, an even stream of cash flow for a number of periods.

In Illustration 9-5, Gianni Pasta has secured a loan of $10,000 from First Savings at a 10% annual rate of interest amortized over five years. The resulting annual debt service payment is $2,637.97, with $3,189.85 being paid as interest over the term of the loan. If the bank required monthly payments, the debt service payment would be $212.47, with a total interest of $2,748.20 being paid over the term of the loan.

AMORTIZATION RATE

As noted earlier, the amortization rate is a critical element of a loan agreement and a primary negotiating point. While you want to negotiate the longest term for your loan, more importantly, you want to negotiate the longest amortization period. The longer the amortization period, the lower your debt service payments will be. Let's look at Illustration 9-6 as an example. As Project A's amortization rate increases from ten to fifteen years, the annual debt service payment decreases. Similarly, the monthly debt service payment for Project B decreases when the amortization period increases from twenty to twenty-five years.

It's important to understand that the lower your debt service payment, the more you can borrow. Recall the debt service coverage ratio shown in Illustration 9-1. The lower the debt service, the higher the debt service coverage ratio. Thus, your lender should be more apt to lend you more money. The more you can borrow for any project, the less equity you will need. The less equity you need, the higher your ROI and IRR. The higher your ROI and IRR, the less

Gianni Pasta negotiates a loan with First Saving at a 10% interest rate for 5 years with debt service payments due at the end of each year. What would be the annual debt service and the total interest paid on this loan?

PV = 10,000
N = 5
I/Y = 10
CPT PMT

PMT = $2,637.97

Total interest = total payments – principal
= 2,637.97 × 5 – 10,000
= 13,189.87 – 10,000
= 3,189.85

What would the debt service and total interest payments be if debt service were paid monthly rather than annually?

PV = 10,000
N = 5 × 12
I/Y = 10 / 12
CPT PMT

PMT = $212.47

Total interest = total payments – principal
= 212.47 × 60 – 10,000
= 12,748.20 – 10,000
= 2,748.20

ILLUSTRATION 9-5

Calculating Debt Service Payments

Project A   Project B
PV = –100,000   PV = –150,000
I/Y = 10   I/Y = 12/12 (1% per month)
N = 10   N = 20 × 12 (240 months in 20 years)
CPT PMT   CPT PMT

PMT = 16,274.54   PMT = 1,651.63

If N is now 15   If N is now 25
PV = –100,000   PV = –150,000
I/Y = 10   I/Y = 12/12 (1% per month)
N = 15   N = 25 × 12 (300 months in 20 years)
CPT PMT   CPT PMT

PMT = 13,147.38   PMT = 1,579.84

In project A, the entrepreneur saves $3,127.16 per year with a higher amortization rate.
In project B, the entrepreneur saves $71.79 per month with a higher amortization rate.

ILLUSTRATION 9-6

Amortization Rate Calculation

ownership you need to offer your equity investor in return for his equity investment. The less ownership you have to offer your equity investor, the more ownership is left for you and your existing owners.

Equity Questions

The process of raising equity is similar to the process of raising debt. Your success depends on how much future cash flow you can realistically generate, how quickly you believe you can generate it, the amount of inherent risk involved in the deal, the amount of equity you are seeking, and the percentage of ownership you are prepared to offer your equity investors.

HOW MUCH EQUITY CAN YOU RAISE?

The maximum amount of equity that can be raised is primarily a function of the deal's cash flow projections and the equity investor's hurdle rate (ROI goal). To calculate the maximum amount of equity you can raise requires a present value calculation similar to the maximum amount you can borrow, as in the calculation previously discussed.

For example, Siu Ling, an entrepreneur, is projecting cash flows as shown in Illustration 9-8. Her investor's hurdle rate, which equates to her cost of equity, is 15%, with NPV computing to negative ($1,928). Based on these calculations, the maximum amount of equity Siu Ling can raise from this investor is $128,072, or $1,928 short of her $130,000 goal. If Siu Ling can find another investor who has a lower hurdle rate, she still might be able to raise the $130,000 of equity she is seeking.

Because Investor B, as shown on Illustration 9-7, has a hurdle rate of only 13%, Siu Ling would be able to raise her $130,000 with another $8,093.89 of equity to spare.

THE IRR AN EQUITY INVESTOR WOULD EARN

As we discussed in chapters 7 and 8, the internal rate of return is the discount rate that makes the cost of your project equal to its present value and NPV equal to zero. Illustration 9-7 shows that if the hurdle rate is 15%, NPV is negative, but a 13% hurdle rate makes NPV positive. Based on your understanding of IRR, you should conclude the IRR for this project is somewhere between 13% and 15%. Illustration 9-8 shows the IRR for this project to be 14.6%. An investor with a 15% hurdle rate would not invest in this deal because it does not meet his hurdle rate, while an investor with a hurdle rate of 14.6% or below might.

If the IRR you compute is higher than your equity investor's hurdle rate, there is extra value in the deal that can be applied to a **carried interest,** a **promoted interest,** or an **equity kicker** for yourself with no capital investment on your part. A carried interest is the ownership percentage the sponsor or promoter of the deal receives with no equity investment on his part. A promoted interest is ownership awarded the sponsor or promoter after a business venture

Siu Ling is trying to raise $130,000 to start her catering business. The cash flows she projected for the next 5 years are as follows:

Year	Cash Flow
1	10,000
2	12,500
3	14,000
4	18,550
5	21,250 + sale value of 160,000

In addition, she expects to be able to sell her business for $160,000 at the end of the 5-year period.

Investor A has a hurdle rate of 15%. Can Siu Ling raise the amount of equity she needs for her venture?

To answer the question requires a net present value (NPV) calculation with CF0 as −150,000 and CF1 to CF5 as 10,000, 12,500, 14,000, 18,550, and 181,250 (21,250 + 160,000) respectively at a hurdle rate of 15%.

Using the calculator or Excel, NPV is −$1,928 which means that cash flow is $1,928 short of justifying the $130,000 investment.

Investor B has a lower hurdle rate at 13%. With this hurdle rate, NPV computes to be $8,093. Thus, with a lower hurdle rate, Siu Ling could raise the amount of money she needs.

ILLUSTRATION 9-7

Raising the Optimum Amount of Equity

Siu Ling is trying to raise $130,000 to start her catering business. The cash flows she projects for the next 5 years are:

Year	Cash Flow
1	10,000
2	12,500
3	14,000
4	18,550
5	21,250 + 160,000

If she is seeking $130,000 in equity, what is the IRR?

Using the IRR calculation sequence on the calculator or the Excel formula, the answer is 14.60%.

ILLUSTRATION 9-8

IRR Analysis

achieves the equity investors' hurdle rate (ROI). An equity kicker is the percentage of the profit on sale awarded the sponsor or promoter of the deal after the equity investors receive the return of their initial investment. It is important to note that the higher your venture's IRR, the more ownership you can retain.

AMOUNT OF OWNERSHIP TO OFFER INVESTORS

The calculation to determine how much ownership to offer an equity investor and still meet his hurdle rate is similar to the calculation to determine the maximum amount of equity that can be raised. However, this particular calculation focuses on the future cash distributions or payouts to the investor, including the sale of the asset at the end of the analysis period.

In Illustration 9-9, Hannah projects the future cash flow for her limited-service hotel venture at $60,000 per year. She plans to hold the hotel for seven years and then sell the property. She estimates the hotel will sell at that time for approximately $1.2 million. She knows investors are expecting at least 12% as their hurdle rate. If she needs to make sure she meets but does not exceed the expectations of her equity investors, she should offer them an ownership interest of no more than 61%.

Use of Sensitivity Analysis

Sensitivity analysis is a method of analyzing investment opportunities by altering the assumptions on which the projections are based. For example, refer to Hannah's deal, shown in Illustration 9-9. Cash flow is projected to be $60,000 each year for seven years, with a sale price of $1.2 million at the end of the seventh year. This represents the base case scenario.

What impact would it have on the deal if actual occupancy were lower than projected? What if the actual occupancy were higher than projected? What if the average daily rate of rooms sold were higher in years five, six, and seven? What if it were lower? What if any of the actual costs for payroll, utilities, or insurance were higher than projected? This can happen and, often does. Any changes to the assumptions will change the project's PV, NPV, and IRR—and, as a result, the return on the equity investment. Normally, investors perform a sensitivity analysis on each investment opportunity he reviews by changing each key projection assumption by +10% and −10%. The objective is to calculate the deal's upside potential and downside risk and see if it still meets the investor's hurdle rate using more conservative projection assumptions.

When performing a sensitivity analysis, after each new NPV is calculated it can be plotted on a graph. The slope of the graph indicates how sensitive the deal is to the changes made to the assumptions. The steeper the slope, the more sensitive the deal is to changes in the assumptions. If an investor is comparing one project with another, the project with the steeper slope is considered more risky than the one with the more gradual slope.

Hannah projects cash distribution to her equity investors to be $60,000 per year. She plans to hold her hotel for 7 years, then sell the property. She estimates that a sale at the end of Year 7 will bring in $1.2 million. She knows her investors are expecting at least a 12% annual return on their investment. To meet, but not exceed, the financial goals of her investors (their hurdle rate) and raise $500,000 in equity, how much ownership should Hannah offer her equity investors in return for their investment of $500,000?

Step 1. PV of the investment opportunity

Option 1 is to use the NPV function computing a total present value of the cash flows and netting it with a zero present value:

CF0 = 0
C01 = 60,000
F01 = 6
C02 = 1,260,000 (1,200,000 + 60,000)
F02 = 1
CPT NPV
Enter I = 12
[↓]
CPT
NPV = $816,644.45

Option 2 is to use the present value of an annuity calculation and the present value of a single lump sum calculation and add the two answers together:

PV of cash flow:		PV of sale:	
N = 7		N = 7	
I/Y = 12		I/Y =12	
PMT = 60,000		FV = 1,200,000	
CPT PV	PV = $273,825	CPT PV	PV = $542,819

Total PV of projected cash distributions: 273,825 + 542,819 = 816,644

Step 2 The Amount of Ownership to Offer
Based on an equity investment of $500,000, a hurdle rate of 12%, annual cash distributions of $60,000, and a 7-year hold with a sale at the end of Year 7 for $1.2 million, how much ownership does Hannah need to give up?

Cost = $500,000
Total PV of projected cash distributions = $816,644
Amount of Ownership:
Cost /PV = 61.23% (The % ownership Hannah should offer for $500,000 of equity).

ILLUSTRATION 9-9
Amount to Offer Investors

Hospitality Applications

Time value of money calculations are used in basic calculations, such as loan amortization, to slightly more involved ones, such as hotel appraisals, lease versus purchase analysis, and multiple investment analysis.

PREPARING A LOAN AMORTIZATION SCHEDULE

You learned how to prepare a simple loan amortization schedule in chapter 7. Let's look at another example. The owner of a chain of restaurants knows you are a hospitality student and therefore approaches you to do a quick analysis for him. He would like to purchase new deep fat fryers for his restaurants for $25,000 each. However, he can only afford a down payment of approximately 20% and therefore needs to finance the balance. His bank offers to make him a five-year loan at an interest rate of 5.0%. He wants you to calculate what his debt service payment would be and to prepare an amortization schedule for him.

Illustration 9-10 shows the steps involved in the preparation of an amortization schedule using a business calculator.

Year	Payment	Principal	Interest	Balance
1	36,956	28,956	8,000	131,044
2	36,956	30,404	6,552	100,640
3	36,956	31,924	5,032	68,716
4	36,956	33,520	3,436	35,196
5	36,956	35,196	1,760	0

Note that while the debt service payment remains fixed over the amortization period, the amount of the principal repayment component increases while the amount of the interest component decreases.

8 restaurants $\times$ \$25,000 per fryer = \$200,000 purchase

With a 20% down payment, the loan is therefore 80%
$200,000 \times 80\% = \$160,000$

Terms of loan: 5%, 5-year

Step 1. Payment Calculation for Debt Service
160,000 [PV]
5 [N]
5 [I/Y]
[CPT] [PMT]
Answer computed as $36,955.9677*

Step 2. Amortization Functions
Once the display shows the payment amount, you need to invoke the
Amortization function *AMORT* which is above the [PV] button:

[2nd] [PV]	Display shows P1 = 1.0000
	P1 stands for the beginning of a period, and thus the calculator is now looking at the beginning of period 1 or the first year. If the display does not show P1=1.0000, enter [1] [ENTER]
[↓]	Display shows P2 = 1.0000
	P2 stands for the end of a period, and thus the calculator is now looking at the end of period 1, or the first year. If the display does not show P1=1.0000, please enter [1] [ENTER]. Now, the calculator is looking at all values of Year 1
[↓]	Display shows BAL = 131,044.0323
[↓]	Display shows PRN = −28,955.9677
[↓]	Display shows INT = −8,000.0000
[↓]	Display shows P1 = 1.0000
2 [ENTER]	Display shows P1 = 2.0000
[↓]	Display shows P2 = 1.0000
2 [ENTER]	Display shows P2 = 2.0000
[↓]	Display shows BAL = 100,640.2662
[↓]	Display shows PRN = −30,403.7661
[↓]	Display shows INT = −6,552.2016
[↓]	Display shows P1 = 2.0000
3 [ENTER]	Display shows P1 = 3.0000
[↓]	Display shows P2 = 2.0000
3 [ENTER]	Display shows P2 = 3.0000
[↓]	Display shows BAL = 68,716.3118
[↓]	Display shows PRN = −31,923.9544
[↓]	Display shows INT = −5,032.0133
[↓]	Display shows P1 = 3.0000
4 [ENTER]	Display shows P1 = 4.0000
[↓]	Display shows P2 = 3.0000
4 [ENTER]	Display shows P2 = 4.0000
[↓]	Display shows BAL =
[↓]	Display shows P1 = 4.0000
5 [ENTER]	Display shows P1 = 5.0000
[↓]	Display shows P2 = 4.0000
5 [ENTER]	Display shows P2 = 5.0000
[↓]	Display shows BAL=0.0000, indicating loan has been paid off
[↓]	Display shows PRN = −35,196.1597, same as the balance left after Year 4
[↓]	Display shows INT = −1,759.8080

ILLUSTRATION 9-10
Loan Amortization Calculation Using a Business Calculator

Loan Amortization Schedule Generated:

Year	Payment	Principal	Interest	Balance
1	36,956	28,956	8,000	131,044
2	36,956	30,404	6,552	100,640
3	36,956	31,924	5,032	68,716
4	36,956	33,520	3,436	35,196
5	36,956	35,196	1,760	0.00

ILLUSTRATION 9-10
(Continued)

To prepare a loan amortization schedule using a business calculator:

1. Perform the annuity calculation to determine the annual debt service payment. The view window should show $36,956 on your calculator.

2. Next, look for the *AMORT* function. On business calculators, it is usually set as a second function directly above the PV button.

3. Once you are in amortization mode, you will be asked to enter P1 and P2. P1 stands for the beginning of the period, and P2 stands for the end of the period. For example, if you are looking for the first year (Year 1) debt service components, enter *1* as P1 and *1* as P2.

4. As you scroll the worksheet using the down arrow, you will see principal, interest, and balance of Year 1. If you want to calculate the aggregate of the loan through Year 5, enter *1* as P1 to begin the period and *5* as P2 to end the period. By doing so, you will obtain the following information:

Principal	Interest	Balance
160,000	24,779.84	0

While the term of the loan and the amortization rate in the previous example were the same, in the real world the term of the loan is usually much shorter than the amortization period. This allows for a substantially lower debt service payment, which allows you to borrow more money but forces you to either sell the asset after five years to pay off the balance of the loan or to refinance the loan for an additional five years or so.

USING THE INCOME APPROACH TO DETERMINE CURRENT MARKET OR APPRAISED VALUE

If you or your company wanted to acquire an existing hotel, renovate it, improve its financial performance, and sell it in a few years, how much should you pay for it today, and how much would it be worth today if your turn around plan proved successful? The answer to the question, "How much should I pay for it today?" is fairly basic. You simply cap or divide the trailing twelve months' cash flow by the market cap rate. The market cap rate today is between 6% and 10%.

Answering the question, "How much could it be worth today if my turn around plan is successful?" is somewhat more involved.

Hotel appraisers who have earned the designation **MAI** are eligible to become members of the Appraisal Institute. Appraisers use three methods of valuation to estimate market value: the cost replacement approach, the comparable sales approach, and the income approach. MAIs are to the valuation profession as CPAs are to the accounting profession. MAIs become certified after taking examinations and satisfying a stringent set of criteria.

The **cost replacement approach,** as its name implies, places a value on the property based on the current value of the land, the current cost to rebuild the physical structure, and the current cost to replace the existing furniture, fixtures, and equipment. The word *replacement* is the key. It is not the market value of the property or its original cost, but rather the cost required to replace the hotel as is. Thus, any physical deterioration or functional obsolescence is included in the analysis.

Consider the example in Illustration 9-11, a limited-service hotel built three years ago, one block from a major highway. The value of the land on which the hotel resides is worth $250,000. All improvements, including furniture, fixtures, and equipment, total another $700,000. However, a few things that occurred during the prior three years must be factored into the calculation. First, due to wear and tear and a poor preventive maintenance program, a physical inspection indicates the property's value has decreased by $50,000. In addition, when the hotel was built, its owner cut corners and used outdated technology in the plumbing and heating systems. Therefore, functionally, although the building is only three years old, an additional $25,000 adjustment is warranted. Finally, during the prior three years, six more limited-service hotels were built right along the highway, while the subject hotel is located one block from the highway. Thus, economically, another $35,000 deduction must be taken to arrive at the appraised value of $740,000.

As you can see, this method yields a rough estimate of the property's value. It's used primarily to provide a reasonableness test for the other two approaches to value.

The **comparable sales approach** values a hotel property based on recent comparable sales. Selling prices of properties of similar size, quality, and market are used to estimate the approx-

---

Formula to Cost Approach

Estimated Additions		
+ Land	$	250,000
+ All improvements (if new)		500,000
+ Furniture, Fixtures, and Equipment		200,000
Estimated Deductions (depreciation)		
− Physical		(50,000)
− Functional		(75,000)
− Economic		(85,000)
= Value of Hotel	$	740,000

ILLUSTRATION 9-11
Cost Approach to Hotel Valuation

Today's date: November 30, 2008

Sale date of other three full-service hotels:
Hotel Orion   January 18, 2008
Moon River   March 24, 2005
Blue Marlin   June 22, 2000

Sale date of hotels of comparable competitive markets and attributes:
Jade Garden   March 13, 2008 (full-service airport hotel)
The Esmeralda   April 4, 2008 (full-service same clientele)

In this case, the sale price of the above five hotels will be averaged and adjusted to derive a price for International Airport Hotel.

ILLUSTRATION 9-12
Sales Approach to Hotel Valuation

imate market value of the subject property. While this approach may appear easy, if there have been few comparable sales in recent months, comparisons can be difficult. Substitute hotel sales or less current sales may need to be used as surrogates to estimate market value.

In Illustration 9-12, of the ten hotels proximate to the International Airport, four are full-service hotels, and the remaining six are limited-service properties. Your company is looking at one of the full-service hotels as a potential investment. Only one of the other three full-service hotels has sold during the prior year. In this situation, you may need to work with the appraiser to seek less current comparable sales to estimate the current market value of the subject hotel.

The **income approach** is preferred by most appraisers, buyers, and sellers, as it takes into consideration the future income potential of the hotel. The income approach estimates the future stream of cash flow, including an assumed sale at the end of the analysis period, to capture ongoing value, and it discounts the resulting cash flow using WACC as the discount rate. The resulting present value (PV) is the appraiser's estimate of current market value.

FEATURE STORY

STEVE RUSHMORE–HOTEL APPRAISAL PIONEER

Steve Rushmore is the president and founder of HVS International, one of the leading hospitality appraisal and consulting firms. He founded Hospitality Valuation Services (HVS) in 1980 during the Golden Age of hotel development, when lenders and investors were busy financing hotels across the United States.

During the early 1970s, after receiving his BS from the School of Hotel Administration at Cornell University and his MBA from the University of Buffalo, Rushmore went to work for a hospitality real estate brokerage firm, where he learned to prepare hotel appraisals, feasibility studies, and deal structuring from his mentor, Steve Brener. Brener also taught Rushmore about hard work and how to market and sell professional services. These lessons proved invaluable to Rushmore a few years later when he decided to venture out on his own.

Rushmore recognized that most hospitality consultants lacked real knowledge of the real estate aspect of the hotel business. Seizing the opportunity, he opened his appraisal oriented consulting firm in 1980. He recognized that in the consulting business, he would be retained by clients only if they were convinced of his expertise in his specialized area. Therefore, prior to opening HVS, Rushmore established his credentials by authoring a book for the Appraisal Institute on hotel valuations. To compete against larger and more established consulting firms, Rushmore marketed himself as the first member of the Appraisal Institute with a degree in hotel administration. To further differentiate himself, he provided feasibility studies with financial projections and valuations at the same price as others charged for a market study.

Over his thirty-five-year career, Rushmore has provided consultation services to owners and lenders involved with more than 12,000 hotels throughout the world. His firm has provided market studies, feasibility studies, valuations, and litigation support for thousands of clients in all fifty states and more than sixty foreign countries. Steve is also a leading authority and prolific author on the topics of hotel feasibility studies and appraisals and is a frequent speaker at hospitality conferences and seminars.

SOURCES

"In Demand: Stephen Rushmore Learned from the Best to Create HVS International, a Full-service Consulting Firm. Now His Goal is to Pay It Forward." *Hotels' Investment Outlook.* http://www.hotelsmag.com/investment-outlook/2000/12/Default.asp, December 2001.
http://www.hvsinternational.com/Personnel/Profile.aspx?Id=47&Bp=377.

Note, however, that just because a certain market value is estimated for the hotel, this is not necessarily the price a buyer should pay for the property. The appraised value represents the current value of the hotel based on all the assumptions made by the appraiser. These assumptions could include some or all of the following:

1. Ownership change
2. Major renovation
3. Brand change
4. Management change
5. Changes in future market conditions

The current market value, or present value (PV), more correctly represents the potential present value of the hotel, assuming the successful execution of the action plan and the anticipated future market conditions. The buyer should therefore buy on historic performance and value on future performance.

As the deal is analyzed by the potential buyer, she compares the asking price of the seller with both the current market value, based on the capitalization of the trailing twelve months' cash flow, and the potential present value of the asset, assuming the successful execution of the action plan. If the current asking price is reasonably close to the capitalization approach to value and significantly less than the present value assuming the successful execution of the action plan, she will likely pursue the deal.

THE REAL DEAL

If the income approach to hotel valuation is the best one, why would you spend time estimating the cost replacement approach or the comparable sales approach to value? The answer is that the cost and sales approaches are used to test the reasonability of the income approach. Where do appraisers find the necessary information to make these estimates? Appraisers often obtain information from public records and tax assessors. Many sources publish construction costs and furniture, fixtures, and equipment estimates. HVS International is one reputable source that surveys and publishes construction cost per room for hotels of different types. Construction companies and real estate developers are also excellent sources.

The **IRR approach** can also be used to determine whether or not the asking price yields an IRR that is equal to or exceeds the equity investor's hurdle rate. This is done by inputting the asking price as the cost in year zero and then inputting each year's cash flow, including the assumed sale, at the end of the analysis period. Let's look at the example shown in Illustration 9-13.

Maui Ocean Hotels has been in business since the early 1990s. It has a strong corporate management team and is well known for acquiring underperforming properties, turning them into profitable ventures, and selling them in five to seven years, maximizing return on investment for their equity investment partners.

Hotel Independent was identified by one of Maui Ocean's executives last year. Maui Ocean's plan is to acquire Independent, renovate it, convert it to a Hilton hotel, operate it professionally for about five years, and then sell it. It is estimated that by the end of the fifth year, operating cash flows of the subject hotel will be stabilized. Maui Ocean uses the income approach to estimate current market value.

After final negotiations, Maui Ocean signs a contract to acquire Independent for $3,000,000. Maui Ocean believes the hotel, during renovation, will achieve a net cash flow after debt service and reserve for capital improvements of $500,000 and that the subject hotel will be able to achieve revenues of $1,400,000 in year two after a major renovation of $2,000,000 and conversion to a Hilton. It also estimates a growth in sales of 8% per year for the next four years, beginning in Year 2. At the same time expenses, including a 4% reserve for capital improvements, are estimated at $825,000, beginning in year two, with a growth rate of 6%. At the end of the five-year period, Maui Ocean expects the subject hotel's cash flow to have stabilized and will cap the fifth-year cash flow at the market cap rate of 10% to calculate a sale price for the hotel. The hotel will be financed with 50% debt and 50% equity. Maui Ocean can obtain a loan from

	A	B	C	D	E	F	G	H
1		*Input and assumptions*						
2	3,000,000	Purchase price						
3	2,000,000	Renovations						
4	500,000	Estimated net cash flow during renovations						
5	1,400,000	Revenues beginning Year 2						
6	8%	Percentage increase in sales per year						
7	825,000	Expenses beginning Year 2						
8	6%	Percentage increase in expenses per year						
9	50%	Debt ratio						
10	50%	Equity ratio						
11	7%	Cost of debt, including tax effect						
12	20%	Hurdle rate						
13	10%	market cap rate						
14		*Process*						
15								
16		2. Cost of capital						
17		wacc = wdkd(1-T) + wake						
18		= (50%)(7) + (50%)(20%)						
19		= 13.50%						
20								
21		3. Cash Flow Calculation						
22		Annual Operating Cash Flow	Year 0	Year 1	Year 2	Year 3	Year 4	Year 5
23		Revenues			1,400,000	1,512,000	1,632,960	1,763,597
24		- All Expenses			825,000	874,500	926,970	982,588
25		Net Cash Flow		500,000	575,000	637,500	705,990	781,009
26		Purchase price	-3,000,000					
27		Renovations		-2,000,000				
28		Sale Price						7,810,086
29		Total Cash Flow	-3,000,000	-1,500,000	575,000	637,500	705,990	8,591,095
30								
31		*Output*						
32	1. NPV	$1,547,293.89						
33	2. IRR	22%						

ILLUSTRATION 9-13

Maui Ocean Hotel Projection of Cash Flow for the Renovated Hilton for 5 Years its bank at an interest rate of 7%, with a twenty-five-year amortization rate. The equity investor's hurdle rate is 20%.

Using the income approach to value and an Excel spreadsheet, as shown in Illustration 9-11, Maui Ocean first projects cash flow for the renovated Hilton for five years. It then discounts these cash flows back to the present using a discount rate of 13.5% (WACC). The estimated sale value of the Hilton at the end of Year 7 is $7,810,086, based on Year 7's cash flow and assuming a market cap rate of 10%. The net sales is then discounted back to the present using a 13.5% discount rate (WACC). The PV of the annual cash flows and the PV of the net sales proceeds are then added to become the current market value of the subject hotel. It is then compared to the market value with the $3 million asking price plus the $2 million renovation. The NPV is then determined to be a favorable value of $1,547,284 and IRR is computed to be 22%. Because 20% is Maui Ocean's hurdle rate, the deal appears favorable to Maui Ocean and its equity investors. Illustration 9-13A shows the Excel formula for the spreadsheet calculations.

NPV APPLICATION OF LEASE VERSUS PURCHASE DECISION

Time value of money calculations can also be applied to lease versus purchase options. The calculation steps are quite simple. In Illustration 9-14, the owner of the Lancashire Hotel is considering whether to purchase a set of new computers or lease them. The purchase price is $25,000, while the annual lease payment is $6,000 for five years with an initial payment of $2,000. Given that Lancashire's cost of capital is 8%, is it better for Lancashire to purchase the computers or lease them?

The calculation steps are as follows:

1. Determine the cost of capital if you were to purchase the asset (I/Y).
2. Input the amount of the annual lease payment (PMT).
3. Input the number of years of the lease (N).
4. Calculate the present value (PV) of the lease payments, using the cost of capital as the discount rate.
5. There is no future value to this lease; therefore, (FV = 0).
6. Compare the present value of the lease payments with the cost to purchase the asset.

The answer, in this case, is to purchase, as the PV of the lease is greater than the purchase price. It is important to take into consideration the PV of any salvage value when calculating the present value of both the lease and the purchase options. If the present value of the lease payments is less than the cost to purchase the asset, leasing is the economic way to go. On the other hand, if the present value of the lease payments is greater than the cost to purchase the asset, purchasing makes more sense.

ANALYSIS OF ALTERNATIVE INVESTMENTS

Thus far, we have looked at one investment opportunity at a time, using both NPV and IRR techniques. In the business world, life is not that simple. An equity investor may have only

	A	B	C	D	E	F	G	H
1	*Input and assumptions*							
2	300000	Purchase price						
3	200000	Renovations						
4	50000	Estimated net cash flow after year 1 during renovations						
5	1400000	Revenues beginning Year 2						
6	0.08	Percentage increase in sales per year						
7	825000	Expenses beginning Year 2						
8	0.06	Percentage increase in expenses per year						
9	0.5	Debt ratio						
10	0.5	Equity ratio						
11	0.07	Cost of debt, including tax effect						
12	0.2	Hurdle rate						
13	0.1	market cap rate						
14	*Process*							
15								
16	2. Cost of capital							
17	wacc = wdkd(1-T) + weke	= (50%)(7) + 50%)(20%)						
18		= A9*A11+F10*A12						
19								
20								
21	3. Cash Flow Calculation							
22		Annual Operating Cash Flow	Year 0	Year 1	Year 2	Year 3	Year 4	Year 5
23		Revenues			=A5	=E23*(1+$A$6)	=F23*(1+$A$6)	=G23*(1+$A$6)
24		- All Expenses			=A7	=E24*(1+$A$8)	=F24*(1+$A$8)	=G24*(1+$A$8)
25		Net Cash Flow		=A4	=E23-E24	=F23-F24	=G23-G24	=H23-H24
26		Purchase price	=A2					
27		Renovations		=A3				
28		Sale Price						=H25/A13
29		Total Cash Flow	=SUM(C25:C28)	=SUM(D25:D28)	=SUM(E25:E28)	=SUM(F25:F28)	=SUM(G25:G28)	=SUM(H25:H28)
30								
31	*Output*							
32	1. NPV	=+C29+NPV(B18,D29:H29)						
33	2. IRR	=IRR(C29:H29, .1)						

ILLUSTRATION 9-13a

Excel Formulas for Projection of Cash Flow Calculations

Lancashire is a boutique hotel that is looking into either purchasing a set of new computers or leasing them. The purchase price is $25,000, while the lease is $6,000 per year payable for five years and payable at the end of each year with an initial down payment of $2,000. Because Lancashire's cost of capital is 8%, is it better for Lancashire to purchase or lease the computer equipment?

The steps for the calculation are as follows:

1. Input your cost of capital if you were to purchase the asset (I/Y).
2. Input the amount of your annual lease payment if you leased the asset (PMT).
3. Input the number of years of the lease (N).
4. Calculate the present value (PV) of the lease payments using your cost of capital as the discount rate.
5. Because there is no salvage value to this lease, (FV = 0).
6. Compare the present value of the lease payments with the net cost to purchase the asset.

Calculation:
I/Y = 8
PMT = 6,000
N = 5
CPT PV = 23,956,26

Because there is a required initial payment of $2,000, the total cost of the lease is $25,956.26, which is $956.26 more than the purchase price. Thus, direct purchase versus leasing would be the better economic choice.

ILLUSTRATION 9-14
Lease Versus Purchase

$100,000 to invest, and if he is considering three deals requiring varying amounts of equity, generating varying amounts of cash flow, over different time periods, how can he decide which one to choose?

In Illustration 9-15, Jeffrey and Jose are both trying to convince Jorge to invest in their hotel deal. Jorge has limited funds and must select one deal to invest in. Jeffrey is seeking an equity investment from Jorge of $10 million, while Jose's proposal is for Jorge to invest $15 million. Jeffrey and Jose both present their cash flow projections to Jorge. Jorge's hurdle rate is 12%. Which proposal should Jorge choose?

In the first scenario, Jeffrey's project would yield an NPV of $1,124,377.54 and an IRR of 12.59%. Jose's project would yield an NPV of $2,946,425.65 and an IRR of 15.39%. Jose's proposal is superior to Jeffrey's on both counts. Thus, Jorge should focus on Jose's proposal and consider investing $15 million with Jose.

However, in the second scenario, Jeffrey's numbers look a lot better, now yielding a NPV of $2,649,166.99 and an IRR of 15.62%. Comparing these with Jose's numbers, Jeffrey's deal yields a higher IRR. Which one should Jorge choose? While some might say, "Go with the higher NPV," as Jorge must invest $15 million to receive $2.95 million with Jose, while he needs to invest only $10 million to receive $2.65 million from Jeffrey, most investment analysts would recommend Jeffrey's deal because it offers the higher IRR.

The cash flows and sale values of Jeffrey's and Jose's proposals are presented below:

First Scenario

Timeline	Jeffrey's Hotel San Rio	Jose's Kawai Sunset
Year 0	(10,000,000)	(15,000,000)
1	500,000	500,000
2	770,000	775,000
3	1,000,000	1,000,000
4	1,100,000	1,750,000
5	1,250,000	2,900,000
Sale	14,000,000	
6		3,260,000
7		4,000,000
Sale		22,000,000

Based on Jorge's hurdle rate of 12%:

NPV of Jeffrey's project is $1,124,377.54 with an IRR of 12.59%
NPV of Jose's project is $2,946,425.65, and the IRR is 15.39%

If the cash flow projections for Jeffrey's project are modified as follows:

Time Line	Jeffrey's Hotel San Rio	Jose's Kawai Sunset
Year 0	(10,000,000)	(15,000,000)
1	500,000	500,000
2	770,000	775,000
3	1,500,000	1,000,000
4	1,600,000	1,750,000
5	1,750,000	2,900,000
Sale	15,000,000	
6		3,260,000
7		4,000,000
Sale		22,000,000

NPV of Jeffrey's project is $2,649,166.99 with an IRR of 15.62%
NPV of Jose's project is $2,946,425.65 with an IRR of 15.39%

ILLUSTRATION 9-15
Alternative Investment Analysis

Using ROI, NPV, and IRR

Now that you are familiar with ROI, NPV, and IRR as investment analysis methods, which do you believe is the best analysis method to use? ROI, NPV, and IRR all have their advantages and disadvantages.

The biggest advantage of the return on investment (ROI) method is that it is easy to calculate because it requires nothing more than dividing annual cash flow by the equity investment. The higher the ROI, the better the deal. The biggest disadvantage of this approach is that it does not take into consideration either the time value of money or the potential sales value of the asset at the end of the analysis period. Thus, while it is easy to use, it is not the most popular method of investment analysis.

The net present value (NPV) approach is the second easiest to calculate and understand. As long as the PV is greater than the cost, the investment is favorable based on the discount rate (WACC) used in the calculation. While NPV is a better and more popular analysis tool than ROI, because it takes into consideration the time value of money and the potential sales value of the asset at the end of the analysis period, its primary limitation is its ability to compare investment alternatives of varying costs.

For this reason, the internal rate of return (IRR) method of analysis is preferred by most investment analysts. It not only takes into consideration the time value of money and the potential sales value of the asset but also it allows you to compare investments requiring varying amounts of capital. The investment offering the highest IRR is the one favored by the equity investor. The disadvantage of the IRR method is that it assumes that cash distributions received can be reinvested at the IRR rate. This becomes a bigger issue as the life of the project increases. Many contend it is not feasible to assume that year after year the cash flow can be reinvested at the same rate as the IRR. In addition, if a negative cash flow is projected for any of the forecasted years, multiple IRRs may be computed, with only one being correct.

The bottom line is this: Use the investment analysis method that suits your purpose, situation, and needs the best, recognizing that each of the three methods has advantages and disadvantages. At the end of the day, we recommend that you learn all three and apply each to your investment opportunities.

Finance in Action

Mantle's Loan Amortization Schedule

The Mantle Restaurant Co. specializes in owning and operating franchises of national restaurant brands. Mantle is currently evaluating expansion possibilities and is looking into opening a trendy diner concept restaurant in a ski resort area. Mantle has enlisted the help of a partner, Jeff Smithson, who will be responsible for daily operations of the restaurant. Jeff is not investing any money; however, he will receive a 30% ownership position for his commitment to the development and operation of the project.

Total start-up and construction costs for the restaurant are estimated to be $450,000. Based on current market conditions, banks are willing to fund up to 70% of the total project cost to start a new restaurant.

1. How much money is the bank willing to lend the Mantle Restaurant Co.? How much equity capital does the company need to secure?

   To calculate how much the bank is willing to loan Mantle, simply multiply $450,000 by the loan-to-value ratio of 70%, which equals $315,000. This means the company needs to secure $135,000 in equity capital.

   Mantle has decided to invest the remaining 30% of the project cost with its own funds; therefore, it will only be necessary to secure financing from a lender. The Sumoon Bank has agreed to lend the company $315,000 at an annual interest rate of 8.5% for a term of five years, with an amortization rate of ten years.

2.   Create an amortization schedule for this loan.

The first step in creating an amortization schedule is to determine the loan payment. As you learned in chapter 7, you can compute the payment by identifying the number of compounding periods (10), interest rate (8.5%), and present value ($315,000). By inputting these into either an Excel spreadsheet or your financial calculator, you will determine that the annual payment on this loan equals $48,008. When you reach this point, begin setting up your amortization schedule as shown in the following table. It will help you determine which numbers need to be calculated.

Year	Payment	Principal	Interest	Balance
1	$48,008	$21,233	$26,775	$293,767
2	$48,008	$23,038	$24,970	$270,728
3	$48,008	$24,997	$23,012	$245,732
4	$48,008	$27,121	$20,887	$218,611
5	$48,008	$29,427	$18,582	$189,184
6	$48,008	$31,928	$16,081	$157,256
7	$48,008	$34,642	$13,367	$122,615
8	$48,008	$37,586	$10,422	$85,028
9	$48,008	$40,781	$7,227	$44,247
10	$48,008	$44,247	$3,761	$ (0)

Let us look at Year 1. You have already computed the payment, which will remain the same throughout the life of the loan. The next column to calculate is the interest column. Simply multiply the original loan amount by the interest rate ($315,000 × 8.5%), which equals $26,775. Next, compute the principal payment by subtracting the interest amount from the annual payment ($48,008 − $26,775), which equals $21,233. The final number to compute is the ending balance, which is the beginning balance less principal paid, or $293,767 ($315,000 − $21,233). Continue these calculations to complete the amortization schedule. (Remember, interest is calculated by multiplying the previous year's ending balance by the interest rate.)

3.   How much money does the company owe in Year 5 at the end of the loan term?

The ending balance in Year 5 is $189,184. The company must either pay this amount in full by selling the asset or by refinancing the loan for an additional term.

4.   If Mantle Restaurant Co. was willing to pay only $40,000 a year in debt service payments, what amortization rate would it need to negotiate?

Before calculating anything, identify the information you have. First of all, you know that Mantle Restaurant Co. wants an annual debt service payment of $40,000 [PMT]. You also know the current interest rate is 8.5% [I/Y] and Mantle requires a loan of $315,000 [PV]. Now, all you need to do is calculate the number of compounding periods [N], which represents the amortization rate. When you calculate *for the amortization period you should get 13.57 years, so Mantle would prefer a fourteen- or fifteen-year amortization in this scenario. (If you did not get this answer, go back and make sure you put a minus sign in front of the loan payment amount.)*

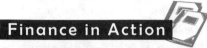

Finance in Action

A Hotel Appraisal Using the Income Approach to Value

Angela Drake Properties is planning to purchase the Parker Hotel, a 270-room property in a suburb of Abbottsville, a major metropolitan city. The acquisition price is $13,500,000, or approximately $50,000 per key, which is substantially below replacement cost. Replacement cost is estimated to be approximately $125,000 per key. The present owners purchased the hotel a few years ago for $18 million and have spent $6 million upgrading the guest rooms, lobby, restaurant, meeting rooms, and exterior. This equates to approximately $20,000 per room. The renovation won several design awards and is one of the best renovations in many years.

Parker Corporation, a major hotel brand, presently manages this hotel. Angela Drake Properties believes the fact the hotel is managed by a brand means there should be significant management upside opportunities to reduce operating costs and increase profit margins. Angela Drake Properties developed the following five-year pro forma to assist in their investment decision. At the end of year five, Angela Drake management believes they will be able to sell the property for $18,882,900. The sale price has been determined based on Year 5's cash flow and assuming a market cap rate of 12%.

Income and Expense Statement
Five-year Pro Forma

	Year 1	Year 2	Year 3	Year 4	Year 5
Revenues	6,697,832	7,019,529	7,764,415	8,333,949	8,832,677
Total departmental expenses	2,531,300	2,613,622	2,799,253	2,917,063	3,021,245
Departmental profit	4,166,532	4,405,907	4,965,162	5,416,886	5,811,432
Total undistributed operating expense	1,940,066	2,012,018	2,152,355	2,255,715	2,350,593
Gross operating profit	2,226,466	2,393,889	2,812,807	3,161,171	3,460,840
Total fixed expenses	823,324	842,396	875,424	903,453	929,911
Net operating income	1,403,142	1,551,493	1,937,383	2,257,718	2,530,928
Reserve for replacement	200,935	210,586	232,932	250,018	264,980
Cash flow from operations	1,202,207	1,340,907	1,704,451	2,007,700	2,265,948

1.   You have been hired by Angela Drake to conduct an appraisal on this property. Utilizing the income approach to valuation, determine the value of the property in Year 5 based on a WACC of 14%.

   Let us review the steps for determining valuation utilizing the income approach. The first step is to estimate future streams of cash flow; these were provided by Angela Drake Properties in the five-

year pro forma. Second, a terminal selling price must be determined; this is $18,882,900. The final step is to calculate the present value of each of these cash flows, utilizing the WACC (14%) as the discount rate. This is a simple calculation where 14% is the interest rate [I/Y], the year is the compounding period [N], and the cash flows are the future values [FV]. The following chart provides the breakdown of cash flows and present value of cash flows for each year. Notice that the Year 5 cash flow includes both operating cash flows of $2,265,948 and a terminal selling price of $18,882,900.

Year	Cash Flow	Present Value
1	$ 1,202,207	$ 1,054,568
2	$ 1,340,907	$ 1,031,784
3	$ 1,704,451	$ 1,150,456
4	$ 2,007,700	$ 1,188,720
5	$21,148,848	$10,984,049

When the present values of future cash flows are added, the present value equals $15,409,576.

2. Based on the project's present value, would you recommend that Angela Drake continue with this project? Why or why not?

Yes, based on the income approach to valuation, you would recommend that Angela Drake Properties invest in this hotel. Given that the company is paying only $13.5 million for a hotel with a present value of nearly $15.5 million, it is getting a good deal.

Finance in Action

Multiple Investments for Mancini

After many years of successful operation management, The Mancini Group, which already owns one hotel in the Northeastern United States, has decided to purchase a second hotel to add to its portfolio of real estate investments. The company's first investment was in a branded hotel that had been suffering from neglect and mismanagement. It took several years to renovate and turn the hotel around, but now that the challenge has been met, management is looking to the future and additional earnings potential.

Mancini is looking to purchase another hotel in the vicinity. Management feels the market demand is strong in the area during the peak seasons of winter, summer, and early fall, and either an existing property or a new build would fit their needs.

The group has hired a consultant to review their options and provide advice about which property he thinks is the best option to meet their investment specifications. The developer of the business park where the new build would be is ready to move forward, and other offers are on the table.

The Mancini Group will be providing $1.5 million to whichever option is the best investment for their company. The company's WACC is 12%, and the current market cap rate is 10%.

OPTION #1–NEW BUILD

The Mancini Group has the option of purchasing a parcel of land located one exit away from the property they already own. Currently, the site is adjacent to a business park void of existing hotels. It is a major access point to local activities such as hiking, boating, and skiing. The proposed seventy-five-room hotel would be a limited-service property, and the business park developer has assured the Mancini Group that a family-style restaurant will be located adjacent to the hotel site. The group feels that a brand would be essential to the success of the property, and they are currently in the process of finding one that would be consistent with a good-quality limited-service property. The total cost of this project would be $4.7 million. The following table provides the five-year projections presented by the Mancini Group management.

	Year 1	Year 2	Year 3	Year 4	Year 5
Available rooms	75	75	75	75	75
Occupancy	50%	55%	65%	70%	75%
Occupied room nights	13688	15056	17794	19163	20531
Average daily room rate	$55.00	$60.00	$65.00	$65.00	$65.00
Revenues	$752,813	$903,375	$1,156,594	$1,245,563	$1,334,531
Total departmental expenses	$203,259	$243,911	$312,280	$336,302	$360,323
Departmental profit	$549,553	$659,464	$844,313	$909,261	$974,208
Total undistributed operating expense	$180,675	$216,810	$277,583	$298,935	$320,288
Gross operating profit	$368,878	$442,654	$566,731	$610,326	$653,920
Total fixed expenses	$67,753	$81,304	$104,093	$112,101	$120,108
Net operating income	$301,125	$361,350	$462,638	$498,225	$533,813
Reserve for replacement	$22,584	$27,101	$34,698	$37,367	$40,036
Cash flow from operations	**$278,541**	**$334,249**	**$427,940**	**$460,858**	**$493,777**

1. Calculate the project's ROI, NPV, and IRR.

   First, calculate the return on the investment for the first five years of the property.

   The calculation for ROI requires dividing the annual cash flow by the equity investment. The following chart breaks down the calculation:

Year	Annual Cash Flow	÷	Equity Investment	=	ROI
1	$278,541		$1,500,000		18.6%
2	$334,249		$1,500,000		22.3%
3	$427,940		$1,500,000		28.5%
4	$460,858		$1,500,000		30.7%
5	$493,777		$1,500,000		32.9%

The table indicates that the ROI ranges from 18.6% to 32.9% during the five years of operation. Unfortunately, the ROI does not take the time value of money or the terminal sale price into consideration, so we must also calculate the NPV and IRR of the project.

Net present value and IRR are similar valuation methods used to analyze cash flows. In order to compute the NPV, input the cash flows for years 1 through 5. Remember to include the terminal sale price in the cash flow for Year 5, which would be $4,937,766 ($493,777 ÷ 10%). The terminal sale price is calculated utilizing the capitalization method of valuation. The other variable needed to calculate NPV is the cost of capital, which, in this case, equals 12%. When you compute NPV, you get a negative $505,356. Then, calculate the IRR using the same cash flows, and you should receive an answer of 9.1%. The new build does not look like a good option, so consider option #2, which is an existing property that needs renovations.

Option #2—Existing Hotel

Across the street from the Mancini Group's hotel is a 112-room property, Mountain Lodge, which is similar to the current operation. The lodge operator is not willing to share data regarding market position or performance, but the company believes the property is operating at only 20% occupancy, with an ADR of $50. The Mountain Lodge has fallen on hard times, gone through foreclosure, and is now owned by the bank. It is in desperate need of both hard and soft goods renovation. The property does not have a restaurant but occupies a prime location just off a major freeway. The total cost of this project would be $4.875 million, slightly more than the first option. The following table provides the five-year projections prepared by Mancini Group management.

	Year 1	Year 2	Year 3	Year 4	Year 5
Available rooms	112	112	112	112	112
Occupancy	30%	45%	60%	70%	75%
Occupied room-nights	12264	18396	24528	28616	30660
Average daily room rate	$55.00	$60.00	$65.00	$70.00	$75.00
Revenues	$674,520	$1,103,760	$1,594,320	$2,003,120	$2,299,500
Total departmental expenses	$202,356	$331,128	$478,296	$600,936	$689,850
Departmental profit	$472,164	$772,632	$1,116,024	$1,402,184	$1,609,650
Total undistributed operating expense	$202,356	$331,128	$478,296	$600,936	$689,850
Gross operating profit	$269,808	$441,504	$637,728	$801,248	$919,800
Total fixed expenses	$67,452	$110,376	$159,432	$200,312	$229,950
Net operating income	$202,356	$331,128	$478,296	$600,936	$689,850
Reserve for replacement	$20,236	$33,113	$47,830	$60,094	$68,985
Cash flow from operations	**$182,120**	**$298,015**	**$430,466**	**$540,842**	**$620,865**

2. Calculate the project's ROI, NPV, and IRR.

As in the first option, start with the return on investment for the first five years of the property. The calculation for ROI requires dividing the annual cash flow by the equity investment. The following chart breaks down the calculation:

Year	Annual Cash Flow	÷	Equity Investment	=	ROI
1	$182,120		$1,500,000		12.1%
2	$298,015		$1,500,000		19.9%
3	$430,466		$1,500,000		28.7%
4	$540,842		$1,500,000		36.1%
5	$620,865		$1,500,000		41.4%

The table indicates that the ROI ranges from 12.1% to 41.4% during the five years of operation. Next, look at the calculations of NPV and IRR for this project.

As stated in the explanation for option #1, in order to compute the NPV you must input the cash flows for years 1 through 5. Remember to include the terminal sale price in the cash flow for year 5, which would be $6,208,650 ($620,865 ÷ 10%). The terminal sale price is calculated by using the capitalization method of valuation. The other variable needed to calculate NPV is the cost of capital, which in this case equals 12%. When you compute NPV, you get a positive $50,546. Calculate the IRR; your answer should be 12%.

3. Which option would you recommend for the Mancini Group, and why?

When comparing the two options, it is obvious that the Mancini Group should not invest in option #1 because that project has a negative net present value and a low internal rate of return. The second option is a better investment for the Mancini Group because it has a positive net present value and the project's internal rate of return meets the company's cost of capital.

Finance in Action

Brownell Country Club—Lease or Purchase

The Brownell Country Club is in the process of upgrading its catering management system and trying to determine whether to purchase system software or go with an online version. Over the past decade, online software providers or application service providers (ASP) have become popular because the provider owns and operates the software, operates and maintains the application servers, and allows users to access the program from any computer with an Internet connection. Upgrades for ASPs are also automatically installed from the provider's end without any interruption for the users. These are all pluses for Brownell management, but they are still concerned about the overall cost of the online program.

In order to purchase the program and maintain it at the Brownell Country Club, it would cost $20,000, with another upgrade required at the end of five years. Brownell's current cost of capital is 9%. The ASP option requires an annual fee of $5,000, which provides access to the catering management program, maintenance, and upgrades. The ASP provider also requires an initial setup fee of $1,000. This is a one-time fee that will not be repeated at future renewals.

Evaluate the software purchase versus the ASP model and determine which is right for the Brownell Country Club. Explain your choice.

Determining the more beneficial option for Brownell Country Club is a simple present value calculation. First, identify the variables, and then calculate the cost of the ASP model. Brownell's cost of capital is 9% [I/Y], the annual lease payment equals $5,000 [PMT], the time period is for five years [N], and there is no future value to the lease option. Input these numbers into either a financial calculator or an Excel spreadsheet and compute the present value [PV]. The present value of the payments for the ASP model is $19,448. This is just under the $20,000 it costs to purchase and maintain the software, but you must also add the $1,000 setup fee to the cost of the ASP model, bringing the total to $20,448.

When analyzing the two totals, $20,000 for purchase of the software and $20,448 for the ASP program, the required investments are very close. Based on the numbers alone, purchasing the software would be the best option, but for the additional $500, management may choose the ASP model because it appears easier to maintain.

WHERE WE'VE BEEN, WHERE WE'RE GOING

The applications of time value of money are indeed varied and endless. Now that you have some practice, continue to work on the application exercises and the concept checks at the end of this chapter. Once you complete them, you will be ready to explore the elements included in an investment package and how lenders and investors value each of these elements.

Key Points

> Time value of money calculations are important calculations to consider when preparing a loan application and negotiating a loan.

> Time value of money calculations are quite helpful in structuring and negotiating a deal with an equity investor when factoring in issues such as a preferred return, a carried interest, a promoted interest, and an equity kicker.

> NPV and IRR are two calculations used to analyze potential investment opportunities.

> NPV calculations help determine whether it is more advantageous to lease or to purchase an asset.

➤ An appraiser uses time value of money calculations to estimate the market value of a hotel or other hospitality asset.

➤ NPV and IRR calculations help a potential investor perform multiple investment analyses to determine if an investment will be profitable.

Key Terms

PRINCIPAL: The amount of money borrowed.

DEBT SERVICE: The amount of the regular fixed payments to the bank in repayment of the loan.

INTEREST RATE: The percentage of the loan balance the lender charges the borrower for the use of the money.

AMORTIZATION RATE: The number of years the debt service payment is based on.

LOAN-TO-VALUE RATIO: The percentage of a venture's estimated value for which a lender will approve a loan. For example, if the value of your new venture is estimated to be $1.0 million and your lender's loan-to-value ratio (LTV) is 60%, the maximum he will lend you is about $600,000.

LOAN-TO-COST RATIO: Same as the loan-to-value ratio with the cost of the project substituted for value in the calculation.

DEBT SERVICE COVERAGE RATE: Cash flow divided by debt service.

CARRIED INTEREST: Ownership percentage the sponsor or promoter of a deal receives with no equity investment on his part.

PROMOTED INTEREST: Ownership awarded to the sponsor or promoter after the business venture achieves the equity investors' hurdle rate (ROI).

EQUITY KICKER: Percentage of profit on sale awarded the sponsor or promoter of the deal after the equity investors receive the return of their initial investment.

SENSITIVITY ANALYSIS: Method of analyzing investment opportunities by conservatively altering the assumptions on which the projections are based.

MAI: Member of the Appraisal Institute.

COST REPLACEMENT APPROACH: A way to estimate the value of a hotel property based on the cost to replace the property in its current state. This includes the current value of the land plus the current market price to replace the building, furniture, fixtures, and equipment.

COMPARABLE SALES APPROACH: A way to estimate the value of a hotel based on recent sale prices of comparable properties.

INCOME APPROACH: A way to estimate the current market value of a property by discounting projected future cash flows, including the estimated sale price of the property at the end of the analysis period.

IRR APPROACH: A way to estimate the current market value of a property by calculating the percentage yield of the projected future cash flows, given the investment cost.

Application Exercises

1. What is the maximum amount of loan Jose Luis can obtain if projected cash flows from his proposed project for the next five years are as follows and the lender is requesting a 12.5% interest rate?

Year	Cash Flow
1	5,000
2	5,800
3	6,900
4	9,500
5	12,650

2. What is the monthly debt service payment on Marco's loan if Enrique lends him $15,000 for four years at 8% interest?

3. Tanya is trying to prepare her loan amortization schedule for the renovation of her bed-and-breakfast facility. Her banker is quoting her an interest rate of 12% for four years. The loan amount is $25,000. Prepare the loan amortization schedule.

4. Juan would like to add a shuttle service for his hotel guests to nearby shopping centers. The van has a price tag of $35,000. His bank will give him a loan for $25,000 at only 6% interest, compounded monthly, If Juan pays $10,000 as a down payment. What is Juan's loan amortization schedule for the first five months?

5. What will be the total interest expense that Tanya (exercise 4) and Juan (exercise 5) will have to pay for their loans over the entire term?

6. Efren is considering buying some new equipment for his restaurant for $30,000. However, the restaurant supply store says they also lease equipment. The supply store will offer him a five-year lease with no down payment, four annual lease payments of $6,000 per year, and a final payment of $10,000. If Efren's cost of capital is 8%, should he select the lease or purchase option? If there is a salvage value of $1,000 if he buys the equipment but no salvage value with the lease option, will his decision change?

7. Mary has been approached by Ian to invest $75,000 of equity in a project that projects the following cash flow. If Mary's hurdle rate is 15%, should she invest in the deal?

Year	Cash Flow
1	20,000
2	10,000
3	10,000
4	45,000

8. Milton is offering Bernard an opportunity to invest in his deal. He is asking for an equity investment of $125,000 and promises to pay Bernard the following cash flow:

Year	Cash Flow
1	25,000
2	30,000
3	35,000
4	40,000
5	20,000

Bernard's hurdle rate is 14%. Does Milton's proposal meet Bernard's investment goal?

9. **ETHICS** ✳ Cathy is an accountant with a major corporation that is on the list of corporations to be audited under the new Sarbanes-Oxley law. She knows that one of the directors, Aaron, wants to start a hotel business of his own but is having a hard time coming up with the needed funds. She overhears another director suggesting to Aaron that he take out a personal loan from the company and pay it back later. Aaron trusts Cathy's judgment and asks her opinion. If you were Cathy, what would you tell Aaron?

10. **EXPLORING THE WEB** ✳ Visit the American Institute of Certified Public Accountants (AICPA) website at www.aicpa.org and view the information regarding Sarbanes-Oxley, especially Sections 401 to 404. Compose a 1,000-word document on how these four sections attempt to regulate financial reporting in the hospitality industry. Does Sarbanes-Oxley affect subsidiaries of American firms?

Concept Check ✓

The Star Takeover

The Star Restaurant Company owns and operates Chinese restaurants throughout the northwestern United States. Paris Brown, vice president of development, has been analyzing a new metropolitan market for expansion opportunities. The company's best option would be to acquire a distressed property at a low price and turn it into a money-making venture. Ms. Brown is contemplating taking over a restaurant that recently failed and is currently closed. The restaurant is located in the parking lot of a large regional shopping mall. The mall owner is anxious to reopen the restaurant, as in its current state it is an eyesore and a deterrent to attracting retail customers.

Ms. Brown asks the previous owner for historical operating results for the failed restaurant, and she is provided with the following information:

Siesta Restaurant
Operating Results
(000)

	2002	2003	2004	2005	2006
Revenue					
Food	$900	$925	$950	$975	$1,000
Beverage	350	360	365	370	375
Total	1,250	1,285	1,315	1,345	1,375
Operating expenses					
Food cost	240	255	270	285	300
Beverage cost	50	53	54	57	60
Labor cost	550	585	615	650	685
Travel	120	120	120	120	120
Marketing	60	50	40	20	10
Utilities	60	65	70	75	80
Rent	160	162	163	165	150
Total	1,240	1,290	1,332	1,372	1,405
Operating Profit (Loss)	**$10**	**$(5)**	**$(17)**	**$(27)**	**$(30)**

Based on Paris's market analysis, tour of the competition, inspection of the subject property, and interviews with the prior owner, she concludes a Star Restaurant would work in the subject space, but it would require approximately $200,000 of renovation and conversion cost in addition to the land purchase price of $2,000,000. By Year 5, the restaurant could generate $2.5 million in annual food revenue and $1.5 million in annual beverage revenue. Ms. Brown estimates the following cash flows for the first five years of operations, with cash flows leveling off in Year 5.

Year	Cash Flow
1	$695,000
2	876,250
3	1,057,500
4	1,238,750
5	1,420,000

1. Calculate the IRR and NPV of this project utilizing a 12% discount rate and a 15% cap rate. Ms. Brown was able to secure a loan for $1,540,000, and an equity investor agreed to invest the remaining $660,000 in exchange for 20% ownership in the project.

2. What is the loan-to-value ratio for this project?

3. What would the investor's ROI be for this 5-year project if the restaurant achieved its budgeted operating results for the year?

4. If the investor has a hurdle rate of 15%, does this project meet or exceed the investor's requirements?

Concept Check ✓

The Tennyson Borrowing Power

Tennyson Investments, a hotel investment company, has identified a potential midscale branded hotel prospect located in a major metropolitan area. The Mason Hotel, a franchised property, is on the market, and the owners are looking to sell the asset quickly because they need cash to invest in other projects they currently own and operate.

The Mason Hotel is located next to a midscale limited-service hotel, across the street from a historic conference center and an upscale full-service hotel and adjacent to a new major-league baseball stadium. The property consists of a 124-room full-service hotel with a leased restaurant, a forty-space parking garage in the basement, a gift shop, an exercise room, and meeting rooms.

The property is currently being marketed at an asking price of $6.4 million. Tennyson Investments offered $5 million, which was accepted by the sellers, and has secured a new non-recourse first mortgage with a 6.4% interest rate for 70% of the total project cost of $5,977,335. Tennyson has estimated the following cash flows for the first five years of the project.

Mason Hotel

Five-year Pro Forma

	Year				
	1	2	3	4	5
Revenues					
Rooms	$ 1,886,850	$ 2,216,640	$ 2,362,320	$ 2,454,960	$ 2,501,280
Telephone	$ 7,980	$ 8,160	$ 8,415	$ 8,745	$ 8,910
Restaurant lease	$ 104,160	$ 106,800	$ 109,395	$ 113,685	$ 115,830
Other income	$ 101,010	$ 68,400	$ 69,870	$ 72,610	$ 73,980
Gross income	$ 2,100,000	$ 2,400,000	$ 2,550,000	$ 2,650,000	$ 2,700,000
Departmental expenses					
Rooms	$ 547,941	$ 594,946	$ 613,022	$ 629,452	$ 634,074
Telephone	$ 32,696	$ 34,083	$ 35,830	$ 37,959	$ 39,425
Restaurant utilities	$ 30,133	$ 31,495	$ 32,895	$ 34,844	$ 36,197
Other	$ 0.00	$ 0.00	$ 0.00	$ 0.00	$ 0.00
Total departmental expenses	$ 610,770	$ 660,524	$ 681,747	$ 702,255	$ 709,696
Gross operating income	$ 1,489,230	$ 1,739,476	$ 1,868,253	$ 1,947,745	$ 1,990,304

Undistributed expenses

Administrative and general	$ 234,150	$ 275,040	$ 293,250	$ 304,750	$ 310,500
Franchise fee	$ 55,230	$ 56,640	$ 57,885	$ 60,155	$ 61,290
Marketing	$ 180,810	$ 185,520	$ 189,720	$ 197,160	$ 200,880
Energy	$ 103,530	$ 106,080	$ 108,630	$ 112,890	$ 115,020
Repairs and maintenance	$ 123,480	$ 134,400	$ 138,210	$ 139,655	$ 142,560
Total undistributed expenses	$ 697,200	$ 757,680	$ 787,695	$ 814,610	$ 830,250
Gross operating profit	$ 792,030	$ 981,796	$ 1,080,558	$ 1,133,135	$ 1,160,054
Fixed charges					
Management fee	$ 63,000	$ 72,000	$ 76,500	$ 79,500	$ 81,000
Real estate taxes	$ 83,580	$ 85,680	$ 87,720	$ 91,160	$ 92,880
Insurance	$ 83,580	$ 85,680	$ 87,720	$ 91,160	$ 92,880
Reserve for replacement	$ 63,000	$ 72,000	$ 76,500	$ 79,500	$ 81,000
Total fixed	$ 293,160	$ 315,360	$ 328,440	$ 341,320	$ 347,760
Net available for debt	$ 498,870	$ 666,436	$ 752,118	$ 791,815	$ 812,294

1. How much money has Tennyson Investments borrowed for this project based on a 70% loan-to-value ratio?

2. What is the maximum amount available for debt service in the first year if the lender requires a 1.25 debt service coverage ratio?

3. Utilizing the debt service payment calculated in the previous question, calculate the ideal amortization rate for the first mortgage at the 6.4% annual interest rate.

4. Tennyson Investments has hired Geoff Strips Management Co. to operate the hotel. The Strips Co. has negotiated a 10% equity kicker on the sale of the property if the hotel meets or exceeds projected cash flows. If the property is sold in Year 5, what dollar amount would Geoff Strips Management receive? Utilize the capitalization rate method of valuation based on a 10% cap rate.

5. Calculate the NPV for this project based on a 12% cost of capital. What is the IRR?

THE INVESTMENT PACKAGE

IAN SCHRAGER—THE PIONEER OF BOUTIQUE HOTELS

Ian Schrager is a man of many contradictions. He is a straight, shy man, but his first claim to fame was a glamorous, hedonistic New York City discothèque called Studio 54, which he cofounded with close friend Steve Rubell, a flamboyant gay. He studied commercial law but was sent to the federal penitentiary for tax evasion. He and Rubell conceived their first boutique hotel, Morgans, in the early 1980s. It was so successful that they expanded the concept rapidly and borrowed heavily, so much so that when the economy went south, Ian had to file for bankruptcy protection. He recovered, however, and went on to develop many successful deals on his own. Perhaps because of these circumstances, the man has built an aura of invincibility that impels investors and lenders to plunge their money into his projects.

Schrager's first brush with business came during the 1970s, a decade associated with pop groups such as the Village People, the Bee Gees, and ABBA, and with the movie *Saturday Night Fever.* He remembers, "It was a very exciting time—a period when people were waiting in line to get into discos. A time when I realized that without a lot of capital, this could be my access into the economic system."

In 1974, he and Rubell opened the legendary Studio 54 on West 54th Street in Manhattan, New York. The discothèque was a cash generator from the start. It made the partners as famous as the celebrities who were waved past the velvet ropes. Fame and success, however, must have gone to their heads, because in 1979 the Internal Revenue Service raided Studio 54 and had the men arrested for not reporting $2.5 million of club revenue.

For most people, having a criminal record would spell an end to their career. Indeed, after serving their time in federal penitentiary, Schrager and Rubell struggled for a while.

> *When we got out we were below ground zero because we couldn't get a liquor license, couldn't get credit cards, couldn't even open a checking account. . . . They took everything from us, but I'm not complaining. That's just the way the system works. We lost our way, but that didn't affect my enthusiasm or my ambition. As my mother and father used to say, "There's no real harm in falling down. The harm is in not picking yourself up and moving forward." Any success I have today is the result of being relentless.*

Luckily, they still had the infamous discothèque, which they sold for $4.75 million. With that money, they bought a dilapidated hotel on lower Madison Avenue, renovated it in a style consistent with their unconventional style, and opened it for business in 1985. Like Studio 54, the Morgan was an instant hit with the in crowd.

Even when Rubell passed away in 1989 and the lenders foreclosed on the Morgan and Royalton hotels a few years later, Schrager took his defeats in stride. He bought back the hotels from the lender and continued to expand the boutique concept throughout the United States and Europe. By then, his hotels had acquired a cult following and frequently experienced full occupancy in spite of the high room rates. His original hotels became tourist attractions because of their unique trend style and the celebrities they attracted. In an effort to capitalize on his hotels' popularity, Schrager and his investors expanded rapidly and borrowed heavily, banking on Schrager's ability to deliver publicity and the hope that each hotel would gain an instant reputation as a hot spot that would generate immediate cash flow through high room rates and occupancies.

But once again, Schrager's luck ran out. Beset by the weak economy and the travel anxieties that followed the 9/11 disaster, the hotel industry suffered through its worst years in recent memory, with boutique hotels hit particularly hard. According to Smith Travel Research, RevPAR of boutique hotels dropped 18% following 9/11 from their peak in 2000. Likewise, the boutique hotels that Schrager owned, namely the Royalton, the Paramount, the Delano, the Clift, and the Mondrian, saw RevPAR fall by as much as 40%. As a result, Schrager found himself seeking bankruptcy protection for his Clift Hotel when he could not convince his lender to agree to a work-out of his $57 million mortgage. Yet, within a year, he pulled himself out of the insolvency mess by refinancing $475 million of debt at a lower cost and selling his Paramount and Clift hotels for close to $200 million.

Since then, Schrager has turned his attention from hotels to ultra-luxury residential condominium and co-op projects, including Gramercy Park North and Bond Street in Manhattan, New York. Will he finally get it right this time, or will the housing market turn ugly as interest rates climb? We will have to wait and see.

SOURCES

"Life After Studio 54." http://sumagazine.syr.edu/summer01/features/enterprisezone/index.html, 2001.

Hamilton, W. L., and M. Rich. "Familiar Face at the Hard Times Hotel." *New York Times,* Style Desk, August 10, 2003.

"Ian Schrager Files Bankruptcy Protection for Clift Hotel in San Francisco; No Reprieve on Hotel's $57 Million Debt." http://www.hotel-online.com/News/PR2003_3rd/Aug03_SFClift.html, August 21, 2003.

"The Morgans Hotel Group, Formerly Known as Ian Schrager Hotels, Completes $475 Million Recapitalization." http://www.hotel-online.com/News/PR2004_3rd/Aug04_MorgansReFi.html, August 18, 2004.

Bagli, C. V. "Schrager Quits Hotel Company for Apartments." *New York Times,* Metropolitan Desk, July 12, 2005.

"Steve Rubell." http://en.wikipedia.org/wiki/Steve_Rubell, January 28, 2006.

"Studio 54." http://en.wikipedia.org/wiki/Studio_54, January 28, 2006.

Learning Outcomes

1. Identify the need for an investment package when seeking approval to spend ownership's capital or when attempting to raise capital for a new project or business venture.
2. Determine the components of a professionally prepared investment package.
3. Describe how an investment package is reviewed and evaluated by ownership, a potential lender, and a potential equity investor.

Preview of Chapter 10

The Investment Package

1. THE NEED FOR AN INVESTMENT PACKAGE

2. THE COMPONENTS OF AN INVESTMENT PACKAGE

    a. Executive summary

    b. Fact sheet

    c. Business plan

    d. Source and use of funds

    e. Photographs and renderings

    f. Third-party confirmation

    g. Line item project budget

    h. Qualifications of the project team and management

    i. Financial analysis

    j. Personal financial data

3. EVALUATION OF AN INVESTMENT PACKAGE

a. Lender
  i. Loan to value
  ii. Loan to cost
  iii. Debt service coverage ratio
  iv. Risk of project
b. Owner/Investor
  i. Amount of investment
  ii. Return on investment (ROI)
  iii. Exit strategy

THE NEED FOR AN INVESTMENT PACKAGE

When capital is needed to finance the renovation or expansion of an existing hospitality asset, a new start-up business venture, the acquisition of an existing hotel, the development of a new restaurant, or even a public stock offering, the first and perhaps most important step in gaining approval for funding is the preparation of a professional investment package. When requesting approval to spend your owner's capital, the investment package may be only a few pages long. However, when seeking public financing, the investment package may be over 100 pages long.

The investment package should tell your story. It should sell your project or new venture to capital sources from which you are seeking funding. The capital source may be the existing owner of your business, a prospective lender, or a prospective equity investor. The investment package for an initial stock offering is called a *prospectus*. Illustration 10-1 shows what is normally included in a prospectus and a representative table of contents.

The better you tell and sell your story, the more likely your request for capital funding will be approved—and on terms favorable to your business. While the contents of your investment package may vary based on the size and type of project to be financed, the basic contents of every package are the same and should include the following components:

1. **Executive summary:** A brief recap of the project clearly stating its operational benefits, its financial benefits, and the amount of capital being requested. When seeking debt financing for a new business venture, the loan terms being requested should also be included.

2. **Fact sheet:** A one-page description of the key components of the project or venture.

3. **Business plan:** A summary of your full business plan that describes what your project is all about and how you are going to make it successful.

4. **Source and use of funds:** While this may sound complicated, it's really not. A source and use of funds statement presents when, and from whom, the capital is coming from (sources), how and when you intend to spend it (uses), and, most important, how and when you intend to pay the money back.

A prospectus should answer the following questions:
- Type of investment
- Parties involved
- Amount to be invested
- Charges and fees
- Expected risk and return
- Exit strategy
- Further contact information

A sample table of contents from an IPO prospectus is shown below:

1) Key Dates and General Information
2) The Offering: Investment Highlights
    i) Purpose of the Operation
    ii) Number and Origin of Shares
    iii) Valuation of the Company
    iv) Terms and Conditions of the Offering
    v) Cost and Net Proceeds of the Offering
3) Industry Overview
4) Overview of Company
    i) General Information
    ii) Competition and Market Analyses
    iii) Board of Directors
    iv) Senior Management
5) Financial Information
    i) Risk Factors
    ii) Independent Accountants Report
    iii) Consolidated Financial Statements
    iv) Pro Forma Financial Statements
    v) Recent Developments and Prospects
    vi) Dividend Policy
6) Additional Information
7) Glossary of Terms and References
8) Corporate Directory

ILLUSTRATION 10-1
Prospectus: What Should Be Included

5. **Photographs or renderings:** Any available photographs or renderings of the project, plus preliminary architectural or interior design plans. Remember the old adage, "A picture is worth a thousand words."

6. **Third-party confirmation:** When seeking outside financing, a report from a well-known and reputable consulting firm affirming the feasibility of your project is usually expected or even required by the prospective lender or equity investor. The report could take the form of either a market study or an appraisal.

7. **Project budget:** A line-item budget detailing hard costs (bricks and mortar), soft costs (fees and other pre-opening expenses), and an operating reserve to fund cash shortfalls until the project begins generating a positive cash flow.

8. **Qualifications of the project team:** Résumés, curriculum vitae, and company brochures presenting the qualifications of each key member of your development and management team.

9. **Investment analysis:** A pro forma operating statement presenting projected sales, expenses, cash flow, annual return on investment, net present value, and internal rate of return for the project or venture.

> 1. Executive Summary
> 2. Description of project that funds are being requested for
> 3. Project budget
> 4. Pro forma statement of cash flow for five to ten years
> 5. Source and use of funds statement
> 6. Drawings and rendering
> 7. Project team
>   a. Architect
>   b. Interior designer
>   c. Contractor
> 8. Investment analysis
>   a. Annual ROI
>   b. Payback period
>   c. Net present value analysis
>   d. Internal rate of return analysis

ILLUSTRATION 10-2

Sample Table of Contents for In-House Request for Capital Funds

10. **Personal financial data:** This is required only in situations where the lender requires the loan be guaranteed. The financial data required includes copies of balance sheets and prior-year tax returns for the guarantors of the loan.

Illustration 10-2 shows a table of contents for a typical investment package.

Executive Summary

The executive summary may be the only section of the investment package your owner, lender, or investor reads. It therefore must be complete and concise. It should state how much capital you need, why your request should be approved, and the major benefits of the deal right up front.

When seeking private debt financing from an outside source, the executive summary should also include the key loan terms you are requesting, such as the interest rate, amortization rate, and length of the loan. It should also highlight your project's loan-to-cost, loan-to-value, and debt service coverage ratios. Illustration 10-3 provides an executive summary for a sample investment package.

Fact Sheet

The fact sheet—no more than one page long—should succinctly answer the basic questions the reader of your investment package wants answers to with regard to your project. For example, a loan package for the development of a new hotel, or the acquisition of an existing hotel, might include the following information:

Executive Summary

Overview

Months of economic contraction worsened by the events of September 11 have created significant opportunities to acquire distressed assets within various segments of the U.S. hotel industry. A proliferation of evidence suggests that the dramatic decline in revenue per available room has undermined the capacity of many hotel owners to meet their debt service obligations. Based on research, it is estimated that 30% of U.S. hotels will be unable to meet their debt service obligations from operations in 2004. In fact, over the 80 years that TWL Research has tracked the U.S. hotel industry, the magnitude of RevPAR decline in 2001 through 2003 is the greatest seen since the Great Depression of the 1930s. TWL Research believes that this RevPAR decline will have a substantially greater impact on those hotels experiencing declining occupancies prior to the macroeconomic downturn.

Milton Hotels, Inc. ("Milton") intends to take advantage of this unfavorable environment by acquiring distressed upscale and midscale limited-service hotels properties on a national basis, and through its rehabilitative and operational expertise reposition each asset thereby enhancing value (the "Venture"). Milton will target only high-quality brands and rebrandable assets. Milton will also evaluate portfolio acquisitions as such opportunities are defined.

Milton believes it can acquire a minimum of 20 assets over the next 18 months and estimates the initial aggregate portfolio size to exceed $200 million depending upon opportunity flow, individual submarket conditions, the outlook for the travel and lodging sectors, and the rapidity of a macroeconomic recovery.

Sponsorship

Milton is a REIT based in Houston, Texas, that develops, acquires, and rehabilitates upscale, premium limited-service and high-end extended-stay hotels. Milton's management took its portfolio of ten hotels public in 1996, raising approximately $50 million. Today, Milton trades on the New York Stock Exchange under the symbol MTN. The company has an ownership interest in 60 hotels comprising 7,390 rooms in 15 states across the country. Milton's current portfolio is over $150 million in annual revenues, and Milton has a 49% joint venture interest in three of these properties. The average age of the properties in the Milton portfolio is approximately ten years, representing one of the youngest portfolios within its peer group.

Milton's senior management will devote significant time and effort to the Venture. Ethan Kinneman, CEO, Daniel Mader, president and COO, and Charles Franco, CFO of Milton, will be personally involved in the acquisition, finance, asset management, rehabilitation/repositioning, and, ultimately, disposition of each asset acquired by the Venture.

To supplement overall company growth and enhance shareholder value, Milton's management team has made the Venture the cornerstone of its future growth strategy.

Investment Strategy

The targeted assets will fall into three general categories: 1) assets acquired for repositioning, 2) assets acquired for rehabilitation, and 3) mismanaged assets primarily requiring more effective management, Milton believes each asset will cost about $10 million to $30 million. The Venture will acquire assets on a nationwide basis, but acceptable assets should be in markets of a minimum population of 500,000 with great economic growth potential, regional air-traffic volume, and proximity to a national or regional transportation hub.

The Venture's acquisition parameters target an all-in cost per asset of less than 85% of replacement cost, with the internal rate of return in the range of traditional opportunistic investments. Given the current debt market environment, Milton believes the Venture can achieve debt levels of approximately 65% of total cost. Milton expects to acquire assets over at least an 18-month period and intends to hold each asset for approximately three and a half years. From the first acquisition through the final disposition, the life of the Venture should be about six years.

ILLUSTRATION 10-3
Sample Executive Summary for an Investment Package

The Venture intends to acquire and reposition assets at the bottom of the lodging cycle and dispose of assets as RevPAR recovers, cash flows stabilize and increase, and capitalization rates decrease from current levels.

Value Creation
The Venture anticipates that value will be created in four different ways:
1) income growth from assets rehabilitation / repositioning and implementing effective management practices
2) enhanced leveraged cash flow created by historically low mortgage rates
3) decreasing capitalization rates and increasing values resulting from an upturn in the lodging cycle, and
4) income growth resulting from a broad macroeconomic recovery.

Investment Timing
Based on its own projection as well as those of TWL Research, Milton expects the window of opportunity will remain open for at least the next 12 months. However, the depth and duration of the current recession will define the length and magnitude of the opportunity targeted by the Venture. If the current downturn proves more persistent, the window of opportunity may be longer resulting in a greater opportunity to acquire distressed assets.

Milton believes the sellers of targeted assets will include large lodging companies and smaller ones. Milton also believes there will be opportunities to acquire assets out of foreclosure or assets that lenders have forced distressed borrowers to sell. Milton intends to monitor the major hotel lenders and CMBS servicers that may consider liquidating their positions. In addition, the Venture will seek out distressed opportunities created by experienced developers and investors that acquired assets during the market upswing but lack the financial resources during the downturn.

Acquiring Transactions
Given the limited window of opportunity, the Venture will require immediate nationwide access to potential transactions. As such, Milton has already begun actively sourcing transactions for the Venture, which has resulted in a pipeline of potential assets. To ensure complete market coverage, Milton will employ a three-level strategy: 1) as a nationally prominent owner of premium limited service and upscale hotel properties in the United States, Milton maintains an extensive network of contacts among owners and operators of similar assets, and thus enjoys broad access to potential transactions; 2) Milton has engaged W&S Consulting to exclusively provide the Venture with access to potential transactions through its nationwide client base and network of relationships within the lodging industry; and 3) Milton will employ its team approach to sourcing transactions where it will identify a qualified regional or local partner to source potential transactions within a given geographic region and perform daily operational activities with the acquired property.

Exit Strategy
Milton believes the assets comprising the Venture will vary in size and price, which should provide maximum flexibility during the disposition process. It is also expected that the aggregate portfolio will be large enough and of sufficient quality to attract primarily institutional buyers such as hotel REITs and C-corporations.

Financial Analysis
Please see appendix I for details.

Capitalization Request
Milton is seeking joint venture programmatic equity capital to execute the Venture set forth in this proposal.

ILLUSTRATION 10-3
(Continued)

Hotel Information

Location
The Huntington Hotel is located in downtown Charleston, on the peninsula, one mile northwest of the city's historical district. The hotel enjoys a wonderful location overlooking the river and is only one block from the city's minor-league baseball park. The Citadel is one mile to the north, and the state's largest medical complex is only half a mile to the south. US Highway 17, the main highway providing access to the peninsula from the surrounding Charleston region, is directly to the south of the hotel.

Year Opened
1980

Rooms
300 guest rooms

Description
The full-service hotel features a 14-story guestroom tower and 15,000 square feet of high-quality meeting and banquet facilities with 15 meeting rooms. Food and beverage facilities at the hotel include a full-service restaurant and lounge. Additional guest amenities include a gift shop, an outdoor swimming pool, an exercise room, and a business center.

Site Acreage
7.13 acres

ILLUSTRATION 10-4
Sample Fact Sheet of a Hotel Investment Package

- Location
- Age of facility
- Number and mix of guest rooms
- Number and size of restaurants and bars
- Other amenities, such as swimming pool, tennis, golf, and spa
- Proposed brand affiliation
- Development team
- Management team
- Ownership entity
- Equity participation of promoter

A fact sheet for a new restaurant or other hospitality project is similar in content. A fact sheet for a sample hotel loan package is presented in Illustration 10-4.

Business Plan

A summary of your full business plan is another important component of your investment package. While the readers of your package will likely want to receive a complete copy of your business plan, they will carefully read your summarized version and make a preliminary judgment on the merits of your capital request. Your investment plan, therefore, must answer the following questions:

- What is the project or business for which you need the capital?
- Is the market and business climate favorable for such an investment, and will it continue to be favorable?
- What are your site's major advantages and disadvantages?
- How would you compare the advantages of your site and location within the market with your competition?
- Who is your competition, and how are they doing?
- Is any new competition planned? If there is, how will it impact your business?
- Who is going to develop your project, and what are their credentials?
- Who is going to manage your project, and what are their credentials?
- What are you projecting for payback period, return on investment, net present value, and internal rate of return?
- What factors might prevent you from achieving these projections?
- Why should your owner, lender, or equity investor provide capital for your project rather than putting money in another deal?
- In summary, why do you believe your project will be successful?

Source and Use of Funds

If the reader of your investment package likes your business plan, these are the next questions he will ask:

- How much new capital is required to execute the business plan?
- Where is the remaining capital to finance the project coming from besides my money?
- How much equity is the sponsor investing in the deal?
- Whose money is going into the deal first?
- Whose money is coming out of the deal first?
- How soon will I receive a return on my capital, and what is the exit strategy?

A professionally prepared source and use of funds statement can answer these questions. Illustration 10-5 presents a sample source and use of funds statement.

The JC
Hilton Head, SC

Date Prepared: 7/15/2006

PURCHASE SUMMARY

Purchase Price

		$ 13,500,000
Number of Rooms	296	
Price per Room	$45,700	
Room Revenue Multiplier	3.1x	
Total Revenue Multiplier	2.3x	
Going-in Cap Rate on Trailing-12 as of 2005	2.1%	
Current Value of the Property	$18,180,000	

SOURCES and USES SUMMARY

Total Uses / Acquisition Costs

Cost per Room		$50,085
Purchase Price		$13,500,000
Third-party Inspection Reports	(appraisal, environmental, engineering and cost reports, etc.)	25,000
Financing Costs	(mortgage loan fee + lender's expenses: legal fees, documentations, etc.)	120,500
Legal Costs	(consultants fees, liquor license consultants, etc.)	65,000
Closing Costs	(closing prorations/adjustments, due diligence expenses, etc.)	100,000
Operating Funds	(start-up working capital)	300,000
Franchise Application Fees	$500	(per room- initial fees)	$118,400
Mortgage Brokerage Fees	1.00%	(of the mortgage amount) - Neptune Hospitality Advisors	$96,400
Brokerage/Advisory Fees	0.00%	(of the purchase price) - Neptune Hospitality Advisors	$0
Equity Placement Fees	0.00%		$0
PIP Costs / Renovation Costs			$500,000

Total Sources			$ 14,825,300
65.0%	Mortgage Loan Amount		$9,636,400
35.0%	Equity Required		$5,188,900
100.0%		Equity Partners	$5,188,900

ILLUSTRATION 10-5
Sample Sources and Uses Statement

Photographs or Renderings

Because lenders and equity investors receive hundreds of investment packages each year, making your package stand out from the others is a challenge. One way to meet the challenge is to include a few photographs and/or architectural renderings of your project in your package. The colors alone may make your package distinctive. A photograph or rendering brings your project to life in the eyes of the reader of your package. See Illustration 10-6.

ILLUSTRATION 10-6
Sample Art for Investment Package

THE REAL DEAL

Location, location, location. Have you ever noticed that some locations, no matter what type of restaurant is opened there, don't seem to make it? Location is critical to every hospitality project. Astute lenders and investors focus much of their due diligence on the proposed location for the project. Some investors and lenders may even look at the feng shui of the location and hire a feng shui master to assess whether or not the business will succeed at the proposed site. After all, if the last few restaurateurs were not successful, the chance of all of them being poor managers is quite low. There may be other factors preventing the subject site from being a profitable venture.

Third-party Confirmation

An important component of an investment package is an affirmation from a well-known third party accounting or consulting firm that the proposed investment is feasible. The reader of your investment package wants to learn why you believe the deal will be successful, but he also wants to be assured by an independent third party, experienced in the hospitality industry, that his investment will be safe and yield favorable financial results.

A third-party affirmation can take the form of a **market study** or a full **appraisal.** A market study provides information on the local economy, evaluates the location of the project, researches supply and demand, comments on the appropriateness of the proposed facilities, and presents projected operating results, usually for ten years. A full appraisal includes a market study but also provides an estimate of the project's present value based on financial projections, recent comparable sales, and the approximate replacement cost of the project. Illustration 10-7 shows the table of contents for a sample appraisal.

Most sophisticated lenders and investors prefer an appraisal over a market study. While an appraisal is more costly and requires more seed money be spent by the deal sponsor, it increases the probability that funding for the deal will be approved.

Project Budget

When the reader of your investment package is satisfied that your business plan will result in a feasible project and generate favorable financial results, he will then focus on the cost of your project. To assist the reader in evaluating and becoming comfortable with the cost of your deal, a detailed line item project budget is recommended. Illustration 10-8 shows a sample project budget for a proposed new hotel.

The goal of the project budget is to convince the reader you have included all costs in your budget and that those costs are reasonable. When a project budget is low-balled, or understates budgeted costs in an effort to make the projected return on investment appear more favorable

1) Introduction
    i)   Identification of the subject property
    ii)   Legal description
    iii)   Purpose and use of the appraisal
    iv)   Property rights appraised
    v)   Important dates
    vi)   Property ownership history
    vii)   Definition of values
        (a) Market value
        (b) Prospective market value
        (c) Going-concern value
    viii) Scope and methodology of the appraisal
    ix)   Competency provision of the uniform standards of professional appraisal practice

2) Area review and neighborhood analysis
    i)   Introduction
    ii)   Los Angeles area regional conclusion and economic outlook
    iii)   Economy
    iv)   Employment
    v)   Regional infrastructure
    vi)   Tourism indicators
    vii)   Los Angeles county lodging market

3) Neighborhood review
    i)   Beach overview
    ii)   Local economic and demographic trends
    iii)   Commercial office space
    iv)   Airport
    v)   Beach Convention Center
    vi)   Development and redevelopment projects
    vii)   Conclusions

4) Property descriptions
    i)   Site description
    ii)   Improvements description
    iii)   Conclusions

5) Hotel market analysis
    i)   Introduction
    ii)   Market performance of the competitive market
    iii)   Rooms demand for the competitive market
    iv)   Projected growth in demand
    v)   Estimated market performance of the proposed hotel

6) Highest and best use
    i)   Definition of highest and best use
    ii)   Highest and best use as if vacant
    iii)   Highest and best use as improved

7) Valuation
    i)   Discussion of the three approaches to value
    ii)   Valuation of the subject property

8) Income capitalization approach
    i)   Introduction
    ii)   Methodology
    iii)   Basis for cash flow projections
    iv)   Operating statistics on comparable hotels
    v)   Stabilized year estimate
    vi)   Undistributed operating expenses
    vii)   Fixed charges
    viii) Presentation of estimated annual operating results
    ix)   Estimated annual operating results for the holding period
    x)   Additional operational analysis
    xi)   Valuation using direct capitalization
    xii)   Capitalization rate
    xiii) Discounted cash flow analysis
    xiv) Net proceeds upon sale/reversion

9) Reconciliation and final estimate of value

ILLUSTRATION 10-7
Sample Table of Contents for an Appraisal

The JC
Hilton Head, SC
Date Prepared 07/15/2006
INCOME AND EXPENSE STATEMENT
5-YEAR PRO FORMA

	Year 1 PRO FORMA				Year 2 PRO FORMA				Year 3 PRO FORMA				Year 4 PRO FORMA				Year 5 PRO FORMA			
	Amount	% of Dept.	$ PAR	$ POR	Amount	% of Dept.	$ PAR	$ POR	Amount	% of Dept.	$ PAR	$ POR	Amount	% of Dept.	$ PAR	$ POR	Amount	% of Dept.	$ PAR	$ POR
Percentage of Occupancy	57.5%				59.0%				64.0%				67.0%				69.0%			
Average Daily Rate	$77.00				$78.91				$81.12				$83.55				$86.06			
RevPAR	$44.28				$46.56				$51.92				$55.98				$59.38			
Number of Rooms	296				296				296				296				296			
# of Rooms Sold	62,293				63,744				69,146				72,387				74,752			
# of Rooms Available	108,336				108,336				108,336				108,040				108,336			
REVENUES																				
Rooms	4,796,576	71.6%	16,205	77.0	5,030,227	71.7%	16,994	78.9	5,608,973	72.2%	18,949	81.1	6,048,050	72.6%	20,433	83.6	6,433,023	72.8%	21,733	86.1
Food	1,391,007	20.8%	4,699	22.3	1,455,163	20.7%	4,916	22.8	1,576,812	20.3%	5,324	22.8	1,670,668	20.0%	5,644	23.1	1,753,462	19.9%	5,924	23.5
Beverage	361,662	5.4%	1,222	5.8	377,759	5.4%	1,276	5.9	407,109	5.2%	1,375	5.9	430,456	5.2%	1,454	5.9	451,015	5.1%	1,524	6.0
Telephone	124,586	1.9%	421	2.0	131,337	1.9%	444	2.1	145,621	1.9%	492	2.1	156,382	1.9%	528	2.2	165,463	1.9%	559	2.2
Other Operated Dept.	24,000	0.4%	81	0.4	25,042	0.4%	85	0.4	26,901	0.3%	91	0.4	28,392	0.3%	96	0.4	29,713	0.3%	100	0.4
Total Revenues	6,697,832	100.0%	22,628	107.5	7,019,529	100.0%	23,715	110.1	7,764,415	100.0%	26,231	112.3	8,333,949	100.0%	28,155	115.1	8,832,677	100.0%	29,840	118.2
DEPARTMENTAL EXPENSES																				
Rooms	1,151,178	24.0%	3,889	18.5	1,181,990	23.5%	3,993	18.6	1,290,064	23.0%	4,358	18.7	1,341,066	22.2%	4,531	18.5	1,383,232	21.5%	4,673	18.5
Food	1,105,851	79.5%	3,736	17.8	1,147,049	78.8%	3,875	18.0	1,209,005	76.7%	4,084	17.5	1,262,298	75.6%	4,265	17.4	1,311,856	74.8%	4,432	17.5
Beverage	180,831	50.0%	611	2.9	187,437	49.6%	633	2.9	197,113	48.4%	666	2.9	205,532	47.7%	694	2.8	213,418	47.3%	721	2.9
Telephone	93,440	75.0%	316	1.5	97,147	74.0%	328	1.5	103,164	70.8%	349	1.5	108,177	69.2%	365	1.5	112,739	68.1%	381	1.5
Other Operated Dept.	0	0.0%	0	0.0	0	0.0%	0	0.0	0	0.0%	0	0.0	0	0.0%	0	0.0	0	0.0%	0	0.0
Total Departmental Expenses	2,531,300	37.8%	8,552	40.6	2,613,622	37.2%	8,830	41.0	2,799,253	36.1%	9,457	40.5	2,917,063	35.0%	9,855	40.3	3,021,245	34.2%	10,207	40.4
DEPARTMENTAL PROFIT	4,166,532	62.2%	14,076	66.9	4,405,907	62.8%	14,885	69.1	4,965,162	63.9%	16,774	71.8	5,416,886	65.0%	18,300	74.8	5,811,432	65.8%	19,633	77.7
UNDISTRIBUTED OPRTG EXP.																				
Administrative & General	569,316	8.5%	1,923	9.1	589,826	8.4%	1,993	9.3	621,884	8.0%	2,101	9.0	649,477	7.8%	2,194	9.0	674,905	7.6%	2,280	9.0
Franchise Fees	275,803	4.1%	932	4.4	289,238	4.1%	977	4.5	322,516	4.2%	1,090	4.7	347,763	4.2%	1,175	4.8	369,699	4.2%	1,250	4.9
Sales & Marketing	385,125	5.8%	1,301	6.2	399,000	5.7%	1,348	6.3	420,686	5.4%	1,421	6.1	439,352	5.3%	1,484	6.1	456,554	5.2%	1,542	6.1
Repairs & Maintenance	351,636	5.3%	1,188	5.6	364,304	5.2%	1,231	5.7	403,516	5.2%	1,363	5.8	421,083	5.1%	1,423	5.8	438,905	5.0%	1,483	5.9
Utility Costs	358,186	5.3%	1,210	5.8	369,651	5.3%	1,249	5.8	383,753	4.9%	1,296	5.5	397,140	4.8%	1,342	5.5	410,300	4.6%	1,386	5.5
Total Undistributed Oprtg Exp.	1,940,066	29.0%	6,554	31.1	2,012,018	28.7%	6,797	31.6	2,152,355	27.7%	7,271	31.1	2,255,715	27.1%	7,621	31.2	2,350,593	26.6%	7,941	31.4
GROSS OPERATING PROFIT	2,226,466	33.2%	7,522	35.7	2,393,889	34.1%	8,087	37.6	2,812,807	36.2%	9,503	40.7	3,161,171	37.9%	10,680	43.7	3,460,840	39.2%	11,692	46.3
FIXED EXPENSES																				
Management Fees	234,424	3.5%	792	3.8	245,684	3.5%	830	3.9	271,755	3.5%	918	3.9	291,688	3.5%	985	4.0	309,144	3.5%	1,044	4.1
Equipment Leases/Rents	20,000	0.3%	68	0.3	15,000	0.2%	51	0.2	11,250	0.1%	38	0.2	8,438	0.1%	29	0.1	6,328	0.1%	21	0.1
Property Taxes	387,200	5.8%	1,308	6.2	396,378	5.6%	1,339	6.2	404,306	5.2%	1,366	5.8	412,392	4.9%	1,393	5.7	420,640	4.8%	1,421	5.6
Insurance	181,700	2.7%	614	2.9	185,334	2.6%	626	2.9	188,114	2.4%	636	2.7	190,936	2.3%	645	2.6	193,800	2.2%	655	2.6
Total Fixed Expenses	823,324	12.3%	2,782	13.2	842,396	12.0%	2,846	13.2	875,424	11.3%	2,958	12.7	903,453	10.8%	3,052	12.5	929,911	10.5%	3,142	12.4
NET OPERATING INCOME	1,403,142	20.9%	4,740	22.5	1,551,493	22.1%	5,242	24.3	1,937,383	25.0%	6,545	28.0	2,257,718	27.1%	7,627	31.2	2,530,928	28.7%	8,550	33.9
Reserve for Replacement	200,935	3.0%	679	3.2	210,586	3.0%	711	3.3	232,932	3.0%	787	3.4	250,018	3.0%	845	3.5	264,980	3.0%	895	3.5
CASH FLOW FR OPERATIONS	1,202,207	17.9%	4,062	19.3	1,340,907	19.1%	4,530	21.0	1,704,451	22.0%	5,758	24.7	2,007,700	24.1%	6,783	27.7	2,265,948	25.7%	7,655	30.3

ILLUSTRATION 10-8

Sample Project Budget for a Proposed New Hotel

than it actually is, the reader will pick up on these tricks and often turn the deal down for this very reason. It is best to take a conservative approach to project budgeting, making sure the project can be developed for the cost projected and allowing for contingencies to fund possible construction overruns and operating losses during the early years of operation.

THE REAL DEAL

Most deals in the hotel industry are not financed with capital provided by the developer of the deal. Instead, most are promoted by the developer who puts the deal together, forms the project team, prepares an investment package, and secures both debt and equity capital to construct the new project or acquire an existing one. Raising the required capital has become both an art and a science. Usually the promoter provides 5% to 10% of the required equity, with a wealthy investor or investment group providing the balance of the equity needed. The equity investors are usually rewarded with the first cash-out, which is called a *preferred return,* until they reach their return-on-investment goal. The targeted rate of return is called a *hurdle rate.*

Qualifications of Project Team

The experience and track record of the project team is another important part of your investment package. Owners, lenders, and equity investors all want to feel confident your team can deliver the proposed project on time, on budget, and generating the operating results projected.

The project development team for a new hotel normally comprises the following members:

- Developer
- Architect
- Interior designer
- Construction company and subcontractors
- Structural engineer
- Hotel brand
- Hotel management company
- Lender
- Equity partner
- Law firm
- Accounting firm

In the case of a public offering, an investment banking firm is also an important member of the team. The role of the investment banker is to monitor the preparation of the prospectus, gain approval of the prospectus from the Securities and Exchange Commission, market the public offering to both institutional and retail investors, price the stock or bonds, and manage the overall public offering process.

Because the hardest deal for a new company to finance is its first deal, putting together an extremely strong project team is a very good idea. While a start-up company may not be able to present extensive experience of its own, it can leverage the experience and favorable track record of its project team members.

Investment Analysis

The investment analysis section of your investment package should provide the detail supporting the summary financial projections. Projected sales, expenses, and cash flow, plus the assumptions they are based on, should be included. In addition, estimates of annual return on investment, payback period, net present value, and internal rate of return should be highlighted, including their underlying assumptions. You may remember all these from the last two chapters.

At the end of the day, assuming there is a market for your project or venture, your costs are in line, and your project management team is qualified, most capital requests are approved or denied on the merits of the financial returns the deal is projected to yield. Therefore, the investment analysis component of your package is vital and should not be taken for granted.

Personal Financial Data

When a lender requires the borrower and, in some cases, an additional person or entity of substance, to guarantee the repayment of a loan, copies of the guarantors' current balance sheet and prior-year tax returns must be provided. These are required to verify the guarantors' prior-year income, establish a favorable credit rating, and provide the lender with confidence in your group's ability to fund construction or operating shortfalls that may occur.

EVALUATION OF THE INVESTMENT PACKAGE

Understanding how a lender or equity investor will evaluate your investment package is critical to obtaining the financing you are seeking. Being able to anticipate questions and answer them before they are asked makes you look smarter and more experienced than you may actually be and will help you sell your deal.

Lenders: Debt

Most lenders will ask themselves three major questions as they evaluate your investment package:

1.   How strong is this project, and is it really feasible?

   ▪   Your business plan and story therefore must be persuasive and should be confirmed by a credible third-party source.

2.   Is the project team really qualified?

   ▪   The credentials of your team must be outstanding. If you are attempting to finance a start-up business with no track record and your management team lacks experience, make sure you surround yourself with seasoned professionals and reward them well. Your investment in their talents will serve you well on later deals and help you establish a favorable track record for your company.

3.   What is the risk of this venture failing?

   ▪   Lending is all about risk, so don't ignore it. You must clearly state, in your own words, the risks of the proposed project and how you plan to minimize them.

   ▪   Risk can be minimized by providing additional collateral or personal guarantees, or, preferably, by showing the lender that it is a conservative loan with low loan-to-cost and loan-to-value ratios and a high debt service coverage ratio and that the loan can easily be paid back out of future cash flows.

   ▪   The **debt service coverage ratio** is calculated by dividing projected annual cash flow by the amount of your annual debt service. For example, if your projected cash flow for Year 1 is $100,000 and your debt service for the year is $50,000, your debt service coverage ratio is 2:1, which means you can pay your debt service two times over ($100,000/$50,000), which is a very safe ratio. On the contrary, if your projected annual cash flow is only $50,000 and your annual debt service is $50,000, you can meet your debt service obligation, but with no room to spare. The resulting 1:1 debt service coverage ratio would be considered very risky by the lender, and your loan would likely be denied.

   ▪   The **loan-to-value ratio** (LTV) is another important metric for lenders. From a personal perspective related to a mortgage on your house, LTV is the relationship between the amount owed on the mortgage loan and the appraised value of the home. If a home carries a mortgage of $90,000 and an appraised value of $100,000, the LTV ratio is 90%. In finance, this principle applies to commercial proportion. The LTV ratio is the amount of the loan requested divided by the value of the project as estimated by an independent third-party appraiser. If the appraiser values your project at $500,000 and you are seeking a $300,000 loan, the LTV ratio is 0.6 to 1 ($300,000/$500,000). First-mortgage hotel lenders today will loan up to about 60% of appraised value.

If your prospective lender is comfortable with the answers to the three questions noted above, your chances of receiving the debt financing you are seeking are excellent.

THE REAL DEAL

It is difficult to obtain a loan for your first hotel or restaurant from a commercial bank. However, if you establish a favorable track record of success, securing a loan to open your second and third restaurant is normally easier. What's the secret of securing the necessary capital for your first restaurant? Persevere. Just because one bank turns your loan request down does not mean all banks will. One entrepreneur in Houston had to meet with over 160 lenders before he was able to secure a loan to build his first limited-service hotel. If he had stopped after the tenth or even the hundredth lender, he would have never opened his business. Second, try all potential sources of financing, including contacting your local SBA office and apply for an SBA loan. Third, consider putting together a larger group of small equity investors. You may have to put up with several people owning most of your restaurant, but you can negotiate a buy-back provision that allows you to buy out your partners based on an agreed-to formula when you have sufficient funds to purchase their share of the business.

Owner/Investor: Equity

Your owner or prospective outside equity investors will evaluate your investment package in a similar manner to your lender, but with more of an eye toward the upside potential of the deal. In addition to evaluating the overall feasibility of the project, the qualifications of your project management team, and the risk associated with you achieving your financial projections, owners and prospective equity investors are also interested in answers to the following questions:

1. How much equity is the sponsor group investing in the deal?
   - This is a tough question to answer, particularly if your group has a limited amount of capital to invest in the venture or has elected not to invest its own funds in the deal. But remember, a primary goal of finance is to use other people's money to make money for you and your company.
   - If your group is able and willing to provide 5% to 10% of the equity required, the outside equity investor will usually be comfortable. You now have, as they say, skin in the deal.
2. What annual return on investment (ROI) can I expect to receive, what's the payback period, what is the net present value (NPV) of the deal, what is my projected internal rate of return (IRR), and how much is the sponsor group making on the deal?
   - ROI, payback period, NPV, and IRR were discussed in chapters 7, 8, and 9.
   - As long as your owner or prospective equity investor is confident she will achieve her targeted goals and hurdle rates for ROI and IRR, she will usually be okay with the sponsor group earning a nice bit of change as well.
   - The key, as we discussed earlier, is for the cash equity investors to receive their return before the sponsor group reaps significant rewards from the deal.

3. What is the **exit strategy?**

   ■ This is an important question. An equity investor's strategy, particularly an equity fund, is often to invest the equity, make a quick killing, and look for another opportunity to do it again.

   ■ The shorter and more clearly defined the exit strategy is, the more likely the outside equity investor will be to invest in your deal.

   ■ Also, as you should have noted in chapters 8 and 9, your investor's IRR is primarily driven by the exit strategy (i.e., the assumed sale at the end of the investment period). The shorter the period until the assumed sale, the higher the projected IRR will be.

If you provide your owner and/or equity investor with credible answers to these three questions, she is likely to invest equity in your deal. If you reward her with the ROI and IRR she is seeking and execute the exit strategy well, you will also have a likely source of equity for your next deal.

FEATURE STORY

P.F. CHANG'S CHINA BISTRO—HOW TO TAKE AMERICA'S FAVORITE ETHNIC FOOD NATIONWIDE

When we think of Chinese food, what usually comes to mind is the small family-owned and -operated neighborhood restaurant. All seem to offer dumplings and Hunan beef with a heavy dose of Asian hospitality. Major restaurant companies have often tried to break into this market, but with little or no success. One of the most famous failures was the China Coast concept pioneered by Darden Restaurants in 1990. By the mid 1990s, the company had to make a hasty retreat from its new Chinese restaurant concept when huge cash losses and a significant drop in its stock price resulted. In the end, Darden was forced to take a $44.8 million write off and close all of its China Coast restaurants.

In spite of this failure, one company has risen to the challenge, successfully differentiated itself from the traditional neighborhood Chinese restaurant, and built a nationwide restaurant chain featuring a blend of high-quality Chinese cuisine and American hospitality in a sophisticated, contemporary bistro setting.

P.F. Chang's China Bistro is the creation of Paul Fleming, a creative restaurateur. In 1993, Paul was living in Scottsdale, Arizona, and dismayed that he could not find a local restaurant that offered Asian food to his liking. To solve the problem, Paul Fleming (P.F.) teamed up with his longtime friend and Chinese cuisine expert, Philip Chiang (Chang), to create an upscale restaurant serving select Asian dishes that captured the distinct flavors and styles of the five major culinary regions of China: Canton, Hunan, Mongolia, Shanghai, and Szechwan. They named their new restaurant P.F. Chang's China Bistro, using Fleming's initials and a modified version of Chiang's last name.

In addition to its upgraded level of service, one of P.F. Chang's points of difference was its active promotion of liquor sales. The restaurant offered an extensive wine menu and sold high-quality wines by the glass. This distinction contributed to the restaurant's bottom line, as alcoholic beverages have higher profit margins than food offerings. In fact, 20% of the bistro's sales were liquor, with 10% generated by wine sales alone.

Fleming attributes much of P.F. Chang's phenomenal success to its policy of requiring management to invest in the company. He believes this requirement has played a major role in instilling an entrepreneurial spirit in all of its managers. P.F. Chang's offers three levels of partnerships. At the regional level, the market partner (regional manager) is required to invest $50,000 and sign a five-year contract for the right to develop P.F. Chang restaurants in a designated market. In return, the market partner receives 7% of the cash flow from the restaurants developed in his territory. At the restaurant level, the operating partner (restaurant manager) is required to invest $25,000 and receives 6% of the restaurant's cash flow. In addition, to further align the interests of ownership and management, P.F. Chang's requires each executive chef to invest $8,300, which entitles the chef to receive a 2% interest in his restaurant's cash flow.

Based on its exceptional first five years of success, P.F. Chang's went public in December 1998 and raised $50 million to fund its future growth. Since going public, the chain's operating results have been impressive. In 2005, the company reported a return on investment of 15%. As of January 2006, the market value of its stock totaled $1.35 billion. Between 1998 and 2005, the chain grew from 23 restaurants to over 180. To complement its upscale Chinese full-service restaurant concept, P.F. Chang's recently added a limited-service version called Pei Wei Asian Diner, which is likened to a P.F. Chang Express. With no apparent competition in sight, the future for P.F. Chang's appears bright.

SOURCES

Papiernik, R. L. (1997, March 31). Darden Faces Up to its Problems, Finds its Own Solutions–Darden Restaurants Inc. Nation's Restaurant News.

http://www.fool.com/ddouble/2000/ddouble000522.htm. (2000, May 22). P.F. Chang's Good Fortune.

http://www.fool.com/foolaudio/transcripts/2000/stocktalk000525_pfcb.htm. (2000, May 25). TMF Interview with P.F. Chang's China Bistro Chief Financial Officer and Secretary Robert Vivian.

http://finance.yahoo.com/q/ks?s=PFCB. (2006, January 30). PF Chang's China Bistro Inc. (PFCB): Key Statistics.

http://finance.yahoo.com/q/pr?s=pfcb&partner=mf. (2006, January 30). PF Chang's China Bistro Inc. (PFCB): Profile.

Finance in Action

The Condor–A Good Deal?

Jeremy Oats, an experienced hotel investor, has identified a possible purchase located in a midscale metropolitan market. The Condor Hotel is on the market, and the owners are looking to sell the asset because they are in the process of focusing their business on retail establishments and feel the hotel does not fit well in their portfolio of properties.

The Condor Hotel, built in 1976, is located on a 4.5-acre lot on Fifteenth Street in downtown Hooverville. This is a densely industrial area next to a major amusement park and across the street from a U.S. historical site. Other hotels in the area include a budget hotel and an upscale full-service hotel. The property consists of a 155-room full-service hotel with a restaurant, an 80-space parking lot, an exercise room, a clothing boutique/gift shop, and 21,000 square feet of meeting rooms.

The asking price for the project was $7.2 million, but Mr. Oats offered $6 million for the property because he felt it was overpriced for the current operating numbers. The offer was accepted because the current owners truly wanted to be out of the hotel business. Mr. Oats is now in the process of securing financing for the project. He has contacted a local bank and is requesting a new non-recourse first mortgage with a 9% interest rate.

Condor Hotel
Five-Year Pro Forma

	Year					
	1	2	3	4	5	6
Revenues						
Rooms	$ 2,215,500	$ 2,358,563	$ 2,569,917	$ 2,732,370	$ 2,896,313	$ 3,070,091
Telephone	$ 10,750	$ 9,975	$ 9,461	$ 9,733	$ 10,317	$ 10,936
Restaurant Lease	$ 139,000	$ 130,200	$ 123,821	$ 126,531	$ 134,123	$ 142,171
Other Income	$ 134,750	$ 126,263	$ 79,301	$ 80,815	$ 85,664	$ 90,804
Gross Income	$ 2,500,000	$ 2,625,000	$ 2,782,500	$ 2,949,450	$ 3,126,417	$ 3,314,002
Direct Costs						
Rooms	$ 782,736	$ 684,927	$ 689,766	$ 709,050	$ 742,615	$ 778,268
Telephone	$ 43,206	$ 40,870	$ 39,515	$ 41,443	$ 44,783	$ 48,391
Restaurant Utilities	$ 41,422	$ 37,667	$ 36,515	$ 38,048	$ 41,109	$ 44,428
Other	$ 872	$ 729	$ 271	$ 266	$ 282	$ 299
Total Direct	$ 868,236	$ 764,192	$ 766,066	$ 788,807	$ 828,788	$ 871,386
Gross Operating Income	$ 1,631,764	$ 1,860,808	$ 2,016,434	$ 2,160,643	$ 2,297,629	$ 2,442,616
Indirect Costs						
Administrative and General	$ 327,500	$ 292,688	$ 318,875	$ 339,187	$ 359,538	$ 381,110
Franchise Fee	$ 76,000	$ 69,038	$ 65,667	$ 66,953	$ 70,970	$ 75,228
Marketing	$ 195,750	$ 226,013	$ 215,087	$ 219,439	$ 232,605	$ 246,562
Energy	$ 138,250	$ 129,413	$ 122,987	$ 125,647	$ 133,185	$ 141,176
Repairs and Maintenance	$ 160,000	$ 154,350	$ 155,820	$ 159,860	$ 164,762	$ 174,979
Total Indirect	$ 897,500	$ 871,500	$ 878,435	$ 911,085	$ 961,061	$ 1,019,056
Gross Operating Profit	$ 734,264	$ 989,308	$ 1,137,998	$ 1,249,558	$ 1,336,569	$ 1,423,561
Fixed Charges						
Management Fee	$ -	$ 78,750	$ 83,475	$ 88,484	$ 93,793	$ 99,420
Real Estate Taxes	$ 111,500	$ 104,475	$ 99,335	$ 101,461	$ 107,549	$ 114,002
Insurance	$ 111,500	$ 104,475	$ 99,335	$ 101,461	$ 107,549	$ 114,002
Reserve for Replacement	$ -	$ 78,750	$ 83,475	$ 88,484	$ 93,793	$ 99,420
Total Fixed	$ 223,000	$ 366,450	$ 365,621	$ 379,889	$ 402,683	$ 426,843
Net Available for Debt	$ 511,264	$ 622,858	$ 772,378	$ 869,669	$ 933,886	$ 996,717

Condor Hotel
Cost of Project

Purchase Price	$ 6,000,000
Renovation	$ 500,500
Acquisition Fee	$ —
Financing Fee	$ 80,000
Franchise Fee	$ —
Working Capital	$ 75,000
Legal	$ 45,000
Contingency	$ 25,000
Inspection/Closing Costs	$ 24,000
Total Project Cost	**$ 6,749,500**
Cost per Room	**$ 54,431**
Capitalization	
First Mortgage	$ 4,724,650
Equity	$ 2,024,850
Total Capitalization	**$ 6,749,500**

QUESTIONS

1. Develop a fact sheet to be utilized in an investment package for this project.

   The following is a sample fact sheet for the Condor Hotel. When developing an investment package, always remember that you are trying to sell someone on your project but keep it factual.

Condor Hotel—Fact Sheet

Location

The Condor Hotel is located on Fifteenth Street in downtown Hooverville. The subject property is conveniently situated in a densely industrial area next to a major amusement park and across the street from a U.S. historical site. Other hotels in the area include a budget hotel and an upscale full-service hotel that do not offer direct competition for the property. Highway 45, the major highway that divides Hooverville in half, runs directly in front of the property, with convenient exit and entrance ramps.

Year Opened

1976

Rooms

155

Description

The property consists of a 155-room full-service hotel with a restaurant, an 80-space parking lot, an exercise room, a clothing boutique/gift shop, and 21,000 square feet of meeting rooms.

Site Acreage

4.5 acres

2. Calculate the loan-to-value ratio for this project if an appraiser recently valued the property at $6,500,000.

    $ 4,724,650 divided by $6,500,000 = LTV of 73%

3. Calculate the loan-to-cost ratio.

    $4,724,650 divided by $6,749,500 = LTC of 70%

4. Calculate the debt service coverage ratio for the first year of this project if the annual debt service payment is $481,000.

    $481,000 divided by $511,264 = DSCR of 0.94

5. Based solely on the information provided, would you lend money for this project? Why or why not?

    Based on the proposed LTV, LTC, and DSCR, a lender should not provide a loan for this project. The LTV and LTC are near 70%, which is too high for current lending practices. Most hotel lenders will loan up to 60% of the appraised value. Also, the DSCR is nearly 1:1, which means that during the first year the Condor Hotel can barely cover its debt service. Maybe a better option would be to find more equity investors for this project and lower the debt amount.

WHERE WE'VE BEEN, WHERE WE'RE GOING

A professional investment package is the foundation for seeking funding for an in-house capital project or financing for a new business venture. A clear description of the project or venture noting its merits and cost, the qualifications of the management team, and the numerous financial projections and analysis are important elements to gain the attention of ownership, lenders, and investors. In the case of a new venture, however, this is only the beginning to successfully developing a new business venture. You also need to select the best form of business entity, decide on the proper mix of debt and equity, and successfully negotiate your loan agreement with your lender and your equity agreement with your investor. Chapter 11 focuses on these topics and discusses the use of certain negotiating skills to help you negotiate a favorable deal for yourself.

Key Points

➤   The key elements of an investment package are an executive summary, project fact sheet, business plan, source and use of funds statement, photographs and renderings of project, third-party confirmation, line item project budget, qualifications of the project team, and personal financial data on the sponsors of the deal.

➤   Lenders and investors evaluate investment packages in slightly different ways. While both are interested in the financial feasibility of the project, the qualifications of the project team, third-party confirmation of the merits of the deal, projected operating results, and the potential risk factors that could negatively impact the project, lenders focus on the following three ratios:

   a. Loan to value

   b. Loan to cost

   c. Debt service coverage

➤   Equity investors focus on:

   a. Return on investment

   b. Internal rate of return

   c. The exit strategy

Key Terms

FACT SHEET: A one-page description of the key components of the project or venture.

BUSINESS PLAN: A summary of your full business plan describing what your project is all about and how you are going to make it successful.

PROJECT BUDGET: The estimated cost of a project, including hard costs, soft costs, and cash reserves.

MARKET STUDY: A report, written by an independent third party, that estimates the future financial performance of a proposed project.

APPRAISAL: A valuation of an income-producing asset, prepared by a professional appraiser.

DEBT SERVICE COVERAGE RATIO: Cash flow divided by debt service.

LOAN-TO-VALUE RATIO: The amount of the loan compared to its appraised value.

EXIT STRATEGY: The event (and its timing) that is to provide the return of capital to the equity investor.

Application Exercises

1. Explain the differences between an executive summary and a fact sheet in an investment package.

2. Describe the items that might be included in a business plan.

3. What is a third-party confirmation, and why is it important in an investment package?

4. Who are all the parties that must be included in a project development team? Explain the significance of each.

5. If you are the sole owner of a project, the lender will normally ask you for your personal financial data. What elements are covered in this category, and why would your lender need to know about your personal finances?

6. If an independent third party valued your project at $1,000,000 and you are requesting an $800,000 loan, what is the loan-to-value ratio? What are the chances of this loan being

approved? What is the loan-to-value ratio if you asked for a $400,000 loan? What would be the chances of this loan being approved?

7. What are three key items that lenders focus on when evaluating an investment package? Explain.

8. What are three key items that investors focus on when evaluating an investment package? Explain.

9. **ETHICS** ✳ After reading the market study from a third-party firm, Ben did not like its negative tone and projected operating results. As Courtlan is his friend and Courtlan works for another firm that specializes in market studies, Ben gives the first study to Courtlan and asks him to fix it for him. Ben promises Courtlan that if the results are good, he will give him a 1% ownership position in the proposed restaurant as a friendly gesture. Is Ben ethical in doing so? What should Courtlan do in terms of being ethical?

10. **EXPLORING THE WEB** ✳ Search the Internet for firms that perform market studies and appraisals for the hospitality industry. Contact them to find the approximate cost for a market study and appraisal for a 200-room full-service hotel in a major metropolitan city.

Concept Check ✓

The Right Hotel for the Right Market

Nicole Sharp, director of acquisitions for Sahara Hotels Corp., has discovered a promising location for a future hotel. The subject property is located in a densely populated urban setting and borders the business district in Shepard City. Ms. Sharp is in the process of developing an investment package for potential equity investors and has put together the following fact outline:

- The location of the proposed hotel is excellent, as it is located in one of the fastest-growing market areas in Shepard. Businesses have been readily moving to Shepard because of favorable tax incentives. Along with increased business development, local hotels have experienced an increase in ADR and revenue per available room.

- The acquisition price of the land will be $3.5 million, with an additional $15 million needed for construction costs for the proposed 197-room property. In total, the project will cost $18.6 million.

- The city is currently in the process of building a major freeway in front of the proposed build site, which will increase land values and traffic.

- The hotel competition in the immediate area consists of two major branded hotels and one independently operated property. Competitor A is a budget hotel, Competitor B is a midmarket property without food and beverage facilities, and Competitor C is an upscale independent property with food and beverage facilities.

Ms. Sharp is proposing to build a 197-room upscale full-service property to meet the underserved business travelers currently visiting the area. The following is a pro forma for the first six years of operation. Ms. Sharp has projected six years because she has set a timeline to sell the property in Year 6 at an 11% cap rate.

6 Year Pro Forma

	1	2	3	4	5	6
Revenues						
Rooms	$ 2,252,500	$ 2,388,776	$ 2,557,424	$ 2,737,978	$ 2,902,257	$ 3,076,392
Telephone	$ 9,500	$ 9,713	$ 9,461	$ 9,733	$ 10,317	$ 10,936
Restaurant Lease	$ 141,750	$ 107,625	$ 129,386	$ 120,927	$ 128,183	$ 135,874
Other Income	$ 96,250	$ 118,913	$ 86,258	$ 80,815	$ 85,664	$ 90,804
Gross Income	$ 5,500,000	$ 5,720,000	$ 6,063,200	$ 6,245,096	$ 6,682,253	$ 7,216,833
Direct Costs						
Rooms	$ 765,850	$ 804,062	$ 852,221	$ 903,263	$ 947,885	$ 994,710
Telephone	$ 28,310	$ 28,654	$ 27,631	$ 28,143	$ 29,534	$ 30,993
Restaurant Utilities	$ 49,613	$ 37,292	$ 44,384	$ 41,068	$ 43,096	$ 45,225
Other	$ 1,444	$ 1,766	$ 1,268	$ 1,176	$ 1,234	$ 1,295
Total Direct	$ 845,216	$ 871,774	$ 925,504	$ 973,651	$ 1,021,749	$ 1,072,223
Gross Operating Income	$ 4,654,784	$ 4,848,226	$ 5,137,696	$ 5,271,445	$ 5,660,504	$ 6,144,610
Indirect Costs						
Administrative and General	$ 720,500	$ 741,827	$ 778,473	$ 793,809	$ 840,882	$ 899,071
Franchise Fee	$ 167,200	$ 172,149	$ 180,653	$ 184,212	$ 195,136	$ 208,639
Marketing	$ 430,650	$ 452,355	$ 484,291	$ 503,808	$ 544,465	$ 593,903
Energy	$ 304,150	$ 319,479	$ 342,034	$ 355,818	$ 384,533	$ 419,449
Repairs and Maintenance	$ 352,000	$ 362,419	$ 380,323	$ 387,815	$ 410,812	$ 439,241
Total Indirect	$ 1,974,500	$ 2,048,229	$ 2,165,774	$ 2,225,462	$ 2,375,828	$ 2,560,302
Gross Operating Profit	$ 2,680,284	$ 2,799,997	$ 2,971,922	$ 3,045,983	$ 3,284,675	$ 3,584,307
Fixed Charges						
Management Fee	$ —	$ 171,600	$ 181,896	$ 187,353	$ 200,468	$ 216,505
Real Estate Taxes	$ 245,300	$ 227,656	$ 216,456	$ 214,831	$ 229,869	$ 248,259
Insurance	$ 245,300	$ 227,656	$ 216,456	$ 214,831	$ 229,869	$ 248,259
Reserve for Replacement	$ —	$ 171,600	$ 181,896	$ 187,353	$ 200,468	$ 216,505
Total Fixed	$ 490,600	$ 798,512	$ 796,704	$ 804,368	$ 860,674	$ 929,528
Net Available for Debt	$ 2,189,684	$ 2,001,485	$ 2,175,217	$ 2,241,615	$ 2,424,001	$ 2,654,779

QUESTIONS

1. Is any information missing that should go into an equity investment package? If so, list the information missing.

2. Calculate the return on investment in Year 1 for an equity investor who provides 45% of the total project cost.

3. Calculate the internal rate of return for this project with a sale in Year 6. (Utilize the cap rate method for sale price in Year 6.)

4. Would you invest in this project? Why or why not?

Concept Check ✓

Tex's Home-Style

Tex's Home-style Steakhouse Executive Summary

This is an investment opportunity to be an owner of a new restaurant to be located in a new high-rise marketplace in a major metropolitan city. The marketplace will be a multi-use retail and entertainment center with over 200 retail shops. The restaurant would be developed and owned by a limited partnership, to be formed. The general partner would be a corporation owned by Brad Lee and Lydia Lopez, who are veteran operators of restaurants and nightclubs in the United States. The general partner would have the responsibility for all development and operations of the restaurant.

This investment opportunity is available in limited partnership units of $25,000 each. Limited partners would have no financial obligation beyond the initial investment in the property. Once adequate working capital reserves have been established, 75% of distributable cash flow will be paid quarterly to the limited partners and 25% to the general partners. Upon return of their initial capital contributions, the limited partners will then receive 50% of the distributable cash flow, and the general partner will receive the remainder.

Tex's Steakhouse is an established restaurant franchise with a reputation for high-quality steaks and barbecue, making the restaurant instantly recognizable to potential customers. Projected annual sales are expected to fall between $3,200,000 and $4,200,000. Based on these sales projections, the pro forma projection of pre-tax cash flow from this restaurant ranges from $375,000 to $680,000 annually, for a cash-on-cash return ranging from 65% to 115%.

The capital budget to construct and open this restaurant is $1,600,000, of which the general partner will procure the sum of $1,000,000 in the form of a real estate tenant allowance. The remaining $600,000 is required in the form of limited partner equity. The monthly rental is the greater of $15,000 or 9% of sales. In this instance, percentage rent will begin when annual sales exceed $2,000,000.

TEX'S STEAKHOUSE
Source and Use of Funds

Source of Funds

Cash Equity	$600,000
Tenant Improvement Allowance	$1,000,000
Total	$1,600,000

Use of Funds

Leasehold Improvements	$972,000
Furniture, Fixtures, and Equipment	$355,250
Pre-opening, Marketing, and Inventory	$272,750
Total	$1,600,000

QUESTIONS

1. Analyze the source and use of funds information provided. Is there enough information to answer all of the questions asked below? If sufficient information is provided, please respond. If not, what is missing?

    ▪ *How much new capital is required to execute the business plan?*

    ▪ *Besides the money provided by equity investors, where is capital to finance the project coming from?*

    ▪ *How much equity is the sponsor investing in the deal?*

    ▪ *Whose money is going into the deal first?*

    ▪ *Whose money is coming out of the deal first?*

    ▪ *How soon will the investors receive a return on their capital, and what is the exit strategy?*

2. Analyze the equity structure being proposed. How many limited partnership units are available? If you were the general partner, would you structure the deal in a different way?

3. Calculate the return on investment in Year 1 for each limited partnership unit if the restaurant earns a net operating income of $425,000. How much money would the general partners earn in Year 1?

CRAFTING AND NEGOTIATING THE DEAL

STEPHEN BOLLENBACH—THE CONSUMMATE HOTEL FINANCIAL ENGINEER

Stephen Bollenbach, the current chairman of Hilton Hotels Corporation, is not your typical hotelier who worked his way up through the ranks of a company to eventually be rewarded with a corporate management position. He jokingly admits, "Unlike my great friend, Bill Marriott, I have never checked the temperature of the hot water in the chafing dish that keeps the bacon warm. I feel lucky that I can run a public company and rely on others to check in our guests."

Although Steve may lack hotel operating experience, over the last twenty-five years he has more than made up for it with his innovative financial engineering abilities and leadership skills. He has been the architect of two major hotel company restructurings and the savior of two hospitality companies facing potential financial disaster. His latest financial coup was the successful acquisition of an international hotel company that bears the same family name as his current employer.

After he graduated from the University of California, Los Angeles, and California State University, Northridge, Steve's first job was in the savings and loan industry, where he gained experience in real estate and finance. Working for real estate tycoon Daniel K. Ludwig, Bollenbach helped acquire thirty banks and also served as the chief executive officer of an Arizona savings and loan company. Through further acquisitions, Ludwig's company became the largest banking institution in the state of Arizona, financing tract homes, office buildings, and large construction deals.

After his time in the savings and loan industry, in 1982 Bollenbach was lured by the Marriott Corporation to serve as its treasurer and senior vice president of finance. As Mr. Bollenbach recalls, hotel development at the time was at its peak: "At one point we were opening one Marriott hotel a week."

This was the first of his two tenures at Marriott, and it lasted five years. His second tenure propelled Bollenbach to the center stage of hotel wheeling and dealing. When he rejoined Marriott in 1992, the lodging operator/owner was in serious financial trouble. Negatively impacted by hotel overbuilding, an economic recession, and declining lodging demand and real estate values, Marriott found itself unable to service the $3.6 billion of debt it had accumulated. Market conditions made disposing of its assets a hard sell, as buyers were scarce and foreclosed hotels plentiful. As a result of these negative factors, Marriott's stock plunged from $40 to about $8 a share. Bollenbach's task was to craft a plan to save the ailing company and put it back on its feet. Steve came up with an ingenious plan to divide Marriott Corporation into two companies. Marriott International became a pure management and franchise company with no owned hotel assets and no debt on its balance sheet. All of the existing real estate and debt was spun off into a new company called Host Marriott.

After convincing Wall Street and Marriott shareholders of the merits of his plan and completing his mission at the expense of Marriott's lenders, who were forced to restructure Marriott's debt and absorb millions of dollars of write-downs, Bollenbach moved on to the Walt Disney Company. At Disney, his main accomplishment was the creation and implementation of a plan to finance Disney's international growth. His plan was successful, resulting in a significant increase in shareholder value for Disney's owners.

Steve's next major financial benchmark occurred in 1996, when Barron Hilton approached him with an invitation to join Hilton Hotels Corporation and orchestrate the spin-off of Hilton's gaming business. "While I was still at Disney, I met with Barron for early breakfasts once a week listening to Barron's plan to spin off his gaming business from his hotel business. We kept talking, and after a while he asked me to come and be the CEO of his company."

The opportunity to lead and restructure Hilton proved too good an opportunity for Steve to pass up. Even though he had been with Disney for only nine months, he decided to accept Barron's offer.

During his first ten years with Hilton, Bollenbach carried out Barron's plan to spin off the company's gaming business from its hotels in a tax-free transaction that created Park Place Entertainment (now part of Harrah's Entertainment, Inc.), created the successful Hilton Garden Inn product, and led to Hilton's $3.0 billion acquisition of the Promus Company and its 1,700 hotels, making it one of the top five hotel franchisors in the world. The acquisition of Promus expanded Hilton's product mix to include a limited-service, extended-stay, and all-suite product. Today Hilton owns the Hilton, Hampton Inn, Homewood Suites, Embassy Suites, and Doubletree brands.

In the first quarter of 2006, Bollenbach made headlines again by negotiating the $5.7 billion transaction which, after forty years of separation, reunited Hilton Hotels Corporation (USA) and Hilton International (Overseas). Prior to selling off the international rights to its brand, Hilton Hotels Corporation owned the rights to its name worldwide. Hilton Hotels Corporation's acquisition of Hilton International will open up new opportunities for Hilton to expand its brands overseas and better compete on a global basis.

With his targeted 2008 retirement date rapidly approaching, Bollenbach's last challenge with Hilton will be to select a successor to follow in his footsteps. Although no one has been identified, Steve has assured Mr. Hilton that his successor will surely be "a student of the numbers" and "a friend of Wall Street." He says, "I find it hard to imagine that someone with a background solely related to checking in guests would be able to figure out when to file a 10Q or know what a proxy statement is."

While Mr. Bollenbach's comment may seem harsh to the purest of hoteliers, as you climb the corporate ladder or go into business for yourself, you will frequently be presented with difficult financial challenges. The better prepared you are to face these challenges, the more successful you are likely to become.

SOURCES

Higley, J. "Hilton Buys Hilton: U.S., International Companies Reunite After 40 Years." *Hotel and Motel Management,* January 9, 2006.

Weinstein, J. "Corporate Hotelier of the World Stephen Bollenbach: Opportunity Knocked." *Hotels* 39(11): 50–54.

Higley, J. "Hilton Executives Realign Focus, Prepare for Future." *Hotel and Motel Management,* June 9, 2005.

"Global Update: Hilton Delivers on Promus." http://www.hotelsmag.com/archives/1999/10/gu-hilton-promus-Bollenbach.asp, October 1999.

Bollenbach Leaves Disney to Become Hilton CEO, Prexy—Stephen F. Bollenbach, Walt Disney Co." http://www.findarticles.com/p/articles/mi_m3190/is_n7_v30/ai_17995947, February 12, 1996.

Allen, R. L. "Marriott Turns to Bollenbach to Cure Ills; Former Finance VP Returns to Hotel Chain in Hopes of Reducing Mounting Debt—Stephen F. Bollenbach." *Nation's Restaurant News,* February 24, 1992.

Learning Outcomes

1. Determine how to select the most appropriate form of business entity for a new venture.
2. Explain how to determine the optimal mix of debt and equity for a new business.
3. Identify and explain the keys to successful loan negotiations.
4. Identify and explain the keys to successful equity negotiations.
5. Identify and explain other negotiating skills.

Preview of Chapter 11

Crafting and negotiating the deal

1. THE NEW BUSINESS VENTURE

2. THE BUSINESS ENTITY

    a. Sole proprietorship

    b. Partnership

    c. Corporation

    d. S-Corporation

    e. Limited liability company

3. THE DEBT-EQUITY MIX

4. NEGOTIATING LOANS

    a. Loan size—principal

    b. Interest rate

    c. Points charged

    d. Collateral

    e. Personal guarantees

    f. Other lender issues

    g. Deal sponsor's goals

5. NEGOTIATING EQUITY INVESTMENT

    a. Amount of equity

    b. Percentage of ownership

    c. Probability of achieving an investor's targeted ROI and IRR

    d. Exit strategy and decision-making power on when to sell

6. NEGOTIATING SKILLS

    a. Be well prepared.

    b. Communicate in a professional manner.

    c. Use proven selling and negotiating skills.

THE NEW BUSINESS VENTURE

Creating a new business venture is arguably the most difficult career path a hospitality entrepreneur can elect to pursue. It can also be the most rewarding. It is risky, time-consuming, expensive, and challenging. It requires not only book smarts but street smarts as well. It involves finding a new business niche, proving its feasibility, preparing financial projections, estimating project cost, recruiting a superior project and management team, packaging the story, and, most important, financing the venture. How to finance a new business venture is the subject of this chapter.

Most lenders and equity investors will read your investment package and listen to your story if your deal is a good one. A good deal is one that is feasible, makes financial sense, and meets the lender's and investor's investment parameters. You learned in chapter 10 how equity investors and lenders evaluate an investment package. In this chapter, we further explore what they look for in a deal, how to approach them, how to determine ownership percentages, and how to make the deal profitable for not only the lender and investor but also for the sponsor of the deal.

The Business Entity

When embarking on a new venture, the first task is to decide which form of business entity is right for the venture. While a sole proprietorship is the easiest form of entity to establish, it does not provide the flexibility and personal protection needed to manage and grow a business. Better choices are a form of partnership, a form of corporation, or a limited liability company.

The key issues to consider when selecting the legal form of business entity are:

- The ability to easily add outside investors
- Liability protection
- Tax advantages
- Management control

SOLE PROPRIETORSHIP

A **sole proprietorship** is the simplest, least expensive, and easiest form of business entity to establish. As its name implies, a sole proprietorship has but one owner. All one needs to do to establish a sole proprietorship is to file with the proper authorities and register "doing business as" (DBA).

A sole proprietorship offers several advantages. It allows the proprietor the freedom to make all the decisions. There is no red tape, no need for approvals, and no bureaucracy. As soon as a decision is made, it can be carried out with no questions asked by others. In addition, when profits and cash flow are generated, the sole proprietor reaps all the rewards and doesn't have to share them with partners. The income that a sole proprietor earns is simply added to his personal income tax return and taxed only once.

There are, of course, several downsides to being a sole proprietor. His knowledge base is limited; his ability to raise capital is limited; he doesn't have a partner to provide checks and balances; and he is exposed to **unlimited liability.** For example, if the business is not doing well, the sole proprietor bears all the losses. In addition, due to the nature of unlimited liability, creditors may seize his personal assets to settle their claims. Moreover, a sole proprietorship has **limited life.** Because there is only one owner, if that person dies or becomes unable to work,

Advantages	Disadvantages
Simple and inexpensive to form	Unlimited liability
Flexible	Responsible for all losses
Freedom to make decisions and changes	Expertise and resources of only one individual
No red tape or bureaucracy	Limited life
Keep all profits	
Profits are not taxed twice	

ILLUSTRATION 11-1
Advantages and Disadvantages of a Sole Proprietorship

the business will no longer exist. Illustration 11-1 summarizes the advantages and disadvantages of the sole proprietorship form of business organization.

PARTNERSHIPS

Before the creation of the limited liability company (LLC), partnerships were a popular form of business entity for new ventures. A **partnership** is formed when two or more persons or entities come together as co-owners of a business. Under the Uniform Partnership Act, a partnership is a legal entity that can own property, borrow money, and take actions, just as individuals can. A partnership can also sue or be sued.

There are two types of partnerships, general and limited. In the case of a **general partnership**, the law requires that all partners be general partners with unlimited personal liability for the actions and decisions of the venture. The law also grants each partner the right to comanage the business. Because most entrepreneurs want to maintain management control over their venture and outside investors do not want unlimited liability, this form of partnership is not appropriate for a growing business utilizing outside equity investors.

A **limited partnership** is a more appropriate form of entity. It must have one general partner but can have several limited partners. A limited partnership offers the same tax advantages of a general partnership but protects limited partners from personal legal liability for obligations and actions of the business. It also limits their ability to participate in the management of the business. While a limited partnership is preferable to a general partnership, it has two major drawbacks. First, it does not limit the personal liability of the general partner. Second, it does not automatically provide for the continued existence of the business in the event of the death or disability of a partner. Partnerships do, however, allow for profits and losses to be distributed directly to the partners to avoid paying income tax at the partnership level. Partners can also add value to the venture by providing new ideas, business contacts, financial resources, and counsel on major decisions.

As noted earlier, a major disadvantage of a partnership is its limited life. If any partner violates the partnership agreement, the partnership is in jeopardy. A partnership may also need

Advantages	Disadvantages
Relatively easy to establish	Limited life
Limited partners have limited liability	General partners have unlimited liability
Profits are not taxed twice	One partner can obligate entire partnership
Relative flexibility in decision making	
Low level of bureaucracy and red tape	
Share resources and expertise with partners	

ILLUSTRATION 11-2

Advantages and Disadvantages of a Partnership

to be dissolved when new partners are asked to join or old partners elect to sell their partnership interest.

Another disadvantage of a partnership is that all general partners are exposed to unlimited liability. Like sole proprietors, each general partner is personally liable for the liabilities of the partnership. While **mutual agency** is good in that one partner can act on behalf of the entire partnership to make decisions, when the decision is a poor one, the entire partnership is obligated to honor it.

Illustration 11-2 summarizes the advantages and disadvantages of a partnership.

CORPORATION

A **corporation** is a legal entity, created by the state in which it is located, that avoids the drawbacks of a limited partnership. A corporation is a separate legal entity that can act on its own or on behalf of the shareholders. It can borrow money, acquire assets, and enter into legally binding contracts. It, too, can sue or be sued. McDonald's, Hilton, Starwood, Darden, Landry's, and Hyatt are all examples of hospitality corporations.

Corporations can be publicly or privately held. A publicly held corporation sells its shares of stock to the general public through an organized stock offering. A privately held corporation's stock is sold to a relatively few number of investors, often family members. Privately held corporations are usually small companies but can be large companies as well. Hyatt Hotels Corporation is a good example of a large yet privately held company.

There are several major advantages to the corporate form of business. A key advantage is the limited liability all of its shareholders enjoy. The personal liability of all owners is limited to their equity investment in the corporation. While anyone can sue the corporation, the payment of business obligations is limited to the assets of the corporation.

When it comes to raising large quantities of capital, corporations also have an edge over sole proprietorships and partnerships. Large amounts of equity capital can be raised by selling stock to the general public, which is usually easier than selling partnership units. A corporation can

Advantages	Disadvantages
Continuous life	Double taxation
Limited liability	Somewhat complicated to form
Separate legal entity	
Ease in raising capital	
Ease in transferring ownership	
Monitored by a board of directors	
Significant red tape and bureaucracy	

ILLUSTRATION 11-3
Advantages and Disadvantages of a Corporation

also use its stock to acquire other companies and offer sellers a tax-free exchange. The tax due on the seller's capital gain or profit on sale is deferred until the stock is sold.

Another advantage of a corporation is ownership transferability. While it can be difficult to sell partnership units, the sale of capital stock by owners via a stock exchange is much easier. Also, the life of a corporation continues irrespective of the death of a shareholder. As noted earlier, that of a sole proprietorship or partnership does not continue.

The primary disadvantage of the corporate entity is double taxation. A corporation itself pays taxes on its profits to the state it resides in and the federal government, while its shareholders are also taxed on the dividends they receive. While the U.S. Congress is reviewing this apparent unfairness, double taxation of corporations is still the law of the land today (see Illustration 11-3).

S-CORPORATION

An **S-corporation** is a popular form of legal entity for small businesses. The S-corporation derives its name from "Subchapter S" of the Internal Revenue Code. It provides limited liability for the owners of the corporation and tax advantages similar to a partnership. The profits of an S-corporation are distributed directly to its shareholders and are not taxed at the corporate level. You may be thinking, "If this is such an attractive option, why don't all businesses choose to be an S-corporation?" The answer is that not all corporations qualify. To qualify as an S-corporation, your company must:

- Have seventy-five or fewer stockholders.
- Be a domestic corporation that is not a subsidiary of a larger company.
- Have only one class of stock.
- Have only individuals, estates, and certain trusts as shareholders.
- Have only U.S. residents as shareholders.

Limited Liability Company (LLC)

Another relatively new form of legal entity popular with small businesses is the **limited liability company** (LLC). The qualifications to become a limited liability company are similar to those of an S-corporation. A limited liability company, however, can have more than seventy-five shareholders and a broader variety of owners than an S-corporation. Another advantage of an LLC is the avoidance of double taxation. As its name indicates, all shareholders of a limited liability company enjoy limited liability.

As in the case of a partnership, however, an LLC has limited life. When setting up an LLC, a date of dissolution must be specified. To admit a new partner to an LLC, the permission of all existing partners must be obtained.

Selecting the form of legal entity for the new venture may seem easy, but it can be somewhat complicated. A qualified and experienced business attorney should be retained to help select the most appropriate form of legal entity, prepare the necessary legal paperwork, and comply with all legal requirements.

THE REAL DEAL

Partnership Versus LLC

The LLC is a popular form of business entity for small businesses. In certain states, however, forming a limited partnership may actually be more advantageous. In Texas, a state franchise tax is levied on corporations and LLCs. However, such a tax is not applicable to limited partnerships. The Texas franchise tax rate is 4.5% of the business's taxable income plus any director and officer compensation. The general partner in a limited partnership, however, is still subject to unlimited liability, so you may elect to pay the 4.5% franchise tax rather than take this risk.

FEATURE STORY

Yum! Brands: Evolution of Quick-service Restaurants in the Twenty-first Century

The form of a company's ownership often changes as the company grows and enjoys financial success. Most businesses start small as a sole proprietorship or partnership. As the business expands and the need for capital increases, the business sometimes goes public to raise money to finance its growth. But the company's story does not always end there. During its life as a public company, other financial twists and turns may occur. Some companies get larger by expanding their operations or by acquiring other companies; others may cease to exist under their original name and get swallowed up by larger entities, while still others choose to revert to private ownership to regain control of their future destinies.

Yum! Brands is a company that has undergone several entity changes over the years, so much so that while it is currently the second-largest restaurant company in the world, it is relatively unknown to the general public. Even though the name Yum! Brands is foreign to most of its customers, its restaurant divisions—KFC, Pizza Hut, Taco Bell, Long John Silver's, and A&W—are all household names. Under an earlier incarnation, Yum! Brands was known as Tricon Global Restaurants, which was an offshoot of PepsiCo.

Four of its five restaurant concepts were once privately owned businesses. KFC (Kentucky Fried Chicken) was created during the 1950s when founder Colonel Harland Sanders took to the road with his monthly Social Security check of $105 to franchise his secret fried chicken recipe to individual restaurant owners. Pizza Hut was founded by two enterprising brothers, Frank and Dan Carney, at a family friend's suggestion and with a $600 loan from their mother. Taco Bell was the creation of Glen Bell, who decided to introduce tacos at his hotdog and hamburger take-out stand in San Bernardino, California, to better compete with the nearby McDonald brothers. A&W was established on the foundation of its famous root beer formula by founder Roy Allen. Only Long John Silver's was a concept developed in 1969 by its then parent company, Jerrico, Inc., a public restaurant company.

As these companies evolved, their ownership and forms of business entity changed. Except for Pizza Hut and Taco Bell, ownership of these companies changed at least twice prior to being acquired by PepsiCo. PepsiCo acquired Pizza Hut in 1977, followed by Taco Bell a year later. PepsiCo acquired KFC in 1986 for $840 million. During this period, the restaurants were part of a much larger corporation better known for its soft drink products than its restaurants. In October 1997, PepsiCo spun off its restaurant division to focus on its soft drink and snack divisions. The result was a new public company, Tricon Global Restaurants, named for its three iconic restaurant brands—Pizza Hut, Taco Bell, and KFC.

While these three restaurant concepts were under the control of PepsiCo, they achieved limited success. The soft drink giant basically operated each brand autonomously, leaving each brand's management alone to make its own decisions. Under the direction of Tricon's top executive, David Novak, the new company began to pay more attention to its franchisors, an important group of stakeholders, which PepsiCo had previously ignored. As a result, the three restaurant concepts began to establish better rapport and synergies. During the first five years following the spin-off, Tricon increased systemwide sales by 8%, more than doubled earnings per share, and increased the return on invested capital by 10 percentage points.

In March 2002, Tricon acquired Long John Silver's, A&W, and their parent company, Yorkshire Global Restaurants, and renamed the company Yum! Brands to better reflect its expanding portfolio of restaurants. Yum! Brands' long-term growth strategy is to continue to expand its multibranding program, a concept that provides consumers with more choices and convenience at a single location hosting a combination of KFC, Taco Bell, Pizza Hut, A&W All-American Food, and Long John Silver's restaurants. The company also plans to continue its highly successful international expansion into Asian markets, particularly China.

SOURCES

KFC. "About KFC: Colonel Harland Sanders." http://www.kfc.com/about/colonel.htm (accessed October 10, 2004).

Pizza Hut. "About Pizza Hut: Our Story." http://www.pizzahut.com/about/ (accessed January 22, 2006).

Taco Bell. "History." http://www.tacobell.com/ourcompany/history/default.htm (accessed January 22, 2206).

A&W Restaurants, Inc. "The First Frosty Mug." http://www.awrestaurants.com/about/default.htm (accessed January 22, 2006).

"Special Report: Yum! Brands—Fast Food's Yummy Secret." http://www.economist.com/markets/bigmac/displayStory.cfm?story_id=4316138 (accessed January 22, 2006).

"David C. Novak 1953—From PepsiCo to Tricon to Yum! Brands." http://www.referenceforbusiness.com/biography/M-R/Novak-David-C-1953.html (accessed January 22, 2006).

Byrne, J. A. "PepsiCo's New Formula: How Roger Enrico Is Remaking the Company . . . and Himself." *Business Week,* April 10, 2000.

The Debt and Equity Mix

After the form of business entity is selected, your next task is to fine-tune your financial projections and determine the optimum **debt and equity mix** for your new venture. Once you're satisfied that projected cash flow before debt service is right on the money, it's time to work backward and calculate how much ownership of the venture you need to give to your equity investors and how much ownership you can carve out for yourself. In other words, you need to begin calculating your equity position.

The first step in determining the optimum debt and equity mix is to calculate the maximum amount of money you can borrow based on the interest rate and amortization rate your lender is proposing and his required debt service coverage ratio (cash flow before debt service divided by debt service). Next, subtract the amount of the loan from your total project cost. The resulting dollar amount represents the amount of equity you need to raise. Your next step is to calculate the annual return on investment and the internal rate of return of your venture based on your cash flow projections, your debt service payments, and the amount of equity you need from your investor. Your final step is to see if the ROI and IRR meet or exceed your equity investor's hurdle rates. If they exceed the hurdle rates, your cash flow projections will support a carried interest in the deal for yourself. A **carried interest** is ownership in the venture with no cash investment on your part. In other words, you do not have to allocate all of the cash flow that your venture will generate to your investor to meet his financial goals. The better negotiator and salesperson you are, the larger your carried interest in the deal. Illustration 11-4 shows how to determine if a carried interest is possible.

When you have updated your investment package to incorporate the debt and equity mix and your carried interest, and have convinced your lender and equity investor your deal is feasible, the real fun begins. It's now time to sit down face to face and negotiate the loan and equity agreements.

NEGOTIATING LOANS WITH LENDERS

Before meeting with potential lenders to negotiate your loan agreement, ask yourself the following questions: What loan issues and provisions are probably most important to the lender? What loan issues and provisions are most important to me?

Given Facts:
- Total Project cost; $30,000,000
- Lender's standards:
  - Interest rate 7.5%
  - Amortization rate 20 years
  - Debt service coverage ratio 1.5
  - Debt-to-cost ratio 60%
- Projected annual cash flow of project $2.75 million
- Investors' hurdle rate 15%
- Tax rate 35%

1. Calculate the maximum amount of money you can borrow based on the lender's debt to cost ratio and debt service coverage ratio:

   - 60% × $30,000,000 = $18,000,000, which represents the maximum amount of the loan

2. Calculate the amount of annual debt service based on the loan terms offered:
   - N = 20 (amortization rate)
   - I/Y = 7.5 (interest rate)
   - PV = 18,000,000 (amount of loan)
   - CPT PMT = $1,765,660 (annual debt service)

3. Confirm that the debt service coverage ratio required by the lender is met:
   - $2,750,000 (annual cash flow) divided by $1,765,660 = 1.56, which exceeds the lenders' required debt service coverage ratio

4. Calculate the amount of equity required:
   - $30,000,000 – $18,000,000 = $12,000,000

5. Calculate the weighted average cost of capital:
   - Cost of debt as given = 7.5%
   - Cost of equity = 15% (investor's hurdle rate)
   - Cost of capital:
     - 60% × 7.5% (1 – 35%) = 2.925% (weighted cost of debt)
     - 40% × .15 = 6.0% (weighted cost of equity)
     - 5.93% + 6.0% = 8.925% (WACC)

6. Calculate the present value of the project:
   - Assuming a sale of the project at the end of Year 10 and a terminal market cap rate of 10%, the project sale price would be $27,500,000 ($2.75 million divided by 10%)
   - Present value of $27,500,000 at the end of Year 10 computes to be:
     - N = 10
     - I/Y = 8.925 (WACC)
     - FV = 27,500,000
     - CPT PV = 11,696,529
   - Present value of $2,750,000 annual cash flow for 10 years computes to be:
     - N = 10
     - I/Y = 8.925
     - PMT = 2,750,000
     - CPT PV = 17,706,970
   - Present value of project:
     - $11,696,529+ $17,706,970 = $29,403,499
   - Net Present Value = –$30,000,000 + $29,403,499
         = –$596,501

ILLUSTRATION 11-4
Determining the Possibility of a Carried Interest

In this example, as the net present value of the project is negative, the cash flows generated are less than the cost of $30,000,000. Not only is there no opportunity for a carried interest but the deal does not even meet the investor's 15% hurdle rate. In reality, a project of this nature would generate annual cash flows that would increase from an initial $2.75 million to a Year 10 cash flow as high as $6.0 million. For practice, see if there would be an opportunity for a carried interest based on the following 10-year projected annual cash flows in millions of dollars: 2.75, 3.5, 4.0, 4.5, 5.0, 5.5, 6.0, 6.0, 6.0, 6.0.

If your answer indicates an opportunity for a carried interest, now estimate how much of a carried interest the sponsor of the new venture could carve out for himself. Calculations for this problem are presented in the Finance in Action case at the end of this chapter.

ILLUSTRATION 11-4
(*Continued*)

Once you have answered these questions, ask yourself these further questions: Which issues and provisions that are most important to me will my lender be likely to negotiate on? Which issues and provisions that are most important to me are likely to be harder to negotiate and therefore will require my very best negotiation skills?

The terms common to most loan agreements are principal, interest rate, **points** paid up front (a point is the equivalent of 1% of the loan), length of loan, amortization rate (number of years the repayment schedule is based on), collateral, personal loan guarantee, and prepayment penalty.

While each lender's priorities may vary, the following are usually the primary terms of the loan that are most important to lenders and what you need to know in the negotiation:

- Principal
- Interest rate
- Points charged
- Collateral
- Personal guarantees
- Other lender issues
- Deal sponsor's goals

Principal

Once you understand that lenders make their profit by loaning money, you will understand that your lender wants to loan you all the money you can afford as long as he is comfortable with your deal and the loan conforms to industry guidelines. The more he loans you, the more interest income he makes. Therefore, don't think that by borrowing less money from him you are doing your lender a favor. Both you and your lender want to maximize the amount of the loan as long as you both agree that you can comfortably pay it back.

Interest Rate

The interest rate is a priority issue for lenders. The interest rate is the price of the lender's product, which is money. The amount of money he loans out represents his volume. Volume times price equals revenue. By making loans, lenders generate revenue for the owners of their financial institution. The more money lenders loan out at favorable prices, the more cash flow they generate and the higher the ROI they achieve for their owners. Does that sound familiar? Here's the point: Recognize that your lender is a businessperson just like you. His business is making loans. If he does not make loans, he does not make money. So don't be afraid to be a little aggressive when you negotiate with lenders—and never be defensive. Remember, it is just as important for lenders to make you the loan as it is for you to secure it.

Also, remember that because the interest rate is critical to the lender, if you agree to pay him a slightly higher rate than you would prefer to pay, you might get him to back down on another issue that may be more important to you. Your loan, of course, must conform to the standards of the banking industry, which bank examiners monitor. As long as a lender negotiates within these standards, he can be flexible if he wants to be.

Points Charged

As noted earlier, a point is equal to 1% of the loan. Lenders charge points at the time the loan is approved to raise the effective rate of interest. For example, if a lender offers you a $100,000 loan for five years at 10% annual interest plus 5 points up front, what is the effective rate of interest? In reality, the lender is loaning you $95,000 and charging you 10% interest on $100,000. He is loaning you the points. In this case, the effective rate of interest would be approximately 12%. Illustration 11-5 details the calculation.

The moral of the story is, "Be alert to lender points." Make sure you fully understand the effective rate of interest your lender is charging before you sign the loan agreement.

Additional Collateral

One risk to avoid, if you can, is additional collateral. Additional collateral is an asset your lender asks you to put at risk in the event you default on your loan. While it is the norm to mortgage the asset you are acquiring to secure the loan, it is not the norm to provide additional collateral to close the loan. When your lender asks you for additional collateral, this should raise a red flag. It should tell you that:

1. The lender is getting greedy, or
2. The loan-to-value ratio is too high and the lender is looking for more security, or
3. The lender is not totally comfortable with your deal.

If it is the latter case, the lender is raising an objection. How you respond to the objection is important to your negotiations. We address objections later in the chapter.

A five-year loan of $100,000 at 10% interest rate with a 5 point up-front clause. What is the effective interest rate of this loan?

1. $100,000 × .05 = $5,000 (The $5,000 is treated as interest and allocated over the life of the loan, which is 5 years.)
2. $5,000 divided by 5 years = $1,000 additional interest per year
3. Debt service of principal and interest on the $100,000 loan for 5 years at 10% is $26,379 per year or $131,898 over the five years
   PV = 100,000; N = 5; I/Y = 10; CPT PMT; PMT as computed = $26,379
   $26,379 x 5 years = $131,898
4. Net loan amount = loan – points = $100,000 – $5,000 = $95.000
5. Calculate effective rate
   PV = 95,000; N = 5; PMT = 26,379; CPT I/Y; I/Y as computed = 12.04%

ILLUSTRATION 11-5
Effective Interest Rate with Points Negotiation

Personal Guarantees

Another risk to avoid is personal guarantees. A personal guarantee allows your lender to look not only to the asset you are mortgaging for repayment of the loan but also to all of the personal assets of the guarantor as well.

Every effort should be made to negotiate out of personal guarantees. When your lender asks for a personal guarantee, he is really telling you he is not comfortable that your venture can stand on its own and that it requires extra protection. Your task, at this point in the negotiation, is to find out what is bothering your lender about your deal and fix it.

Other Lender Issues

The length of the loan, the amortization rate, and prepayment penalties are usually less important to your lender than the other issues previously discussed. They are, however, issues that you must address.

The length of the loan is often dictated by its purpose, conformity guidelines, or the trend in market interest rates. As long as your lender is comfortable that you will be able to **service your loan** (stay current with your debt service payments), the length should not be a critical issue for him unless he anticipates that the market rate of interest will increase significantly.

The amortization rate determines the speed by which you are required to repay your loan. The longer the amortization period, the lower the amount of debt service you are required to pay each month and the more interest income your lender will earn on the loan. If your lender is not comfortable with a relatively long amortization period, he is once again raising some objection to your project. The shorter the amortization period, the faster you must pay off your loan and the higher your monthly debt service payments will be. Be careful not to lock yourself into too short an amortization period. Also, remember that the first few years of a new business venture are the most critical. During this start-up period, you are building your business and making a name for yourself. The last thing you need is to have a high monthly debt service payment take you and your business under.

If your lender asks for a prepayment penalty, he may be anticipating that the market rate of interest will decline during the term of the loan and wants to prevent you from refinancing the loan before the term expires. To avoid a prepayment penalty clause in the loan agreement, you could suggest making the interest rate float (fluctuate with the market rate), with a ceiling and floor mutually agreed to.

Deal Sponsor's Goals

As a businessperson seeking to leverage the equity in your deal and maximize ROI and IRR, you should negotiate hardest for these two loan provisions—the amount of the loan and the amortization rate. If you are able to maximize the amount of the loan and minimize your monthly debt service payments by negotiating a favorable amortization rate, you will have succeeded in using other people's money to make money for yourself. More specifically, you will have:

- Reduced the amount of equity you need to raise.
- Reduced your cost of capital (WACC), as debt is less expensive than equity.
- Maximized your ROI and IRR.
- Reduced the percentage of ownership you need to give to your investors.

Because neither the size of the loan nor the amortization rate is a **hot button** of most lenders, a favorable loan amount and amortization rate are less difficult to negotiate than you might think. If you can win on the amount of the loan and the amortization rate, you can afford to pay a slightly higher interest rate and maybe even a point or two up front as long as your debt service payment is in line with your projections. The term of the loan is critical only if you require a relatively long period for your project to reach its stabilized level of performance. Also, while you may prefer a long-term permanent loan with no prepayment penalty, a mini-perm loan with a long-term amortization rate is usually satisfactory.

As noted earlier, every effort should be made to avoid providing additional collateral and personal guarantees. If your lender requests you to do so, try offering to pay a slightly higher interest rate or even lowering the amount of the loan to avoid having to place additional collateral and personal assets at risk. Another approach is to offer some additional collateral and/or personal guarantees but to have them **burn off** (be eliminated) as soon as the business achieves a certain level of performance. You could also ask to have the additional collateral and/or personal guarantees apply only to the top 10% or 20% of the loan amount to limit your exposure. This, in essence, reduces the amount of the loan the lender has at risk, improves the effective loan-to-value ratio, and improves the debt service coverage ratio. The most important elements of the loan negotiation process are summarized in Illustration 11-6.

1) Pre-Negotiation Issues:
   a) What loan issues and provisions are probably most important to the lender?
   b) What loan issues and provisions are most important to me?
   c) Which issues and provisions that are most important to me will my lender be likely to negotiate on?
   d) Which issues and provisions that are most important to me are likely to be harder to negotiate and therefore will require my very best negotiation skills?
2) Principal: Both you and your lender want to maximize the amount of the loan as long as you both agree that you can comfortably pay it back.
3) Interest rate
   a) Priority issue for lenders
   b) If you agree to pay a slightly higher rate than you would prefer to pay, you might gain on another negotiating issue that may be more important to you.
4) Points charged
   a) A point is equal to 1% of the loan.
   b) Lenders charge points at the time the loan is approved to raise the effective rate of interest.
   c) Be alert to lender points.
5) Additional collateral
   a) Avoid if possible.
   b) May be a signal that lender is not comfortable with your loan.
6) Personal guarantees
   a) Avoid if possible.
   b) Lender is obviously not comfortable with the loan and wants extra protection. Your task, at this point in the negotiation, is to find out what is bothering your lender about your deal and fix it.
7) Other lender issues
   a) Your ability to service your loan
   b) A prepayment penalty to discourage you from refinancing the loan if interest rates fall
8) Deal Sponsor Goal
   a) Maximize amount of the loan
   b) Minimize monthly debt service payments by negotiating a favorable amortization rate

ILLUSTRATION 11-6
Important Elements of Loan Negotiations

NEGOTIATING THE EQUITY INVESTMENT

Prior to sitting down face to face with your potential equity investors, it is important that you first identify the issues you believe are most important to them. Your primary objective in negotiating the equity agreement is simple: Give up as little ownership as you can and save as much as you can for yourself. These are the issues that are usually most important to equity investors:

- Amount of equity they are asked to invest
- Percentage ownership they will receive
- Probability of achieving the projected ROI and IRR hurdle rates
- Exit strategy
- Decision-making power on when to execute the exit strategy

Amount of Equity

While equity investors may have a substantial amount of equity to invest, their investment strategy is usually to leverage their equity and spread their risk over as many investments as possible.

For example, rather than investing $2 million in one deal, an investor would likely prefer to invest $500,000 in each of four deals. Your ability to maximize the amount of debt you can raise reduces the amount of equity required. Also, the more equity you need to raise, the more cash flow you need to generate to meet your investor's ROI and IRR hurdle rates.

Percentage of Ownership

Early in the negotiation process, equity investors may request 100% ownership of the project in return for providing 100% of the equity. Your task is to convince them that because you are investing an extensive amount of your personal time to make the deal happen, you deserve a share of the deal as well.

The following are a few ideas to help you negotiate a favorable ownership position for yourself:

1. Convince your investors you deserve sweat equity for putting the deal together. **Sweat equity** is equity with no cash investment. By finding the deal, securing the debt, and creating the opportunity for investors to make a favorable return on their investment, you deserve ownership in the deal.

2. Advise your investors that you will, however, agree to place their equity (ownership percentage) in a preferred position (ahead of yours) until they achieve their hurdle rate, or targeted return on investment. In other words, if your investors' hurdle rate is 15%, all cash flow would go to them until they achieved a 15% return on their money. Once they achieved their hurdle rate, you would begin to receive your proportionate share of cash flow.

3. If your investors reject your offer, try raising their hurdle rate as an incentive for them to grant you a piece of the deal. This will delay the timing of your cash flow distribution but may get you some sweat equity.

4. If that doesn't work, try lowering the amount of sweat equity you would agree to receive.

5. If your investors *still* reject your proposal, tell them you would agree to have them own 100% of the deal until they achieve their targeted return on investment. When this occurs, however, you would earn a **promoted interest** in the deal. In other words, you would be promoted to an ownership position only after their investment goal was reached.

6. If that fails, try this approach: Offer your investors all of the cash flow until they receive all of their equity back. At this point, you would receive your promoted equity interest.

7. Finally, if all else fails and you are desperate for their equity, agree to grant them 100% ownership until you sell the business. Convince them on sale that you at least deserve an **equity kicker.** An equity kicker provides you with a portion of the profit on sale after the outstanding loan balance is paid and your investors receive all of their initial equity back.

8. If the investors still say no, it is time to meet with another investor group.

As you can see, the ability to market, sell, and negotiate are important in the world of finance. While the first investor you approach may reject your deal, be persistent. The more you keep trying, the more likely you are to succeed.

Investor Hurdle Rates

One of the key factors that investors analyze carefully is the probability of their ROI and IRR hurdle rates being achieved. Your investment package should emphasize the likelihood of your financial projections being achieved and provide all the assumptions and support for those projections. If your investors are going to be your partners, you need to be open and honest with them and gain their trust.

Exit Strategy and Decision-making Power on When to Sell

Investors are also interested in the deal's exit strategy, the timing of the strategy, and who controls the exit decision. The longer investors have to wait to get their capital back, the less likely they are to invest in your venture. Investors prefer projects that offer high returns on equity and quick exit strategies. If your deal provides them with both features, you are likely to obtain the equity you are seeking.

NEGOTIATING SKILLS

Selling and negotiating skills can help you secure the debt and equity capital you need. Here are a few you need to learn.

Be Prepared

Do your homework before you begin your negotiations. Learn as much about whom you are going to negotiate with as you can. Understand the issues you are prepared to compromise on and make sure you know the issues you need to stand firm on. In other words, know when to hold 'em and know when to fold 'em. If you know the rules of the game and play your cards right, the winning pot can be yours.

Being prepared also means anticipating the questions your lender or equity investor is going to ask and having the answers ready and rehearsed before they are asked. This demonstrates that you are professional, thorough, and on top of your game. Using a sports analogy, it is like having a copy of your opponent's playbook before you play them. If you design your game plan around your potential lender's and investor's strategy, you have a much better chance of winning.

Be Professional

Think and dress like a lender and equity investor when you meet with them, and speak their language. In other words, talk the talk and walk the walk. If you present yourself well and look and speak like a seasoned professional, you might just be accepted as one even though you may lack the depth of knowledge and experience of the person with whom you are negotiating.

When you dress professionally, you convey to the person you are negotiating with that you are serious about your business and committed to making it successful. Have you heard the phrase "Dress for success"? This is what we're talking about. On the other hand, if you dress like a novice and come across like you are unfamiliar with the language of finance, your chances of success are poor.

Use Proven Selling Skills

There are a number of proven selling skills that you can use when negotiating with investors and lenders. For example, always begin your presentation with an initial benefit statement noting the primary reasons your lender or investor should provide you with the capital you are seeking and the benefits of the deal from their perspective. This will start the negotiations off on a positive note.

Always be alert to any objections raised. When the person you are negotiating with raises an objection, repeat what you believe the objection to be before you address it. The person may be objecting to something other than what you think. Also, what you think is an objection may not be an objection at all but rather a minor misunderstanding that you can easily clarify.

If the lender offers a soft-ball objection, answer it directly and introduce another benefit or two of your deal. Always have your list of benefits close at hand and use them at the appropriate time. If the lender throws you a hard ball (an objection that is hard to overcome), repeat it, but never agree with it. Don't be defensive; try to answer it the best you can, and move on.

You do not want the negotiation to drag. You also do not want to do all the talking. Listening is a critical skill to acquire and the mark of a good salesperson. The more your lender and equity investor speak, ask questions, and raise objections, the better you can understand their position and the better you can sell the benefits of your deal. A technique called a **trial close** is suggested as early in the negotiation as possible. A trial close summarizes the benefits of your deal and offers two favorable options. Presenting a trial close to a lender might go something like this:

We both agree that my deal is a home run. It's a conforming loan that meets your loan-to-value and debt service coverage requirements. I have agreed to pay an interest rate that is actually above market. The amortization rate is fair. I have mitigated your risk by personally guaranteeing the loan during the construction period. Shall we sign the loan documents over lunch tomorrow, or meet back here at the bank?

No matter which alternative the lender chooses, you have won. Congratulations! You have closed the deal!

On the other hand, if the lender hesitates and tells you he needs more time to think about it, you have not closed the deal and have more work to do. He is not yet on board and has more objections that are still bothering him. Your job is to discover the objections, address them, introduce a few more benefits, and try another trial close.

The second trial close should begin with an open question and might go something like this.

"What is it that you are not comfortable with about the deal?" Here is the hard part—say nothing until he speaks. This is hard to do but essential to being a good negotiator. You want to answer his objection and talk about all of the other benefits of your deal—but don't. Remember, a good salesperson lets her customer do most of the talking. Let your lender do the talking. The more he talks, the more you will understand what he likes about your proposal and what he is still uncomfortable with.

Once you understand his objection, repeat it, address it the best that you can, and try another trial close. You may be surprised; he may say, "Okay, let's have lunch and close the deal today. Do you think we might also have time for eighteen holes?"

THE REAL DEAL

More Tips for Making Deals

What is a good deal? Is it good for the investor, the lender, or the sponsor of the deal? Experienced attorneys normally advise their clients that certain clauses or conditions be made part of a deal. Once a deal is agreed on, always include some of the following conditions so that any further discussion or negotiations can move smoothly. "An agreement to negotiate in good faith in the future" is a good clause to add. It does not cause the businessperson any problems and is a gracious gesture. All it means is that if there are any future negotiations, both parties agree to come to the table with a good will at heart. "The right of first refusal" is another good clause to add. In the case of equity investors, the clause means that when you would like to expand, you agree to first approach the existing equity investors to see if they would like to invest further in your business. You are giving your equity investor the right and the option to say yes or no before you approach other outside investors. This will ensure that your current investors' percentage ownership in the business is not diluted. It is also a strong statement of faith. These two clauses are good business practices.

Finance in Action

Carried Interest

Illustration 11-4 calculates the possible amount of carried interest for a series of uneven cash flows. This example will walk you step by step through the calculations to reach the answer. The following was information provided for your calculations.

Given Facts:

- Total project cost: $30,000,000
- Lender's standards:
    - Interest rate: 7.5%
    - Amortization rate: 20 years
    - Debt service coverage ratio: 1.5 times
    - Debt-to-cost ratio: 60%
- Projected annual cash flows of:
    - Year 1: $2,750,000
    - Year 2: $3,500,000
    - Year 3: $4,000,000
    - Year 4: $4,500,000
    - Year 5: $5,000,000
    - Year 6: $5,500,000
    - Year 7: $6,000,000
    - Year 8: $6,000,000
    - Year 9: $6,000,000
    - Year 10: $6,000,000
- Investors' hurdle rate: 15%
- Tax rate: 35%
- Sale in Year 10 with market cap rate of 10%

Steps 1 through 5 remain the same as in Illustration 11-4, but Step 6, Calculating Present Value of the Project, is much more complicated because you are not dealing with an even stream of cash flows.

QUESTIONS

1. Calculate the net present value of the project.

   Two methods can be utilized in calculating the NPV of a project. The first method presented takes you step by step through the process, and the second method utilizes the NPV calculation in Excel.

Method #1

Step #1

The first step in calculating the present value of the project is determining the sales price in Year 10. The calculation is as follows.

$6,000,000 divided by a 10% cap rate = $60,000,000

Now calculate the present value of the terminal sale price of $60,000,000. If you utilize your financial calculator, your inputs would be: N = 10, I/Y = 8.925 (WACC), FV = $60,000,000, CPT PV. The present value of $60,000,000 is $25,519,700.

Step #2

Calculate the present value of the uneven cash flows. If you utilize Excel, this is a simple calculation, as seen in the following chart. The present value of the terminal sale price could also be calculated in Excel utilizing this method. Remember, in this type of calculation, PMT is entered as 0 and you need to put a negative sign in front of the FV; otherwise, your PV computation will be negative.

	A	B	C	D	E
	I/Y (WACC)	**N (Year)**	**FV (Annual Cash Flow)**	**CPT PV**	**Calculations**
1					
2	8.925%	1	$ 2,750,000	$2,524,672.94	=PV(A2,B2,0,-C2)
3	8.925%	2	$ 3,500,000	$2,949,938.13	=PV(A3,B3,0,-C3)
4	8.925%	3	$ 4,000,000	$3,095,118.53	=PV(A4,B4,0,-C4)
5	8.925%	4	$ 4,500,000	$3,196,702.64	=PV(A5,B5,0,-C5)
6	8.925%	5	$ 5,000,000	$3,260,860.06	=PV(A6,B6,0,-C6)
7	8.925%	6	$ 5,500,000	$3,293,042.06	=PV(A7,B7,0,-C7)
8	8.925%	7	$ 6,000,000	$3,298,057.86	=PV(A8,B8,0,-C8)
9	8.925%	8	$ 6,000,000	$3,027,824.52	=PV(A9,B9,0,-C9)
10	8.925%	9	$ 6,000,000	$2,779,733.32	=PV(A10,B10,0,-C10)
11	8.925%	10	$ 6,000,000	$2,551,970.00	=PV(A11,B11,0,-C11)

Step #3

Add the present value of all cash flows, and you will get $55,497,620.

$55,497,620 = PV of all annual cash flows + PV of terminal sale price

Step #4

Now, determine if the net present value of this project is positive. If you subtract the total project cost of $30,000,000 from $55,497,620, you are left with $25,497,620.

Method #2

Step #1

Type all of the cash flows, from −30,000,000 to 66,000,000, in the correct sequence. It does not matter whether you type them in a row or column.

Step #2

Type [=] and then highlight the total project cost of −30,000,000, the initial cash outflow.

Step #3

*Next, type [+] and then [npv] and the open bracket [(]. As soon as [(] is typed, Excel displays: npv(**rate**,value1, value2,. . .); the word rate is bolded to prompt you to enter the rate. Now enter the WACC in decimal form and type a comma [,]; value1 will then be highlighted. Simply highlight all the values from $2,750,000 to $66,000,000. Because you have entered all variables, the operation can be completed by typing [)], then hitting the enter key. The cell will now display the value of $25,497,620.*

2. Determine if there is an opportunity for a carried interest.

Because you already know that the net present value of the project is positive, you know there is a possibility of carried interest. To determine if there is an opportunity for carried interest, you must determine if the project meets your equity investor's hurdle rate by calculating the project's internal rate of return (IRR). The IRR calculation is a simple computation in an Excel spreadsheet. Just type [=], [irr] and then an open bracket [(]. After you type the open bracket, Excel displays: IRR(values, [guess]). The word values is bolded, and all you have to do is highlight all of the cash flows, starting with −$30,000,000 and going through $66,000,000; then type [)] and hit enter. You should now see 18.73% displayed in the box.

	A	B
1	Year	**Annual Cash Flow**
2	0	-$30,000,000
3	1	$ 2,750,000
4	2	$ 3,500,000
5	3	$ 4,000,000
6	4	$ 4,500,000
7	5	$ 5,000,000
8	6	$ 5,500,000
9	7	$ 6,000,000
10	8	$ 6,000,000
11	9	$ 6,000,000
12	10	$ 66,000,000
13	WACC	8.925
14	NPV	$25,497,620
15	NPV Calculation	=B2+NPV(B13, B3:B12)
16	IRR	18.73%
17	IRR Calculation	=IRR(B2:B13)

Because the IRR for the project is 18.73%, it meets the investors hurdle rate of 15%.

3. Estimate how much of carried interest the sponsor of the new venture could carve out for himself.

    If the equity investor requires a 15% return on her investment, then the sponsor of the deal could carve out up to 3.73% of the deal, which is the difference between the IRR and investor's hurdle rate (18.73% − 15%).

WHERE WE'VE BEEN, WHERE WE'RE GOING

Creating the idea for a new business venture may be easy, but the details to make it a reality are difficult. It is risky, time-consuming, and expensive, but at the same time it has the potential to be rewarding and challenging. You need knowledge, a lot of common sense, and people skills. A good business deal is one that is feasible, makes financial sense, and meets the lender's and investors' investment parameters. This chapter explored what lenders and investors look for in an investment.

The last chapter of the book summarizes everything that has been covered in this text and ties together all components to provide you, a future hospitality manager, with a complete view of hospitality finance. Remember, skills you learn in this course are not simply for serving your employer. You can use the knowledge and skills you gain from this book for your own personal finances. Who knows? Perhaps you may start your own deal one of these days.

Key Points

➤   The major types of business entities are the sole proprietorship, partnership, corporation, S-corporation, and limited liability company. Selecting the right form of business entity may seem easy but can be difficult. Retain a qualified and experienced business attorney to help select the most appropriate form of legal entity, prepare the necessary legal paperwork, and comply with all other legal requirements.

➤   Using a simple spreadsheet, the optimum debt and equity mix can be determined. A computer model can calculate the maximum amount of money you can borrow and still meet your lender's debt service coverage requirement based on the proposed interest rate, amortization rate, and your cash flow projections.

➤   After determining the amount of equity you need, the return on investment and internal rate of return also must be calculated to see if they meet the investor's hurdle rates based on the amount of cash flow available after debt service.

➤   If the resulting ROI and IRR exceed your investor's hurdle rates, there may be room in the deal for a carried interest for the deal sponsor.

➤   While lenders' priorities may vary, the following are the key issues most lenders focus on: the amount of the loan, the interest rate, the number of points charged, collateral, personal loan guarantees, and conformity with lending standards.

➤ To an equity investor, the following issues are usually most important: the amount of equity they are asked to invest, the percentage ownership they are to receive, the probability of achieving their ROI and IRR hurdle rates, plus the exit strategy and decision-making power on when to initiate it.

➤ Selling and negotiating skills can help you secure the debt and equity capital you need. A few skills to learn include being prepared, presenting yourself professionally, listening, and using proven selling skills.

Key Terms

SOLE PROPRIETORSHIP: Simplest form of business organization, and the easiest to establish.

UNLIMITED LIABILITY: When the owners of a business are personally liable for the debts of the business.

LIMITED LIFE: A disadvantage of both a sole proprietorship and a partnership. When a partner dies or sells his interest, a new partnership must be formed for the business to continue.

PARTNERSHIP: Formed when two or more partners come together as co-owners to establish a business. Under the Uniform Partnership Act, a partnership is a legal entity for certain purposes.

GENERAL PARTNERSHIP: When all partners are general partners and have unlimited liability.

LIMITED PARTNERSHIP: When all partners are limited partners, with liability limited to their investment in the partnership. A limited partnership must have at least one general partner.

MUTUAL AGENCY: Allows a partner to act on behalf of the entire partnership and make decisions the partners are obligated to honor.

CORPORATION: A legal entity, created by the state in which it is located, that avoids the drawbacks of a limited partnership. There are two major types of corporations: publicly held and privately held.

S-CORPORATION: Derives its name from "Subchapter S" of the Internal Revenue Code. It provides limited liability for the owners and tax advantages similar to a partnership. To qualify as an S-corporation, a company must have seventy-five or fewer stockholders; be a domestic corporation that is not a subsidiary of a larger company; have only one class of stock; and have only U.S. residents, individuals, estates, and certain trusts as shareholders.

LIMITED LIABILITY COMPANY (LLC): The qualifications to become a limited liability company are similar to those of an S-corporation. However, LLCs can have more than seventy-five shareholders and more types of owners than an S-corporation.

DEBT AND EQUITY MIX: The proportion of debt and equity to the total amount of capital required for a deal.

CARRIED INTEREST: Ownership awarded the sponsor of a deal without any cash investment on the sponsor's part.

POINT: Equal to 1% of the principal of a loan.

SERVICING A LOAN: Staying current with debt service payments.

HOT BUTTON: An issue that is vital to someone.

BURN OFF: A personal loan guarantee that is released when an agreed-on amount of annual cash flow is generated.

SWEAT EQUITY: Equity awarded with no cash investment. Earned by the sponsor of a deal in return for his efforts in formulating the idea, finding the deal, securing the debt, and creating the opportunity for the investor to make a favorable return on his investment.

PROMOTED INTEREST: Ownership awarded the sponsor of a deal after the venture achieves cash flow sufficient to provide an agreed-on return on investment for the cash investors.

EQUITY KICKER: Provides the deal sponsor with a portion of the profit on sale after the loan balance is paid and the outside investors receive all of their initial equity back.

TRIAL CLOSE: A technique used in selling to try to get the customer to agree to and sign the deal.

Application Exercises

1. Explain how an S-corporation and a limited liability company can be formed. What are their restrictions and characteristics?

2. What are personal loan guarantees and additional collateral? How can they be avoided?

3. If a lender asks for 2 points on a loan that has a principal of $250,000, what does this mean? How does it impact the effective interest rate on the loan?

4. What is sweat equity, and how can the sponsor of a deal convince his equity investor he deserves some when negotiating an equity investment agreement?

5. Identify and explain the four key issues that equity investors focus on during a negotiation.

6. A five-year loan for $500,000 with a 10% interest rate requires that 3 points be paid up front. What is the effective interest rate of this loan?

7. If the loan in exercise 6 requires that 5 points be paid up front, what would the new effective interest rate be?

8. What are the four basic goals a borrower should set when negotiating with a lender?

9. **ETHICS** ✳ While negotiating a loan, Christian is hitting some roadblocks. The lender wants to charge him 5 points on the loan and asks him for a personal guarantee and additional collateral. Christian senses the lender has some objections to his deal. While he was preparing for the loan negotiation, a friend told Christian that if he senses anything negative from the lender, the lender is just bluffing and Christian should tell the lender that the pro forma numbers are strictly the worst-case scenario and that he will go back and rework them for further discussion. In his heart and mind, Christian knows the numbers as presented are realistic. Is there anything wrong with his friend's suggestion?

10. **EXPLORING THE WEB** ✳ Visit www.governmentguide.com and look under the heading "Small Business." Identify at least two sources from which a small business can obtain a business loan.

Concept Check ✓

Expanding Gregory's

Fergus and Freya Eneas have owned Gregory's Greek Restaurant for over thirty years in Greg-orytown, a small scenic town in the country. The restaurant overlooks a river and offers visitors a lovely view of the countryside. Over the years, the restaurant's popularity has grown through word-of-mouth advertising, and now guests often wait up to two hours on the weekend before being seated.

Fergus and Freya have been approached by Divina Developers, which wants to use the Gregory's Greek Restaurant concept in a mixed-use development it is putting together. It seems that one of Divina's managers ate at Gregory's and loved the concept.

Divina Developers put together an investment proposal for Fergus and Freya requesting to use their concept and cash equity for the deal.

The following are excerpts from the offer sent by Divina:

- Use of the Gregory's Greek Restaurant name in exchange for limited partnership units in the new restaurant.
- A request for a 45% equity investment from Fergus and Freya on the total project cost of $3,000,000. In return for their investment, they will receive 25% ownership and 25% of all cash flows, with Divina reserving 75%.
- With an estimated $175,000 in cash flows in Year 1 and a 10% growth rate over the next decade, the return on equity looks very promising.
- Divina Developers, as the general partner, will retain all operating rights, including the right to decide when the restaurant and property will be sold.

QUESTIONS

1. Identify and explain the positive and negative aspects of the proposed business entity for Fergus and Freya.
2. Calculate the IRR for this project based on a sale in Year 6 with a 10% cap rate.
3. Analyze the structure of the equity proposal. If you were Fergus and Freya, would you accept this offer as it stands? If not, what would you negotiate?

Concept Check ✓

Star or Prize: Which Bank?

Dean Hotel Investments, an S-corporation, has identified a potential investment property near a major New England airport. The 302-room Blackstone Hotel is a recently defranchised upscale hotel asset that has been lender-owned for several years and fallen on hard times. Dean Hotel Investments is proposing converting the independent hotel to a major limited-service brand, which would provide brand recognition and an increased customer base.

The property has been on the market for two years and the current asking price is $8,000,000, which is well below comparable sales in the area. The airport market has seen a slight drop in occupancy and ADR over the past couple of years due to the struggling economy. Experts have estimated that as soon as the economy begins to rebound, so will occupancy and ADR.

Dean Hotel Investments plans on converting the property to a limited-service brand, thereby creating the market leader in a price-sensitive marketplace. The planned renovations and reflagging the investment should result in a total project cost of $11,535,000. Dean Hotel Investments has identified an equity investor willing to invest 35% of the total project cost. Dean has also found a lender, Star Bank, willing to provide 50% of the project cost, and a second lender, Prize Bank, to provide a mezzanine loan for the remaining 15%.

The following terms were offered by Star Bank:

- Interest Rate: 7%
- Loan Term: 10
- Points: 4 points up front
- Collateral: Hotel owned by Dean Hotel Investments

The following terms were offered by Prize Bank:

- Interest Rate: 12%
- Loan Term: 5
- Points: 2 points up front
- Collateral: Subordinated claim of the Blackstone Hotel

QUESTIONS

1. Calculate the amount of the loan from Star Bank, payment amount, and effective interest rate.
2. Calculate the amount of the loan from Prize Bank, payment amount, and effective interest rate.
3. Analyze the terms offered by both banks. If you were Dean Hotel Investments, what terms would you negotiate, and why?

Concept Check ✓

Carried Interest for Emily Ali

Ms. Emily Ali, a restaurant developer, is in the process of developing a new upscale Thai restaurant. The restaurant is in a prominent neighborhood in a large metropolitan city. The particular area where the restaurant is being built comprises residents with diverse cultural backgrounds. Ms. Ali estimates the total project cost will be $6,000,000 and that she will be able to fund 65% of the project with debt; the remainder will be in the form of equity.

Currently, lenders are providing loans with a 6.5% interest rate and a twenty-five year amortization period, and requesting a debt service coverage ratio of 2.0. Ms. Ali has been able to locate a wealthy investor willing to provide 35% of the total project cost for a required return of 16%. The investor is not looking for a long-term investment and would like to see a sale in Year 5, at which time the cap rate is estimated to be 11%. Ms. Ali has also estimated that cash flow in Year 1 will be $700,000 and will grow 6% each year through Year 5. The current tax rate is 30%.

QUESTIONS

1. Calculate the net present value of the project. (For calculations, refer to Illustration 11-4 and the end-of-chapter Finance In Action case study.)

2. Determine if there is an opportunity for a carried interest.

3. Estimate how much of a carried interest the sponsor of the new venture could carve out for herself.

TYING IT ALL TOGETHER

F E A T U R E   S T O R Y

ARCHIE BENNETT JR. AND MONTY J. BENNETT— RIDING THE ECONOMIC CYCLE

Archie Bennett Jr. is a seasoned veteran of the hotel development, finance, and manage-ment business. Having made his mark in the hotel business with companies based in Texas, he is now a semi-retired multimillionaire residing in Ireland. Archie recently passed the baton to his son, Monty, who now manages the Bennett-owned and -operated com-panies. Like many of the entrepreneurs profiled in this book, Archie has experienced his fair share of ups and downs during his business career. As he gained experience, how-ever, he grew astute at predicting real estate cycles and taking advantage of the eco-nomic conditions prevailing at the time. His opportunistic style and extraordinary salesmanship have earned him considerable wealth over the years.

Archie got his first break while attending the University of Houston during the 1960s. His fishing companion, the late Houston oil and real estate tycoon, R.E. (Bob) Smith, took a liking to Archie and helped him start his own business following Archie's graduation from the university. Mr. Smith introduced Archie to a wealthy investor friend of his named James Greer, who owned a glass company in Houston. Mr. Greer provided the collateral for Archie's first loan, which financed the development of Archie's first hotel, the Holiday Inn—Galveston, Texas. With Archie as the operating partner and Mr. Greer as the limited financial partner, they created a company called Mariner Corporation that went on to develop, own, and manage several hotels around the country.

The partnership, however, was abruptly liquidated in 1976 when the partners got into a dispute over how the company should be managed. As part of the settlement, Archie was awarded two of the Holiday Inns he had developed, and he continued to manage them under the Mariner name. Taking full advantage of the hotel real estate boom at that time, Archie was able to develop and acquire a large portfolio of Holiday Inn, Hilton, and Marriott hotels with the capital provided by a large insurance company and several Houston high-net-worth individuals by leveraging his business experience and the relationships he established during his partnership with Mr. Greer.

With large amounts of debt and equity capital readily available, Archie was able to negotiate several sweetheart deals with his insurance company partner and equity investors who were eager to become part of the exciting and expanding hotel industry. One of his early multiple-hotel development deals required the insurance company to provide 100% of project cost (80% debt and 20% equity); award a 50% carried interest in each hotel to Archie, and sign a management contract with Mariner for 3% of total revenue to operate the hotels for the partnership.

The Tax Reform Act of 1986, however, brought new hotel development to a screeching halt and created financial problems for those involved in the building frenzy of the late 1970s and early 1980s, including Archie. In 1988, millions of dollars of hotel loans Archie had personally guaranteed fell into default. He was forced to liquidate the company and file for personal bankruptcy. Still only fifty-one at the time, Archie was not about to concede defeat and immediately founded a new company called Remington Hotels.

As part of the fallout from the Tax Reform Act, the U.S. federal government created the Resolution Trust Corporation (RTC) to assume ownership of all failed savings and loans and dispose of their underlying collateral. Much of this collateral consisted of foreclosed hotels, which the RTC offered for sale at deeply discounted prices, much lower than their replacement cost. Archie saw this as an opportunity to acquire the hotels for pennies on the dollar, with favorable financing provided by the federal government. His plan was to acquire the hotels, operate them for a few years, and then resell them at a much higher price when the economy improved. Archie convinced several wealthy investors to provide the equity he needed for these transactions, and he was off to the races once again. By the early 1990s, Remington Hotels was the largest owner of RTC hotel assets. At its peak, Archie's company owned a portfolio of 200 hotels. By the late 1990s, after the hotel industry had recovered, Remington sold most of its portfolio at a substantial profit. Once again, Archie's knack for timing paid off handsomely.

Today, as noted earlier, Archie's son, Monty, is in charge of the business, although Archie still has a financial stake in the company. Monty joined Remington after graduating from the School of Hotel Administration at Cornell University with a degree in hotel administration and an MBA. After rotating through various executive positions at Remington, he became his father's personal assistant and learned how to make deals, read the market, and seize opportunities as they arose. His first opportunity to increase the family's wealth came in 2001 following the 9/11 disaster and the resulting downturn in the U.S. hotel business.

"Values fell sharply, and we started considering how we were going to position ourselves for the likely future upswing in hotel values." The answer was to create a real estate investment trust (REIT). In 2003, Monty created Ashford Hospitality Trust to acquire undervalued hotel assets. Ashford was the only hotel company to go public in 2003, raising approximately $200 million in a blind equity pool. A blind pool differs from the more traditional equity fund in that the manager of the pool—in this case, Remington—can invest funds without the approval of the equity investors. Monty further expanded the fund by contributing eight of Remington's solely owned hotel assets to Ashford, thereby increasing its war chest to $550 million. Ashford's first acquisition was a $250 million twenty-one-hotel portfolio owned by Fisher Partners, the Gordon Getty Trust, and George Soros. By September 2005, the trust owned $1.4 billion of assets comprising seventy-seven hotels and $100 million in mezzanine loans.

Monty's strategy for the near future is to continue to buy hotels at the right price and sell hotels that have achieved their stabilized value. He believes:

> In hospitality, it's important to not only buy right but also to sell right. . . . Since 2001, growth in hotel demand has been almost nonexistent, which has contributed to very little growth in hotel supply. In 2005, however, while new supply grew by a meager 0.6%, growth in hotel room demand was 3.7%. That's a huge gap that will drive hotel values upward.

Archie taught Monty to be flexible and to develop multiple business strategies in order to fully capitalize on changing market conditions. Applying this strategy to Ashford, the trust has deliberately diversified across capital structure, geography, and asset types. It has access to both the public market and private investors and lenders. It owns hotels in twenty states in both primary and secondary markets. Ashford is also a mortgage and mezzanine lender.

On the subject of his company's future growth strategy, Monty recently commented, "Within the next twelve to eighteen months, we'll shift and buy fewer properties and focus on developing and cranking up our first-mortgage and mezzanine lending business. That's how we're going to continue to grow."

The father-and-son team's track record for predicting business cycles has been excellent most of the time. Will it be correct this time as well? Only time will tell.

SOURCES

"The Remington Story." http://www.remingtonhotels.com/story.html

"Sixty-second Profile: Monty Bennett—Timing Is Everything." Lodging Magazine 29(9): 11.

Higley, Jeff. "Purchase, Conditions Whets Ashford's Hunger." *Hotel and Motel Management* 220(7): 1, 30.

"Ashford Hospitality Trust Rides the Hotel Cycle to Success." http://www.nareit.com/portfoliomag/05sepoct/reitsnapshot.shtml, September/October 2005.

Learning Outcomes

1. Highlight and review the key financial concepts, skills, and tools presented in this text.
2. Provide a reference guide to study for your final examination and a resource to refer to as new business opportunities and challenges present themselves throughout your hospitality career.

Preview of Chapter

INTRODUCTION

Now that you have read each chapter and completed the related exercises and case studies, you should have a clear understanding and working knowledge of what hospitality finance is all about. You should also now possess the financial knowledge, tools, and skills to assist you on the career path of your choice. In this final chapter, we recap the most important financial tools and skills we believe will help accelerate your rise up the business ladder in the hospitality industry. We also provide page references to the chapter where the tool or skill was originally presented and illustrated.

HOSPITALITY INDUSTRY FINANCIAL CHALLENGES

As a hospitality manager, you will face numerous industry challenges. You will be working in an industry characterized by:

1. Low profit margins
2. Fluctuating sales volumes
3. A labor-intensive environment
4. The need for capital to grow
5. Dependence on the discretionary income of your customers

The practical application of the financial concepts, skills, and tools you have learned in this book will help you address these challenges and serve you well during your business career.

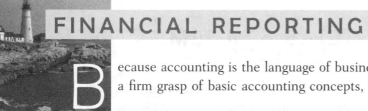

FINANCIAL REPORTING

B ecause accounting is the language of business, you, as a hospitality manager, must have a firm grasp of basic accounting concepts, which include:

1. **Generally Accepted Accounting Principles (GAAP):** A working knowledge of these principles will help you understand the logic, foundation, and rules of accounting that the financial statements that you will be reading and analyzing are based on. While each principle is important, please make special note of the **cost principle,** which requires all transactions to be recorded at their actual cost, as opposed to their **market value.** The application of this principle can result in the market value of a company's assets, as shown on its balance sheet, to be understated, particularly if the company owns a large amount of real estate and uses accelerated depreciation. Also, remember that in finance, market value is the basis of most business decisions.

2. **Uniform System of Accounts:** Nearly all hotels, restaurants, and clubs in the United States use the Uniform System of Accounts designed for their segment of the hospitality industry, and they present their financial statements in the format recommended. It is therefore important to be knowledgeable about the system of accounts for your segment of the industry and fully understand the revenues and expenses included in each account. Without this knowledge, the reading, interpretation, and analysis of your business's income statement and balance sheet is, for all practical purposes, impossible.

3. **Financial Statements:** Knowing how to read an **income statement** is a must. You should also become comfortable with the format of the income statement recommended by the Uniform System of Accounts for your segment of the hospitality business. As your career advances, your ability to read and understand a business's **balance sheet** and **cash flow statement** will become increasingly important.

4. **Management Reports:** All hotel managers should be familiar with and able to read, analyze, and, in some cases, prepare the following management reports:
   a. **Daily revenue report**
   b. **Daily payroll cost report**

  c. **Rooms revenue forecast**

  d. **Accounts receivable aging schedule**

  For food and beverage managers, the **menu abstract report** and the related calculation of theoretical **food cost** is also a must.

5. **CP³ Management System:** When your career advances to the point that you can dictate the management systems and reports you want for your business, don't forget about the CP³ system. It will not only help you maximize your bottom line but also make better managers out of your department heads. In the interim, consider applying portions of the CP³ system to your individual area of responsibility where you are currently employed.

ANALYSIS OF FINANCIAL STATEMENTS AND MANAGEMENT REPORTS

Not only is it important for you to know how to read and understand financial statements, you must also know how to interpret and analyze them. The better you become at analyzing income statements and balance sheets, the better business decisions you will make. It is important for a hospitality manager to be able to compare actual results with the current-year budget, prior-year results, the competition, and industry norms. By comparing current actual results to these **benchmarks,** you will be able to flag problem areas for further analysis and appropriate follow-up actions.

Analysis of Financial Statements

Vertical analysis focuses primarily on the relationship between variable expenses and their respective revenues. **Horizontal analysis** is used to identify operating trends over time. At a minimum, you should be able to calculate the following ratios, understand what they indicate, and know the approximate industry norm for each:

- **Occupancy**—Rooms sold divided by rooms available
- **Average daily rate**—Rooms revenue divided by rooms sold
- **RevPAR**—Rooms revenue divided by rooms available
- **Food cost percent**—Food cost divided by food revenue
- **Beverage cost percent**—Beverage cost divided by beverage revenue
- **Payroll cost percent**—Payroll cost divided by departmental or total revenue
- **Profit margin**—Profit divided by departmental or total revenue
- **Accounts receivable turnover**—Total revenue divided by average accounts receivable
- **Inventory turnover**—Departmental revenue divided by cost of goods sold
- **Return on investment**—Cash flow divided by equity

Analysis of Industry Reports

As your career advances, the other ratios presented in the text may also be valuable to you. If you elect to pursue a career in lodging, a thorough knowledge of competitive analysis reports like the Smith Travel Research *STAR Report,* TravelCLICK's *Hotelligence Report,* and the annual lodging trends published by hospitality consulting firms is also essential.

Applications of Financial Analyses

Once you are confident that you know how to read, interpret, and analyze financial statements and management reports, your next goal should be to apply this important information to your particular area of responsibility. A few critical application areas for a hospitality manager to master include:

- Employee scheduling
- Labor cost control
- Food and beverage pricing
- Revenue management
- Profit flexing

A final critical tool for you to master is **cost-volume-profit** analysis. This skill will be invaluable to you in preparing **operating budgets, profit flexing,** and **computer modeling** of alternative business strategies.

MANAGING WORKING CAPITAL

I f you ever go into business for yourself, **managing your cash** and minimizing the amount of **working capital** you require to operate your business will be extremely important. In the interim, striving to minimize the amount of working capital needed by the company you work for will earn you the respect of top management and ownership. Here are a few proven ways to minimize your business's need for working capital:

- *Offer a **discount on cash sales:*** This saves your business the commission it would otherwise have to pay the credit card company.
- *Minimize **inventories** and turn them over as quickly as possible:* Stock only those products that are truly in demand, and minimize the amount of money tied up in inventories.
- *Establish a good **credit rating** with suppliers and vendors:* This allows you to receive more favorable payment terms on your purchases, receive more frequent deliveries of product, and reduces your need for working capital.

▪ **Manage accounts payable** *effectively:* Pay your suppliers on time, but use your credit to its maximum.

The best way to determine how much working capital your business needs is to develop a **ninety-day rolling cash forecast.** At the beginning of each month, estimate your cash inflows and outflows for the next ninety days. The difference between your cash inflows and cash outflows represents the amount of working capital you need and becomes your working capital budget.

GROWING THE BUSINESS

Whether you work for yourself, a public company, a private company, a large company, or a small company, growing your business is essential to its long-term success. Owners of private companies expect profits, cash flow, and return on investment (ROI) to increase each year. Stockholders of public companies expect the market value of their stock to increase each year. To be considered a growth company, a company's earnings must increase by at least 15% annually. This is a major challenge for most companies and becomes even harder to attain the larger the company becomes. The primary goal of management, therefore, is to increase shareholder value.

Shareholder Value

Shareholder value is the **market value** of the company. Market value for a **public company** is the current market price of its common stock multiplied by the number of shares of its common stock outstanding. Shareholder value for a **private company** is the price the company could be sold for on the open market.

The relationship between **earnings per share** (EPS) and the current market price of a company's common stock is referred to as its **multiple.** The multiple is calculated by dividing the current market price of a company's common stock by its earnings per share. The higher a company's earnings per share, the higher its multiple. If you own stock in a company, you want a high multiple because for every dollar that earnings per share increases, the market value of the company's common stock should increase not only by the amount of its EPS but by the multiple of EPS.

Increasing Shareholder Value

Shareholder value increases when:

1. Revenues increase and costs are controlled.
2. Expenses are reduced and the current level of revenue is maintained.
3. The company's stock multiple increases.

The challenge for most companies is to achieve steady growth without requiring large amounts of new capital. The more new capital a company requires for growth, the slower its growth rate, as raising capital takes time. The slower the company's growth, the slower its shareholder value increases.

Other Benefits of Growth

In addition to increasing shareholder value, growth can also help a company:

1. Establish exciting career paths for its existing employees.
2. Attract qualified new employees.
3. Reduce employee turnover.
4. Increase market share.
5. Limit new competition.
6. Reduce risk by diversifying into new products and/or markets.

Growth Strategies

Hospitality companies can choose from a variety of business strategies to achieve and sustain steady earnings growth, including the following:

1. *Increase sales:* Generate more sales volume from the current operations while maintaining the current percentage profit margin.
2. *Decrease expenses:* Reduce expenses while maintaining the current level of sales:
   a. Reduce labor cost as a percentage of sales by increasing productivity.
   b. Lower food and beverage cost as a percentage of sales by reducing waste.
   c. Lower energy cost by initiating an energy conservation program.
   d. Lower credit card commissions by renegotiating credit card rates.
3. *Expand facilities:* Add to the company's present facilities, construct new facilities, or acquire existing facilities.
4. ***Franchise*** *brand rights:* License the rights to a company's brand for a specific location or market for an initial franchise fee and ongoing royalty payments. Franchising increases the company's distribution system, provides for rapid growth without the need for large amounts of capital, and results in higher profit margins, as the real estate is owned by the franchisee rather than the franchisor.
5. *Secure **management contracts:*** Negotiate contracts to operate facilities owned by others who do not have in-house professional management capabilities. Fees paid to the management company

range from 3% to 5% of total sales plus an incentive fee based on a percentage of gross or net operating profit.

6. **Merge** with or **acquire competitors:** This strategy not only achieves growth but also eliminates competition and increases market share.

THE REAL DEAL

It has always been important to control energy cost in the hospitality industry. A walk down the main thoroughfare of a city such as Las Vegas can cast a very bright light on this issue. To help combat escalating energy use, the United States government passed the Energy Policy Act of 2005, which sets a number of higher efficiency standards for new commercial products. For instance, by January 1, 2006, all lighted exit signs must meet the Energy Star Version 2.0 standard—that is, they should have input power of 5 watts or less per face. This law also offers many tax incentives in the forms of deductions and credits for businesses that purchase and install high-efficiency products and appliances. The total amount allotted is about $2.7 billion. Electric companies are also helping by offering free inspection and advice. Savings are always just a phone call away!

Source: Kiesner, S. "Time to Turn on Energy Efficiency." *The Bottomline* 20(8): 10, 12.

FEATURE STORY

JOE R. LEE–FROM FARM BOY TO CEO OF THE WORLD'S LARGEST CASUAL RESTAURANT COMPANY, DARDEN RESTAURANTS, INC.

Joe R. Lee has come a long way from his humble beginnings as a cotton picker on a sharecropper's farm in Blackshear, Georgia. While many people change employers frequently to advance their careers, Mr. Lee joined Red Lobster Restaurants in 1967 and stayed with the company until his retirement in December 2005. During his thirty-seven-year tenure, he witnessed Red Lobster becoming a unit of General Mills, Inc., in 1970, as well as its spin-off from General Mills to form Darden Restaurants, Inc., in 1995.

Many use restaurant jobs to fund their college expenses, never focusing on restaurant management as a lifetime career. The long hours and low pay deter many from pursuing such a career. As soon as what they consider a "real job" comes along, they take it and move on. At the National Restaurant Association Educational Foundation's Salute to Excellence event in 2002, where Lee was honored, he explained to the students in attendance that the restaurant industry *does* provide terrific career opportunities for those who are not afraid of hard work. "These are not dead-end jobs," he said.

This was not just casual rhetoric, as Mr. Lee was speaking from his personal experience. A college dropout, Lee started his career in the restaurant business acting as a waiter, bartender, and cook at the Marriott, Ramada Inns, and Holiday Inns. With these experiences under his belt, Lee was ready for a management position. At age twenty-eight, he became the restaurant manager of the first Red Lobster restaurant in Lakeland, Florida. When General Mills acquired the fledgling chain of three seafood restaurants two years later, he elected to stay with the restaurant.

This man had big dreams. When General Mills acquired Red Lobster, General Mills was generating $1 billion dollars in annual revenue. During his first meeting with the General Mills financial team, Lee made the bold prediction that his restaurant division would generate at least that much volume within twenty years. Everyone in the room laughed at his audacity. But Lee had the last laugh. Red Lobster reached the $1 billion mark in revenue in just thirteen years instead of his predicted twenty-year target.

After making his wild prediction, Lee moved up the corporate ladder at a phenomenal pace. In June 1972, he was promoted to president and chief executive officer of Red Lobster. In March 1976, he was elected vice president of General Mills. In January 1979, he was elected president of the General Mills restaurant division, overseeing all of General Mills' restaurant operations, which included Red Lobster and the Olive Garden chain. In December 1980, Mr. Lee became executive vice president of General Mills, and in September 1985 was elected to the corporation's board of directors.

Mr. Lee also served General Mills as its chief financial officer and vice chairman. When Red Lobster spun off, the new public company was named Darden Restaurants, Inc., after Red Lobster's founder, Bill Darden. Lee led Darden Restaurants, Inc., for the next ten years, and sales increased from $3 billion to $5.4 billion. Today, Darden Restaurants, Inc., is the world's largest casual dining restaurant company based on market share, revenue, and the number of company-owned and -operated restaurants. The company operates more than 1,300 Red Lobster, Olive Garden, Bahama Breeze, Smokey Bones Barbeque and Grill, and Seasons restaurants in North America, employing more than 150,000 people who serve 300 million meals each year.

For a farm boy and a college dropout, Mr. Lee's 2005 induction into the Hospitality Hall of Honor at the Conrad N. Hilton College in Houston was quite an achievement. During the induction ceremony, Mr. Lee explained his success this way:

> I'm reminded of a story back in my farming days. If you found yourself walking along a country road and saw a fencepost with a turtle sitting on top of it, you may not know how that turtle got there but you know he didn't get there by himself.

Based on his quote, Mr. Lee clearly understands the meaning and value of teamwork.

SOURCES

Lee, Joe R. Acceptance speech, Conrad N. Hilton College Hospitality Industry Hall of Honor, October 11, 2005.

Hayes, Jack. "Joe Lee: Chairman, Chief Executive, General Mills Restaurant Corp., Orlando, Florida—The NRN Fifty: Profiles of Power." *Nations Restaurant News* (January 1995).

Kroll, Lisa. "Clawing Back." *Forbes* (July 26, 1999).

Zuber, Amy. "Annual Salute to Excellence Honors Joe R. Lee, Dave Thomas—Special Report: NRA Wrap-Up." *Nations Restaurant News* (June 10, 2002).

http://investor.dardenrestaurants.com/ir_ReleaseDetail.cfm?ReleaseID=141470.

http://www.yaf.org/conferences/college/2005/joe_lee.htm.

http://finance.yahoo.com/q/pr?s=DRI.

FINANCING GROWTH

As most hospitality industry companies rely on real estate to house their businesses, the hospitality industry is deemed to be capital intensive. Therefore, in order to grow, most hospitality companies require large amounts of capital to fund expansion. Whether you are directly involved in raising capital or the beneficiary of capital raised by others, it is important that you understand how new projects are financed, the cost of these funds to your business, and the sources of the capital. As your career advances, knowing how and where to seek capital will become more and more important to you and your business success.

Types of Capital

There are two types of capital: debt and equity. **Debt** is a fixed obligation or liability of the business that must be paid back over a specified period, plus interest. **Equity** is ownership in the business that does not require immediate repayment but expects a return on the capital invested.

Cost of Capital

The **cost of debt** is calculated by dividing interest expense by the amount of the loan. The **cost of equity** is calculated by dividing the portion of cash flow allocated to the equity investor by the amount of equity provided. Equity is almost always more expensive than debt because equity is riskier and therefore commands a higher return by the investor.

Mix of Capital

The mix of capital is called **WACC** (weighted average cost of capital). Because debt is usually less expensive than equity, the greater the percentage of debt used to finance a project or venture, the lower the WACC and the higher the return on investment enjoyed by the owners. This concept is called *financial leverage*.

SOURCES OF CAPITAL

Numerous types of debt are used for varying business purposes. While it is not critical for you as a hospitality manager to become an expert on each type of loan, you should understand:

1.   The terminology common to all loans
2.   The relative cost of each type of loan
3.   The sources of both debt and equity

It is also important to keep up to date on the new financing vehicles for you and your business to consider, such as **real estate investment trusts** (REITs), **real estate mortgage investment conduits** (REMICs), **condominium hotel financing,** and **timeshare schemes.**

THE REAL DEAL

REITs are still going strong in 2006. In early 2006, the second-largest REIT, CNL Hotels and Resorts, Inc., entered into an agreement to acquire the 500-acre Grande Lakes Orlando Resort. This is a high-end resort with three major elements. First, it has a Ritz-Carlton of about 600 rooms. It is also an AAA Four Diamond property with an Italian design and standard rooms, suites, and club-level rooms. It also has a 40,000-square-foot spa with forty treatment rooms. The second part of the resort is also an AAA Four Diamond–rated J. W. Marriott of about 1,000 rooms and over 100,000 square feet of meeting space with a Spanish décor. Tying the two properties together is an eighteen-hole championship golf course designed by none other than the Shark himself, Greg Norman. How much is this transaction worth? A mere $735 million. The Mickey Mouse magic of Orlando still has its touch!

INVESTMENT ANALYSIS

Once you know how to raise capital, you must also become adept at investing it wisely. As a hospitality manager, understanding the time value of money concept, and possessing the necessary **investment analysis** skills based on this concept, is important to your future success. Investment analysis skills will be immediately valuable to you as soon as you enter the workforce. They will help you, for example, present and justify a capital request to fund a new meeting room, a guest room expansion, a restaurant renovation, or the purchase of new computer equipment. When requesting capital, you will need to demonstrate that the money you are asking for will generate a favorable return on investment for your company. This is critical whether you are requesting capital from your general manager, owner, lender, or public shareholders.

The Time Value of Money

The **time value of money concept** (TVM) is the cornerstone of investment analysis. It is based on the premise that the value of money is not limited to its face value but also includes the interest or profit that can be earned by investing it wisely. Therefore, an asset's market value is deemed to be the **present value** of the sum of the future cash flow it is likely to generate over its life, factoring in:

- The amount of annual cash flow projected
- When the cash flow will be received
- The **risk** associated with the generation of the cash flow
- The WACC required to finance the project

Understanding what a discount rate is, being able to calculate the WACC, and being able to estimate market value using the **capitalization method of valuation** are essential to your being able to understand and use net present value (NPV) and internal rate of return (IRR) to analyze real-world business investment opportunities.

Investment Analysis Methods

The payback period, net present value (NPV), and internal rate of return (IRR) are the three most popular methods used to analyze investment opportunities. It is essential for you as a hospitality manager to know how to use each method of analysis and to be able to perform the necessary calculations on the business calculator and computer spreadsheet.

- The **payback period** is the length of time an investment takes to generate cumulative cash flows after debt service equal to the initial equity investment.
- The **net present value** of an investment is the difference between its present value and its initial cost.
- The **internal rate of return** of an investment is the discount rate that makes its present value equal to its initial cost. It could also be described as an investment's ROI, taking into consideration the time value of money.

Favorable or Unfavorable?

A project is deemed to be favorable when its:

- Payback period is less than the minimum allowable period.
- NPV is equal to or greater than zero.
- IRR is more than the investor's cost of capital (WACC).

Conversely, a project is deemed to be unfavorable when its:

- Payback period is more than the targeted period.
- NPV is less than zero or negative.
- IRR is less than the investor's cost of capital.

The higher the NPV and the IRR, the more favorable the investment opportunity.

Factors Impacting the Analysis

Four primary factors can impact the present value, net present value, and internal rate of return of a potential investment.

- **Weighted average cost of capital:** The lower the weighted average cost of capital (WACC), the lower the discount rate and the higher the NPV.

- **Terminal cap rate:** The lower the cap rate used to calculate the terminal sale price of the asset at the end of the analysis period, the higher the sales price and the higher the PV, NPV, and IRR.

- **Timing of cash flow:** The more cash flow projected for the early years of an investment, the higher the PV, NPV, and IRR.

- **Development or acquisition cost:** The lower the acquisition price of the asset or, in the case of a new development, its total project cost, the higher the NPV and IRR.

Hospitality Industry Applications

When you fully understand the time value of money concept and have mastered the investment analysis tools, you are ready to apply your new skills to real-world situations. Your skills, for example, can help you negotiate debt and equity agreements and structure new business ventures.

Debt and Equity Negotiations

Your new investment analysis skills will assist you in successfully negotiating a loan agreement and answering questions like:

1. What is the maximum amount of loan I can afford based on my cash flow projections and loan terms offered by the bank?
2. What is the maximum interest rate I can afford to pay based on the amount of loan I need and the amortization rate offered by the bank?
3. How much will my annual debt service payment be based on the amount of the loan, interest rate, and amortization rate being offered by the bank?
4. What amortization rate do I need to ask for based on the amount of loan I need and the interest rate being offered?

These skills can also assist you during your equity negotiations with a potential investor and help you determine:

1. How much equity you can raise based on your cash flow projections and your investor's IRR **hurdle rate.**
2. What your equity investor's IRR would be based on the percentage of ownership you are planning to offer him, how much he is investing, and the cash flow you are projecting.

3. Working backward, the minimum percentage ownership you need to offer your equity investor to meet, but not exceed, his IRR hurdle rate.

In addition to helping you answer these questions, you can also use these skills to prepare loan amortization schedules, estimate the market value of your business, make lease versus purchase decisions, and analyze multiple investment opportunities to determine the most favorable one.

THE INVESTMENT PACKAGE

When additional capital is required to finance a renovation or expansion of the business where you are employed, or finance a new start-up business venture, or finance the acquisition of an existing hospitality asset, or finance the development of a new restaurant or hotel, the first, and perhaps most important, step in gaining funding approval is a professional investment package.

The investment package should tell your story and sell your project or new venture to the capital sources from which you are seeking funding. The capital source may be the owner of your business, a prospective lender, or a prospective equity investor. The better you tell and sell your story, the more likely your request for capital funding will be approved and on terms favorable to you and your company.

THE REAL DEAL

An investment package should tell your story and sell your project. Consider the Grand Emperor Hotel in Macao, where one part of its signature is its Golden Avenue. It is a real gold pavement in the lobby of this casino hotel made with seventy-eight pieces of 1-kilogram gold bars placed below the ground. Do not worry about the security; there is a twenty-four-hour security system and guards! This hotel/casino has over 300 slot machines with many new games offering an exciting experience—and not just for the high rollers. The hotel already has many movie stars as its visitors, including the ambassador of tourism of Hong Kong, Jackie Chan. With the Golden Avenue alone, the story is not hard to sell! And, with Macao being marketed as the Las Vegas of the Orient, the return on investment should not be an issue.

What Lenders Want to Know

Your investment package should answer the following questions that lenders are most interested in:

1. How strong is the project, and is it really feasible?

   - Your **business plan,** story, and feasibility study must be persuasive and confirmed by a credible third-party source.

2. Is the project team really qualified?

   - The **credentials of your team** must be outstanding. If you are attempting to finance a start-up business and your management team lacks experience, make sure you surround yourself with seasoned professionals and reward them well. Your investment in their talents will serve you well on later deals and help you establish a favorable track record for your company.

3. What is the risk of the venture failing?

   - Lending is all about risk, so don't ignore it. You must clearly state what the risks of the proposed project are and how you plan to minimize them.
   - Risk can be minimized by providing **additional collateral, personal guarantees,** or, more preferably, by showing the lender that it is a conservative loan with low **loan-to-cost** and **loan-to-value** ratios, a high **debt service coverage ratio,** and that the loan can easily be paid back out of future cash flows.

If your prospective lender is comfortable with the answers to the three questions noted above, your chances of receiving the debt financing you are seeking are excellent.

THE REAL DEAL

For a small-scale start-up company or a limited-service franchise, funding may still be obtainable through one main source or a few sources, including some financing assistance through the franchisor. However, in financing growth of a mega-project, more and more of the deal takes a form of a syndicate. The W Las Vegas Hotel, Casino, and Residences is a mixed-use project and receives its predevelopment credit facility of over $230 million through a syndicate of banks led by the Société Generale Corporate and Investment Banking with first-lien and second-lien term loans. It also takes a long time just to have all the financing finalized. This $230-plus million is only the predevelopment credit; financing is still needed for the construction of the project, and the entire process may take another nine months to a year. This credit facility is privately rated by Standard and Poor's and Moody's and has received a good rating, as the $232.5 million is considered a low loan to value ratio, with the property acting as the collateral.

What Equity Investors Want to Know

Your owner or prospective equity investor will evaluate your investment package in a similar manner to that of your lender, but with more of an eye toward the upside potential of your deal.

In addition to evaluating the overall feasibility of the project, the qualifications of your project management team, and the risk associated with achieving your financial projections, prospective equity investors are also interested in the answers to the following questions:

1. How much equity is the sponsor group investing in the deal?
   - This is a tough question to answer, particularly if you have a limited amount of capital to invest in the venture or if you have elected not to invest your own funds in the deal.
   - If you are able and willing to provide between 5% and 10% of the equity required, the outside equity investor will usually be comfortable.
2. What annual return on investment (ROI) can I expect to receive, what's the payback period, what is the net present value (NPV) of the deal, what is my projected internal rate of return (IRR), and how much profit is the sponsor group making on the deal?
   - As long as your owner or prospective equity investor is confident that he will achieve his targeted IRR hurdle rate, he will usually be okay with you earning a portion of the cash flow as well.
   - The key is for the equity investors to receive their return first before you reap any significant rewards from the deal.
3. What is the **exit strategy**?
   - An equity investor's strategy is often to invest their equity, make a fast profit, and look for another opportunity to do it again.
   - The faster the exit strategy, the more likely the outside equity investor will be to invest in your deal.

If you provide your owner and/or equity investor with credible answers to these three questions, they are likely to invest equity in your deal. If you reward them with the IRR they are seeking and execute your exit strategy well, you will also have a likely source of equity for your next deal.

CRAFTING AND NEGOTIATING THE DEAL

Creating a new business venture is arguably the most difficult career path a hospitality manager can elect to pursue. It can also be the most rewarding. It is risky, time-consuming, expensive, and challenging. It requires not only book smarts but street smarts as well. It involves finding a new business niche, proving its feasibility, preparing financial projections, estimating project cost, recruiting a superior project and management team, packaging the story, and, most importantly, securing financing for the venture. Crafting and negotiating the deal is the ultimate test for a hospitality entrepreneur.

Most lenders and equity investors will read your investment package and listen to your story if your deal is a good one. A good deal is one that is feasible, makes financial sense, and meets the lender's and investor's investment parameters. Knowing how to approach equity investors, how to determine what ownership percentage to offer them, and how to make the deal profitable not only for the lender and investors but yourself as well is the true test of a hospitality entrepreneur.

Business Decisions to Make

When sponsoring a new venture, you must make smart business decisions related to the following:

1. What form of business entity is best suited for the venture?
2. What is the optimum mix of debt and equity?
3. How much of a **carried interest** will the deal support?
4. What deal points are most important to the prospective lender?
5. What deal points are most important to prospective equity investors?

Negotiating the Loan

When seeking debt financing, you should always seek to leverage your equity and maximize your IRR. The two loan provisions that should be negotiated the hardest are the **amount of the loan** and the **amortization rate.** If you are able to maximize the amount of the loan and minimize your monthly debt service payments by negotiating a favorable amortization rate, you will have succeeded in using other people's money to make money for yourself.

Negotiating the Equity Investment

When seeking equity financing, your primary goal should be to raise the equity you need while giving up as little ownership as you can. The issues that are usually most important to equity investors are the:

- Amount of equity they are asked to invest
- Percentage ownership they will receive
- Probability of achieving their IRR hurdle rate
- Exit strategy
- Decision-making power on when to execute the exit strategy

If your investor is going to be your partner, you must be open and honest with him and gain his trust. At the same time, you need to negotiate the best possible deal for yourself.

Negotiating Skills

Selling and negotiating skills can help you secure the debt and equity capital you need for your new venture. When negotiating the deal, remember to always:

1. Do your homework on the person you are meeting with and be prepared to answer any question you think he or she might ask.
2. Dress professionally and present yourself and your deal in a professional manner.
3. Use proven selling skills: State the benefits of your venture, address any objections raised, and close the deal.
4. Think like an owner and act like a manager.

We hope you have learned from this text and have grasped the financial concepts, skills, and techniques presented. If you have, we are confident they will serve you well as you move up the corporate hospitality ladder or go into business for yourself. Good luck!

INDEX